This new, comprehensive examination of Turgenev's fiction challenges traditional assumptions of both Eastern and Western critics. It begins by outlining the writer's life and sketching his personality, provides a brief survey of his poetry and plays as the prelude to the fiction, and reviews some aspects of his literary criticism in their bearing upon it. It offers readings of the individual works, focussing principally on the complexity and subtlety of Turgenev's portrayal of the psychology of his characters. The book is designed to be accessible not only to Slavists, but to other literary scholars interested in one of Dostoevsky's most important but undervalued contemporaries.

CAMBRIDGE STUDIES IN RUSSIAN LITERATURE

Turgenev

Turgenev

A Reading of his Fiction

FRANK FRIEDEBERG SEELEY

Emeritus Professor of Russian and Comparative Literature,
State University of New York, Binghamton

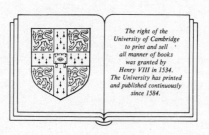

The right of the
University of Cambridge
to print and sell
all manner of books
was granted by
Henry VIII in 1534.
The University has printed
and published continuously
since 1584.

CAMBRIDGE UNIVERSITY PRESS

CAMBRIDGE

NEW YORK   PORT CHESTER

MELBOURNE   SYDNEY

Published by the Press Syndicate of the University of Cambridge
The Pitt Building, Trumpington Street, Cambridge CB2 1RP
40 West 20th Street, New York, NY 10111, USA
10 Stamford Road, Oakleigh, Melbourne 3166, Australia

First published 1991

Printed in Great Britain at the University Press, Cambridge

British Library cataloguing in publication data
Seeley, Frank Friedeberg
Turgenev: a reading of his fiction. – (Cambridge studies in Russian literature).
1. Fiction in Russia. Turgenev, I. S. (Ivan Sergeevich),
1818–1883
1. Title
891.733

Library of Congress cataloguing in publication data
Seeley, Frank Friedeberg.
Turgenev: a reading of his fiction / Frank Friedeberg Seeley.
p.   cm. – (Cambridge studies in Russian literature)
ISBN 0 521 36521 X
1. Turgenev, Ivan Sergeevich, 1818–1883 – Criticism and
interpretation. I. Title. II. Series.
PG3443.S37   1991
891.73'3 – dc20   90-1442   CIP

ISBN 0 521 36521 X hardback

CE

To the memory of my parents,
Emil Friedeberg and Lilly Seeley

Contents

Preface

This book is a reading of Turgenev's fiction, preceded by a chapter outlining his life and sketching his personality and another chapter surveying his poetry and his plays, as the prelude to his fiction, and glancing at certain aspects of his literary criticism in their bearing on his fiction. It does not attempt to consider his other writings: his memoirs, his translations into and out of Russian, his correspondence – which already comprises more than six thousand published letters and is constantly being augmented by new discoveries – or what might, somewhat broadly and vaguely, be called his journalism.

It may be asked, why 'a reading' rather than, for instance, 'a study'? I am not sure what the distinction may be, or if there is any hard-and-fast distinction, but I suspect that a study would have required me to argue my departures from accepted assumptions and traditional categories. That would have made the book much longer – and as it is, it may already seem too long.

My main focus has been on the complexity and subtlety of Turgenev's characterization – of the psychology of his personages – which has attracted less attention and occupies much less space in the critical literature than it deserves. Here if anywhere there is room as well as need for a variety of readings.

At the risk of boring Slavists with elementary general information, I have tried to make the book readable for non-Slavist and non-Russian lovers of literature and of Turgenev: by simplifying dates and spelling of Russian words (see below), and by giving the titles of his works in English (with plays and narrative poems italicized regardless of whether or not they have been translated). On the other hand, my treatment of the fiction (though not of the poetry, plays or criticism) assumes that the reader is familiar with Turgenev's texts or will reread them before attacking my commentary.

After reading about Turgenev and lecturing about him for more than forty years, it would be hopeless to try to detail one's indebtedness to all one's predecessors in the critical field; I have acknowledged in my text and notes the debts of which I am still conscious. But no one writing on Turgenev today could fail to pay tribute to the 28-volume edition of his *Collected Works and Correspondence* published between 1961 and 1968 by the Soviet Academy of Sciences, supplemented by a further five volumes of *Turgenev Miscellanies*. This edition (of which an updated version – unfortunately, not available to me – has now been launched) brought together not only the fullest and most thoroughly edited texts of Turgenev's works and letters but, in the introductory commentaries, the notes and the articles, an unprecedented wealth of literary-historical information: on the genesis and composition of each work, the first and subsequent editions in Turgenev's lifetime, variants in the Mss, proofs and early editions from the last version approved by the author, critical reactions in Russia and foreign translations in Turgenev's day, besides copious notes on his correspondents and on references and allusions likely to be unfamiliar to non-specialists. My readings are based on the texts in this edition, supplemented, where necessary, by reference to materials published since 1968; dates and other materials of literary history have been drawn from or checked against it.

Acknowledgments

I gladly record my gratitude to the University of Texas at Austin for issuing me a 'Special Reader's Card', without which this book could not have been written, and to the editors of the *Slavonic and East European Review*, London, and those of the *Annali dell'Istituto Universitario Orientale (sezione slava)*, Naples, for permission to re-use the following articles which first appeared in their pages:

'The Heyday of the "Superfluous Man" in Russia', *SEER*, December 1952;
'Theme and Structure in *Fathers and Sons*', *Annali*, 13, 1970; and
'Thematic Counterpoint in "Poezdka v Poles'e"', *Annali*, 16–17, 1973–4.

Warm personal thanks I owe to: Professor Henri Granjard of the Sorbonne for the gift of two of his books; Dr Rimgaila Salys of the State University of New York at Binghamton for a volume of Soviet papers on Turgenev; Professor N. Kauchtschischwili of the University of Milan for the volume of papers on my author, edited and contributed to by herself, which she graciously sent to me; Professor Alessandro Ivanov of the University of Udine for the gift of a similar volume of essays; to Professor James L. Rice of the University of Oregon for directing my attention to some letters of Turgenev's mother; to Dr Helen Rapp, London, for reading my first four chapters in draft and making valuable suggestions; and particularly to Professor Malcolm V. Jones of the University of Nottingham for reading the whole of the typescript and responding with most helpful suggestions and comments.

Dates

The Russian (Julian) calendar in the nineteenth century was twelve days behind the (Gregorian) calendar of Western Europe and America. Turgenev uses either date or both, depending on context; the 1961–8 edition mostly uses both; with one or two special exceptions, I have everywhere used the Gregorian alone. Where both are given, the Julian precedes the Gregorian.

Spelling

Transliteration of Russian names and words varies widely. Where the spelling of historical names has been standardized for English texts, I have kept to those forms: Dostoevsky, Tolstoy, Nicholas I (not Nikolai), Alexander II (not Aleksandr), etc. For names of fictional characters and for all other Russian words and phrases I have used what seems the simplest and least misleading rendering, dispensing with the professional diacritics and *j* of the International Phonetic Alphabet; so: ts, ch, sh, shch, zh (pronounced like s in 'pleasure'); 'i' for *i*, *ij*, or *j* after a vowel other than *i*, 'y' for *y*, *yj*, or *j* before a vowel.

References

All my references to Turgenev's writings are, unless otherwise specified, to the Soviet edition mentioned above:

I. S. Turgenev, *Polnoe sobranie sochineni i pisem* (*Collected Works and Correspondence*), Moscow–Leningrad, Izdatel′stvo

Akademii Nauk SSSR (Soviet Academy of Sciences), 1961–8. The *Works* are numbered I–XV; the *Correspondence* is in fifteen books numbered I–XI, XII/1, XII/2, XIII/1, XIII/2. For the benefit of those who read Turgenev in earlier editions or in translation, references to the fiction are to the chapter as well as to the page of this Academy edition. References to works other than fiction or to the critical apparatus are by volume and page, preceded by *W*. References to letters are by the number in this edition, preceded by 'L' and followed by the name of the addressee and by the date (the Gregorian date, regardless of whether Turgenev used only the Julian date and of the fact that this edition gives both). For example: XII, 89; *W*, v, 503; L. 70, to Pauline Viardot, 1 Dec. 1847.

Since 1968 three volumes of letters not included in the Soviet edition have been published in the West: H. Granjard and A. Zviguilsky, *Lettres inédites de Tourguénev à Pauline Viardot et à sa famille*, Edition l'Age d'Homme (Lausanne, 1972); and Alexandre Zviguilski, *Ivan Tourguénev: nouvelle correspondance inédite*, Librairie des Cinq Continents, 2 vols. (Paris, 1971, 1972). Letters from these collections are referred to respectively as GZ and Z, followed by the number of the letter and its date.

INTRODUCTION
Turgenev and his antinomies

As recently as 1969 an Italian scholar could begin an article on Turgenev with the words: 'In our day and age Turgenev's books are hardly read any more.'[1] In the Winter 1974 issues of *The Yale Review* a well-known Dostoevsky scholar calls for a return to Turgenev, comparing and contrasting his aesthetic and his standing in the West with those of Dostoevsky.[2] But after reading in this accomplished article that in Turgenev's view nature 'provides a model for art and the artist', one is startled by the assertion that 'for Turgenev middle-class values appear to be precisely those of nature' – with the clear implication that the values of Turgenev's art are middle-class. No less striking is the traditionalism of the article's approach: Turgenev and his writing are presented in categories which would have been perfectly understood and accepted by his contemporaries: which could surely not be said of the best of modern Dostoevsky criticism or even Tolstoy criticism.

By way of contrast, here is a sentence from an article, antedating both of the above citations, by a Russian critic: 'His [Turgenev's] material is everything that disproves the accepted code and the idea of an integrated personality, everything that illustrates his sense of relativity and instability and his implicit suggestion that sickness is not so much the price of civilization as of self-consciousness.'[3] As I read Turgenev, this article comes considerably closer to appreciating the protean nature of his art than do the traditional approaches that must have contributed to the neglect or depreciation of him deplored in the Italian and American essays referred to above.

Contrary to received assumptions, the antinomies and paradoxes which permeate Turgenev's literary work are matched by those in his critical writings and by the contradictions between his literary professions and practices. In a letter of 1875 he reluctantly offers this definition of his *Weltanschauung*:

I will say summarily that I am pre-eminently a realist – and what interests me most is the living truth of the human physiognomy; I am indifferent to everything supernatural, I don't believe in any absolutes or systems, I love freedom above all else – and, so far as I can judge, I am sensitive to poetry. All that is human is dear to me. Slavophilism is alien to me, as is every orthodoxy.

But this attempt to satisfy his correspondent is characteristically preceded by a deprecatory warning: 'It would be no less natural and truthful to say, "the Lord alone knows!" – I don't know my own face.'[4]

Actually, his self-definition is open to challenge on all but one of its main points. All that is human is dear to him: granted. But he loves freedom above all else – and he mortgages his freedom for forty years to his fantastic love for Pauline Viardot. He does not believe in any systems or absolutes: whereas, in fact, he does have his own system of ethics, pivoted on self-respect, loyalty and duty, and he does revere beauty and love as absolutes. He is indifferent to everything supernatural; yet at least half a dozen of his stories (about one in five) are officially designated 'mysterious' or 'fantastic' and appear to hinge on the supernatural. What interests him most is the living truth of the human face (not 'soul'); but though observation of what is open to the senses (the 'physiognomy') is indeed one of his master talents, it is wedded to an intuition which accounts for the depths and complexities of his portrayals.

No doubt the crucial article of his literary creed is that he is a 'realist'. What does that mean? Many or most critics would agree that Turgenev began as a Romantic poet. In a letter of 1848 he advances the Romantic thesis that suffering is to be welcomed as an ennobling force and that impassioned despair may or should form the core of great art.[5] In his 1845 review of a translation of Goethe's *Faust* he writes: 'The first and last word, the alpha and omega of all his [Goethe's] life was, as it is with with all poets, his own ego.'[6] And as late as 1856 he can write: 'By nature an aesthete, in spirit an idealist, in language a Romantic – I would fain have sung mighty heroes, inspired fighters.'[7] It is true that in the 1845 review just cited he goes on to declare – faithful to Belinsky's teaching – that in this later age poetry is no longer enough: aesthetic enjoyment must give place to social concern. But his own mature work only half conforms to his preaching: parallel with *A Sportsman's Sketches* and the novels runs the long train of his stories, innocent (with only few exceptions) of social history and of social problems. Of course he did not remain a Romantic poet. But the perfume of his poetry was absorbed into his prose, and the realism of his mature work soared beyond the narrow bounds of the reality penned within the limits of mid-nineteenth-century science, as represented by French Naturalists and prescribed by Russian radicals.

It is generally held that the 1860 essay 'Hamlet and Don Quixote' offers a useful key to much of Turgenev and his writings. It is less often realized that the key will be most useful if one attends to what the essay fails to say or glides over or mis-states. Turgenev is obviously so much more *reasonable* than Tolstoy or Dostoevsky that readers are apt to take the intellectual components of his work at face value. They should be warned by his own admission in 1869: 'Whenever I am not dealing with images, I become quite confused and am at a loss how to proceed. I always feel as if one could equally well assert the opposite of all I am saying.'[8] This is indeed reflected in his incapacity for effective argument, especially polemical argument – whether in life (against Tolstoy) or in his fiction (most damagingly in *Fathers and Children*).

In the essay Turgenev opposes Hamlet to Don Quixote: as egoism to devotion, as critical irony to enthusiastic faith, and as intelligence to heart and will. Note the curious failure to oppose them as realist to fantast: Turgenev glances at these categories, but shies away. This is interesting both in itself and inasmuch as it may well be due to his delusion that the makers of history are the Don Quixotes, while the Hamlets cannot make history except through their disciples, the Horatios. The truth is just the opposite: not only in Shakespeare and Cervantes but in Turgenev's own work. It is Don Quixote who cannot make history except through his disciple, Sancho Panza; Hamlet – however tardily, clumsily and bloodily – does make history: he liquidates the Old Order, including himself, and so clears the way for a New Order in the person of Fortinbras. So, too, no history will be made by Insarov, unless through his disciple, Elena, while history, of a sort, will be made by Bersenev and Shubin.

Meanwhile, the antithesis realist–fantast is directly relevant, in more ways than one, to Turgenev and his writings. He admits that his Hamlet and Quixote are abstract types – one might almost say, symbols – and that in most men both are present in varying degrees. He himself may be said to represent an interesting combination: a realist at heart or (perhaps, better) in intuition, he is a fantast intellectually.

While 'realist at heart' may meet with wide assent, the following clause is likely to raise not a few eyebrows. But not only is it implicit in the 1869 quotation above (about his confusion when not dealing with images and his sense that contrary statements could be equally valid), it informs his antinomial views of every major aspect of life. Here two examples may suffice. His view of love certainly appeared fantastic to his French friends when he tried to persuade them that it was a unique and mysterious feeling; that he could see a divinity in the eyes of his beloved; and that love in general melts us down, delivering us from the trammels of individuality and uniting us with the infinite.[9] One guesses that they will have been less resistant to his alternative view of love: as a sickness, a bondage, a scourge of fate. Then again: who would not regard as fantastic his view of nature as a paragon of harmony and moderation, which turns a blind eye alike to her physical cataclysms and to her biological monstrosities? This also is a view that he was ready to exchange for its opposite, concentrating in dismay on the destructiveness of that same nature.

Turgenev's intellectual fantasy is projected into many of his stories in the guise of the illusions on which the personages wreck themselves or others: illusions concerning either their own character or rôle or the character or attitude of others. Though an undistinguished satirist, as Gershenzon points out,[10] Turgenev is a master of irony – above all, the ironies of character and of situation.

In virtue of his realism of heart, or intuition, Turgenev is a superb psychologist – hardly, if at all, inferior in this to Dostoevsky or Tolstoy, although many readers fail to recognize the fact. That may well be because he requires from his readers the kind of collaboration expected by the poet rather than by most fiction-writers. That is, his effects are achieved by touches so subtle that casual reading will often discern only the simple conventionality of which so many complain. In fact his work is steeped in antinomies and paradoxes, both psychological and philosophic; the reader who is prepared to look out for them can discover that Turgenev's surface harmony and transparency are likely to prove as deceptive as nature's: they quite often overlay themes of many-layered richness.

1

Life and reputation

What an important year 1840 has been for me! How much I have lived through in these nine months! Just fancy – at the beginning of January [I am] galloping in a hooded sledge over the snows of Russia. The ferment in [me] has hardly begun; [I am] troubled by vague thoughts, timid, given to futile musing . . . [I][1] spend ten days in Austria's opulent capital and arrive in Italy, in Rome. – In Rome I find Stankevich.[2] Do you understand the upheaval, or rather – that beginning of my soul's development! How eagerly I listened to him – destined as I was to be the last friend he would initiate into the service of Truth by his example, by the Poetry of his life, or his words! . . . I saw in him the outcome and result of a great struggle and was able – without regard to its beginning – to give myself up without qualms to tranquil contemplation of the world of art. Nature smiled on me. I had always had a lively sense of her enchantment, of the presence in her of a God; but she had seemed in her beauty to be reproaching me – poor, blind, filled with vain doubts. Now I could stretch out my arms to her joyously and swear at my soul's altar to be worthy of life!

This is from a letter addressed by Turgenev, aged 21, to some of his fellow students at the University of Berlin, and in particular to Mikhail Bakunin, who was about to replace the dead Stankevich as his friend and mentor.[3] In a further instalment of the same letter, he writes (in German now): 'To form (*fassen*) a philosophic conviction is a supreme work of art, and philosophers are the greatest of masters and artists. Actually, this is where art ceases to be art – it is merged in philosophy.'[4]

Thirty-five years later, at the age of 56, Turgenev responds, reluctantly, to an appeal to define 'in writing, concisely' his philosophy of life (*Weltanschauung*): 'let me say in short that I am primarily a realist – and what interests me most is the living truth of human physiognomy; I am indifferent to everything supernatural, I don't believe in any absolutes or systems, I love freedom above all else – and, so far as I can judge, I am sensitive to poetry. All that is human is dear to me. Slavophilism is alien, as is every orthodoxy.'[5]

And about midway between these two dates, at the age of 39, in a

5

sympathetic reply to a 21-year-old student who had evidently begged for advice as to how to order his life, Turgenev offers as a central principle: 'you are faced by a great duty to yourself: you must make *yourself*, make a man of yourself – and then, whatever becomes of you, wherever life may lead you – you can leave it to your nature [to cope]: you will have done right by yourself'.[6] In these three revealing passages we are offered a glimpse of Turgenev's lyrical and Romantic starting-line; of the seemingly serene objectivity of his maturity, and of the way he thought he had taken from the initial to those final positions.

Turgenev's biography can be seen as dividing into five periods. First, the *Lehrjahre*, the period of his apprenticeship to life, of his education in the broad sense, extending over his first twenty-four years: the years of childhood and youth, of home, school and university, of travel abroad, of first friendships, of abortive loves, of juvenile writing. Next, the 'remarkable decade',[7] in which the whole course of his further life was determined by his meeting with Pauline Viardot and the course of his writing was set by his meeting with Vissarion Belinsky: a decade of happiness in love and of the first fine efflorescence of his literary powers. Then comes a decade 'in limbo', when Turgenev is separated from Pauline Viardot – first physically, later spiritually: a period of growing unhappiness and ill-health, which appears, however, to concentrate and ripen his creativity.

Finally, the last twenty years of his life comprise a 'German period' of about eight years and a 'French period' of about twelve. The German period is marked by a full reconciliation with Pauline and growing closeness with her family, the French period by what amounts to a symbiosis.

The five biographical periods are roughly paralleled by five periods of literary history. To the *Lehrjahre* (1818–42) corresponds the period of *Juvenilia* (1834–42) – mainly Romantic lyrical poetry. To the 'remarkable decade' (1843–52) corresponds a period of experimentation in genres, themes and styles, culminating in the publication of his first major work, *A Sportsman's Sketches*. The years 'in limbo' (1853–62) coincide with a climax in productivity: his four best novels and nine stories, including three or four of the finest. The German period (1863–70) produces nine more stories, including at least one masterpiece, but only one novel; the somewhat longer French period (1871–83) adds one more novel, nine stories (though two of these might better be classified as sketches) and three additions to the *Sportsman's Sketches* of thirty years earlier.

Birth, family and education: 1818–42

Ivan Sergeevich Turgenev was born 28 October/9 November 1828 in the town of Orël in central Russia as the second of three sons of Sergei Turgenev and his wife Varvara, née Lutovinova. The parents were an ill-assorted couple: the father thirteen years younger than his wife,[8] an impoverished noble, a retired colonel of the Horse Guards and a handsome fellow; the mother a wealthy landowner, a provincial without looks or graces, though not without intelligence and culture. The Turgenevs belonged to the ancient nobility, they figure in the pages of Russian history; the Lutovinovs were undistinguished country gentry. The opposition of background was matched by an opposition of temperament: the colonel – cool, reserved, controlled (though capable of flashes of rage on occasion) and masterful; his wife – possessive, tyrannical, passionate in the dark and violent tradition of her family. She kept the administration of her estates in her own hands, while her husband led his own life of hunting, card-playing and amorous adventures, largely outside his home. He died, at only 41, when Ivan was 16.

At the age of 4 Turgenev accompanied his parents on a tour of Western Europe, in the course of which he would have tumbled into the bear-pit of the Berne zoo if his father had not caught him at the last moment; but most of his first nine years he spent at Spasskoe, his mother's principal estate, in a large two-storey manor house surrounded by a vast park, partly landscaped, with a pond, tree-lined paths (forming a patterned XIX in reference to the century), flowerbeds and a hothouse, partly overgrown with many kinds of trees and bushes – the pond stocked with various species of fish, the woods filled with the songs of many sorts of birds. Here Turgenev soon loved to wander or to lie and observe, to feed the fish and snare the birds; here were laid the foundations of his love and exceptional knowledge of nature and his later, paradoxical passion for hunting.

Turgenev's mother ran her estates as a small kingdom with herself as sovereign. The serfs were her subjects, over whom she wielded an absolute power, unchecked by law and untempered by sympathy or imagination. Her childhood and youth had been embittered by lack of love, by fear and humiliation; her marriage was soured by her husband's infidelities; and she found compensation for her past sufferings in making others suffer. She was an emotional woman, a woman of moods, and she vented her every frustration in cruel punishment of her serfs – and her sons. The boys were birched – 'most days', according to Turgenev's later recollections; the serfs were flogged, separated from their families and banished to estates in other provinces, arbitrarily paired in marriage, assigned to work that stultified their native abilities.

Ivan was roughly two years younger than his brother Nikolai and three years older than his brother Sergei (who was to die in his teens), but although the boys may have been drawn together by a common dread of their mother, Sergei was too young and Nikolai too different in temperament and outlook to provide Ivan with the affection and comfort he needed. How he hungered for his father's affection we read in 'First Love'; how ready he was to pour out his heart to anyone who showed feeling for him appears touchingly in the five letters – the only ones to survive from his childhood – addressed, at the age of 12, to his uncle Nikolai.

But it was to the serfs he would have had to turn most of the time. It was a serf who helped him to break into the old library next to his nursery and who initiated him, at the age of 8, into the joys of poetry. It was from serfs he will have learned to snare and perhaps to shoot. Their children will have been his playmates, if he was allowed to play. It was to a serf-girl that he lost his virginity when about 15. And always his heart must have yearned to the serfs for their sufferings at the hands of the woman in whose shadow he too lived.

In 1827 the Turgenevs moved to Moscow, and Ivan and Nikolai spent the next two years in boarding-schools while their parents travelled in Western Europe, seeking medical advice and treatment for the father. When the parents returned to Russia, the boys too came home, where they continued their studies under a succession of tutors of varying quality. These studies comprised the usual history, geography, mathematics and drawing, besides Russian, French and German language and literature, to which were added, as Turgenev approached his mid-teens, English, Latin and Greek. At the age of 15 he entered the University of Moscow, but spent only one year there, as the family then moved to St Petersburg and he transferred to the university of that city.

However, Russian universities at that time could not compare with those of Western Europe, particularly Germany. This was the finishing school to which the most intelligent and independent-minded of Turgenev's young contemporaries gravitated; and after taking his degree at St Petersburg in 1837, he set himself to win his mother's consent to his completing his education abroad. It took the best part of a year; but in June 1838 he arrived in Berlin. In the following three years, he spent 27 months in Germany – most of that time in Berlin, where he studied at the university: classical languages and literatures, history and philosophy. He studied with enthusiasm, looking forward to a career as professor of philosophy, and after his return to Russia in May 1841 he prepared for the examinations required for the degree of Master of Philosophy. He actually passed these examinations, oral and written, in the first half of 1842, but never finished the dissertation: whether because, as he stated later, he was carried away by a passion for hunting or, more probably, because he came to realize the hopelessness of a career in philosophy in Russia, where it had become something of a taboo subject since the Decembrist Rising of 1825.

Meanwhile, his three years in the West had operated great changes in his mind and outlook. His two years at Berlin University, under renowned scholars, gave him a solid grounding in the classics, history and philosophy and fitted him to emerge as the best-educated Russian writer of his generation. His two months in Italy – where he visited not only Rome, but Naples, Leghorn, Genoa and the Lago Maggiore – moved him to new appreciation of nature and art and provided him with material for several later works. His social contacts with cultured Germans and with Russian families in Germany and Italy provided further intellectual and emotional stimulation. And his friendships with Stankevich and, later, Bakunin fired him with a sense of purpose and helped crystallize the values still latent or only partly formed in him at home.

None of the relationships lasted long (Stankevich died, Bakunin remained abroad and plunged into revolutionary activity); and if their contributions – especially Stankevich's – to the later Turgenev were significant, the groundwork had been laid and the materials assembled long before: in his childhood home, on his ancestral estate, under the rule of the woman he 'feared like fire'.

Varvara Turgeneva was no mere sadist. She was a woman who had been starved of love all her life, and craved it all the more for that. She had loved her husband – and discovered that he did not love her. She had probably come to doubt, at least unconsciously, whether she was capable of inspiring love; and so urgent was her need to find out that, a couple of years before her husband's death, she gambled her reputation in an affair with the future father of Tolstoy's future wife and risked her life, at 53, to bear his daughter (whom she brought up as her 'ward').

Varvara Turgeneva loved her sons – in her own fashion – and Ivan was her favourite. When he was abroad, or away from home, she yearned for his presence, trembled for his safety, demanded regular bulletins on his health and doings, enforcing her demands with the threat that for every post that brought no bulletin she would have one of her serf-boys whipped. When Ivan came home on a visit, the whole household breathed more freely, knowing that the mistress would be in her softest mood.

Power for her was a means of testing the love and devotion of her family and 'subjects' and/or a surrogate for the love of which she could never be sure. She held the purse-strings, and she kept her sons short of money almost on principle. But from the time Nikolai went into the army and Ivan went abroad, her authority and influence began a long, slow process of decline, though it was not till the end of the 1840s, in the last year of her life, that her sons freed themselves from her completely.

She is often blamed for 'breaking her son's spirit', for having been the cause of that 'weakness of will', which Turgenev in later life was to claim or proclaim rather than extenuate or excuse. Incidentally, he himself offered a much more appealing aetiology. According to him, he had been, as a child, short, obstinate and mathematically inclined; but at puberty he underwent a mysterious illness, which kept him in bed for several months and from which he arose almost full-grown, warm-hearted and sensitized to literature and art, while crippled in will. In other words, he had outgrown his strength and paid the price in a reversal of personality.

Be that as it may, we must beware of making too much of this 'weakness of will'. Turgenev's self-denigration on this score tends to be couched in hyperbolic terms; and his friends tend to attribute to weakness of will conduct they disapprove, such as his relation with Pauline Viardot, where will-power was not the issue.

Turgenev was inexperienced and inept in practical matters, excessively sensitive, much of the time, to other people's feelings, and painfully insecure: and these traits, separately or in combination, fully explain most or all of the failures to keep engagements, the occasional insincerities, the wavering intentions and changes of plan, the delusive time-tables that were a constant trial to his friends – and his editors.

The insecurity may have been a legacy from his mother (or both parents): he was childishly incapable of exercising authority and of rejecting appeals for help, support or subsidies, and was therefore grossly exploited by the unscrupulous. But if his mother's despotism was at the root of his insecurity, it was also at the root of his abiding hatred of oppression and all forms of inhumanity and of his cult of freedom and self-respect: so that, paradoxically, she gave him (unintentionally) far more than she was able to take from him.

As for infirmity of will, that played a part in the trivia of everyday existence; but in the fields that were most important to him – love and friendship, art and literature, political principles – his integrity remained unsullied. And anyone observing his persistence in social and literary activities amid the excruciating physical sufferings of his last years can only marvel at the courage and resoluteness she was then able to muster.

A 'remarkable decade': 1843–52

Early in 1843 Turgenev was introduced to the critic Belinsky. To the intellectually awakened and forward-looking of his generation Belinsky was what Stankevich had been to his little circle of friends: a conscience and a model of moral and intellectual integrity. But Stankevich was gentle and taught mainly by example; Belinsky was a preacher and fighter, and spared neither others nor himself in his criticism. Stankevich had been an amateur poet and an amateur philosopher; Belinsky was a professional critic of literature and, through literature, of society.

Turgenev appeared to Belinsky like manna in the desert. Here was a young man (seven years his junior) with whom he could talk for hours on all the subjects that interested him, an intellectual peer, but one far more widely read than he and with that solid grounding in philosophy and foreign literatures which he lacked. One, moreover, who had as much to learn from him in the field of life as to teach in the field of books. Turgenev's character was still far from formed: he was to write later that he had had no 'face' of his own till he turned 30; and Belinsky dealt severely with his young friend's aristocratic foibles, childish inconsiderateness and literary dilettantism. Turgenev accepted the mockery and chiding with characteristic humility and good humour; he looked up to Belinsky during the five years of their friendship and revered his memory to the end of his own life. And if Belinsky did not live quite long enough to see him with a face of his own, to Belinsky must go much or most of the credit for transforming him from an amateur to a professional writer: that is, a writer who saw literature as his life's work and committed all his powers to his writing.

This might be disputed by those who hold that everything in Turgenev's adult life took second place to his love for Pauline Viardot, whom he met towards the end of that same fateful year, 1843. But – apart from the fact that Pauline's own sense of vocation and example of professional commitment can only have reinforced Belinsky's teaching – this is an unprofitable dispute: it begs too many questions, and there is too much we still do not know about their relation in its various phases.[9]

What we do know is that the 22-year-old *diva* came to Russia with an Italian opera company for the winter seasons of 1843–4, 1844–5 and 1845–6; that she took St Petersburg and Moscow by storm; and that Turgenev fell desperately in love with her and continued to love her through the remaining 40 years of his life. We know that in 1845 he followed her to the West and spent five or six months in France – all but a fortnight between Paris and Cour-tavenel, the Viardots' country estate, some 60 km south-east of Paris. We know that between the beginning of 1847 and the middle of 1850 he spent over three years in the West – all but a few weeks between Paris and Courtavenel, where, during the absences of Pauline and her husband on tour, he kept her mother company, learned Spanish, steeped himself in Spanish literature of the Golden Age, and wrote Russian sketches, stories and plays in greater numbers than ever before or after. It was evidently a happy period.

But although we have nearly a hundred letters written by Turgenev to Pauline Viardot in the first ten years of their friendship (as compared with only just over two hundred published for the following thirty years), we still have no clear idea of the character of their relationship then (or at any subsequent period). Were they ever lovers? Did Turgenev father any of the three children born to Pauline in the 1850s? These questions have been answered both positively and negatively; but we do not know – and that is obviously because Turgenev and Pauline wanted nobody to know. Only a dozen or so of her letters to him have been published, though she must have written hundreds. His published letters to her must represent only a small fraction, considering that in many, if not most, of their periods apart he bound himself to write to her at least once a week. And what are we to make of the fact that for some periods we have not a single published letter from him to her? Did the letters of 1860 to mid-1862 reflect too deep an estrangement? Did those of 1875–8 and of 1881 betray too great an intimacy?

If Turgenev's letters to her tell us too little of the everyday texture of their relationship, they do make plain his feelings and his attitude towards her. It is a feeling of romantic worship, reminiscent in some respects of the courtly love of the Middle Ages. He prostrates himself before her. He kisses her hands or her feet innumerable times or for hours on end. He treasures her nail-clippings. When she is on tour, he follows her in imagination hour by hour, projecting himself into the opera houses where she is achieving her new triumphs. Although he does not use the term (no doubt because it had become too trite), it is plain that she is a sort of goddess to him. Her will is his law. He consults her on all the major decisions of his life and adopts her counsel unquestioningly. Yet, on a more mundane level, he reports to her his daily doings, his plans, and later on the vicissitudes of his health, in intimate detail; he worries about her physical wellbeing and comfort, advises her how to take care of her health, and, in the early years, discusses her music and even ventures to offer suggestions on the playing of certain rôles.

Of the dozen or so published letters from Pauline to Turgenev, only three date from their first decade, and two of these are followed by notes from her husband, while the third is incomplete. She writes with affection, but – not surprisingly in the circumstances – with none of Turgenev's extravagance. Like his, her letters consist largely of accounts of her activities and surroundings; each assumes that every detail of his/her life will be precious to the other. It is not clear that she is in love, but she loves him – and enjoys his adoration.

Her two letters in the second decade are brief and, at best, coolly friendly – though there is a touch of pique when she suspects that he may have written to one of his lady friends sooner than to her. Her three letters of the third decade are also brief – a businesslike summary of her doings. The remaining four letters – towards the end of their fourth decade – seem slightly longer and distinctly warmer: owing perhaps, at least partly, to her evident fear that he may be tempted to stay in Russia for good: she does not want to lose him.

For Turgenev the first decade of his love was certainly a period of growth and mainly happy. It quickened and matured his creativity: his four long poems, all his ten plays, all but five of his twenty-five (or twenty-seven) sketches and nine of his thirty-three stories were written in those ten years. He was drawn, for long periods, to the West, where he broadened his literary, political and cultural horizons in ways that set him apart from his great contemporaries. He extended his repertory of languages and literatures by the inclusion of Spanish, paid tribute to the alien genius of Calderón, while adding Cervantes to his personal pantheon, to join Homer, Shakespeare, Goethe, Pushkin and Gogol. He made more than a start in the process of familiarizing himself with foreign peoples and ways of life, which is a necessary condition of achieving a serene and equitable vision of one's own country and culture. And he lived through the crisis and collapse of the French Revolution of 1848, which shattered the illusions and hopes of so many of his contemporaries. It shattered Turgenev's youthful illusions too; and since his political mentor, Belinsky, had died before the *débâcle*, he had to work out a new creed and course for himself.

He did not embrace the *status quo*, as did all too many, nor did he seek refuge in the apocalyptic populism of a Dostoevsky or the radical populism of a Herzen. He formed the view that the salvation of Russia could not come from the people and would not come by revolution – at any rate, in his lifetime. It must come from 'above', and gradually, and through education. That is what he meant in calling himself 'a convinced Westerner', and to this faith he adhered for the rest of his life in the teeth of contumely from both Left and Right.

In the middle of 1850 Turgenev returned to Russia. This was not just a yielding to the pressures of financial stringency, which his mother had been applying throughout his absence: he went back firmly resolved – with the backing of Pauline Viardot – to come to a financial arrangement that would set him free to live where he chose (and to deliver his brother Nikolai, now married, from his even more miserable dependence). The old lady tried to play for time, but the brothers presented a united front; Ivan – with Pauline to report to – stood unusually firm, made the issue one of self-respect, and withdrew with Nikolai and his family to their father's small estate. Varvara Turgeneva prepared to take vengeance on the rebels but, fortunately, died before her plans could be carried out.

So Turgenev was now his own master and – although he left it to Nikolai to settle the division of the inheritance, stipulating only that Spasskoe should be his – in easy circumstances. Or rather, he should have been in easy circumstances. Nikolai was to die a millionaire in rubles; Turgenev was, through the rest of his life, often short of money, reduced several times to borrowing consider-able sums, forced in the 1860s to sell his Baden-Baden villa at a loss and in the 1870s to sell his collection of paintings at a loss and his horse and carriages. This was not due to vice or folly. He did not gamble or speculate. It was due partly to his uncalculating gener-osity, but even more to his complete lack of practical sense: he once described himself as 'as stupid as a saint and as inexperienced as a baby'. Discovering that he was incapable of running his estates himself, he put them in charge of a succession of stewards who proved as incompetent as he was and/or robbed and swindled him.

Turgenev's 'remarkable decade' was rounded off by two events of major significance. In February 1852 Gogol died – Gogol, the leading Russian writer of the preceding fifteen years, revered by Turgenev only less than Pushkin; and Turgenev, incensed by the indifference to such a loss of government and high society, wrote an obituary in which he proclaimed Gogol 'a great man'. When the article was banned by the St Petersburg censorship, Turgenev sent it to Moscow, where it was passed and published. The government, on the instructions of the Emperor himself, decided that such 'open insubordination' must be punished: by a month of gaol, in a local police station, to be followed by relegation to his estate under police surveillance for an indefinite period. Turgenev bore his reclusion with fortitude and resolved to make the best of his banishment to the country, though he realized that as long as the Emperor lived he would not be able to leave Russia. He was at last

on his own as he had never been in any previous period of his
existence.

Storm-tossed: 1853–62

The confinement on his estate lasted only a year and a half, but it
was during that time that Pauline Viardot paid her last visit to
Russia. She sang in St Petersburg and Moscow; and Turgenev,
braving the severe penalties which would have attended discovery,
stole up to Moscow with a borrowed passport to spend a few days
with her. The reunion evidently failed to restore the closeness of
the years in France. His letters grow short, the intervals between
them grow longer, and within a year he is lamenting that he feels
their relationship now holds only by a thread. And he had to wait
till after the death of the Emperor and the end of the Crimean War
to return to the West.

We do not know what happened between them when Turgenev
finally arrived in Paris in August 1856. He had to face the fact that
during their separation Pauline had given birth to two children and
that within some two months of his return she was pregnant again.
When, after his mother's death, he had stayed on in Russia instead
of hastening back to her – had she turned back to her husband, after
a ten years' break in childbearing? Or were these children the
offspring of a lover (or lovers) who had supplanted Turgenev? In
any case, Pauline must have made him understand that he could not
hope to win her back to the kind of relationship they had had before
1850. There is no doubt that his health – always apt to give trouble
in one form or another – was seriously affected. For the next three
years he was tormented by bladder or kidney trouble (stone?), and
while it is true that his father had suffered similarly at an even
earlier age, it is worth noting that in Turgenev the onset coincided
with Pauline's latest pregnancy.[10]

Paradoxically, this decade (1853–62) of his estrangement from
Pauline Viardot – when their relationship reached its lowest point:
after she had turned for comfort and children to another man (or
other men) and he had first fallen back on an affair with a serf-girl
and then played with the idea of marrying a distant cousin (who
seemed willing) – this decade marked a peak in his creativity.
Turning away from the genres with which he had experimented in
the preceding twenty years – lyric and narrative poetry, plays and

sketches – he now concentrated his mature powers on only two, the story and the novel, and within these ten years produced nine stories, including at least three of his best, and his four best novels: a genre that was new to him and that did not come easily.

Between Turgenev's stolen ten days with Pauline in 1853 and his return to France, perhaps the most curious event was his meeting with Tolstoy in November 1855, which inaugurated a relation as peculiar in its way as that with Pauline. Tolstoy, ten years younger than Turgenev, came to St Petersburg straight from the siege of Sebastopol, which he had helped to defend for a year against the armies and fleets of Britain, France and Turkey. He knew and admired Turgenev's writing; Turgenev knew and admired his and divined in him, even before they met, the future greatest writer of his generation. Though still only in his thirties, Turgenev already felt it part of his literary mission to foster and promote the genius of his Russian contemporaries: he read voraciously and was constantly discovering 'new talents' and recommending them, with sometimes excessive enthusiasm, to his editors. He had himself 'launched' the poetry of Tyutchev and Fet, acting as editor-in-chief of a first edition of Tyutchev's collected poems and of a revised version of Fet's original and translated poetry.

It was natural for him to fall into an attitude of this kind towards Tolstoy, who was still sowing his wild oats and still by no means certain of his vocation as a writer, and this alone might have sufficed to set them at odds: Tolstoy's reaction to any form of authority was apt to be fierce rebellion. Whatever was generally accepted, he was impelled to question or reject; and in argument Turgenev's charm and urbanity were no match for the younger man's often arrogant aggressiveness. But they loved each other: both were convinced of that. In the winter of 1855–6 Tolstoy stayed in Turgenev's apartment; early in 1857, when Tolstoy came on his first visit to Western Europe, Turgenev was his guide around Paris and accompanied him on a short trip to Dijon. They continued to correspond, and during Turgenev's sojourns in Russia in 1858 and 1859, they met occasionally and briefly, while both becoming more and more convinced that they could love each other only at a distance. In 1860 they did not meet; when they did, in 1861, Tolstoy provoked Turgenev into insulting him so that a duel between them was only narrowly avoided. Both recognized that they had overstepped proper limits and apologized; but after that, all direct relations between them were suspended, though Turgenev continued to follow Tolstoy's writing with warm concern. In 1878 Tolstoy proposed a reconciliation; Turgenev responded eagerly, and on his last four visits to Russia stayed briefly with Tolstoy and his family at Yasnaya Polyana.

No simple explanation will fit this odd love–hate relationship. Turgenev opined that they were made of different clay – which may have been true but was hardly enlightening. He also fumed that Tolstoy hated everything he (Turgenev) loved and *vice versa*, but this was demonstrably untrue: they both loved hunting and music and literature and (though in different ways) the Russian peasant, not to mention that they both had their roots in the same area of Central Russia and were both members of the same social class. And if they differed in their literary tastes and their philosophy of life – Turgenev's tolerance and pliancy enabled him to remain friends with men who differed from him no less.

When Turgenev returned to the West in 1856, it was not without serious misgivings, and his unhappiness was soon evident enough to embolden old friends to urge on him the folly of staying in France (meaning, on the edge of the Viardot nest) and the need to settle down in Russia if he was ever to have a normal life of his own. He recognized the force of their arguments and was torn between conflicting feelings – between his unhappy love and the prospect of growing old in exile and loneliness, on the one hand, and, on the other, his longing for a home and family of his own in the midst of his own folk.

At first he drifted helplessly back to Courtavenel; but the sight of Pauline as a happy mother for the third time in five years must have seemed more than he could bear, for after less than two months he set off abruptly for Italy; and after five months there and flying visits to Paris and London, in the middle of 1858 he headed back to Russia. There he remained for eleven whole months; and though he spent the summer of 1859 in France – two of the four months at Courtavenel – by September he was in Russia again and remained there for seven and a half months. These were his two longest visits home in the last twenty-seven years of his life (i.e., after 1856); but their duration was not wholly due to distress about his relation with Pauline.

The new Emperor, Alexander II, had opened to public discussion the question of the emancipation of the serfs, which during the preceding forty years had been only whispered about or sighed for in Russia, and by the end of 1857 it was clear that emancipation was coming; its modalities were yet to be debated, for another three years.

Turgenev had hated serfdom since his boyhood, its cruelties had horrified and disgusted him, its flagrant flouting of human dignity had made it appear to him the greatest and most intolerable evil of Russian life – an enemy to be combated relentlessly until it was destroyed. His *A Sportsman's Sketches* had dealt that enemy a heavy blow, opening the eyes or stirring the consciences of his generation (Alexander himself, as Heir Apparent, was said to have read and been moved by it). And now 'the face of the live new dawn' could be descried on the horizon. Turgenev was, as he wrote, 'happy to have lived to see' this great event – and not disposed to wait for the conclusion of the debates. He would free his serfs ahead of time, and on terms so generous that no Emancipation Act was likely to grant more, or perhaps even as much.

That is what he did. To Tolstoy he wrote from abroad: 'I have decided to devote the whole of next year to a settlement with the peasants; even if it means giving them everything – I will cease to be a serf-owner.'[11] And, a little later, in asking a friend to precede him to Spasskoe and have all the legal procedure and papers prepared in advance of his arrival, he summarizes his instructions in the words: '*I am ready for any and every sacrifice!*'[12]

The settlement, in spite of Turgenev's disregard for his own interests, was neither quick nor easy. Though he informs Pauline Viardot as early as November 1858 that he has reached an agreement with the peasants, it is only fourteen months later that he is able to inform his brother of the details. He admits then that the new arrangements will cost him about one-quarter of his income in the first year; but this estimate, as well as his hope that the loss would prove only temporary, turned out to be too optimistic, for the peasants, transferred from labour-service to quit-rent, failed to pay their dues either regularly or in full, and he was not the man to apply legal or other pressures.

Once this business was concluded, he was again drawn irresistibly westward. He spent nearly half of 1860 in France without staying at Courtavenel for any length of time, and it was in the last weeks of that year that his relations with Pauline Viardot evidently came to crisis point. Two letters written in December of that year give us some idea of its seriousness, if only vaguely of its nature.

[T]he other day my heart died. I am telling you this as a fact – I don't know how to express [*nazvat'*] it. You understand what I am trying to say. The past fell away from me once and for all, but when I had parted with it, I saw that I had nothing left, that my whole life had fallen away from me together with that [past]. – I felt wretched – but soon I turned to stone; and now I feel that I can go on living in this state. But if the slightest hope of a return were to spring up again, it would shake me to the depths of my being. I have experienced such numbness before, like a crust of ice overlaying a voiceless grief . . . once the crust hardens, the grief beneath will vanish.[13]

A key to this lament may perhaps be found in two sentences addressed three weeks later to the same correspondent:

Above all, never seek to utter or hear a *last* word in any matter, however just and sincere that last word may be: such last, final words usually lead to fresh misunderstandings. Be as satisfied as possible with approximations to happiness . . . nothing on earth is certain and clear except unhappiness.[14]

Taking these two outbursts together, it seems difficult not to deduce that Turgenev had rashly demanded of Pauline a clear definition of the status of their relationship and that her 'final word' had proved shatteringly different from what he had hoped. For the period between January 1860 and June 1862 no letters from Turgenev to Pauline have been published. Though this does not prove that none were written, it does suggest that, if any were, they were not such as Pauline would have wished to keep or to share with posterity. But in the second half of 1862 there are signs that her attitude is changing again: the Viardots spend several months in Baden-Baden, no doubt to explore the possibility of settling there, as they actually did the following year – and Turgenev stayed there for nine weeks at the same time. One might even try to date the sealing of the new entente by a drawing of Pauline's representing two interlaced triangles with the legend in Turgenev's handwriting (in Russian): 'This figure was drawn by P . . . 6 November/25 October 1862, in the evening, in my room, in Paris, 210 rue de Rivoli.'[15]

The 'German' period: 1863–70

The Viardots' move to Baden-Baden in the autumn of 1863 was prompted by Pauline's decision to give up singing in the big opera houses, as she realized that her voice had passed its peak, and by her husband's rooted detestation of the régime of Napoleon III. They built themselves a villa there, which remained their base for the next eight years, although towards the end of the period they stayed for some months in Karlsruhe and, later, in Weimar, partly in connection with Pauline's musical engagements, partly to secure better art and music teachers for their children. Pauline continued to sing in opera in some smaller musical centres, but she turned to teaching and returned to composing too. Her salon in Baden-Baden became a brilliant musical and social centre, graced by a cosmopolitan élite, in which famous musicians jostled crowned heads (Brahms, Wagner, Clara Schumann; the King and Queen of Prussia, the Grand Duke and Grand Duchess of Baden) and listened, in the little concert hall/opera house built in the grounds of the villa, to concerts and to operettas composed by Pauline, for which Turgenev had written the libretti. They were acted and sung by her pupils; Turgenev also acted in them, evoking contemptuous amusement in some of the royal personages and resentment in some of his Russian friends at such 'humiliation' in the service of his lady.

For Pauline had recalled Turgenev to her side, and this German period was to be the happiest, after 1850, in his relation with her. She called and he came. He had never changed towards her; but why did she call? No doubt there were several factors. Her 'semi-retirement' as a singer meant that she could spend much more of her time at home and left her far more time and energy for a personal life than she had had when constantly on tour in the preceding twenty years. Now she had leisure for her children, she had leisure for friendship – and need of a friend who could share this new mode of existence in a foreign country as her ageing husband could not.[16]

But perhaps, even so, she would not have ventured to reinstate this adorer in her intimacy if she had not felt that now she could, at last, do so safely. In 1856 she had been impelled to thrust him away from her, presumably, because his reappearance threatened to disrupt the closeness with her husband which she had built up in the first half of the fifties. If, six years later, that danger had passed although Turgenev was as much in love with her as ever, was it not (to borrow the delicate formula of one of his lady friends) because her 'female age had passed'?[17] This would be a wild surmise but for a sentence in one of Turgenev's last letters to his daughter[18] (then in her forty-first year, as Pauline had been in 1862): 'I confess I thought you had reached an age at which certain needs of nature cease to be felt.' On what was he more likely to have based such an assumption than on the experience of Pauline Viardot – the woman he knew best and (in his eyes) the paragon of womanhood?

So they were free – he to worship as fervently as in his youth, to share her music, her family and eventually her home; she to abandon herself to a love which, for all its warmth and sweetness, could remain 'innocent' and to share his literary activity inasmuch as he made her the ultimate judge of all his writings. He moved to Baden-Baden in 1863, settled there and built a villa for himself; he followed the Viardots to Karlsruhe in 1868–9 and to Weimar in 1869–70. In the years 1864–70 his visits to France, where his daughter was living, averaged ten days a year; in three of the eight German years he did not go home to Russia at all and in the other five his sojourns there added up to no more than eight months.

Soon his life near Pauline came to seem his only reality: away from her, life took on a dreamlike quality, an aura of unreality;[19] she is the very breath of life: away from her, he cannot breathe, he wilts and sickens.[20]

And in the midst of this family life he discovers a fresh joy, a fresh romance. Claudie (Didie to her family) was Pauline Viardot's second child, born in 1852. Turgenev later claimed to have fallen in love with her at first sight, when she was 4 years old; but in fact, up till 1862, references to Didie in his letters to her mother barely single her out from the other children. In 1862, at 10, she not only becomes a person in her own right, she becomes an object of devotion. In his first surviving letter to her, he draws a portrait of himself and asks: 'Consider whether you would like an old Don Quixote such as this for your future husband!' and adds: 'Be that as it may, this Don Quixote loves you madly and kisses you as hard as he can.'[21] At the same time he writes to Pauline: 'That little person holds a power over me . . . of which she has not remained unaware. I daren't say to her that I kiss her hands, but I do';[22] and, a few weeks later: 'there is only one Didie in the world. Don't read her this: she doesn't need to hear such words to know that I belong to her, but she could put a collar round my neck like Flambeau's [one of their dogs] and the worst of it is that I wouldn't mind at all.'[23]

For the next six years we have no letters to Didie (apart from one humorous missive addressed jointly to her and to (her younger sister and brother) Marianne and Paul. The references to her in his letters to Pauline show that she is still his favourite, but no more. From 1867 on, when she is 15, he starts extolling her beauty (and circulating photographs of her) and her talent (as a painter) to his friends. In 1868 he begins putting aside money for her dowry, and by the time she marries, in 1874, this amounts to 100,000 francs. From 1868 on, he writes to her regularly when they are apart; for the last fifteen years of his life we have several score of these letters, distributed through all but two of those years.[24]

In 1869 she is his 'little idol', he loves her 'inexpressibly', he 'adore[s] her with all [his] might';[25] in 1870 she is his 'dear angel, white as a little lamb', he tells her 'everything that crosses [his] mind';[26] in 1873 he kisses her 'dear hands a THOUSAND times', she 'know[s] how [her] old friend adores [her]'.[27] And there is no change of style when she marries; rather, the expressions of his love can range more freely.[28]

As in his letters to Pauline, many of the more romantic effusions are couched in German – in fact, we find identical or very similar formulas in the letters to mother and daughter. Paradoxically, he is less inhibited in writing to the daughter, regarding his affection for Didie as paternal and therefore, by definition, 'innocent' – a view clearly shared by Didie and her husband. But who could have expected a master of language like Turgenev to have stylized in such similar terms two feelings which he must have experienced as radically different?

His affection for Marianne, while warmly fatherly, seems to have had none of the loverlike overtones of his feelings for Didie, though one must bear in mind that only a couple of his letters to her (out of several score extant) have been published. Both girls evidently returned his love and remained close to him to the end of his life.

Happiness, however, did not raise Turgenev's literary productivity. Whereas the years 'in limbo' had brought forth his four best novels, the German period produced only one, and that one regarded by most critics as the weakest. The number of stories is the same, nine, but perhaps only one or two from the sixties should be ranked with the three or four best of the previous period. Nor did he shut his eyes to the fact that he was losing touch with his homeland and that his writing was bound to be affected by this: 'to an artist his native air is essential', he admitted early in the period,

and as time goes on, his lamentations on this theme are repeated
more and more poignantly.

On the other hand, the German period witnessed a rapid spread
of Turgenev's reputation in the West. French and English translations of *A Sportsman's Sketches* go back to the time of the
Crimean War; and from then on, translations of his works
appeared in France every two or three years, keeping fairly
abreast of his new writings. In Germany a similar close following
of his production began in 1862; at this time Turgenev formed personal ties with a number of German writers, artists and critics,
some of whom translated his works, while others celebrated them
in articles and reviews. Paradoxically, this coincided with a slump
in his standing in Russia, following the controversies provoked by
Fathers and Children (1862) and then by *Smoke* (1867), which led
him to see himself as 'probably the most unpopular man in Russia'
just then. Even this failed to poison his happiness, to judge by the
generally satisfactory state of his health and the less frequent inci-
dence of depression, as compared with either the following or the
preceding period.

Back in France, last years, death: 1871–83

The 'German period' was brought to an abrupt end by the Franco-
Prussian War of 1870–1. Though the Viardots hoped (as did Turgenev) that Napoleon III would be defeated and welcomed the fall
of his Empire, they felt they could not stay on enemy territory
while France was being overrun and humiliated – not to mention
that it was more difficult, if not impossible, in wartime for Pauline
to make a living. So they sought refuge in England (attended, of
course, by Turgenev) until the end of the war allowed them to
return, in 1871, to their former house in Paris. Turgenev, who had
always detested Paris, joined them there, occupying four rooms on
one of the upper floors.

In 1874 he and the Viardots jointly acquired a summer home at
Bougival, on the Seine just west of Paris, and these two homes he
continued to share with them for the remainder of his life. Louis
Viardot was now a septuagenarian who had faded almost completely into the background, and it was Turgenev who escorted 'his
ladies' (Pauline and her daughters) everywhere; his friends complained that he was too often unavailable to them because every-

thing and everyone took second place to the 'needs' of those ladies.

Pauline continued to teach, and pupils flocked to her from all parts of Europe. She continued to have regular musical, and occasional literary-musical, parties at her house, in which she and her children often sang or played and which attracted a varied and distinguished audience. Didie and Marianne married, in 1874 and 1881 respectively, but remained close to home, and Turgenev continued to be as involved in their lives and was as anxious and excited about their confinements as if they had been his own children.

These were the people, the events, the settings which formed in large part the fabric of his everyday existence; his private life (writing, visits to Russia, dinners with Flaubert and his circle, etc.) was inserted into the spaces left unoccupied by the Viardots. The death of his brother Nikolai, in 1879, did not affect him greatly, either emotionally or materially. The vicissitudes of his daughter's marriage were a cause of considerable expense and some anxiety, especially in the last two years of his life. His son-in-law was then facing ruin and eventually went bankrupt; Paulinette and her two children sought refuge with Turgenev, who had to find a hiding-place for them (in Switzerland) and assume the whole burden of their financial future, at the cost of selling his horse and carriages and his small collection of paintings. He acted promptly and effectively; he did his duty by his family, as he had always done to the best of his ability, but – except, perhaps, in the few days of crisis – still with a minimum of emotional involvement.

Though more and more reluctant to face separation from Pauline, he continued to travel. Apart from three cures at Carlsbad early in the period and four flying visits to England towards its end, that meant travel to Russia: eight visits in those twelve years, covering about eighteen months. He went home to see his friends, to write in the peaceful solitude of Spasskoe, to keep a hand on the pulse of Russian life – in particular, to observe with a view to the writing of his last novel. He went home, above all, because he still ached for Russia, though the roots he had struck in the West proved too deep and strong to allow of any permanent or even long-term return. But he went home – all the more willingly because of the changed attitude of his public. The decade of nihilism, the sixties, had given place to the decade of populism; and the successors of the angry young who had raged at his portrayal of the 'nihilist' in

Fathers and Children and at the scathing Westernism of *Smoke*
were ready to salute in him the champion of freedom for the serfs
(in *A Sportsman's Sketches*), of moral integrity (in *A Nest of
Gentry*), of youthful heroism (in *On the Eve*) – and in fact
welcomed him with speeches and ovations which astonished,
delighted and humbled him all at once.

But his literary productivity continued to decline. Three sketches
conceived, and perhaps drafted, in the 'remarkable decade' and
now written down for inclusion in a new edition of *A Sportsman's
Sketches*, two others of more recent inspiration, one novel and six
stories – make up the sum of his fiction in the 'French period'.

Yet Turgenev was by no means idle. His conception of his
literary 'mission' had broadened since the fifties. He not only
continued to seek and discover new Russian talents among the
younger generation; he not only exerted himself to cheer the
flagging spirits of such contemporaries as Polonsky and Saltykov:
but he deliberately set himself to promote a knowledge of Russian
literature in the West and to familiarize his countrymen with the
latest works of the leading French writers – Flaubert, Zola,
Maupassant, Daudet, Edmond de Goncourt – who had now
become his friends and admirers. All this required extraordinarily
generous sacrifices of his time. The correspondence – with editors
in Russia to persuade them to publish the works of his established
Western friends and of his unknown Russian *protégés*, with
Western editors and critics to create interest around the translation
and publication of major Russian writers – this correspondence, a
good part of which has survived, probably accounted for only a
fraction of his time and effort. For he not only read the many scripts
submitted to him by beginners – he criticized, encouraged, advised
the young authors, with some of whom he continued to correspond
for years. In some cases he was prepared to subsidize publication or
translation out of his own pocket. He himself translated two of
Flaubert's stories into Russian and collaborated in translations into
French of his own works and some of those of other writers. He did
his best to hearten the young Vsevolod Garshin and came to his
support during and after his mental breakdown. He forced Tolstoy,
whom he considered the greatest Russian writer of his age, upon
the attention of Western readers.

Nor was it only young writers who appealed to Turgenev for help
and advice. Young radicals, political refugees from Russia were

drawn to him as to a familiar centre and source of comfort or support in the midst of an alien and unsympathetic world. He received them, listened to them, argued with them, tried to find work for them, tried to get their political writings published, gave them money or recommendations, raised money for individuals and for the Russian community in Paris,[29] appealed to the Russian authorities on behalf of those who regretted their emigration and wished to go home, warned them of such impending police action against them as came to his knowledge. He referred, perhaps with tongue in cheek, to 'my revolutionaries' and informed P. L. Lavrov, with some complacency, that he was himself under police surveillance and regarded by the police as the 'very fountainhead of nihilism' (*samaya matka nigilistov*).[30] And all these activities were carried on in spite of the ailments of a prematurely ageing body, amid recurring bouts of depression, and finally in the throes of his protracted and excruciating last illness.

Considering Turgenev's undoubted tendency to hypochondria and the limitations of medical knowledge in his lifetime, it would be futile to seek to trace out his medical history. That his big body was basically strong and sound is implied by its capacity to endure fatigue (for instance, in hunting) and its long, stout resistance to the fatal cancer. That some, or perhaps many, of his complaints were psychosomatic is highly probable. This may apply to the cardiac troubles to which there are sporadic allusions in his student days and again, briefly, at the end of the sixties and in the mid-seventies, but which appear to have taken on organic form, as angina pectoris, only in the last few years of his life. It may apply also to the bladder (or kidney) trouble which made his existence a misery at the end of the fifties – at the time of his estrangement from Pauline – but apparently vanished during the German period and reappeared only occasionally and at long intervals during the seventies. And it may be reflected in the premature appearance of physical ageing, foreshadowed in his early thirties when his hair began to turn white.

At the age of 32 we find him writing: 'I am sick of Petersburg – and terribly sick of my body – it is clumsy, old, ugly – and aches into the bargain. Nobody should be allowed to write – to anybody – in a state of mind like my present one.' Here, as so often, bodily disorder goes with mental depression (though he could also be overwhelmed by wretchedness while in good bodily health).[31] In his forties he looked quite grandfatherly. At 50 he regarded himself

as an old man: 'When a man has turned 50, he lives as though in a
fortress that is under siege and will inevitably be taken, by death.'[32]
Not surprisingly, his health gave least trouble and his melancholy
was mostly in abeyance throughout the German period.Even his
gout, which was probably the least psychologically determined of
his ailments, seems to have visited him only rarely in Baden-Baden.

Since the spinal cancer which killed him was discovered only
after his death, we cannot know when the disease set in. Presumably not later than April 1882, when Charcot diagnosed angina
pectoris and Turgenev became immobilized and, realizing that he
was terminally ill, made his literary and financial plans accordingly.
In the sixteen-and-a-half months that followed he yielded on
occasion to illusions as to the probable duration of his malady and
even as to the possibility of a lasting remission; but as the slight
easing during the summer of 1882, in the country, was succeeded by
a return of the symptoms in full force, he braced himself 'to look the
devil in the eye without losing heart'.[33]

The pains that racked his body were such that he could neither
stand nor walk nor lie (during the summer, he had been able to
stand and walk for a few minutes at a time with the aid of some sort
of 'machine' and to take drives); he could lie and sleep in the initial
and final phases only with the help of morphine. Pain was at times
so intense that his 'bellowings could be heard the length of the
street'.[34] The dosages of morphine had to be stepped up as the pain
increased and, as a result of either or both, he had periods of
delirium when he became abusive or violent.

Yet he never relaxed his hold on life or his concern for other
people. He continued to write (though the movement of his arm in
writing became painful) till within a few days of his death: at least
460 letters in sixteen months and, barely a year before the end, his
last story.[35] The letters went to his daughter and granddaughter, to
Didie, to his friends in Russia, to his doctor in Paris (cool, factual
reports of the ups and downs of his symptoms and the details of his
daily routine – even a literary account of the excision of a small
'neuroma' from his abdomen, which, owing to his heart condition,
had to be performed with only ether instead of chloroform); they
went to editors on behalf of unpublished authors; to a young writer
with advice how to write, to a young opera singer with advice how
to act; to various agents about financial and literary business; to
Mariya Savina carrying on their epistolary flirtation,[36] to literary

colleagues with words of cheer, to Tolstoy imploring him to return to literature.

After the end of January 1883 the flow of letters dwindles to a trickle. In May, Louis Viardot dies, after a long illness: Pauline had had to divide her nursing between the two men. A few weeks later Turgenev's suffering has become 'unendurable'; he longs for death – he who all his adult life had lived in terror of death – and asks his friends to wish it may come soon. Pauline's daughters joined her in nursing him. He died 3 September 1883.

It took five weeks for his body, accompanied by Didie and Marianne and their husbands, to travel back to St Petersburg, where he had wished to be buried near Belinsky. It was seen off at the Gare du Nord in Paris by several hundred Russians and distinguished Frenchmen. In Russia the government took stringent measures to regulate and minimize public mourning; but the funeral train was met at every station by sorrowing crowds, and in St Petersburg the funeral procession, with its deputations from 176 cultural and professional organizations, was (except for Dostoevsky's funeral two years earlier)[37] the most impressive public farewell to a private citizen ever seen.

Reputation

Goncourt sees Turgenev as 'a gentle giant', 'a Druid', 'the good old monk in "Romeo and Juliet"'.[38] He was tall and handsome – not because of any special regularity or beauty of feature (he himself insisted that there was nothing 'aristocratic' about his appearance),[39] but in virtue of 'the nobility of his bearing, his pleasant smile, the mane of white hair thrown back from his fine forehead, above all, the attractiveness of his glance. His eyes were not "immense", as Daudet asserts, nor even outstandingly beautiful – but intelligent, honest, kind: the eyes of an exceptionally good human being.'[40] 'His laugh was infectious, childlike.'[41]

His charm of manner attracted young and old, men and women. He loved children, and they responded by treating him as one of themselves. The young revolutionaries who, in the seventies, came to him for help – prickly, on the lookout for the slightest sign of patronizing or condescension – were disarmed by his modest simplicity and his willingness to be of use while not disguising his disagreement with their views.

He was a brilliant conversationalist – or rather, *raconteur* – who could hold spellbound for a whole evening even as sophisticated a company as that of Flaubert and his friends. They were struck by 'the originality of a superior mind (*esprit*)' and by 'his immense and cosmopolitan knowledge',[42] meaning, by 'knowledge', knowledge of both books and life. They were struck also by the differences between Russian and French values, between a Russian and a French view of life, which Turgenev, on one long-remembered occasion, sought to sum up in the pithy formula: 'Oui, vous êtes des hommes de la loi, de l'honneur; nous . . . nous sommes des hommes de l'humanité!'[43]

Flaubert paid tribute to his friend's 'distinction'[44] – for him a quality of supreme importance – and enthused repeatedly over the subtlety of his aesthetic perceptiveness and the sureness of his critical judgment.

Pauline Viardot called Turgenev 'the saddest of men'.[45] And it is evident that a vein of deep melancholy imbues both his work and his life from early on, fed openly and directly by his fear of death and his sense of the precariousness of life, and, less consciously, by a sense of unworthiness or guilt, expressed in his reaction of shame to applause and praise[46] and even to 'being loved so much',[47] and, more generally, by the excessive – and, clearly, unfeigned – modesty which pervades his correspondence. This melancholy grew with the passing of time, complicated by his homesickness for Russia and misgivings about having wasted his youth and sacrificed part of his potential as a writer.

But this was less than half the story. Not only was the gloom kept largely under control and in perspective by intelligence and irony, but Turgenev retained in his make-up, all through life, a great deal of the child and the woman. It was the child in him that continued to enjoy playing games and dressing up and acting and composing scatological stories for the Viardot children. And it was the child that accounted for his insecurity and unpracticalness. Perhaps it was the adolescent (as seen by Pietsch)[48] that radiated the multi-faceted generosity of spirit: the readiness to forgive all personal injuries, the tolerance and the willing devotion not only of material resources but of his time and influence to so many who needed or appealed for help.[49]

The woman in him found expression mainly in tenderness, sometimes loverlike but most often maternal, or a blend of the two.

At the age of 30 he wrote once: 'Since yesterday I am a mother, I am tasting the joys of motherhood, I have a family. Three charming little triplets [...] whom I am feeding myself and taking care of with real pleasure. Three little leverets, which I bought from a peasant [... with] my last franc.'[50] The leverets survived only a couple of days. But he had plenty of later opportunities to mother: Pauline's children and her pupils, the young writers he took under his wing and, no doubt, as many of 'his' revolutionaries as would permit such treatment. His letters to such friends as Polonsky and Borisov when they are in trouble are instinct with a truly feminine gentleness and solicitude.

A man reveals a good deal of himself in his friendships. Turgenev claimed that he did not form attachments easily, but that those he did form were likely to be lasting.[51] That proved true. Through long years of separation he kept writing to his friends; he stood by them when needed; he showed and evoked the most admirable devotion. When Turgenev was dying, Polonsky wished he could have taken his friend's sufferings on himself and died in his stead. And a like selflessness breathes from Turgenev's last, pencil-scrawled note to Tolstoy:

I have not written to you for a long time, for I have been and *am* – to put it bluntly – on my deathbed [...] I am writing to you really to tell you how glad I have been to be your contemporary – and to utter my last heartfelt plea to you. My friend, return to literature! ... Ah, how happy I would be if I could think that my plea would have that effect [...] My friend, great writer of the land of Russia, hear my plea! Let me know if you receive this note. I cannot [write] more, I am tired.[52]

When Gogol's death left the foremost place in Russian literature vacant Turgenev was the first to occupy it, in the late fifties and early sixties (a fact quaintly signalized by his election, in 1859, as a corresponding member of the Imperial Academy of Sciences); and if, in the second half of the sixties, his star began to pale over against the rising glories of Dostoevsky and Tolstoy, he was already the best known and most admired of Russian writers in France and Germany. By the 1870s his reputation had spread throughout the European literary world and even to England and America. In 1871 he was invited to speak in Edinburgh at the commemoration of the Scott centenary, in 1878 he was elected vice-president of the International Literary Congress convened in Paris to discuss authors' rights and, in the absence of the president, chaired several of the plenary sessions. (He was a pathetically ineffectual chairman, but won the hearts of most of the delegates nonetheless.) With typical unconcern for his own interests, he spoke out against international copyright, which would have deprived many translators of a living and raised a barrier to cultural interchange between nations. In 1879 the University of Oxford conferred on him – the first novelist ever to be so distinguished – an honorary degree of Doctor of Civil Law.

His influence on the following generation of writers, in Russia and in the West, has yet to be fully studied. In the West, his art was widely seen and welcomed as a form of realism preferable to that of the French Naturalists; but there too his fame was overtaken and more or less overshadowed by the more overtly challenging work of Tolstoy and Dostoevsky. Perhaps partly for that reason, the study of Turgenev in terms of twentieth-century thinking seems to have lagged behind the study of his great contemporaries. If the 'modernization' of Dostoevsky and Tolstoy studies can be said to date from the first quarter of this century, fresh approaches to Turgenev are hardly discernible before its third quarter, and since then have advanced somewhat tentatively and sporadically. Is it too much to hope that we may be about to be cheered by a new surge of effort to restore Turgenev to his rightful place among the stars of Russian and world literature?

2

Poetry, plays, criticism

Turgenev began writing poetry in his teens – mainly lyrical poetry in a Romantic key, but also translations (of Shakespeare and Byron), some narrative poems, and a dramatic poem, *Steno* (the name of the protagonist), composed at the age of 16. From this early period barely a dozen of the hundred or so lyrics mentioned by Turgenev[1] have survived, and of the longer works, apart from fragments, only *Steno* – a childish echo of Byron's *Manfred*.

But Turgenev continued to write poetry throughout his twenties, and thirty-nine of his lyrics, besides three translations (Byron's *Darkness*, a scene from Goethe's *Faust* and the twelfth of his *Römische Elegien*) were published in various journals at the time, as were two of his four longer poems; the other two appeared in book form.

This poetry of his youth he later disowned, claiming to have developed an almost physical revulsion from it,[2] and none of it was included in any of the editions of his *Works* published in his lifetime. But it has appeared in all posthumous editions of his *Collected Works*; and though he would no doubt be forgotten today if he had died in 1847 (the year in which he ceased to publish poetry), yet it was his long poems of the 1840s which brought him to the notice of Belinsky and to the attention of the Russian reading public. For this reason, and because there must be an organic connection between a writer's early and later work, it seems necessary to say a little about them.

Lyric poetry

Though Turgenev had drunk deep of the Romanticism of Schiller and Byron, he embarked on Russian poetry as a disciple of Pushkin and Lermontov. He continued to extol Pushkin as his master all his life, while saying little or nothing of his debt to Lermontov; but in fact he was, especially in this early period, rather closer to Lermon-

tov in outlook and thematics, while very different in temperament
from both these predecessors. The affinities can be explained by
their closeness in age (only four years apart) and by the fact that
both had imbibed Byron in adolescence and in the original –
Pushkin had come across him later and in translation – but whereas
Lermontov is incisive, intense, bitter, Turgenev is mellifluous and
elegiac. Turgenev would never turn on 'the crowd'

> to fling in their face, defiant, a verse of iron,
> annealed in bitterness and fury![3]

When he addresses the crowd, it is only to reserve his right to
independence and privacy; he may bow before them, but never
love them; he will neither woo them with praise nor offend them
with mockery.[4]

If we add to the thirty-nine lyrics published in the 1840s a dozen
more included in the latest edition of the *Collected Works* (i.e., all
the extant lyrics except the *Juvenilia*) we have a corpus of fifty-one,
of which twenty-six are love poems, nine have nature for their main
subject, four could be classified as ballads, three have a social
or civic theme, the rest do not fit neatly into such categories.
Turgenev's 'social' lyrics continue the tradition of Pushkin and
Lermontov, but with profound differences. Pushkin opposed the
poet to the 'crowd': the poet is a king, he must live unto himself;[5]
the crowd is not worth teaching and/or incapable of learning,
degraded as they are by greed, vice, stupidity and malice.[6] To
Pushkin the crowd is 'you' and 'they'; Turgenev and Lermontov
seek to maintain that distance, but in their most sweeping
indictment of their society 'we' supplants 'they': Lermontov
deplores in 'our generation' what he scorns, struggles against, fears
to succumb to in himself, and Turgenev follows suit. But Lermontov is in deadly earnest; Turgenev can not only see (as Lermontov
also does) that the crowd will not take the poet's sufferings
seriously, he can himself find his own suffering more laughable than
the activities of those around him.[7]

The last of Turgenev's social poems, 'Confession' ('Ispoved'), is
directly inspired by Lermontov's famous 'Meditation' ('Duma') – it
might almost be termed a paraphrase of it. But what a contrast
between Lermontov's lapidary judgments, the taut impetuosity of
his verse, modulating between lines of six, five and four feet, and
the keen, hard edge of his generalizations, on the one hand and, on

the other, the easy, even flow of Turgenev's octaves (made up of two quatrains of iambic tetrameters), the loose, wavering outline of the indictment, the descent into detail in stanzas 3 and 4, and the Delphic enigma of the final quatrain. Turgenev was not a good hater, and, as he was to declare later, despised hardly anyone except himself.[8]

About one-third of the love poems are inspired directly (and several more, perhaps, indirectly) by his brief involvement with Tat'yana Bakunina, sister of his friend Mikhail Bakunin. Turgenev visited the family on his return from Germany in 1841; Mikhail had recommended him fervently to them and them to him; and Tat'yana, who was three years older than Turgenev, fell in love with him. Turgenev, like other visitors, was charmed by the family and responded warmly to Tat'yana, but very quickly – within a few months – discovered he was not in love with her. His awkward attempts to redefine their relation in brother–sister terms only embittered her and led to a complete break, but since her brothers remained his friends, they evidently saw no reason to blame him. The episode gave him material for perhaps a dozen of his love poems and, later, one or two of his stories.

Love was one of the staple themes of Romantic poetry. Turgenev produced about as many love poems in his twenties as had Pushkin and Lermontov in theirs, but the differences in range and tone are interesting. The earlier poets run the whole gamut, from playful to ecstatic and from melancholy to tragic resignation; apart from two very early examples of the playful, Turgenev's tone remains predominantly elegiac. There is one example of near-ecstasy, but it is given as recalled from the past. Pushkin and Lermontov sing of love past, love present and love future; with one or two exceptions (in the present), Turgenev's concern is with past love. There is in Turgenev none of the 'detachment' of Pushkin and Lermontov's portraits of the beloved,[9] nor of the selflessness of their concern for her happiness apart from their own.[10] Nor does Turgenev resort to the device of stylization or dramatization of his love: that is, its presentation through the medium of fictitious lyrical 'I's'.

The poems of the Bakunina cycle comprise a couple in which the poet appeals to her to try out a new, fraternal relation; a couple more in which he evokes a past scene of their togetherness and sadly contrasts his feeling then with his feeling now; and there are several others in which the natural setting around him prompts a mood of gentle regret for what has been and is no more. In these, the music of the verse and the harmony between mood and landscape cast a special, Turgenevan spell upon the reader, which we shall encounter later in the landscapes of his prose works.

Nature seems to have a greater place in Turgenev's love poetry than in that of his predecessors; his nature poems proper tend, like some of the love poems, to be poems of mood, even if the mood is barely hinted at or is relegated to a concluding line or two. The moods are subdued, in consonance with the aspects of nature depicted, as may be inferred from such titles as: 'Evening', 'Autumn', 'Spring Evening', 'Moonless Night', 'After the Storm'. One is titled 'Storm', but it is divided between the storm itself and the peace that follows it. There is a picture of night in the steppe; a second view of autumn at its very end, and a vision of a summer day in and around Spasskoe: the beloved garden and the cornfields and steppes beyond.

The poet insists, as he will do later in his stories (though it is not true), that:

> Like an artist austere and serene, Nature keeps a sense
> Of measure in all things and true to harmonious simplicity.[11]

But if this is not nature's artistic creed, it is already Turgenev's.

Evening leads him to wonder what lies beyond the evening of life; a spring evening brings back childhood's carefree outlook and sense of reverence; amid the summer day at home in Spasskoe he is buoyed up by the sense of boundless freedom breathing from the steppe.

Whereas nature in Pushkin and Lermontov is most often the exotic scenery of the South of Russia and the Caucasus, Turgenev's nature is the quiet, unexciting landscape of his native Central Russia; but what differentiates him even more radically from them is the intimacy of his relation with nature, compounded of the countryman's precise and detailed knowledge of vegetable and animal life and atmospheric conditions and of a sensitivity all his own to every slight variation of colours, shapes, sounds and odours.

This knowledge and love of rural life is displayed in a cycle of nine lyrics under the general heading 'The Country' (*Derevnya* – which also means 'the village'). This includes, besides four of the nature poems already mentioned, a general view of the village at evening; two hunting scenes, one in summer, the other in late autumn; a ballad-like evocation of the poet's dead grandfather out hunting; and the first snow as the signal for a return from country to town. Curiously enough, as the poet enters the village, surveys the scene and gazes at the peasants' faces, it seems to him not only that he understands them but that he would be willing to live their poor and simple life.

So much for matter. As regards form, Turgenev's lyrics offer a respectable variety of the metres, stanzas and rhyming patterns developed by his predecessors. The non-stanzaic poems include several in regular rhymed decasyllables or octosyllables, a couple in blank verse and several in elegiacs. There are two poems in couplets and others in stanzas of four, five, six, eight or ten lines. Far the commonest of these stanzaic forms is the quatrain, used in more than a dozen of the lyrics (about one in four), with almost every variety of metre.

The tints of Turgenev's poetry are the tints of his native forests and fields; its tones suggest the songs of the woodland birds and the sounds of wind among the leaves. There is no thunder and light-ning in this world; there are no blizzards or floods. There is plenty of pain – the pains of parting, of change, of loneliness and the failure of love – but little anger, and despair only once: in the ballad of the old gentleman dying without having known love. And as there are no extremes of nature or of mood, so there are no startling similes or metaphors, no striking coruscations of lan-guage. But a number of these poems have been set to music by well-known composers; a few became popular songs. Music and mood might be said to be the keynote of Turgenev's lyric poetry at its best.

Narrative poems

Between 1843 and 1846 Turgenev published four long poems: *Parasha* (the name of the heroine), *A Conversation* (*Razgovor*), *Andrei* (the name of the protagonist), and *The Landowner* (*Pomeshchik*). Like his lyrics, these continue the traditions of Pushkin and Lermontov; and, like his lyrics, they show consider-able diversity of form. *Razgovor* begins as narrative, but consists mainly of dialogue, all in rhymed iambic octosyllables. The other three poems are in stanzaic forms: *Parasha* in a 13-line, *Pomesh-chik* in a 16-line stanza – both apparently of Turgenev's invention:

the former of 10-syllable, the latter of 8-syllable iambs – while
Andrei is in regular decasyllabic octaves.

Parasha and *The Landowner* are heirs to a tradition that goes
back – through Lermontov (*The Tambov Treasurer's Wife* and
Sashka) and Pushkin (*Count Nulin* and *Little House in Kolomna*) –
to Byron's *Beppo*. *Beppo* was a good-humoured anecdote or jest in
verse, offering a glimpse of Venetian society in carnival time and of
a love triangle without blood or tears – the exotic glitter and bustle
of the scene in piquant contrast to the deromanticized love-story,
and both scene and story enchased in, and set off by, the sardonic
commentary of the narrator.

Pushkin takes over from Byron the form of the anecdote, the
theme of the triangle and the preponderant rôle of the narrator
(who in *Little House in Kolomna* occupies about 45 per cent of
the poem), but deglamorizes the setting as well as the love-story:
Count Nulin is played out on a country estate in the provinces,
Little House in Kolomna in a petit-bourgeois suburb. The point of
both poems is that they are pointless: Pushkin is cocking a snook at
the hack critics who, catering to government views, harassed him
with demands for works with a purpose – meaning, an acceptable
moral and/or political purpose. Lermontov takes up where Pushkin
left off; but his contributions to the genre, if still humorous, are no
longer good-humoured. In *Sashka* we meet the hero in a brothel,
the heroine is a prostitute; we might almost see the poem as a cross
between *Beppo* (in form) and Musset's *Rolla* (in setting and
theme).

In *Parasha* Turgenev opens a new chapter. He retains the rôle of
the narrator – a less sparkling narrator than Pushkin's – whose
self-revelations – biographical, psychological and ideological –
form some 40 per cent of the poem. He retains the provincial rural
setting of *Count Nulin*, but his vision of the country is very different
from Pushkin's: it is the view of the countryman, familiar to us from
his lyrics and later to be developed and enriched in the settings of *A
Sportsman's Sketches*. However, the main innovation is in the
theme, which has kept no trace of *Beppo* or of any of the Russian or
French poems to which it gave rise.

Pushkin averred, whether seriously or not, that he had written
Count Nulin as a parody of Shakespeare's *Rape of Lucrece* – as an
answer to the question, 'What might have happened if Lucretia,
instead of submitting to Tarquin, had slapped his face?' In the same

sense, *Parasha* might be regarded as a parody of Pushkin's *Evgeni Onegin* – an answer to the question, 'What might have happened if Onegin, instead of rejecting Tat′yana's proffered love, had married her?' The answer appears to be that the devil would have chortled.

The heroine, Parasha, grows up as the only child of well-to-do provincial gentry. Her parents are not unlike Tat′yana's parents, perhaps born a decade or two later. Parasha is not Tat′yana: Turgenev goes out of his way to tell us so. She is not beautiful; she could never have become a queen of St Petersburg drawing-rooms. She reads not eighteenth-century Western literature, but contemporary Russians – making little distinction between the great poet Pushkin and the Romantic second-rater Marlinsky. But she might be a younger half-sister to Tat′yana. The narrator portrays her with loving care, devoting nearly one-tenth of the poem to that portrayal. The childlike gaiety, the capacity for passion, the pride and reticence, the blend of velvet and steel in her character – have clearly won his heart. He sees her as destined to great suffering in a world where she is unlikely to meet with any kindred spirit.

There is no plot, and hardly any story. One day Parasha sees a man – a gentleman, evidently a landowner out hunting – sitting in the hollow beyond her garden fence. He finishes his snack and lies down to nap without noticing her; but when he wakes up, he does see her, jumps the fence, asks whose land he is on, and introduces himself as the grandson of a neighbour and old friend of her father. After a brief exchange he withdraws, promising to call on her parents. He does in fact call, the following day, but the interval seems an eternity to Parasha: this is not so much stated as conveyed to the reader by the device of devoting nearly a quarter of the poem, at this point, to the narrator's divagations and a portrait of the hero (somewhat ominously named Viktor).

Viktor is a retired army officer, well-to-do, travelled, intelligent without originality, with a turn for irony, susceptible to feminine charms but incapable of strong passions or deep attachments, good-humoured, good-looking, popular, but self-centred and cool-blooded. He has led a life typical of his class and time: danced, gambled, flirted – forgetting his 'conquests' much more easily than they were able to forget him – clubbed together with his peers to make fun of 'the crowd', yet not above kowtowing to wealth or power. And like many of his type, he has ended up jaded, bored with the world and with himself.

Parasha is not Tat'yana; but we are never quite sure how far she falls short, or whether, if she had met an Onegin and had the chance to educate herself in his library, she might not have come to rival that predecessor. Viktor, however, is only a pale shadow, if not a caricature, of Onegin: he lacks the pride and moral courage to stand alone, the capacity for passion and the originality – and, therefore, the true superiority to his society. Yet he is not only new, he is obviously superior – in culture, experience of the world and intellectual liveliness, at least – to the country bumpkins among whom Parasha had grown up; she is 20 and ripe for love and has no means of measuring or judging him; and she falls in love.

Viktor's first visit occupies another quarter of the poem. It is a very long visit (punctuated, of course, by the narrator's digressions and reminiscences). First there is much talk, then, before supper, a long walk in the gloaming through the vast garden or park which surrounds the house. Viktor is at his best. He senses the fluctuating, growing feeling of the girl at his side and is genuinely moved by it, stirred in his turn; and as he drives home, he muses that it would be a suitable match and realizes that he is ready to settle down.

And that is all. The progress of the courtship and the marriage are screened, blocked out by the narrator's philosophizing. The implications are clear; no facts are vouchsafed. But after a five-year absence the narrator returns to the area. He is welcomed by Parasha, who is faintly disturbed by this return of the past and sheds a few tears, and Viktor, who has grown fat but has come to respect and love his wife sincerely. They have been married less than four years, so the courtship must have been protracted. At first Viktor had tried not to take her seriously, but found he could not give up his visits, and the marriage ensued. Her old father had had a fine house built for them.

The narrator, dismayed and disappointed, hastens to leave the district, intending not to see Parasha again. She is by no means wholly happy, but she is equally far from the unhappiness which the narrator had foreseen for her. She still treasures the innocent dreams of her girlhood and sighs often and long for the joys they had promised; but where, ah where are the great sufferings reserved for her in the narrator's dreams? Her life is now a smooth, if winding, stream: no torrents, no waterfalls, no whirlpools. The narrator has lost his last dream, said farewell to the last star in his sky; it remains only for him to take his leave of the reader.

The down-to-earth *Beppo* triangle has been volatilized into a triangle of a very different kind: between the Romantic narrator and the unromantic, not to say anti-romantic Viktor – Parasha, sadly immolating her dreams on the altar of life.

The Landowner is the last, the shortest and in many ways the closest of Turgenev's four poems to the *Beppo* tradition, although the rôle of the narrator has been reduced here to very little. On the other hand, the ghost of the triangle theme has been grafted onto what is essentially a genre painting of One Day in the Life of Sergei Petrovich.

Sergei Petrovich is a middle-aged, old-style landowner living on his country estate. His wife has gone away for the day to pray at some not too far distant shrine, and he is bent on savouring his ephemeral freedom. After walking his dog to the river and throwing sticks in for him to retrieve, chatting with one peasant about progress and having two other peasants beaten for allowing their cows to stray into his field, he decides he deserves an outing and will visit his neighbour, a merry widow who lives some ten miles away, has made her house the social centre of the district, is visited by men of all classes from the provincial governor down, draws hosts of guests to her family celebrations, and in winter gives balls to which neighbours within a radius of thirty miles eagerly flock.

While the big, lumbering family coach is being made ready for Sergei Petrovich, let us see what kind of man he is. What he wants from life is peace and quiet, freedom from restrictions and freedom to do nothing (*pokoi, prostor i len'*); what he fears – the devil and his wife. He once served in some Treasury records office; reads little and with difficulty; has no use for foreigners; dresses in the outlandish style of the Slavophils; and has sired a motley brood of children – but still has a roving eye.

The satiric picture of the Slavophil landowner is capped by a satiric picture of his Slavophil study; and no less satiric are the accounts of the merry widow and the balls she gives, where the guests appear as a cross between the monsters in Tat'yana's dream in *Evgeni Onegin* and the grotesques in Gogol's *Mirgorod* and *Dead Souls*. Satire was never to be Turgenev's element, and here it is neither much more nor much less effective than it will be, later, in his novels; the introduction into the ball scene of a mysterious 15-year-old Parasha *in erba* does nothing to make the other guests more believable.

The story proper can be told in a few words. Sergei Petrovich sets out in the old coach, leaving his household as relieved to be rid of him for some hours as he had been to be rid of his wife. After a few miles, the back axle breaks and the coach overturns. Nobody is injured; but before help can be summoned and repairs undertaken, his wife, returning early from her pilgrimage, descends upon him, guesses his destination and carries him off in her carriage – back to their home, to render account, for she had always been firmly convinced that it is the function of husbands to be subject to their wives. And so the narrator bows out, claiming the reader's indulgence for the weaknesses of his tale in consideration of its irreproachable morality – for, after all, the protagonist does end up 'united with his own wife'!

Neither of Turgenev's other two long poems has any connection with the *Beppo* tradition, but *Andrei*, the third to be written and the longest of the four, may be viewed as standing in much the same relation to *Parasha* as we saw *Parasha* standing to *Evgeni Onegin*. If *Parasha* offers an answer to the question, 'What could have happened if Onegin had married Tat'yana?' – *Andrei* wrestles with the question, 'What might have happened if Parasha had met her Onegin (i.e., a man truly worthy of her) only when she was already married?'

Andrei, a young man who, like Turgenev himself, had spent three years in the civil service, returns to his native town and his family home in the provinces, where he no longer has either friends or family. He is rescued from his solitude by a neighbour who had known his father and insists on inviting him to his house.

The neighbour is an ordinary man – middle-aged, a gossip, a card-player, but kind-hearted, simple, unexciting. He is married, evidently not very long, to a young wife. Dunya is Parasha's age, but, unlike Parasha, she has had a hard childhood and youth. Orphaned early, she spent some time in an orphanage, then with a deaf and miserly old aunt. Marriage came to her as a deliverance, and she loves her husband warmly – but like a child; she is emotionally unawakened, has no friends and fights shy of social relationships.

Andrei is similarly young for his age, inexperienced, sensitive, bashful, and something of a dreamer. He becomes a regular visitor at his neighbour's house, and the inevitable happens: the young people recognize their affinity, become friends, are drawn closer and closer, fall in love; but they are so innocent that it takes them some time to identify their feeling and then to discover that it is mutual. When they do, they are dismayed, for it is unthinkable for both of them to act dishonourably.

In the two years since the writing of *Parasha* Turgenev's insight into the birth and growth and modalities of love has been strikingly deepened and enriched – no doubt by his experience with Pauline Viardot. Though Dunya is very different in temperament, character and history from Pauline, Andrei can be seen as a less cultured Turgenev, and the situation is almost identical with his. It is doubly interesting therefore that, after the protagonists find out that they love each other, it is to the man that Turgenev assigns the lead in determining their conduct: Andrei leads, Dunya follows – an unusual rôle for a Turgenev heroine. And it is Andrei's reactions to the discovery that Turgenev explores.

What mainly motivates Andrei is not his relation to the husband but his love and understanding of Dunya, which impels him to keep her unsullied and unashamed, and his respect for their love, which he must preserve from contamination by *poshlost'*.[12] Six months of winter pass while Andrei wrestles with the problem of what is to be done. He continues to frequent the house, but the young people take care not to remain alone together. Andrei recognizes that he must go away; while he is still hunting desperately for a pretext, the providential death of a rich uncle in faraway Saratov provides him with the excuse of going to take over his inheritance. Of course, both young people know that he is going for good. They struggle through the ordeal of parting without yielding to their feelings – and Andrei goes abroad.

After wandering in the West for three years, still haunted by his love, Andrei receives, in Italy, a letter from Dunya. This remarkable composition, which constitutes almost one-sixth of the whole poem, conveys in masterly fashion the turmoil and confusion in the poor girl's heart and head. She knows she should not be writing; but she is so unhappy, so horrified by the prospect of living out her life in conditions which had seemed acceptable before she knew Andrei and what love meant. In her misery she almost envies him the novel and varied experiences of his travels, she even suspects him of having loved her less than she loved him and of having forgotten her and consoled himself elsewhere, though the envy and suspicion are only hinted and promptly recanted. She continues to live in the past, to relive his visits day by day. Her head tells her that he had behaved properly, honourably, unselfishly, but her heart whispers that if he had loved her a little more, they could have been happy together.

These wildly contradictory thoughts and feelings are punctuated by tears, by words of love such as they had never allowed themselves while they were together, by covert reproaches and overt self-reproach, and conclude with a solemn last farewell in which she sets him free to love another. But the fact remains that she had reread the letter before sending it and has sent it without changing anything in it. What happens after that we never know: the final stanza is an enigma. In it the narrator tells us that he has seen his personages again, recently,

> But that o'er which I even wept with them
> To me appears now faintly comical.

Where did the narrator see them? Apart or together? Is it their former abnegation at which he now feels like smiling? Or did Andrei read the letter as a summons home?

Although the psychology and atmosphere of *Andrei* are at a far remove from the *anecdote galante*, the poem is written in octaves – the metre of *Beppo* – and has retained both the theme of the triangle and the ironic narrator. But the tragic has ceased to be a joke, has become serious, and the narrator has ceased to be a fully fledged fourth personage: those developments, taken together with the psychology, make this the most original – as well as the most mature – of Turgenev's narrative poems.

It was, however, *A Conversation* which received Belinsky's most unqualified approval – and still earns the most pages of commentary in the latest edition of Turgenev's works. All in virtue of its social criticism – though as an indictment of Russian society, it hardly seems that Turgenev says here anything that Lermontov had not said, more succinctly and more searingly, six years earlier, in his 'Meditation'.

A Conversation is written in the vigorous and not very common metre used by Lermontov in his long poem *The Novice* (*Mtsyri*). *The Novice* was the 'confession' (i.e., the review of his life) of a dying youth; *A Conversation* comprises the confessions, in the same sense, of two men dead to the world. One is an old hermit, near to death; the other, a much younger man, a rootless wanderer, who had known the hermit in his earlier days and returns to pour out his heart to him. The old man is horrified by what he hears and recalls his own past as a contrast and reproach to his visitor's tale.

They belong to different generations; each is quite unintelligible to the other. The old man represents the Romantic generation which had fought in the wars against Napoleon and gone on to form the secret societies that succumbed in the Decembrist Rising. He has drunk deep of the joys of battle and of passionate love; he believes in God and thrills to the beauty of nature; he is a patriot who prays for a happy future for his country – a future which he hopes and almost believes may come soon. 'You are younger than any of us', is the younger man's withering comment.

The younger man represents the post-Romantic generation, characterized by their incapacity to love, to act or to believe. The wanderer has been loved, but has fled from the woman who loved him; he is too alienated from men to be able to form relations with them or influence them; and he believes in a better future only as something he will not live to see and, of course, can do nothing to hasten. He paints a picture of himself and his contemporaries which shatters the old man's faith in life and in the future and he reacts by cursing his visitor. The wanderer listens to his invective, acknowledges the justice of his charges, but retorts by pointing out that the hermit too has withdrawn from worldly life and asking scornfully how much better the older generation had left their world than they had found it.

Some simple-minded critics have taken this to signify an equal condemnation of both generations. Hardly. Within the limits of the poem, the hermit and his peers, who have lived and loved and saved their country from a foreign invader surely have earned more respect, if not admiration, than the wanderer and his kind who have achieved nothing. As for the wider reference – though it might be true that the average man of the 1820s and 1830s had contributed no more to Russian progress than the average man of the following generation, yet it was the élite of the twenties and thirties that had kindled a light and pointed a course for the élite of Turgenev's generation.

But perhaps the most interesting aspect of *A Conversation* is its foreshadowing of motifs in Turgenev's mature work: the clash of generations which was to find its richest expression in *Fathers and Children*; the post-Romantic type immortalized as the 'superfluous man'; the theme of love as bondage; and even the death of Rudin on the barricades.

Similarly, the type of the 'Turgenev heroine' was adumbrated, however faintly, in Parasha and Dunya; the siren of, for instance, 'Spring Torrents' in the merry widow of *The Landowner*; and the major mode of Turgenev's treatment of nature in both the narrative poems and the lyrics. In fine, if Turgenev's poetry does not place him among the greatest Russian poets of his century, it is worth studying at least as the seedbed of major types and themes of his maturity.

Theatre

Turgenev's attitude to his plays never became as negative as his attitude to his poetry, but it did undergo a radical modification. In the decade from 1843 to 1852 when the plays were being written, he evidently expected to make a significant contribution to the development of the Russian theatre. Gogol had just laid the foundations for a modern prose theatre with his two comedies, *The Inspector-General* (*Revizor*, 1836) and *Marriage* (*Zhenit'ba*, 1842), and four of Turgenev's ten plays are in the Gogol tradition, while two or three of the others still owe something to him. But Turgenev was not content to follow in Gogol's footsteps. He set out to endow the infant theatre, which still subsisted largely on translations or adaptations of mediocre foreign (mainly French) imports, with a repertory of good literary quality and comparable in variety to the best of Western theatre.

He experiments constantly: with types and themes – mostly Russian – and with forms (genres) – mostly foreign. His confidence reaches a peak in the winter of 1850/1, when, after seeing a stage production of one of his plays for the first time, he writes: 'This experience showed me that I have a vocation for the theatre and that in time I shall write good plays.'[13] Yet after that, he resolutely turns his back on the theatre (except for his librettos to Pauline Viardot's operettas in the late sixties), writing only one more short play, which remains unpublished and unstaged in his lifetime; he deprecates and discourages any later staging of his plays, insisting that they are not stageworthy, though they may be worth reading;[14] and while he included all but the last of them in the 1869 edition of his *Collected Works*, in preparing and polishing them for that edition he seemed bent on justifying that judgment: that is, a number of his alterations did make them less rather than more stageworthy.

This flight from the theatre was prompted by a combination of adverse factors. First, there were the conflicts with both the literary censorship and the censorship of plays. Of his nine plays submitted to censorship only two were both published and staged within a year of submission.[15] Four others were published within a year.[16] One had to wait nine years for publication,[17] one for seven years,[18] one for five years;[19] the third of these appeared most cruelly mutilated. As for staging: one play had to wait three years,[20] one for six years,[21] one for fourteen[22] and one for twenty-two.[23] Needless to say, the stage versions suffered – similarly or differently – at the hands of their censors.

No less discouraging than the censorship was the generally inadequate level of acting in Russia at the time. There were a few excellent actors, and Turgenev wrote several of his plays as vehicles for some of the best of them, but as his art developed in subtlety and complexity, the gap between the acting talent required and that available must have steadily widened.

Thirdly, there was the consensus of critics and friends that, if admirable as literature, these plays were not suitable for the theatre. None of his readers, it seems, was sagacious enough to allow for the effects of the poor acting. They can hardly be blamed for not realizing that Turgenev was moving ahead of his time; but he, in his excessive modesty, too readily adopted their judgment and made it his own.

Finally, important changes were taking place in the Russian literary scene and in Turgenev's own position in it. The publication of *A Sportsman's Sketches* in 1852 and of his first novel, *Rudin*, in 1856 had made him Russia's premier fiction-writer, while in the same period Ostrovsky had been emerging as a popular and prolific playwright, who could be expected to take over Turgenev's mission of endowing Russia with a national theatre. So Turgenev could feel he was entitled to leave the dramatic field to his successful rival, in order to concentrate on the fiction where he was reaping such rich rewards.

Of his ten plays, seven are one-acters; the other three comprise two, three and five acts respectively. Most of the one-act plays – four out of seven – are farces or near-farces, looking back, in their tone and types, to Gogol's theatre and forward to Chekhov's one-acters. Of the other three, one, as Grossman has shown,[24] was indebted to Mérimée's *Théâtre de Clara Gazul*,[25] the other two to Musset's *Comédies et proverbes*.[26]

Contrary to what might have been expected, Gogol was not Turgenev's first model for playwriting. If we disregard the Byronic 'dramatic poem', *Steno*, the first model was Mérimée, whose collection of short, purportedly Spanish plays had appeared in a third edition the year before Turgenev produced his one-act *An Imprudence*. He owes to Mérimée the Spanish setting, the compactness of the action and the melodramatic *dénouement*, not to mention the smouldering and murderous passion which brings it about.

Dolores d'Esturiz is a young woman of 27, living with a husband twice her age and a grim and even older duenna; Don Pablo, the husband's austere, taciturn 40-year-old friend haunts the house and is their only visitor. Dolores is bored to death. As she sits on her balcony sighing for a glimpse of youth and life, she is overheard by Don Rafael, a handsome young man passing by in the street below who decides, on the spur of the moment, to court her, pretending he has watched and loved her for a long time. They talk; he improvises a serenade, then rashly vaults the high stockade into her garden. The duenna, who has been spying in the background, locks Dolores in her room and the doors from the garden into the house, trapping the intruder. When the husband returns, she reports to him; he panics and delegates to his sinister friend the task of dealing with the young couple (Rafael has, by this time, climbed up to Dolores' chamber). Don Pablo confronts the pair, sends Rafael away and, alone with Dolores, reveals that he has for two years been secretly, desperately in love with her. On discovering that he cannot hope to overcome her dislike and dread of him, he kills her – and evidently gets off scot-free, for in an eight-line 'epilogue – ten years later' he has become a grandee and minister of state (or something of the kind).

This ultra-Romantic concoction, in which the husband and Rafael are stock figures from light comedy – the quaking pantaloon and the dashing young blade, clearly destined to turn into just such

another pantaloon thirty years hence – while Don Pablo and the
duenna are similarly stock figures from melodrama, claims our
interest by its relatively realistic portrayal of Dolores: innocent,
silly, timid, pathetic in her loneliness and helplessness, yet finding
the courage to refuse to sacrifice Rafael – to denounce him, as he
proposes, as a burglar – and to tell Don Pablo the truth about her
feelings even when completely at his mercy. She is a less vital
figure, and more lightly sketched, than Parasha, but her author
observes her with the same mixture of insight and indulgence, even
if, perhaps, with somewhat more of irony and less of tenderness.

The four Gogolian farces (or light light comedies[27]) can be
treated more summarily. *Moneyless* is basically a duet between a
young gentleman, who has spent more than he possesses, and his
old servant – punctuated by visits of sundry creditors, who have to
be fobbed off by the servant while the young master hides behind a
screen. The youth is feather-brained and unteachable: nothing will
persuade him that he has exhausted not only his funds but his
credit. He sends the servant out to buy necessaries and cannot
believe they can only be had for cash; he sends him to friends with a
request for a loan and is indignant to see him return empty-handed;
even while short of necessaries, he is bent on adding to his
superfluities: a hunting dog, a new livery for his servant. The old
man tries to impart a little of his own good sense to his master,
urging that he could live not only free from debt but with all the
comforts he now lacks if he would just return to his home and
family; but the young man regards the 'tedium' of country life as
worse than all the discomforts of the city.

The creditors are a motley crew, and the comedy pivots on the
old man's struggles to get rid of them, if only for a day or two, and
the young man's alternations between deluded bluster and terrified
scurryings behind the screen. But since tradition requires a happy
ending to this sort of composition, our hero is saved, at least for the
time being, by the arrival of a country neighbour, a middle-aged
bumpkin of a landowner, who is prepared to bail him out of his
difficulties in return for being initiated into the wicked delights of
metropolitan life.

Turgenev's cultivation of the Gogolian mode is then suspended
for three years, while he tries his hand at the 'proverb', popularized
by Musset, and at longer plays, that is, plays of more than one act.
He returns to Gogol in the second half of his play-writing decade

with a one-acter that actually reached the stage without delay (though its publication was banned for seven years) and became arguably the most popular of his plays.

Breakfast with the Marshal of the Nobility was revived fourteen times between 1849 and 1912, ran through forty productions between 1912 and 1918, was revived several more times in the Soviet period on stage, and in 1954 as a film (*W*, III, 391–400). The landowner Bespandin and his widowed sister, Kaurova, have been feuding over an estate inherited jointly from a dead aunt. The local marshal of the nobility invites them to come together for a final attempt to mediate their differences; to second his efforts he invites his predecessor as marshal (who arrives halfway through the meeting) and the local judge; two poorer landowners who have dropped in uninvited are co-opted to assist in the mediation. The sister and brother turn up separately.

The sister presents herself as a poor defenceless widow-woman, ready for all concessions, but accuses her brother (before his arrival) of having tried to kill her by suborning her coachman to overturn her carriage. The coachman is called in to testify, and it becomes evident that the whole story has been dreamed up. Then the brother appears, a bluff, good-natured fellow; but even he has lost all patience with his sister.

After both have roundly refused to be reconciled, it is clear that the only way to peace is to divide the estate between them. A map is brought in and the marshal makes a series of proposals as to how this could be done. The brother agrees to each of them; the sister rejects them all, convinced that there must be a catch in each, even though she cannot see it. She evidently suffers (like Korobochka in Gogol's *Dead Souls*) from a pathological fear of being cheated or victimized.

The entrance of the former marshal creates a diversion. Without examining the map, he suggests a completely lopsided division; this time the widow is willing – to take the lion's share – while her brother refuses to be content with a remnant. The marshals spar politely, since each is anxious to be re-elected. The widow accuses their host of favouring her brother in expectation of a requital; indignant at the slur on his honour, he washes his hands of the business and takes refuge in his bedroom; and the party breaks up with nothing achieved – a sort of neo-Gogolian equivalent of the Mad Hatter's tea-party, a counterpoint of quirks and obsessions, served up with *brio*.

The next to be written, though last of the four to be published, was *Conversation on a Highway* – the shortest, slightest and most Gogolian of the four.[28] Designed to be read by a single virtuoso actor rather than staged, it is supposed to be set in a family coach travelling on a rural highway. The cast consists of the coachman, on the box, and the landowner and his valet inside. The sickly, self-pitying master is homeward bound to face the prospect of bankruptcy, of an early death from consumption, and a domineering and unsympathetic wife. His attitude to his two serfs, who are both considerably older than he, fluctuates between childish attempts to stand on his dignity and enforce deference and childish appeals for information, advice or sympathy. The two serfs (obviously derived from Chichikov's coachman and valet in *Dead Souls*, but more fully drawn, and humanized) feel superior to their master, but the coachman's attitude is tinged with pity, the valet's, with contempt. The valet is asthmatic and tries to hold aloof, taking refuge in silence, sulks or sleep; the coachman talks more than twice as much.

The master first upbraids the valet for having paid out too much too readily at their last stop, then the coachman for his driving, offending both; and is then furious at the idea that they should dare to take offence at anything he says (or does). From anger he drops into lamenting that he has been too kind and indulgent a master: that is why they have lost all respect for him – but he will not long be a burden to them; and will they be better off when he dies? So they have to turn and comfort him.

Among the subjects on which the coachman philosophizes are horses, spirits, dreams, the proper relations between husbands and wives. An extra layer is superadded to the comedy by the vagaries of the serfs' thinking and their multifarious misuse of language. Meanwhile, the landowner – unlike the protagonist of the poem *The Landowner* and unlike the landowners in *Breakfast with the Marshal* – is pathetic: in his sickness, his ineptitude, his childish swings of mood, his emotional dependence. But this is still a Gogolian (as distinct from a Dostoevskian) type: we feel sorry for him; we are not tempted to like him.

Finally (in this group of plays), *The Provincial Lady*, which in the sixty-three years preceding the First World War vied in popularity with *Breakfast with the Marshal*, is a hybrid: the setting is Gogolian (Russian provincial), the men and the cook are toned-down Gogolian types, but the theme and the lady are redolent of Musset.

The lady, Dar'ya Ivanovna, is young and bored with the *poshlost'* of life in a small provincial town. She had grown up as the orphaned ward of a rich countess and had acquired in her home a culture and tastes that raise her far above her present setting. The old Countess's son, though some twenty years older, had not disdained to flirt with the quick-witted teenager. But he had gone away to live in St Petersburg, and the old Countess, before dying, had married her ward off to a dull but solid little civil servant, twenty years older than the bride.

Now, twelve years after he left home, the Count has returned temporarily to his estate to repair his somewhat battered fortunes, and the lady determines to meet him, revive his one-time interest in her and charm him into getting her husband transferred to the capital and provided with a job there. How she achieves this is the subject of the play.

At first everything seems against her: her husband is slow-witted and jealous; the Count (who has business with her husband and is manoeuvred into coming to discuss it at her house) does not, at first sight, even recognize her, let alone seem inclined to remember his former dalliance. But the lady, though disconcerted, does not lose heart. She sees at a glance that the Count, though the years have taken their toll, still values himself as a ladykiller (he dyes his hair and rouges his cheeks) and she sets herself to play on his male vanity and on a middle-aged man's sentimental attachment to memories of his youth. She first has to induce him to accept her invitation to dinner (for which she has made timely provision in a style far above her everyday standards), so assuring herself of a few hours in his company. To keep her husband out of the way in that time, she enlists the assistance of a young kinsman living in her house by promising to take him along to St Petersburg if her husband is transferred there.

Once she has the Count to herself, she begins by re-evoking their past, hinting that some of its memories have meant, and mean, more to her than they could to him; she goes on to contrast the kind of life she had led in his mother's house with her present existence; she expresses fear that already this life has set its stamp upon her, changed her beyond recognition (causing him to scrutinize her more closely, eliciting gallant protestations, and flattering him with her confidences). In a short time he is completely conquered, is persuading himself that he has never ceased to think of her and that he is as much moved by their meeting as she appears to be. From here it is only one step to recognizing that it would be a sin to let so fascinating a woman waste away in this backwater – she should be shining in the capital, and he will have her husband transferred there.

Subtly and surely she consolidates her hold. The Count fancies himself as a musician and is composing an opera. While he goes to his lodging to fetch a duet to sing with her, her husband returns, and it takes all her powers of psychological manipulation to convince him that the only way to St Petersburg and promotion is to stay out of sight till dinner-time.

After the love-duet[29] the Count is even more excited, but his declaration is interrupted by another sudden reappearance of the husband; the lady takes her guest out to inspect the garden while the young kinsman talks the husband into withdrawing again. When the protagonists return, the frustrated Count completes his declaration in even more passionate terms and is teased into repeating it on his knees, from which he finds himself too stiff to rise. He is caught in this ridiculous position by the husband, and it looks as if the lady has overplayed her hand. But the Count sees magnanimity as the best way out of his discomfiture: he reaffirms the promise of a post in St Petersburg – and stays to dinner. And – like the Count – we remain charmed by the lady: she is so spirited and resourceful that we only smile at her artfulness, and she is as free from malice and as honest with herself as any heroine of Musset – or Turgenev.[30]

The difference between Musset's *comédies* and his *proverbes* is that the latter are supposed to illustrate – to exemplify – the proverb that gives them their title. Both the comedies and the proverbs pivot on the theme of love and are characterized by their lyricism and fantasy; but Turgenev's first attempt at a 'proverb' is firmly anchored in Russian 'reality'.

A Chain is as Strong as its Weakest Link was written and published in 1848 and staged three years later. It pivots on the theme of love. The scene is laid in Turgenev's favourite and most familiar setting, a 'nest of gentry'. This nest is presided over by a lady who is first cousin to the ladies who preside over similar nests in his first two novels: a widow of middle years, with one nubile daughter and a small retinue of hangers-on, with an affectation of French culture and nothing much in either her head or her heart. And, as in those novels, it is the daughter who is the heroine of the play – at 19, already a fully-fledged 'Turgenev heroine': candid, courageous, single-hearted. Her name is Vera: Faith.

The hero is Evgeni (Eugene) Gorski, the 26-year-old owner of a neighbouring estate. His name would have put Russian playgoers in mind of Evgeni Onegin, the eponymous hero of Pushkin's 'novel in verse', and so have prepared them for a love story similar to that of Onegin and Tat'yana; in fact, Gorski is much more closely akin to Lermontov's Pechorin, hero of the novel *A Hero of Our Time* (1840).[31] His central motive is, like Pechorin's, pride and love of power; like Pechorin, he is incapable of giving himself in love but needs to feel loved; like Pechorin, when crossed, he can be mean and vindictive. But he lacks the passionate intensity, the strength and the recklessness of Pechorin: there is nothing grand and there is nothing 'demonic'[32] about him.

The problem of the play is: whom is Vera to marry? She is drawn to Gorski and he to her. But he fears marriage 'more than fire' – because it will make emotional claims on him which he (though he struggles not to recognize the fact) is incapable of meeting. So he throws up a smoke-screen of wit, setting himself to entertain, in order to steer clear of serious discussion, let alone commitment. He cannot decide in his own mind whether he is in love with Vera (he wants to think he is not), but he is quite determined (he thinks) not to marry her. On the other hand, he has just discovered that he does not want her to marry anyone else.

Until the opening of the play he had been convinced of the contrary – even to the point of introducing her to a neighbour of his as a suitable match. This young man, Vladimir Stanitsyn (the name, again, will have conjured up Vladimir Lenski, Onegin's poet-friend, killed by Onegin in a duel), is the antithesis of Gorski: awkward, shy, modest – and straightforward and good-hearted. As Gorski had anticipated, Stanitsyn falls in love with Vera and decides to propose; but on hearing of this, Gorski suddenly realizes he does not want to lose her, and hurries ahead to prevent her from accepting by courting her himself – but without compromising his freedom.

Vera is eager to live – as distinct from vegetating in her mother's shadow. And for her life means love and love means marriage. She is sure of Stanitsyn and understands him thoroughly, but Gorski puzzles and intrigues her. He is elegant, witty, interesting – all that Stanitsyn is not. But is he capable of true love? What is the mystery behind his deviousness, his romantic hints of emotional confusion and sin? That is what she sets herself to find out in the day-long verbal duel that has to be fitted into the intervals between the activities of the other members of the household. Gorski fences brilliantly; but his rhetoric and cleverness are no match for her simple directness and crystalline truthfulness: she even asks his advice on how to respond to Stanitsyn's proposal; and as he feels the necessity to make a choice and decision closing in on him, Gorski's frustration turns to exasperation and malice. So Vera sees through the smoke-screen and unriddles the mystery: his heart is cold; he lives not by feeling but by imagination; he could not make her happy. And she accepts Stanitsyn – offering Gorski her friendship, which his wounded pride impels him to reject.

This play might be considered the first of Turgenev's psychological studies for the stage. Musset would not have cluttered his stage with the secondary personages or the details of *byt*;[33] but the psychology of the protagonists, though it owes nothing to him directly, would not have been disowned by him and the love-duel would have delighted him.

The other Turgenev play generally regarded as in the Musset tradition, though not literally a 'proverb', was his last: *An Evening in Sorrento* (1852). Turgenev never cared to have it published or staged, and it was, in fact, not staged till 1884 (privately), 1885 (publicly), and not published till 1891. Rather than a play, it is a light-hearted theatrical sketch. But his main reason for keeping it in the drawer may have been that it represents a comedic variation on the main situation and some of the principal characters of *A Month in the Country*.

He takes the principal personages of that play and moves them from their 'nest of gentry' to a foreign setting, unencumbered by *byt* and by the train of secondary characters. The protagonist is again a woman at 'the critical age', as then conceived,[34] but now she is a widow;[35] the 17-year-old ward Vera becomes an 18-year-old niece, Mariya; the young man to whom both women are attracted is not a raw boy but a 28-year-old who has travelled and seen something of the world; and the *cavalier servente* of the protagonist has been transformed from a polished and cultured projection of

Turgenev into a 45-year-old landowner from the wilds of Saratov,
who is so sick of everything foreign and so homesick for Russia that
he has only to doze off to dream himself back home.

So the whole emotional spectrum is shifted from dark to light.
The *cavalier servente* has no reason to feel guilty and is only
moderately disquieted and irritated by jealousy. The young man is
first dazzled by the aunt, but then gravitates naturally to the girl.
The protagonist is not passionately involved and, at the first
challenge to her coquetry and pride, surrenders her prey gracefully
to her young rival and seems inclined to reward the faithful
devotion of the older man.

As we turn to consider Turgenev's longer plays, it is convenient,
for several reasons, to consider *The Bachelor* next, out of chronological order. Although written a year after *The Parasite*, it was
published seven-and-a-half years ahead of the latter and staged
more than twelve years sooner.[36] Secondly, *The Bachelor*, alone
among Turgenev's longer plays, is still Gogolian in setting and, to a
considerable extent, in typology. And thirdly, like the one-act plays
and unlike *The Parasite* and *A Month in the Country*, it has not
travelled beyond the limits of the Russian theatre.

The play is set in St Petersburg, among civil servants of comparatively humble rank.[37] The bachelor of the title, Moshkin, is a
man of 50, who had taken into his home and raised as his ward the
now 19-year-old orphaned daughter of a neighbour. A young
colleague, Vilitsky, whom Moshkin has befriended and taken
under his wing, has fallen in love with the girl, Mar'ya, and become
engaged to her; when the play opens, they are to be married in a
couple of weeks. These are the principal characters; the subject of
the play is the development of the relations between them. Two or
three other personages are brought in for comic relief or diversion:
Mar'ya's widowed aunt; a one-time friend and neighbour of
Moshkin's, who arrives unexpectedly from the country after they
have not seen each other for twenty years; and a grotesque Greek
scribbler, who remains as extraneous to the play as Lupoyarov, ten
years later, to *On the Eve*.

At the outset, all is joy: Moshkin loves both the young people
and is very happy about the approaching marriage and delighted by
the visit of his old friend. But he is also nervous: Vilitski is to bring
to dinner a young colleague who, though junior in rank to
Moshkin, has the privilege of acting as special aide to the minister,

the head of their department. This young fellow, von Fonk,[38] turns out to be a tactless, supercilious snob, whose only concern in life is to make a career. He is blind to the qualities of heart and character in Moshkin and Mar'ya: he sees only the humble background, the lack of sophistication and of worldly assets, and he impresses on Vilitski that such a wife, far from advancing his career, is bound to be a drag that he can ill afford. Vilitski has as much affection as he is capable of for Mar'ya and Moshkin, but he is weak, suggestible and dazzled by von Fonk. He cannot go on with the marriage; but neither can he bring himself to break with his fiancée: he suspends his visits, and when Moshkin comes to enquire about his health, pretends to be out or out of town. Mar'ya writes to press for an explanation of his behaviour, then, too impatient to wait for a reply, takes the bold step of coming alone to his rooms (so anticipating by ten years the boldness of Elena in *On the Eve*). She senses she has lost him and is willing to release him, but he cannot bring himself to admit the truth. Instead, he promises to come and talk things over that evening; when Moshkin catches him a little later, he repeats that promise – but cannot conceal his change of heart and in the end writes to break off the engagement. Mar'ya feels disgraced; and as she has already been criticized for eating the bread of idleness under the roof of a man who is no blood-relation, she proposes to go away and earn her living. Moshkin is in despair at the thought of losing her: to save her face and keep her with him, he asks her to marry him, and in the process discovers that his love is not as fatherly as he had believed. Mar'ya is moved by his measureless devotion to accept; and though she will not easily forget Vilitski, we are left with the impression that it need not long remain a screen-marriage.

The Bachelor is, above all, a vehicle for the virtuosity of the actor who plays Moshkin; it is arguably for his benefit that the play is spun out to its present length. He has to run the whole gamut of emotions, from the initial happiness and pride, through protracted and escalating anxieties, to fury when his darling is rejected, to near-despair when it seems that he can do nothing about it, to chivalrous relief when he lights on the recourse of a nominal marriage, and finally to wild elation when he glimpses the prospect of a real marriage. His is the only fully drawn character. Mar'ya is a faint silhouette of a Turgenev heroine. The other personages (with some reservations for Vilitski) are toned-down Gogolian types.

The Bachelor, together with the immediately preceding *The Parasite*, have been seen as influenced by the sentimental human-ism – the concern for the 'humiliated and abused'[39] – popularized in Russia by Dostoevsky's novel *Poor Folk* (1846).[40] But this was part of a far-flung European trend; both Turgenev and Dostoevsky had drawn inspiration from Gogol's 'The Overcoat' and from George Sand and writers with similar sympathies; in any case, it is Tur-genev's merit to have translated this new orientation to the Russian stage.

With *The Parasite*, written a year before *The Bachelor* though published and staged much later,[41] Turgenev broke new ground in several directions. He freed himself from the limitations of the one-act play, chose a situation of human rather than narrowly national interest, and explored it with a subtlety and poignancy which made it the first – and one of only two – of his plays to establish itself as part of the international repertory. It was first performed in Frankfurt in 1883, in Paris in 1890, and appears to have held the stage in both Germany and Italy[42] well into the nineteenth century (*W*, II, 603).

Parasites – impoverished or destitute gentlemen and ladies – were stock figures in the households of well-to-do landowners. Their lot was an unenviable one: in return for being lodged, fed and clothed they were apt to be treated at best as superior servants, at worst as butts or court jesters, subjected to every kind of humiliation and ignominy. Such had been the fate of Kuzovkin, the protagonist of this play. But Kuzovkin's patron and tormentor had died a couple of decades before the play begins; his widow had survived him only a few years; their daughter and heir had gone away to be educated.[43] Kuzovkin had lived on in their house.

Now, as the play opens, the young mistress is about to return home with her new husband. The whole household is agog. Kuzovkin's friend and neighbour, Ivanov – poor, timid, gloomy – warns him that the new master may throw him out; Kuzovkin scouts the idea: the man Ol'ga has married cannot but be good and humane. The old man[44] recalls fondly the child he used to play with and looks forward eagerly to seeing her again.

When the young couple arrive, Ol'ga does not immediately recognize him and has forgotten his patronymic, but she is very gracious, even friendly, and he is in the seventh heaven. But the husband, Eletski, a high-ranking civil servant, 11 or 12 years older than his wife, is a dry, cool, unsentimental gentleman.

Within the hour a visitor is announced – a neighbouring land-owner, Tropachëv, a vain, vulgar snob and bully, who arrives with his own parasite in tow; he ingratiates himself with his host, who promptly invites the pair to stay to dinner, and grossly patronizes Kuzovkin. At dinner, in the absence of Ol′ga, Tropachëv promises Eletski 'some fun', plies Kuzovkin with liquor and sets himself to draw him out. The old man is too happy to notice what is happening and ignores Ivanov's furtive attempts to restrain him. Prompted by Tropachëv, he embarks on a long, garbled and (for his audience) hilarious account of the legal tangles that have prevented him from getting possession of the tiny estate to which he is heir.

Then, when he seems 'ripe', they try to make him sing and dance, as he had had to do for Ol′ga's father. But that was twenty years ago; now he is old, and they are trying to make a clown of him in front of Ol′ga's husband: he cannot and will not sing or dance. So Tropachëv sends his parasite to make a dunce's cap and slip it onto Kuzovkin from behind. When he discovers it, he breaks down in tears, but then turns to bitter reproaches – not against Tropachëv, whom he despises, but against Eletski, who has not taken an active part in the 'fun', but has supported and enjoyed it. Eletski tries to outface and overawe him; but the old man, emboldened by drink and wounded to the core, is completely carried away and, in response to some further provocation, blurts out: 'Do you know who I am? . . . Do you know whom you have married? . . . You are married to my daughter.' Eletski, thunderstruck, exclaims: 'You are out of your mind'; and Kuzovkin, moaning, 'Yes, out of my mind', rushes away clutching his head. End of Act I.

The second act presents the aftermath, next day. Eletski's only concern is to have Kuzovkin retract in front of witnesses and then depart for ever. Kuzovkin, overcome with shame and remorse, agrees to do so; but Ol′ga had overheard the fateful words and is determined to get to the bottom of the matter. She summons Kuzovkin to say good-bye – and insists on knowing 'everything'. He tries to deny having meant anything – he was drunk and didn't know what he was saying . . . but she will not be gainsaid.

Yet how can he, simple and uneducated, convey to this gently bred girl that her putative father was an adulterer, a despot and a brute, and that her mother, in a moment of supreme humiliation and despair, had turned to him, Kuzovkin, for comfort (with the implication that her mother too committed adultery and that Ol'ga herself is illegitimate)? He does accomplish this feat with truly chivalrous delicacy (referring to his tormentor as 'your father' or 'my benefactor' and implying what will not bear relating) – a *tour de force* of dramatic writing. Ol'ga probes the story, but finds it impossible to doubt him.

She goes to tell her husband what she has learned. Eletski will not believe it: the old man must be a liar and a blackmailer. Or, at any rate, he must be made to appear a liar and a blackmailer: he must not only be sent away, but be sent away with a large sum of money. When Kuzovkin refuses his 10,000 rubles, he infers that the man wants more. Only Ol'ga succeeds in disarming the old man with a show[45] of filial affection, assuring him that she believes him, promising to keep in touch with him, and pressing on him only the money to redeem the little estate of which he has been unjustly deprived all his adult life. To please her and save her embarrassment, Kuzovkin accepts this; and after publicly withdrawing and apologizing for his 'mad words' of the day before and submitting to some more ragging by Tropachëv and his parasite (which Eletski, this time, unceremoniously cuts short), 'the new landowner' is toasted by the assembled company and goes off to 'take possession' of his village with its forty-two serf 'souls' (as male serfs were officially styled).

It may be thought that Turgenev's inclination to write plays for and around a single virtuoso actor (or actress) has weakened the ending of this play, leaving the audience or reader with one or two frustrating questions unanswered. Kuzovkin's character and destiny have been rounded out in masterly fashion; but what of Ol'ga?[46] What had gone on in her mind and heart between the end of Kuzovkin's story and her embracing him as her father? Was her uprush of filial feeling sincere, or was she playing her husband's game: persuading the old man to take the money in the only possible way? Turgenev almost certainly intended her to be sincere; but this can be deduced only from the little we see of her in the rest of the play, not from anything in the immediate context.

In *The Parasite* the surface theme of man's inhumanity to man is interwoven with the more fundamental one of the discrepancy between being and seeming, between reality and appearance – with typical Turgenevan unobtrusiveness, but so that it adds an extra dimension to Kuzovkin. The despised hanger-on is a great gentleman; the rich gentlemen are cads and bullies. The young heiress has no right to the estates she has 'inherited'. And the marriage hailed with such joy in the opening scenes stands revealed as a sad mismatch: can the true-hearted girl continue to respect a man who lives for appearances? Can he ever understand or appreciate her?

Turgenev's last[47] and best play, *A Month in the Country*, marks the full development of the psychological drama, a generation before Chekhov. It has been translated into most Western languages and continues to be produced, not only in the Soviet Union and on the Continent but in England and America. Although there is still a star rôle for the protagonist, who is on stage nearly 60 per cent of the time and is called upon for acting abilities well above average, yet she does not dwarf or eclipse the other personages: the cast includes at least four other fully drawn characters – three of them explored with considerable subtlety and *con amore*.

Since Grossman[48] makes so much of *A Month in the Country*'s debt to Balzac's *La Marâtre*,[49] let us begin by defining the extent of that debt. Turgenev always insisted that he had no powers of invention; he took his materials, as far as possible, from life, but he was prepared on occasion to take a plot from literature (notably in the case of *On the Eve* and 'A King Lear of the Steppes'). For *A Month in the Country* he borrowed from Balzac the plot of an older and a younger woman (stepmother and stepdaughter in the French play) as rivals for the love of a young man; the older woman's devious manoeuvring to ascertain the object of the girl's affections and the nature of the man's feelings for her; and her grim attempt to dispose of her antagonist by marrying her off to a preposterous suitor. Besides the basic situation and plot, the two plays share, in some measure, three of the secondary rôles – those of the vain, clumsy suitor, the observant and meddlesome doctor and the young (12- or 10-year-old) son of the protagonist – and some of the 'business': the group of card-players, with their exchanges counterpointing more serious dialogue, the protagonist on her knees before her young rival.

However, it should be borne in mind that in 1844 – four years before *La Marâtre* was written – Turgenev had tried out the situation of an older and a younger woman contending for the love of one man, in his unfinished play *Two Sisters*, and that, if the rôles of the suitor and the doctor in the French and Russian plays are analogous, the characters of the two personages are significantly different. Turgenev's suitor is middle-aged, graceless, dim-witted; Balzac's is elegant, self-assured and – though he feigns naïvety – 'the shrewdest man in the district'. Balzac's doctor is a man of sterling character and warm affections; Turgenev's is an arrant egoist and is careful not to show his true face in society.

Anyhow, the differences between the two plays are far more fundamental than the similarities. Not only has Turgenev stripped away the melodramatic trappings – disguises, poison, blackmail, suicide – that distort Balzac's initial conception of *drame intime* ('intimate drama', i.e., drama framed in the tenor and norms of everyday life), but the situation and plot common to both plays is set in the context of very dissimilar stories. The stepmother had known and loved the man in dispute long before she met and married her husband; the boy believed by the husband to be his son was in fact fathered by the lover; the stepmother had enrolled the lover in her husband's service in order to keep him near her but he has remained in it in order to be near the stepdaughter, with whom he has fallen in love and who returns his love; the stepdaughter is blackmailed into accepting the suitor's proposal, but has no intention of marrying him and does not do so: none of this corresponds to anything in *A Month in the Country*. And *La Marâtre* contains no analogue to the character and rôle of Rakitin.

Besides, the capital difference between the French and the Russian play lies in the psychology – and this invests similar or even identical elements with radically different meanings. Balzac's psychology is Romantic: his personages are creatures of a single passion (the two women, the lover) or of a system of non-conflicting passions (the husband). Though they speak in prose, not verse, each of them could aptly say, with Hugo's Hernani, '*Je suis une force qui va!*' Turgenev's principal personages are everyday mortals, a little above average in culture and character, but complex, conflicted, capable of surprising themselves as well as an audience. In fine, Balzac's *conception* of 'intimate drama' was realized – in *A Month in the Country*.

A Month in the Country actually comprises only the last few days of the month, in which 29-year-old Natal'ya Petrovna – the mistress of the 'nest of gentry' – and her 17-year-old ward Vera discover that they have fallen in love with the 21-year-old student engaged to tutor the 10-year-old son of the house over the summer. The play opens as 'intimate drama' is supposed to open – with the household seemingly lapped in the peace of routine family life. Only one small black cloud spots the horizon: Natal'ya Petrovna is seen to be unusually restless and irritable. But the small cloud quickly over-spreads the whole sky and generates an emotional storm which does not clear away until it has disrupted the existing tissue of personal relationships and driven half the persons closely involved out of the nest.

The cast of thirteen divides, almost neatly, into two groups: the five principals, on the one hand, seven subsidiary rôles on the other, with, between them, the figure of the doctor, whose rôle is purely auxiliary (that of introducing and promoting the interests of Vera's suitor), but whose character is drawn in the round, whereas the seven are hardly more than silhouettes.

The seven comprise: Natal'ya Petrovna's mother-in-law with her companion, her young son with his German tutor (evidently a fixture in the household, unlike the young Russian engaged for the holidays), two servants and the grotesque suitor. These are essentially stock figures, although Turgenev, with his rooted fondness for youth, does impart a special sparkle to the boy and to the young maidservant; their general function is to lighten the dramatic tension and/or to slow the pace of the action. The suitor and the German tutor are comic figures; the two servants (who are, of course, serfs) are treated, in the tradition of Pushkin, as individuals endued with the dignity of self-respect.

The doctor is an interesting case. His name, Shpigel'ski, suggests the German word for 'mirror' (*Spiegel*) and/or the Polish for 'spy' (*szpieg*) though, if he is of foreign descent, his name and patronym-ic and his racy command of language seem to indicate that he is at least a third-generation Russian. Natal'ya Petrovna sums him up as a 'provincial Talleyrand', that is, a master of intrigue in unprinci-pled and successful pursuit of his own interests; he is cynical and two-faced, but also intelligent and amusing. To his author he must have represented a morally alien type and a class enemy; and it is noteworthy that Turgenev, far from satirizing him, allows him to cut a surprisingly fine figure, especially in the scene of his marriage proposal – to the old grandmother's companion – in which he exposes his own true nature – the face behind the mask – with a ruthlessness of honesty unsurpassed by any of the other personages.

Here again we have a sudden revelation of the reality behind appearances. Who of us would have imagined Dr Shpigel'ski capable of such candour at his own expense? How far is it in character? If we look closely enough, we shall not doubt its being fully so, for it proves to be compounded, in almost equal parts, of calculation (that is, self-interest) and pride. The calculation is that a marriage, to be solid, must be as free from illusions as possible; if his bride discovered the face behind the mask only after marriage, she would be entitled to feel cheated – with all the likely corollaries of resentment and disaffection. As for pride – we have seen evidence of it in his condescending manipulation of the suitor, we have heard evidence of it in Natal'ya Petrovna's complaints of his 'impertinence'; but here we meet an unexpected aspect of it, an aspect akin to self-respect – the determination to be with a wife what he cannot be in society: himself. Finally – and not least convincingly – the 'confession' is in character in its language: the down-to-earth, occasionally crude, hard-hitting realism.

The five principal personages of the play are: Natal'ya Petrovna, 29; her husband, Islaev, 36; her 'old friend', as she calls him on the strength of the platonic relationship they have maintained over the past four years, Rakitin, 30; her son's summer tutor, Belyaev, 21; and her ward, Vera, 17. The interrelationships between these five are complicated enough to form no less than four 'triangles', which, if we take the initials of the personages to designate the 'angles' could read: RNI, RNB, INB, NBV; more simply – Natal'ya Petrovna is loved by three men, loves all three of them in different ways, and in relation to the youngest and newest in her life finds herself in competition with her ward. It is this rivalry that provides the 'action' of the play.

Among these principals it is the women who are the active forces; the men react to them.[50] Hardly less important is the division between the sophisticated characters (Natal'ya Petrovna, Rakitin) and the ingenuous (Vera, Belyaev, Islaev). Obviously these two groupings do not coincide – they intersect: at one level Natal'ya Petrovna is pitted against two of the ingenuous – Vera, Belyaev; at another – against her fellow sophisticate, Rakitin.[51]

Allowing for the differences in age, culture and social background, the husband and the student have a great deal in common. The primary interest of both is in practical activities; both bring to these activities skills and energy which evoke admiration; both are undemonstrative and reticent about their feelings, but capable of feeling deeply; both are strikingly open, honest and direct; both have a stable and defined system of values, thanks to which they know what is right and proper to be done.

Islaev does not appear at all in Act II and has barely two or three minutes in Acts I, III and IV. He has submerged himself completely in the running and development of his estate; but his hint, on his first appearance, that he had once had other dreams, which he has had to lay aside, may suggest an analogy with the student's interest in the ideas of Belinsky's articles.[52] The fullest revelation of his character comes in the fifth act. He has found his wife crying on Rakitin's shoulder and has waited nearly twenty-four hours – vainly – for the promised explanation. Now he is unable to concentrate on any business, and after respectfully fending off his mother's attempts to interfere, he sends for Rakitin. Their brief meeting throws into relief the salient features of Islaev's personality: the moral courage which not only impels him to say and do what is right but nerves him to confront the truth, however painful; his modesty, that is, his realism in regard to himself; and the quality of his love for his wife, whom he is willing to give up if her happiness depends on that, though he does not know if he could live without her. Yet even such self-sacrifice and love are no guarantee against dramatic irony: Islaev sees the threat to his marriage as coming from Rakitin – just when Rakitin has ceased to represent any danger, and never suspects that a much more pressing danger is now embodied in Belyaev.

Belyaev combines the moral and practical virtues of the husband with the glow and dash of youth and has conquered all hearts in the Islaev household with his cheerful friendliness, as Vera tells Natal'ya Petrovna in their first colloquy (Act III). With his peers and inferiors he is warm and unself-conscious, but he is constantly aware of the gulf, in culture and status, that separates him from the gentry, and with them he remains somewhat stiff and aloof – 'awkward', as Natal'ya Petrovna says; but shy, not wary – he responds to their direct approaches or questions with unvarying candour.

In Act I, reporting to Islaev on the progress of work on his dam, he shows that he has missed nothing – and has found all for the best: his sunny satisfaction contrasts with his employer's anxious expectation of omissions and errors. Then he is catechized by Natal'ya

Petrovna and gives her a matter-of-fact picture of his family background, stressing the limitations of his upbringing and education. In Act II, he responds with equal good-humour and less uneasily to further questioning by Rakitin: revealing his attitudes to work and to study, his hobbies and his intellectual interests. Between these two inquisitions we see him briefly with Katya, the young maidservant, who would be in love with him if she dared, and, in a longer talk, with Vera, who is on the point of discovering that she is in love with him. Belyaev is so devoid of vanity that he quite fails to notice the perfectly transparent feelings of the two girls. When Vera confides to him her urges to cry for no reason, he explains them as growing pains; when she wishes she could be in his sister's place, he understands this in terms of location, not of relation to himself. And when he learns, later, that Vera is in love with him, he is astounded, he can hardly believe it.

This is in his crucial colloquy with Natal'ya Petrovna at the end of the third act. So far, in all of the significant dialogues – with Natal'ya Petrovna, with Vera, with Rakitin – he has played a purely reactive part, replying and responding to their initiatives. And so it continues through the first half of this third-act meeting: she speaks, he interjects brief expressions of concern, puzzlement, incredulity. But once he has grasped the situation, he, for the first time, takes the moral initiative: he must leave the house.

Yet, only a few moments later, when the lady has shown she wants him to stay, he reverses himself and agrees to do so. This turnabout is not explained until their final talk, in the fourth act, where the young man conveys, in figurative language very different from his ordinary style, that that had been the moment when he realized he was in love with her. Looking back, we can see that this moment of truth has been prepared (if only tenuously) by his earlier stress (in his conversation with Vera in Act II) on his fear of the lady and his linking of fear with love. Perhaps a further hint in the same sense could be read into his plan to organize a fireworks display for the mistress's name-day.

In their final colloquy he is overwhelmed by her confession that she loves him. His instinctive reaction is again to do the right thing, but when she tries to keep him, he wavers; and in the last act, next day, he needs Rakitin's example – and Rakitin's philosophy of love – to 'screw him to the sticking-point'. He goes away, but not in settled determination – rather in panic flight, not daring to face

Natal'ya Petrovna even to say goodbye. If love has not had time to break his will, love has certainly staggered it. He will return to his former life, carrying with him a few cherished memories, having taken only one or two difficult steps on the road to adulthood.

For Vera those same last four days of the month have sufficed to complete the transition from child to woman. It is true that her ordeal has been imcomparably more severe. First, the struggle with, and efforts to understand, the unfamiliar emotions that have suddenly begun to well up in her. Then the realization, under Natal'ya Petrovna's probing questions, of the real nature of her feelings. She surrenders her secret, unwillingly, to this woman whom she only half trusts but who is her sole substitute for a family (she appears to have no relationship with Islaev, and though she says she is very fond of Rakitin, he sees nothing objectionable in her being married off to the grotesque suitor) – and the woman promptly betrays and humiliates her by blazoning her secret abroad. The humiliation is redoubled and compounded with bitter misery when she finds that her feeling for Belyaev is not returned; and to these pangs is superadded a sense of guilt when she believes (wrongly) that the young man is to be sent away on her account. As certain shocks can 'turn hair white in a single night', so this harrowing of her heart 'ages' her, as she herself asserts – in a single day; nor is it idly that she says to Natal'ya Petrovna: 'From today on, I am a woman . . . I am just as much a woman as you.'

This means, first, that her eyes are opened: she becomes aware that Natal'ya Petrovna is jealous of her – and that must mean that she too is in love with Belyaev. At this point, there is a split between what she thinks and what she feels. She says (and, no doubt, believes) that she does not blame her rival – for deceiving and betraying her, because jealousy (love) excuses everything; but not only does she repay that rival in kind – divulging the secret of the older woman's love as her own secret has been divulged – but she elects to marry the despised suitor and scornfully rejects Natal'ya Petrovna's contrition and pleas for reconciliation – even after she knows that *he* is going, that *he* is lost to both of them. Anything rather than remain in the shadow of the woman she has evidently come to hate.

Is the decision to marry nothing but a blind reflex of hate? Surely all we have seen of Vera's honesty and courage speaks against such a partial interpretation. This marriage *is* an escape from the power of a detested rival; but it is also and, in the long run, above all – a choice of independence: such limited independence as is attainable in her world. It means turning her back on the comforting illusions of childhood. It means facing a life without hope of happiness (but she has already lost that anyway). She is ready to pay the price. It is, after all, the common lot. In seven out of Turgenev's ten plays a young woman marries or prepares to marry; in only one of the seven does she marry a man whom she loves and who truly loves her.[53]

We have it on Turgenev's own authority that in Rakitin he had projected himself.[54] And, although he does not say so, there is an obvious analogy between Rakitin's position on the edge of the Islaev nest and Turgenev's in relation to the Viardots; but this must not mislead us into equating the two families. Admittedly, Pauline Viardot in 1850 was 29 – the same age as Natal'ya Petrovna – but Louis Viardot was then 50, to Islaev's 36. Besides, Islaev and Rakitin were boyhood friends; Turgenev knew the Viardots only since 1843, when he was 25. And however much of feminine psychology Turgenev may have learned from his experience with Pauline Viardot, she was a woman with a vocation, to which everything else in her life was secondary; a vocation is precisely what Natal'ya Petrovna lacks (and perhaps needs?). So one should beware of concluding from the play either that the relation between Turgenev and Pauline had always been platonic, or that in 1850 Turgenev was prepared to write it off as 'sickly and morbid', or that Natal'ya Petrovna's infatuation with Belyaev is based on an infatuation of Pauline Viardot with Gounod (or anyone else). Such equations cannot be either established or invalidated.

Rakitin's four-year-long devotion to Natal'ya Petrovna is an obsession, which has come to absorb all his thoughts and purposes – his entire life. He 'belongs' to her; her will is his will; he cannot imagine life without her. He is aware that such obsession involves a narrowing and impoverishment of personality[55] and he is conscious, at some level of the contradiction between hopes of becoming her lover and the basic decency that would forbid him to deceive his friend.[56] He sees his situation as painful, embarrassing, ridiculous. But he is spellbound – utterly unable to end the relationship which, as soon as she has ended it, he will recognize as sickly, morbid.[57]

Rakitin is, as Islaev attests, the most gifted of the three men.

Highly intelligent, cultured, attractive, sensitive, a lover of nature, an elegant conversationalist – and, in relation to Natal'ya Petrovna, patient, loyal, warm, selfless.[58] What he lacks (apart from the magic of youth) is drive.[59] The husband and the student are men of action. Faced with an equivocal situation, Islaev cuts through the Gordian knot within twenty-four hours. Belyaev, discovering his love is returned, knows that he must flee: because if he stays, he 'cannot answer for' the consequences. Rakitin has let Natal'ya Petrovna play cat-and-mouse with him for four years without even once making her cry – without complaining. How much he has suffered is hinted in the philosophy of love he expounds to Belyaev; how wretched the rewards of such suffering is brought home to him at the end, when his lady lets him leave without as much as a goodbye or a glance.

Returning to the Islaevs' after an absence of several weeks (not 'a few days', as stated in the play, for Belyaev has been there nearly a month and Rakitin knows nothing about him) – Rakitin at once senses an emotional disquiet in Natal'ya Petrovna. It takes him two-and-a-half acts to grope his way to a determination of its nature and cause. From the moment that he understands that she is in love with Belyaev he concentrates his efforts on saving her from herself. He knows that she is capable of being carried away by a sudden impulse or infatuation that would ruin her life (and Islaev's).[60] Of course, neither his decision to give her up himself nor his efforts to ensure that his rival leaves at the same time are disinterested: here his lady's best interests coincide with his own; but he *is* disinterested when he exerts himself to save Islaev from discovering or suspecting his wife's feelings for the young man. We might note that whereas the women – not only Natal'ya Petrovna but Vera too – betray each other to the men, the men studiously refuse to compromise the lady: Rakitin in talking to Islaev and to Belyaev, Belyaev in talking to Rakitin and to Vera.

The philosophy of love which Turgenev puts into Rakitin's mouth is one that crops up a number of times in his works. The love to which a man surrenders completely is a disaster, a disease, a degrading slavery. Rakitin is always severe with himself (and at this point he is intent on scaring Belyaev, which he does); we may wonder if the picture really fits Rakitin – who has neither seduced his friend's wife nor lied to his friend – half as well as it might fit the woman who has cheated and lied to all around her and is now nerving herself either to take a lover under her husband's roof or even to abandon husband and child to follow that lover.

Natal'ya Petrovna is by far the most complex female character Turgenev has yet created.[61] Her central characteristic seems to be her insecurity. She grew up in the shadow of a father who perhaps loved her but of whom she was always afraid. She has never felt young; she has never felt free; she has never been in love. At the age of 18 (presumably just after her father's death) she married a man who loved and was in love with her, but with whom she was not in love and with whom she had no common interests. She had one child soon after her marriage – and for ten years has chosen to have no more. She is fond of her son and her husband, but neither separately nor jointly do they suffice to fill her life.

Seven years into her marriage – four years before the opening of the play – she attached to herself a much more interesting man than her husband and one who, unlike her husband, has devoted all his time and the resources of his mind to her service: that is, he has warmed her with his love, entertained her with his intelligence and shored up her insecurity with his admiration and unconditional submission. In return he has asked for nothing but to be near her: seeing her is enough to make him happy. And she, if not happy, has been content: Rakitin bears witness to the exceptional evenness of her moods – up till now (Act II, following his colloquy with her).

But at a deeper level she has remained unsatisfied, and his brief absence has left her vulnerable to the impact of new and disturbing circumstances: the spectacle of youth and happiness in effervescent interaction. To her conscious eye, her son, her ward and the strange student are all equally 'children' (she is particularly insistent on this in reference to Vera), but subconsciously she is keenly aware that two of the three are ripe for love and marriage. Meanwhile, they represent the joyous freedom she has never had and always longed for.

Their effect on her is, no doubt, considerably intensified by the imminence of middle age: 30 was thought to mark the end of a woman's youth, and Natal'ya Petrovna's constant harping on the theme 'I am old' is not to be dismissed as merely a device of coquetry, but carries poignant undertones of fear and revulsion.

With the timidity stemming from her insecurity, which she habitually masks with a cool aloofness (as she confesses in her first colloquy with Belyaev, Act I), she has repressed her disquiet and kept the young man at arm's length – in four weeks they have not had a single personal talk – while waiting for Rakitin's return. Unconsciously she must have hoped that he would protect her – conjure the danger away. That explains her carping at him in the first act: without fully realizing her own meaning, she is goading him into asserting himself ('I want *you* to want'), into offering her something more satisfying than nature madrigals and endless psychological studies ('Lace is fine – but no match for a draught of cold water on a hot day'). When he fails to understand ('You subtle people – how little insight you show . . .') and proves unable to take command or possession, the repressed begins to break through. The announcement of a suitor brings home to her that Vera is no longer merely a child; the sight of the good feeling between her and Belyaev alarms her jealousy (though she does not yet recognize it as such): she embarks on her first intimate talk with Belyaev and agrees to let the suitor try his luck.

Next day (Act II) Rakitin's anxiety about the change in her keeps pace with her growing irritation with him, which finds its culminating expression in the deliciously cruel commentary on his madrigal about the trees. His insight has not yet pierced to the root of her trouble, of which she herself is still not conscious, although some of her outbursts are quite transparent: nature is much simpler and coarser than he assumes, because it is, thank Heaven, healthy . . . (whereas) he and she are sick or, at any rate, are old. His eyes are finally opened only by the scene of the kite-flying, which takes place off-stage but is described afterwards: there he sees her transfigured – youthful, radiant, following the young man with such joyful and confiding attention as to leave no doubt in Rakitin's mind.

Natal'ya Petrovna, of course, could not see herself as Rakitin had seen her; but the real nature of her feeling can hardly now be far below the level of consciousness. And her first reaction next day (Act III) is to make a clean breast of her feelings, so far as she understands them, and implore Rakitin's support in coping with them. But he fails her once more: jealousy makes him recoil and turn away; and though he returns a little later to try to make amends – it is too late, for Natal'ya Petrovna has already had her climactic talk with Vera, has found out that the girl loves Belyaev and believes he loves her, and has been forced by her own reaction of furious jealousy and misery to recognize that she herself is in love.

This third day (Acts III and IV) is, as Natal'ya Petrovna remarks towards its close, 'a day of revelations'.[62] She has cajoled Vera into revealing her love for Belyaev; she has manoeuvred Belyaev into making it clear that he does not love Vera; she has confessed to Belyaev that she herself is in love with him and so elicited his answering declaration of love. In pursuing her purpose she behaves like someone in the grip of an irresistible force, and that is how she sees herself: '. . . in no case can one answer for oneself or give guarantees for anything', she warns Rakitin before throwing herself headlong into the torrent; and after detailing to Belyaev the lies, the trickery, the disgraceful treatment of Vera that have filled her day – the only explanation she offers is: 'It was beyond my power to control all that' (*Vsë eto ne bylo v moei vlasti*: Act IV, after her avowal that she loves him) – an explanation that is evidently supposed to contain its own justification. Even her display of sincerity to Belyaev is tinged with insincerity, for immediately after professing disgust with her recent dishonesties she proceeds to lie just as shamelessly to Rakitin in order to throw him off the scent and so prevent him from interfering in her further relations with Belyaev. The fact is that everything else has lost all meaning for her: truth, good faith, all other personal relations are expendable. She has already written Rakitin off – so completely that when (in the last act) he walks out of her life, she cannot spare him a word or glance of farewell. She is preparing to write off her husband and son likewise: 'What ever will there be to live for?' she asks forlornly when first admonished that Belyaev must go.

The love to which she capitulates so unreservedly is not simply physical, although it is clear that the physical element plays a very large part in it. It is the young man's physical attractiveness she calls to mind when she first mentions him to Rakitin ('I like him. Slim, shapely, a cheerful look', Act I). Her excitement during the kite-flying must have been largely physical. And when, on the third day, she explains to Rakitin 'the rather powerful impression' Belyaev has made on her, she says: 'The man has infected me with his youth – that is all' (Act III). This has a physical reference, but also points beyond the physical – at any rate, in the sense of the purely sexual: it involves the looming shadow of age. The third major component of her passion is jealousy – a rather frantic jealousy rooted in her basic insecurity. The idea that Belyaev (or, perhaps, any man?) could prefer Vera to her drives her wild. When he convinces her that he is not in love with Vera, she reacts with enormous relief[63] – followed by anger when he proposes to leave: what reason is there now for him to go? And a second surge of relief greets his explanation that he has held aloof from her all these weeks out of awe: she had seemed a creature of some higher world. So it wasn't because something in her had repelled him: she doesn't need to prove herself: she could let him go, after all.

But when, freed from his awe by her declaration of love, he in turn starts to speak the language of love, she changes her mind again. On the first day (Act I) she had lightly asked if it was not possible to love two men at the same time, but, when challenged, had conceded that that would perhaps mean one loved neither. The two men then were no doubt her husband and Rakitin; and in fact she loved neither of them with the all-absorbing, utterly reckless love which was even then fighting its way upward into consciousness. Two days later – it has broken through, and 'everything is shattered, scattered, swept away'. Another two days – and she is left, without joy and without hope, to hide her mourning from those who love but do not know her.

In *A Month in the Country* Turgenev combines two subtle psychological portraits – of a woman in crisis and of a hero of what he will later call 'the Hamlet type' – with the Romantic theme of the impact of nature on culture and the classical theme of love as a sickness, a madness, a curse sent from above.[64] He interweaves these elements into a rich and compelling pattern, and he presents his personages with the respect of a true artist and the impartiality of a true psychologist.

Turgenev's theatre starts from the positions of the Spanish (or pseudo-Spanish) drama and the Gogolian farce (or light light comedy) and moves gradually away from both, reducing or discarding certain elements while incorporating new elements from other sources. In the farces the comic 'business' is reduced (to a minimum in *Conversation on a Highway*) and tinged – with 'sentimental humanism' (*ibid.*) or with the sprightliness and some of the subtlety of the 'proverb' (in *The Provincial Lady*). In the dramas, the action is diluted (almost to vanishing-point in *A Month in the Country*) to make way for 'sentimental humanism' (*The Bachelor*, *The Parasite*) or a post-Romantic psychology, which – for all its originality – has affinities with Musset's (*A Month in the Country*).

Criticism

Turgenev did not consider himself a good critic.[65] Flaubert – no
mean judge – took a different view: 'what a critic! I was dazzled by
the depth and clarity of his judgment. Ah, if those who dabble in
the judging of books could only have heard him – what a lesson.
Nothing escapes him.'[66]

Turgenev was not a professional critic and was as little hampered
by theories of criticism as by theories in other fields. He was
familiar with Hegel's aesthetics, with Lessing and with a great deal
of eighteenth- and nineteenth-century criticism, and he quickly
adopted Belinsky's views on the social obligations of literature;
though many of Belinsky's self-styled heirs had difficulty seeing any
social justification for much of Turgenev's later writing. He read
voraciously all his life and was a man of exceptionally wide literary
culture: he had not only read but absorbed the great works of six or
seven literatures and he kept abreast of the literary productions of
his own time at many levels below the highest, and as far afield as
America. Within the limits of his sympathies he had exquisite taste
and perceptiveness: that is what Flaubert saw and admired in him.

Probably most, and certainly the most interesting part, of his
literary criticism is to be found in his letters; but between 1843 and
1854 he published about a dozen critical articles, essays in the form
of book reviews: the earlier ones redolent of Belinsky, the later
ones more nearly reflecting Turgenev's own interests. The tone is at
times somewhat magisterial, the considerable learning is apt to be
displayed at considerable length,[67] some of the judgments are
youthfully summary, as in this comparison of Schiller and Goethe:
'As a human being and a citizen, he [Schiller] is superior to Goethe,
though inferior to him as an artist and, generally speaking, as a
personality.'[68] Simplistic, perhaps, but arguable and – even more
noteworthy at a time when some ardent young contemporaries
were ready to anathematize Goethe for being 'only a poet' –
equitable.

In his 42-page review of a translation of *Faust*,[69] Turgenev does
not deny that Goethe was 'only a poet' (an uncommitted writer),
but he insists that Goethe was a very great poet, who in his life and
works expressed supremely well and fully the spirit and life of his
people and his time, and is not to be blamed for not having
expressed the needs and interests of a later time. In this (i.e.,

Turgenev's own) age, it is not enough to be a poet: human society takes precedence over the individual; art cannot be divorced from social problems. (This is pure Belinsky.) But recognition of these truths detracts nothing from the greatness of Goethe and his work.

The essay comprises a characterization of Goethe in his relation to poetry, an analysis of *Faust* and a detailed critique of the translation. There cannot have been more than a handful of Russian writers at that date who would have been capable of producing such an essay. The mastery of German, the knowledge and appreciation of German literature, the philosophy of translation and the overall balance combine to constitute a kind of originality.

One of the later reviews was of a four-volume novel written by a woman. Turgenev condescendingly opines that only a woman would venture on such a feat in Russia at this period, because women write with their hearts and therefore have no qualms about going off at a tangent and filling scores of pages with irrelevant chatter. His later life was to contain little to modify such views: the majority of the young writers who submitted manuscripts to him were apparently women, and he was to toil unstintingly to advise, correct and instil into them ideas of measure and relevance. Oddly enough, he seems never to have read Jane Austen.

His 1852 review of Ostrovsky's play, *The Poor Bride*, is noteworthy for its definition of the proper place of psychology in literature.

Mr. Ostrovsky burrows into the soul of each of his personages . . . before our eyes; we would venture to point out to him that this undoubtedly useful operation should be carried out by the author beforehand. He should have his personages completely in his power before they are introduced to us. We shall be told: 'But that is psychology'. Granted; but psychology ought to be hidden within the artist as the skeleton is hidden from our eyes within the warm, living body which it, solidly though invisibly, sustains.

In the second of his two reviews of S. T. Aksakov's book on hunting we find a disquisition on the right and wrong attitude to nature. The wrong attitude is to use nature as a stalking-horse for our own emotions (as the Romantics do) or fantasies (as Rakitin did); what we ought to do is to love her truly, which means disinterestedly.

The criticism, and self-criticism, to be found in Turgenev's letters consist mainly not of long passages, but of a few lines or even single

sentences; but over the forty-odd years of his adult life these enable
us to build up a picture – not complete but surprisingly wide-
ranging and various – of his reading, his enthusiasms and aversions,
his blind spots, his literary principles and creed.

In music he was a conservative: his idols were Gluck, Mozart and
Beethoven; he found it very difficult to digest Verdi, let alone
Wagner; but in music, as in art, it is likely that his judgments were
at times influenced by the attitudes of the Viardots. In literature,
his tastes were probably formed before he met them; they reflect
the successive strata of 'influences' in his own education and –
deriving partly from these, partly from deeper emotional springs –
the conflicts in his own mind and personality.

He had begun as a lyric poet. The earliest influences, in the first
half of the 1830s, were no doubt Byron and Russian Romantics such
as Benediktov, Marlinsky and perhaps already the Pushkin of the
1820s – joined a little later by Shakespeare and Lermontov. Then
came the years in Berlin, when he steeped himself in the classics
and in German eighteenth-century literature, in Goethe. In the
early forties, the lyric poet was called upon to merge his subjectivity
in a sense of social mission; in the later forties he discovered the
literature of the Spanish Golden Age. From all these far-flung fields
he recruited the pantheon of his literary gods, major and minor,
who set the standards by which, whether consciously or not, he
judged other writers of the past and of his own time.

Although, like most amateur classicists, he gradually lost touch
with Greek, he continued to revel in Homer,[70] whom he reread,
and quoted, in Voss's superb translation,[71] and whom he recommended as essential reading to younger writers. While he referred
to Aeschyulus as 'that colossus',[72] his second enthusiasm among the
Greeks was for Aristophanes, 'that father of laughter',[73] whose
Birds and *Frogs* he proposed to read with Pauline Viardot (omitting
whatever might have offended her delicacy).[74]

In the forties he dismisses Latin literature as 'cold and second-
hand' (or: 'artificial'),[75] but in the mid-fifties he is ploughing
through the Roman historians: Sallust ('whom I greatly disliked'),
some of Livy, Suetonius, Tacitus; and in the early seventies he has
returned to Vergil (as witness Polozova's seduction of Sanin in
'Spring Torrents') and Ovid. A little later he informs friends that he
has become addicted to the Romans – he doesn't know why[76] – and
that he is rereading Vergil 'with no little pleasure';[77] with singular

perceptiveness he recognizes in the author of *The Aeneid* 'a daring innovator and a Romantic'.[78] Ovid he defends more tepidly; later in the seventies his references are to the *Tristia*, to which he may have been drawn by the theme of exile and his own homesickness.

From his two visits to Italy, in 1840 and 1857–8, he derived a warm and enduring love of the country – its natural beauties and its works of art – but only a smattering of the language, with which he persisted in sprinkling his writings and, in particular, his letters. The great Italian classics, from Dante to Tasso, he read mainly or wholly in translation; and, in spite of some ingenious speculations to the contrary, there is no evidence that he had any knowledge of, let alone took any interest in, the major Italian writers of his century.[79]

In Spanish he read a number of classics of the Golden Age: Calderón, whose philosophy of life remained utterly alien to him yet impressed him profoundly;[80] probably Lope de Vega and Tirso de Molina, to whom he refers at various times; but the only Spanish writer who won his heart, whom he made a part of himself in a peculiar way and whom he repeatedly thought of translating into Russian, was Cervantes.

In English, 'his' writers were Dickens, whom he greatly admired, George Eliot, whom he knew personally and respected deeply, and, of course, 'Father' Shakespeare, whom he compared to Nature herself, no doubt primarily in virtue of his universality and variety, but explicitly in terms of (their) 'inevitability, truth and . . . the wedding of means to ends (*tselesoobraznost'*)'. Besides *Lear* and *Hamlet*, on which he drew directly in his own writings, his favourite plays, those he advised Tolstoy to read, included *Julius Caesar*, *Coriolanus*, *Henry IV*, *Macbeth* and *Othello*.[81]

In German literature he came to know a number of his contemporaries, but his compliments to or about them need not be taken as literary judgments. The writers he quotes are Schiller, Heine and, most often, Goethe (Lessing he admired only as a critic.)[82]

Of all foreign literatures he probably knew the French best, and he spent about one-third of his adult life in France. But he disliked France (especially Paris); he disliked the French as a people; among his wide range of acquaintances he counted few friends, and none perhaps as close or intimate as his inner circle of Russians; and he constantly castigated French literature as 'literary' (a term

of abuse in his vocabulary). What he meant by this he explained at
some length in his 1867 preface to a Russian translation of Maxime
Ducamp's novel, *Les Forces perdues*. French literature is 'predominantly artificial and imitative'; it is excessively cerebral; 'the
French mind is keen and quick, but the French imagination is
dulled and poor'; 'French taste is discriminating and sure,
especially in negation', but the French lack true poetic feeling, do
not care for simplicity and show little concern with truth to life –
they tend to create types 'which never have lived nor could have
lived'. This last was said specifically of Balzac; but he is taken as a
prime example of 'the coexistence of great talent with inability to
understand artistic truth'. In fine, 'literary' meant too cerebral, too
abstract, too much concerned with form, too little with life, which is
the essence of true 'poetry' or art.

Of course, Turgenev recognized that France had produced great
writers, and he admires some of them. Montaigne and Rabelais
were authors whom he would have liked to translate into Russian if
he ever had to give up creative writing. He responded to Pascal in
something like the same way as he had to Calderón:[83] he was
impressed and moved by the writer's genius while repelled by his
'enslavement' to Catholicism. Molière delighted him. He speaks
with respect of Voltaire, while dismissing Diderot somewhat cava-
lierly.[84] In his own century there was only one writer whom he
regarded as great, even great enough to challenge comparison with
Tolstoy, and that was Flaubert.

Among the younger generation he took a kindly view of
Alphonse Daudet and Anatole France. Zola was a hard case:
Turgenev liked and respected him as a man, recognized his
considerable talent, helped to get him known in Russia, but
deplored his 'literariness', without, however, going to the same
length of condemnation as against Balzac.[85] The younger writer of
whom he spoke with unreserved admiration as the most talented of
his generation was Maupassant.[86] As for poets, it is hardly surprising that he found nothing to say, in a literary-critical context, of
Baudelaire, Verlaine, Rimbaud or Mallarmé; those he commended
to his Russian or German friends were Leconte de Lisle, the first of
the Parnassians, and Jean Richepin.[87]

In Russian literature Turgenev shows little interest in any writing
prior to the nineteenth century. His immediate predecessors,
Pushkin and Gogol, commanded his reverent admiration. Pushkin

is 'my idol, my teacher, my unattainable model';[88] Gogol was 'for us [Russians] more than simply a writer: he had revealed us to ourselves. He was, in more senses than one, the continuer of Peter the Great.'[89] About Lermontov, the third member of the great literary triumvirate of the first half of the century, he has comparatively little to say. He translated Lermontov's poem, *The Novice* (*Mtsyri*) into French prose with the assistance of Mérimée; in the brief preface to the translation he remarks that Lermontov was regarded by the Russian literary world as Pushkin's heir and successor; elsewhere[90] he implies that he shared that opinion. He quotes Lermontov occasionally in his letters, but nowhere does he express his own feelings about him. He shows a generous appreciation of most of the leading Russian writers of his own generation: both those with whom he had early and long-lasting relations, such as Herzen,[91] Pisemsky, Goncharov, and those with whom his relations developed late or remained tenuous, such as Ostrovsky and Leskov.[92] Among writers of the following generation he has praise for Reshetnikov[93] and Gleb Uspensky[94] and, above all, for Vsevolod Garshin, in whom he sees a 'successor' to himself and to whom he awards 'first place among young writers taking their first steps'.[95]

It is perhaps in relation to Russian literature that one perceives most clearly the two factors that were apt to colour, and in some cases to cloud, Turgenev's literary judgments: his personal feelings about individual authors and his own philosophy of writing (if one may dare to ascribe any sort of philosophy to him). Although he acknowledged that the ideal critic would start from the positions of his author and seek to judge how far and how well that author had achieved his purposes,[96] in practice he quite often lost sight of those ideals. It is evident that his sweeping over-estimations of youthful talents were due to personal feelings, and surely the same is true when he extols his friend Polonsky as the sole surviving poet in Russia[97] or when he exalts Fet above Heine.[98] As an example of the impact of a negative feeling on his judgment, one might consider his attitude in the sixties and seventies to Nekrasov's poetry. But in most of his 'negative injustices'[99] personal feeling is combined with, or overlaid by, literary philosophy.

As a convert from Romanticism, having, no doubt, to combat its residues in himself, he seeks to bury it, as far as possible, in silence. He never refers at all to most of the major writers of English and

German Romanticism,[100] just as he never refers to the poetry of such French Romantics as Vigny and Musset.[101] A single reference to the arch-Romantic Jean-Paul[102] speaks for itself: Homer's *Odyssey* will be the most effective antidote to 'that half-sentimental, half-ironic fussing over one's own sick personality which characterizes Jean-Paul ...'[103] His *bête noire* among the French Romantics is Victor Hugo; referring to some 1875 articles of Hugo, he writes: 'I am sorry I don't know any expression forcible enough to convey how much I despise them – as, indeed, *all* his prose.'[104] And that this is no passing flash of irritation is attested by his comments on Hugo's main prose works of the 1860s and 1870s as each appears;[105] and his attitude to Hugo's poetry of the same period is vituperative (with certain reservations for the second series of *La Légende des siècles*).[106] But Romanticism is only one of the deadly sins of his literary philosophy. The other is 'literariness;[107] and the quintessence of literariness was the work of Balzac: 'I have never been able to read more than ten pages of his at a sitting, so repulsive and so alien to me is [his work].'[108]

On occasion literary disapproval is reinforced by personal dislike (of the long-dead as well as of the living): as in the case of Rousseau,[109] or of Lamartine, whose rôle in the Revolution of 1848 Turgenev despises no less than his 'pale, monochrome verses',[110] or of Dostoevsky, whom he defines as 'the Russian marquis de Sade'.[111] Very rarely, Turgenev's personal feelings were in conflict with his literary-philosophical views. The most interesting of such cases was that of Tolstoy. Turgenev was among the first to recognize and rejoice in Tolstoy's genius[112] and to foresee in him the successor of Gogol and the greatest Russian writer of the second half of their century; nor did he ever waver in this assessment. His predominant feeling for Tolstoy as a man was always one of admiring affection. But he hated Tolstoy's injection of ideology into his writing (or perhaps, more precisely, of the particular brand of ideology), and as late as 1874 – five years after the completion of *War and Peace* – he still insisted on regarding *The Cossacks* as 'the masterpiece of Tolstoy and of all Russian narrative literature'.[113] He continues to carp at the 'Muscovite' and 'Slavophil' elements in *Anna Karenina*; and it is not till 1881 that he finally pronounces *War and Peace* 'the greatest of modern epics'.[114]

But Turgenev's inherent humility, candour and sense of justice worked against his emotional and 'philosophical' biases. Thus, in

1877, writing to Dostoevsky to introduce a French scholar in search of biographical and literary materials, he could say – five years after being cruelly lampooned in Dostoevsky's novel, *The Devils* – that their personal differences had not affected his 'opinion of your superior [*pervoklassnom*] talent and of the high place which you deservedly hold in our literature'.[115] This, admittedly, leaves open the question of just how he rated Dostoevsky in relation to other leading writers of the day whom he admired, such as Leskov, Saltykov, Pisemsky, Ostrovsky, or in relation to himself. Actually, he never placed himself in relation to his Russian contemporaries (except to Tolstoy, to whom he unequivocally and repeatedly awarded first place); whereas he explicitly declared himself 'not made of the same stuff' (*non eiusdem farinae*) as Dickens, George Eliot and George Sand.[116]

From his polemics with Tolstoy, Fet and others, and from his preaching to young, untried writers, his own philosophy of writing emerges clearly. At the root of all is literary 'talent' or 'poetic feeling.' But even the greatest literary talent will be perverted or stultified unless directed by 'truth to life', life being richer and more various than any imagination. Truth to life is impossible without 'freedom of spirit', that is, freedom from ideology. There may have been a certain ingenuousness in this: it seems never to have occurred to Turgenev that his own liberalism and Westernism constituted an ideology no less than Tolstoy's or Fet's (different kinds of) conservatism and 'Slavophilism' and that a personage like Potugin in *Smoke* is as much the mouthpiece of his creator's ideas as Levin in *Anna Karenina*. (However, in life Turgenev was no doubt much more broadminded than Fet or Tolstoy, neither of whom would have thought of paying, as he did, for the publication of works that promoted ideas alien, or even opposed, to his own.) And even in his fiction, if we exclude *Smoke*, he does appear to be the most 'open-ended' writer of his generation.

'Truth to life' implies 'realism' – a realism imbued with (not divorced from) 'poetry' and making room for reverence and love for classical antiquity – and simplicity, which is a matter of not merely style but, first of all, perception.

Literature requires the writer to be professional and objective. Professionalism (which Turgenev often called 'specialization') means total dedication to one's writing – meshing in it all one's powers of mind and heart – and involves unremitting hard work:

not only on the writing itself, but on the study of life and books.[117]
The criterion of 'objectivity' is that one would rather describe x
than describe one's reactions to, or feelings about, x[118] or than use x
to promote one's own ideas.[119] Objectivity is a form of disinterestedness or self-effacement. And the contradiction between the
requirement of objectivity and the admission that a writer draws his
materials from within himself[120] is only a seeming one: the issue is
not where the materials originate but how they are treated: 'First
Love' is autobiographical, but the reader would not suspect that if
he did not know of Turgenev's statement, elsewhere, to that
effect.[121]

The writer's own language is a sacred trust, and, as such, must be
kept pure and undefiled.[122] Any writer who writes for publication
in any language other than his own is utterly despicable.[123] It is odd
that Turgenev should have expressed himself so hysterically about
this: he must surely have known of poets, such as Petrarch and
Milton, who wrote and published in Latin as well as in their own
vernaculars. Perhaps it was a response to charges and insinuations
that he had turned his back on, and/or lost touch with, his country.

There are three stages in writing, which should not be rushed or
telescoped: the gathering of experience and knowledge; their
gradual maturation within, and assimilation by, the writer till they
have taken possession of him and demand expression; and the
actual writing: preferably in solitude and tranquillity. The writer
'does not clothe preconceived ideas in images: it all [i.e. his writing
as a whole – the ideas and images] grows out of him, half
unconsciously'.[124] Indeed, it seems as if 'no author really knows
what he is doing'.[125] One might add: 'or what he has done': which is
why all his life Turgenev submitted his writings before publication
to such friends as Annenkov and Pauline Viardot for their criticism
and comments.

A writer should write 'simply, sincerely' about what interests,
delights or even only 'amuses' him: 'If I were to state the real basis
of my activity, I might well say, "I wrote because I myself enjoyed it
[*weil es mich selbst ergötzt hat*]"'.[126] This is indeed probably nearer
to the essence of his art than such (comparatively rare) abstract
formulations as: 'in my work I have constantly based myself on
facts taken from life [*zhiznennye dannye*], striving to the best of my
ability to raise mere chance phenomena to the [level of the]
typical'.[127] But his heroes do, in fact, become types – common

nouns – like those of Shakespeare, while those of Tolstoy and Dostoevsky do not.

For all his self-doubt, Turgenev must have known most of the time that he had 'talent' – possessed the 'poetry' of a true writer – which faltered only when, for lack of direct observation, he was forced to fall back on imagination, on invention. More than any other Russian writer of his generation he cultivated that 'freedom of spirit' that was no more popular, or common, in his days than in ours. He combined a simple directness of perception with a simple beauty of style; his masterly handling of the Russian language was never questioned by critics who attacked him on every other head. His 'objectivity' has recently been called in question again,[128] but if we accept as our yardstick his own conception of objectivity – he surely does *not* use x to promote his own ideas, he *does* describe x rather than his reactions to or feelings about x – it seems arguable that in most of his work, and certainly in his best work, he has effectively concealed himself. And he undoubtedly became a professional: a specialist in the full sense he attached to the word, serving literature – his own writing and that of others, that of his own country and those of other countries – with all the powers of his heart and mind.

3

First stories

Turgenev's 'remarkable decade' (1843–52) saw first the brief, four-year efflorescence of his narrative poetry; simultaneously, but extending beyond that, his ten-year-long experimentation with play-writing that culminated in the psychological drama *A Month in the Country*; and thirdly, his struggles with the genre in which he was to achieve his greatest triumphs: the prose fiction that was to bring him national and international fame.

But the road to fame was no easy one: in fact, when Turgenev left Russia for the West in January 1847, he was sufficiently depressed by the level of recognition he had reached to be ready to play with the idea of giving up literature. Admittedly, this was an idea which was to return to him periodically in the following thirty-odd years; but at this date it was plain to him that he had no great future as a poet and it was not yet plain that he had any future as a playwright (neither of the two plays then written had been staged) or as a writer of fiction (none of his three published stories had won critical acclaim, though the second had won some praise from Belinsky and Apollon Grigor'ev).

Turgenev's fiction in the remarkable decade can be seen to pass through several phases. First, in the roughly three years between the first half of 1844 and the first half of 1847 he wrote five stories, varying in length from about 4,000 to about 13,000 words,[1] at least four of which foreshadow thematic developments of subsequent decades; then, in a little more than four years, between late 1846 and early 1851, he produced the twenty-two sketches republished in book form in 1852 as *A Sportsman's Sketches*; finally, in the three years between the beginning of 1850 and the end of 1852, he completed four more stories, two of which[2] are closely bound up with the main theme of *A Sportsman's Sketches*, while a third[3] represents a variation on the theme of one of those sketches[4] and points ahead to a series of later heroes.

Turgenev began to write fiction only two years after the publication, in 1842, of Gogol's *Collected Works* – the last fiction, as it proved, that Gogol was to publish. Belinsky, the literary lawgiver for progressive young writers, saw Gogol, and presented him to Russia, as a realist, a social reformer and a model for the literature of his age. Turgenev, like his young contemporaries, tried to adopt Belinsky's literary creed and to assimilate whatever he could of Gogol's literary techniques; but his vision of social reality was much wider and more various than Gogol's and in temperament and culture the two had very little in common. The most 'Gogolian' of his works – whether plays, such as *Moneyless* and *Breakfast with the Marshal of the Nobility* or stories such as 'The Jew' – are not among his best, but Gogolian attention to squalid aspects of life and addiction to caricature served to infuse his natural lyricism with a certain astringency or to overlay his original Romanticism with a patina of 'realism'.

Following Byron, Pushkin and Lermontov had endowed the narrator in a number of their narrative poems with an independent or quasi-independent existence, and Turgenev, as we have seen, had followed their example in *Parasha* and, to a lesser extent, in *Andrei*. Similarly, in their early prose tales, not only Pushkin and Lermontov but Gogol too had distanced themselves from their subjects by interposing two narrators between author and text.[5] Turgenev in three of his first five stories adopted the distancing device of hiding the author behind one or more narrators,[6] but discarded the idea of a collection and therefore had no need of an 'editor', or rather, the editor was transformed into an anonymous 'I' who provided the frame for the story proper. His other two early stories are told by an ominiscient author.

The settings are even more varied than the narrative techniques and, in all but one of the five tales, such as to minimize any temptation to subjectivity. One is laid in a 'nest of gentry', but in the last quarter of the eighteenth century, a couple of generations before Turgenev's; two deal with adventures of army officers: in war in 1812, in peace in 1829; in a fourth the scene is provincial lower middle class (though the protagonist is a middle-aged lieutenant). Only the students of the first story project elements of their author's own history.

As a corollary, we have a fair variety of characters, drawn perhaps with less than Turgenev's later subtlety and depth, but already alive and distinctive and representing both sexes, half a dozen social groups, and all ages from late teens to old age (as he conceived old age).

It should be borne in mind that the stories as we read them were thoroughly revised by Turgenev for the first edition (three volumes, 1856) of his *Stories and Tales*. The revision was mainly stylistic, in a broad sense: it involved the excision of prolixities, curtailment of authorial (or narrator's) commentary, including a deal of often heavy irony, besides the usual sort of tidying-up in the interests of precision, conciseness, clarity or elegance; only in one or two cases was new material introduced (for instance, the eighth chapter of 'Petushkov') or a character somewhat modified (e.g., the relation between the heroine and her mother in 'The Duellist': cf. *W*, v, 557). Our concern is, of course, with the stories in their final form.

'Andrei Kolosov'

Turgenev's first play had been a pseudo-Spanish melodrama more redolent of his Romantic past than of his 'realist' future. His first story, 'Andrei Kolosov', can be criticized in analogous terms, although it was not based on any foreign model nor set in an unfamiliar social scene. But it is not only one of the most subjective (in Turgenev's sense) of his stories, it is virtually a *pièce à thèse*, and in both respects it sins against his later artistic creed. Moreover, the subjectivity has impaired the artistry: the two principal figures, seen from too close up, are slightly blurred and fail to carry the 'message', which is spelt out with uncharacteristic bluntness on the last page.

Thus the narrator, who had begun by asserting that 'the most poorly told story is more effective than the most excellent ratiocination', is made to trample on his own principle (and Turgenev's); or are we to say that Turgenev has here sacrificed his own principle to psychological consistency inasmuch as his narrator has been shown throughout to be a mass of contradictions?

Turgenev says somewhere[7] that his failed lovers are always to some extent projections of himself. And this applies to his first story as much as to any later work. A few years earlier he had, as we have seen, briefly fancied himself in love with Tat'yana Bakunina and his attempts to extricate himself from the relationship were relatively protracted and somewhat clumsy. They were variously reflected in a number of his lyrics and in two or three of his stories.

'Andrei Kolosov' was his first prose attempt to *talk out* his experience, and he does not so much come to terms with it as pass judgment on it.

If the narrator is an avatar of Turgenev, the figure of Kolosov is said to owe a great deal to his dead friend Stankevich, and the modalities of Kolosov's break with Varya may have been inspired by those of Stankevich's break with his young German mistress Bertha (though in his relationships with the two Bakunin sisters with whom he had been, successively, in love Stankevich had proved no more immune from Romanticism than the narrator of this story). Of course, the story, as distinct from the characters of the two young men, is, so far as we know, invented: if it contains any autobiographical materials, they have been transposed and radically refashioned. Kolosov and the narrator are students, in or hardly out of their teens; Turgenev and Stankevich, at the time of their respective involvements with Tat'yana and Bertha, were in their mid-twenties; Turgenev and Stankevich were in love with two different girls in two different decades, Kolosov and his friend fall in love with one and the same girl in the space of a single year; and no heroine could have been less like the high-strung, well-educated and intellectual Bakunina or the fun-loving, sharp-witted and mercenary Bertha than the artless little Varya of the story. (Something of Bertha's personality may be hinted in the shadowy Tanyusha to whom the narrator attributes Kolosov's break with Varya.) Perhaps all this concentration and simplification is designed to ram home the point of the tale, which is to exalt immediacy, 'naturalness', over Romanticism with its rôle-playing, rhetoric and self-deception.

In spite of Lenin's adolescent (and later) enthusiasm for 'Andrei Kolosov',[8] the thesis fails to carry conviction because Turgenev tips the scales too blatantly. He is too harsh to the narrator (himself) and too indulgent to his friend Kolosov: that is, he is blind to the significance of the behaviour he reports.

Kolosov uses his friends. He uses Gavrilov to distract Varya's father through the six months leading up to Gavrilov's death; presumably even galloping consumption shows forth some premonitory signs, but Kolosov notices nothing. For six more months he uses the narrator, who, as a poor card-player, suffers not only boredom but embarrassment and is hardly even thanked. The narrator's joy on being chosen to succeed Gavrilov as Kolosov's confidant evokes not an answering surge of warmth but gentle laughter (*Kolosov ... tikhon'ko posmeivalsya*), yet the narrator persuades himself that his idol was touched. Kolosov expects to be followed unquestioningly: when the narrator enquires where they are going, he retorts, 'Gavrilov would not have asked.' When, later, the narrator reproaches him for having deserted Varya, he does vouchsafe an explanation of his conduct, but only after clearly hinting that this is a condescension on his part.

In the narrator's eyes Kolosov was, and has remained, an 'extraordinary' person, simply in virtue of his 'naturalness'. But what is 'naturalness'? On close inspection it appears to mean neither more nor less than a disposition (the narrator might prefer the term 'ability') to act on one's immediate feelings in total disregard of other people's opinions, and feelings.

Kolosov is young, attractive, full of the joy of life. His vitality and unself-consciousness charm his fellow students, make them 'fall head over heels in love with him'. He accepts and enjoys their love, but admits to intimacy only those whose services he needs. He falls in love with Varya and courts her for a year, without looking beyond his immediate enjoyment, without considering the long-term cost to her. She obviously lives in and for him; but 'Kolosov had not relinquished his freedom; when she was not with him, I don't think he even remembered her; he remained the same carefree, cheerful, happy man we had always known.' When he tires of her, he takes the easy way out. Rather than make a clean break, rather than face her and confess his change of heart, he spaces – and finally ceases – his visits, leaving her to pine in uncertainty and hope. He does not even bother to send her word that all is over till stung by the narrator's chiding. And then it does not occur to him to let her know how much she has meant to him: it is only to the narrator he admits he is deeply in her debt. His parting word is cool and dismissive: if not the prince to the beggar-maid, we hear the 'extraordinary' man announcing her fate to the ordinary girl.

It is true we are shown Kolosov only as the narrator sees him; but we look in vain for any slightest hint that the author sees him differently. The narrator, an unreclaimed Romantic, continues throughout life to see Kolosov as a hero. He is a hero because he is able to live and to act, while the narrator is capable only of dreaming and suffering. Yet it is the narrator's devotion that enables Kolosov to continue enjoying his love after Gavrilov's death and that helps Varya to readjust to life after her loss of Kolosov. And Kolosov lives and acts, whenever 'necessary', at the expense of others: he is able to live to the full by pressing others into his service and shutting his eyes to what that service costs them.

Kolosov and his friend are polar opposites. Kolosov is simple: that is, he lives in and for the day, and his desires and motives are unitary or integrated: that is what frees him to live and act; the narrator is inhibited from living and acting for himself by conflicting desires and motives of which he becomes conscious when he needs to pass from dreaming to decision and action. Evidently he feels this defect in himself as so painful that the possession of what he lacks is seen by him as not merely *a* virtue but as virtue *par excellence*, blinding him to the egoism and exploitation in which it is rooted. But we shall meet the types foreshadowed in these two young men often enough in Turgenev's later work not to need to linger over an analysis of the narrator at this point.

'Three Portraits'

Whether Turgenev realized that in 'Andrei Kolosov' he had handicapped himself by choosing a subject too close to him or whether he just followed an artistic instinct, he turned for his next story to the period of his grandparents. If 'Three Portraits'[9] was based on a page of his family history, it dealt with people who had lived and died more than thirty years before he was born.

Belinsky found nothing much to say about 'Three Portraits': in a forty-page review of the miscellany in which it appeared he devoted only four lines to this tale, commending the skill and liveliness of the narration and opining that it read less like fiction than like a memoir of 'the good old days'.[10] Apollon Grigor'ev, one of the most imaginative critics of his generation, not only reviewed the story on its first appearance but felt impelled to reconsider it on two further occasions, nine years and thirteen years after his original assessment.[11] There is a characteristic inconsistency between the three articles, but, first and last, Grigor'ev is fascinated by the figure of Vasili Luchinov, in whom he sees a 'hero of his time', a Russian Don Juan or Lovelace, an eighteenth-century forerunner of Pechorin.

This is to promote Luchinov to very exalted literary company, but the critic's intuition of affinities is near the mark. The trouble is, we are shown too little of Luchinov: enough to convince us of his reckless courage and his ruthlessness, but we have to take his charm on trust. His thoughts and feelings are apparently all reducible to their expression in his behaviour: his suborning of the devoted Yudich, his defiance of his father (which in that day and age could have cost him his liberty, if not his life), his seduction of his mother's ward (no doubt, his half-sister), his pinning his own guilt on the girl's fiancé, and his murder of the defenceless young man.

Here, then, we have a man who lives for his own pleasure and in pursuit of that pleasure will stop at nothing. Such a character can be made interesting if he is endowed with the intelligence and/or emotional complexity of a Pechorin, or if he is pitted, like Lovelace, against a personality of comparable strength and opposite quality. But Luchinov is manifestly all of a piece, impervious to what the narrator of 'Andrei Kolosov' had called 'the petty good feelings of pity and remorse';[12] and he lives and moves among men of straw, shadows, who laugh when he laughs, tremble when he frowns, and who either submit to him unresisting or are broken by him without effort.

The three portraits which give the story its title are matched by Turgenev's three verbal portraits: of the narrator, the murderer and his victim (the other personages are mere sketches). One can detect a subtle counterpoint in both triads. On canvas, the two *lovers* contrast with the *heroine* as man with woman; they contrast with one another both physically and morally inasmuch as their characters are expressed in their faces; and, as symbolized by the hole in the heart of the one, they contrast in the kind of love that relates them to the woman. In the narrative portraits the central position is occupied by Luchinov – a striking villain between two unremarkable good men. At first sight, the narrator and the fiancé have not a little in common: their girth, their good nature, their bucolic mode of life. Yet they too are contrasted: as a country gentleman of the 1840s with a country gentleman of the 1780s: the latter ignorant of French, a collector of butterflies and a man of a single love, the former an assiduous reader of French books and journals, a breakneck hunter of wolves and foxes, and a man who enjoys flirting with all his pretty neighbours while taking care not to get involved with any of them.

The lively flow of the narration is highlighted by three dramatic scenes: the interrogation and flogging of Yudich culminating in the confrontation between father and son; Luchinov's prevailing on his mother to pardon Ol'ga's 'sin' and to attribute it to her fiancé; and Luchinov's compelling Rogachëv to 'fight' and killing him.

Nothing, perhaps, is more impressive than the economy of the means by which the hero achieves his purposes. We are first given a glimpse of the virtually unlimited power – the power of life and death – of the landowner over the members of his household; then the young man enters, acknowledges his responsibility for the theft of the money, overawes the serfs who are holding Yudich, outfaces his infuriated father and checkmates him with the mere gesture of half drawing his sword. In the scene with his mother, he imposes his will with the single word, 'Remember': she is to remember her own sin, which disqualifies her from judging her ward; but he does not say it. The old lady is silenced by his tone; Ol'ga is stunned by his cold-blooded mendacity in accusing her fiancé. In the duel scene, Luchinov toys with his victim as if he had all time at his disposal, when actually – in enemy territory – his own life is hanging by a thread.

There are, incidentally, a few loose ends, as if to show that Turgenev is still learning his craft. Ol'ga is given a birth-date some ten years earlier than the rest of the chronology requires. There is no explanation of how Luchinov was able to return from banishment to St Petersburg. Nor are the three deaths of the final paragraph prepared or justified. Surely, it is not a case of 'The wages of sin ...'?

'The Duellist'

'The Duellist' (or 'The Swashbuckler' – but *Bretër* is more aggressive than the first, less colourful than the second of these renderings) is the longest of the stories in this chapter, and, although not the most original, arguably the subtlest in its psychological portrayals.

It is a commonplace of modern life that any figure who can capture the imagination of any significant section of society – any figure (writer, actor, athlete, political leader, financial wizard) who achieves star status – is liable to become the object of a cult in the form of slavish imitation. Since the imitators lack most or all of the gifts that made their idol a star, they are mostly reduced to imitating

at best, his superficial, at worst, his negative traits. Before the age
of our mass media the cult object was as likely to be a figure in
literature as a person in real life: St Preux rather than Rousseau,
Werther rather than Goethe – but Byron (or Napoleon) no less
than the Byronic hero. The latest analogue of the Byronic hero in
Russia was Pechorin, the protagonist of Lermontov's 1840 novel, *A
Hero of Our Time*.[13] Pechorin, like the Byronic hero, was a man of
dark and complex passions, at war with himself and at war with
society; a man of reckless courage; a brilliant and fascinating
personality, and endowed – like Lermontov and Byron but unlike
the heroes of Byron's 'Eastern' poems – with superior intelligence
and scathing wit.

Conservative critics of the time disapproved of Pechorin's sub-
versive stance, conventional critics disapproved of his donjuanism.
Both groups were only too glad to pretend that Turgenev's
Luchkov was a scaled-down Pechorin or a Pechorin merely stripped
of his surface polish, instead of recognizing in the story a satire on
the Pechorin cult and in its protagonist a satirized product of the
cult.

Luchkov is a poor career officer trying to play Pechorin, when all
he understands of Pechorin is the duelling and the aura of mystery,
and even here his attempts at imitation are caricatural. Pechorin
sought dangers of every kind, for the sake of the excitement or to
test himself and because he held his life cheap, and only occasionally or incidentally to avenge some slight to his pride; Luchkov
seeks to make himself feared, usually risking as little as possible:
provoking and attacking the 'new boys' in his regiment like a school
bully. Pechorin was mysterious because he was really a puzzle,
partly even to himself, whereas Luchkov's taciturnity covers only a
void: he is uneducated, unintelligent, unfeeling. Pechorin was an
original – *rara avis in terris*; Luchkov is a shoddy counterfeit, of a
kind destined to proliferate at least till the turn of the century, as
witness the figure of Solëny in Chekhov's *Three Sisters*.[14]

Kister also represents a type not uncommon in the late 1830s and
early 1840s, the so-called Schillerian idealist. Brought up by
women, construing life in terms of his reading, he surrounds
himself with an orderliness and cleanness which set him apart – as
symbolized by the locks on his doors – from the world of his
regiment.[15] He is the direct antithesis of Luchkov – cultured,
modest, kindly, sensitive, principled.

Masha is another early avatar of the 'Turgenev heroine': less formed, perhaps, than the Parasha or the Dunya of his poems, but much more alive than the passive little Varya of 'Andrei Kolosov'. Her predicament is one which Turgenev was to develop, more maturely and effectively, two years later in the play *A Chain is as Strong as its Weakest Link*. Like Vera in the play, Masha has to choose between a supposed or would-be Byronic hero and a *merely good* man who truly loves her. Both girls nerve themselves to probe the reality behind the mask of the mystery man, both recoil disillusioned from their dreams of romance to embrace sense with friendship, although poor Masha is not allowed to enjoy even that.

And there is poetic justice in the catastrophe. Vera is an extraordinary girl and, therefore, entitled to look for a mate of her own calibre; Gorski was actually above average in many respects; and their duel is conducted with intelligence and spirit, in style. Masha is not an extraordinary girl. She is, of course, not to be blamed for letting Kister mislead her regarding Luchkov's true character and status nor for the youthful clumsiness of her attempts to get past his guard; but she misconceives herself: both as to the kind of man she really wants and needs and as to her fitness to win and keep the interest of a remarkable man (some real-life Pechorin). But, of course, the main responsibility for the tragedy rests on the 'idealist', Kister. He has had ample opportunity to get to know Luchkov, but he has deluded himself, as he later goes on to delude Masha; and he has failed to recognize in time the true nature of his feeling for her. Instead, he sets out to play Providence: to redeem his friend through love and to bestow happiness on the girl at his side in the form of the kind of lover she (thinks she) wants.

This Schillerism costs Kister his life and Masha her happiness; Luchkov, needless to say, emerges from his involvement with no more than a scratch to his vanity which will leave no trace: Masha had turned out to be a silly little chit who didn't know what she wanted, and he had demonstrated his superiority over Kister in the only way that counted for him.

There is an added piquant irony in the fact that, while the educated protagonists fatally misjudge themselves and their closest associates, the rough rude officers of the regiment are able not only to understand and assess Luchkov – a grosser variation on a not unfamiliar type – but to appreciate and admire Kister, to take him to their hearts, although he differs so utterly from their conception of what an officer should be. Even Luchkov is a better judge of himself and (until embittered by his humiliation at Masha's hands) of Kister than Kister is of Luchkov or, arguably, of himself. Luchkov has enough honesty – one might almost say: enough intellectual courage – to recognize that he is not only ignorant but unintelligent (though he perceives that Kister is in love before Kister himself does); while Kister convinces himself that Luchkov is 'a fine and remarkable man', a man with a 'kind heart', and that he, Kister, ought to make a match between the girl he doesn't know he loves and his goodhearted and remarkable friend.

Luchkov is a study in vanity and frustration. Inferior to his peers in looks, brains and emotional resources, he cannot bear to be ignored or despised, and therefore imposes himself on their notice and regard in the only way open to him – through fear. He gravitates towards Kister because Kister is the first man to accept him: Kister in his innocence not only does not judge him but invests him with virtues he does not possess. Left to his own devices, Luchkov has enough sound sense to steer clear of romances; Kister unwittingly makes the mistake of playing on his vanity in persuading him that Masha is interested in him; from there on, events follow their inevitable course.

So whereas in 'Three Portraits' the good are destroyed by an external evil beyond their control, in 'The Duellist' the destruction of the good is due, as in true tragedy, to flaws in their own nature.

'The Jew'

In 'The Jew',[16] written in the same year as 'The Duellist' (1846), Turgenev continues to keep subjectivity at bay by choosing for portrayal a period and setting and events and, presumably, characters from outside the limits of his own experience. The story is told by a veteran of the wars against Napoleon, recalling an incident in his life during the 1813 siege of Danzig.

After winning a large sum at cards, he is approached by a Jewish camp-follower, who offers to bring a beautiful girl to his tent – for payment, of course – and does so. The girl, Sara, is very beautiful, but obviously frightened and quite inexperienced: she takes flight the first time she is kissed. On her second visit, she bursts into tears, and the chivalrous young lieutenant, himself only nineteen, lets her go as she has come. Some time later, while on a foraging expedition, he chances on the village where she and her family live, and saves them from the depredations of his soldiers. She promises to pay him a third visit on the following day; but that very morning the Jew is caught drawing a plan of the Russian camp and condemned by the commanding general to be hanged as a spy. It turns out that Sara is his daughter, and she and the young lieutenant make frantic efforts to secure his pardon; but the sentence is carried out and the girl curses his executioners and collapses.

The whole second half of the story pivots on descriptions of the Jew's abject terror at the prospect of death. He tries to deny what his map clearly establishes; he tries to flatter and bribe his captors; he tells the lieutenant that whereas he had no intention, earlier, of letting him touch Sara, now, if his life is spared, he will hand her over to him. All this is accompanied by a crescendo of pitiful and grotesque manifestations of panic and horror.

In later life Turgenev had rich Jewish friends, interceded with Russian authorities on behalf of poor Jewish victims of administrative action, unreservedly deplored Russian anti-Semitism and condemned the pogroms in private (while declining to speak out against them publicly), and was variously extolled or decried as the most cosmopolitan or least nationalistic of Russian writers; but at this stage he had apparently not emancipated himself from one of the most widespread attitudes of his caste.[17]

If the protagonist, as a personification of cunning greed and comic cowardice, is a stereotype, much the same can be said of the other male characters: the Germanic general with his kind heart at odds with the letter of the law and the gallant narrator with his wild gambling and chivalrous respect for beauty in distress. The latter two are thumbnail sketches, as is the romantic heroine; only the spy is drawn, if not in the round, at something like full length. It is a repellent picture, in spite of the pity professed by the narrator and demonstrated by the general; it makes its impact on the reader in the manner of 'slice of life' journalism.

Oddly enough, its publication was held up by the Imperial censorship for several months. One wonders why. One may also wonder why it never occurred to Turgenev to exclude it from his *Collected Works* (as he excluded all his poetry, for instance).

'Petushkov'

'Petushkov' is the most Gogolian of the six stories. Although the protagonist of 'The Jew' is in some respects a Gogolian figure, there is nothing Gogolian about the setting or the other characters. In 'Petushkov' the urban lower-middle-class setting is distinctly Gogolian; so is the vein of comedy, which sets this story apart from the other five. The same can be said of at least four of the six personages: the major, the aunt of the heroine, the servant and the friend of the hero. Petushkov himself is a Gogolian type viewed through the prism of 'sentimental humanism'. Gogol was notoriously incapable of depicting lifelike girls or young women, but Vasilisa may approximate what Gogol might have produced if he had been able to depict a lifelike girl and had condescended to depict a girl of Vasilisa's social class. On the other hand, the theme of 'Petushkov' is eminently Turgenevan: the theme of love as an obsession that degrades and morally destroys its bearer.

Although it would be rash to read either autobiographical or programmatic intentions into this story at this date, it cannot escape notice that the hero ends up *dreeing his weird* 'on the edge of another man's nest', as Turgenev will later define his situation *vis-à-vis* the Viardots, nor, on the other hand, that Petushkov's 'passion' is not merely unromantic but anti-romantic: so that this story would involve another line of attack on Romanticism, following those in 'Andrei Kolosov' and 'The Duellist'.

The tradition of courtly love, out of which Romantic love developed, posited the excellence of the beloved, her superiority to the lover, and the ennobling effect of such love on the lover; Petushkov's infatuation for Vasilisa runs counter to all three of these postulates. Nor is it a case of quixotic delusion. He does not invest his Dulcinea with imaginary virtues: he sees her as she is; he even comes to see that she does not love him, that she feels nothing for him.

The nature of Petushkov's infatuation may raise some questions in the reader's mind. From the one sentence in which we are informed that he and Vasilisa did become lovers ('Ivan Afanas'e-vich, to put it delicately, attained his purpose') one might infer that his interest in her was predominantly sexual. And this appears to be borne out by the jesting commentary of the following sentences: 'Men are usually cooled by the attainment of their purposes, but

Petushkov, on the contrary, became more and more ardent with every passing day ... Petushkov became passionately attached to Vasilisa. He was completely happy.'

But, first, we have to ask how much of this passage is Turgenev's. The editors of his *Works* assume that the sentence in brackets above is Nekrasov's.[18] But then how can we be sure that Nekrasov's editing was limited to that one sentence? And if one or more of the following sentences are his, how can we take the passage as a basis for characterizing Petushkov's passion?

However, if the whole passage is Turgenev's, how far is an interpretation of the passion as mainly sexual borne out by the rest of the story? The glimpses we are given of the brief happy stage of the relationship seem redolent not of romantic or sexual ardours but rather of a humdrum domesticity.

Petushkov at the age of forty has remained a gentle, childlike soul, too timid to form a close relationship with anybody. Chance causes him to notice the pretty face of 17-year-old Vasilisa, who has just arrived in the neighbourhood to help in her aunt's bakery. Goaded by the strictures of his flighty visitor, Bublitsyn, and of his morose servant, Onisim, both of whom scoff at his lack of enterprise, he pursues the acquaintance, is prompted to visit the aunt, and almost before he (or the reader) knows what is happening, has, as the narrator delicately puts it, attained his purpose (if we can believe that he ever had a purpose).

Bublitsyn, or any of his ilk, would have enjoyed the adventure as a side-line, while continuing to live in his social world; but Petushkov has no social world to hold on to – or return to – and therefore sinks as into a quagmire into the warm squalor of the bakery. He is cold-shouldered by his fellow officers and finally hauled over the coals by his choleric commander for losing caste, but even this somewhat frightening experience fails to rouse him from the trance-like state into which he has lapsed.

What does disturb him is his gradual realization of Vasilisa's unfaithfulness and indifference. His attempts to win her back swing between appeals to sentiment and efforts to assert his dignity, culminating in half-threats of rupture, which sound like nothing so much as a small child's threats to run away from home. When his bluff is called, he backs down; when he is given his *congé*, he goes to pieces. He pines for her, wastes away, and by the time his faithful servant has realized the seriousness of the crisis and goes to fetch her, he has sought relief or distraction in alcohol.

Alcohol is supposed to show a man in his true colours, and that is certainly its effect on Petushkov. When Onisim returns with Vasilisa, he receives her courteously and gently, as an honoured guest. No reproaches to her: only to himself. And no prevarication: it is kind of her to say he is unwell, but the truth is, he is drunk. He is drunk because he is destroyed (*ubit*) – destroyed by her, but he does not hold that against her. It is not her fault, it is his: he loved her and he ought to have offered to marry her in spite of their social disparity. She could have had a good life with him,[19] for he is a goodhearted man. But now he is drunk, destroyed: he has lost his self-respect and turned to vice.

But how could she have wounded him so cruelly, leaving it to her aunt to give him his dismissal? He had loved and respected her. Even now, she has only to say the word and he will marry her. But if not, he is ready to beg her on his knees to readmit him to her life: only to let him visit her again, be with her as before but making no claims on her, leaving her completely free. Finally he breaks down in tears, and Vasilisa and Onisim, though they have not drunk a drop, are moved to weep with him. Evidently his last plea is granted. Vasilisa leads her own life, inherits the bakery, marries a man of her own class (and age, perhaps). Petushkov has come to live in a small closet in the bakery, and continues to drink.

Surely it is plain that if sex brought Petushkov and Vasilisa together, it had ceased to be what bound him to her, at least by the time of his dismissal, if not before. A key word in Petushkov's cogitations is 'orphan' (*sirota*), a word used with less narrow literalness and perhaps more pregnant with desolation in Russian than in some other languages. His intimacy with Vasilisa may have brought home to him in a new and more poignant way the utter loneliness of his existence up till that time. In clinging to her, in sharing her life or even only watching her live, his existence had taken on a new dimension of meaning, which had become essential to his survival. Cut off from her, he would probably have drunk himself to death quite soon; allowed back within the borders of her life, he lives on into old age (as defined by Turgenev), but only with the prop of alcohol, so at the cost of his self-respect, steeped in what he regards as vice.

'Three Meetings'

'Three Meetings'[20] was written towards the end of Turgenev's 'remarkable decade'; it attracted little critical attention and less approval, although it moved Dobrolyubov to tears and Nekrasov and Botkin paid tribute to the poetry of its first half. Between 'Petushkov' and 'Three Meetings' Turgenev produced 'Diary of a Superfluous Man', which looks forward to his writings of the middle and late 1850s and will be considered together with them.

The three meetings on which this story hinges took place in Southern Italy, in Central Russia and in St Petersburg. Observers of life know well that coincidence plays a much larger part in real life than it is supposed to do in 'realistic' literature; but Turgenev was criticized for regressing to the Romanticism of earlier decades. His narrator was seen as too obtrusive and not interesting enough; it was objected that the parts did not hang together: not only was the contrast too strident between the 'poetry' of the first part and the banality of the second, but the suicide of old Luk'yanych appeared a pointless digression, irrelevant and unmotivated.[21]

It must be conceded that the last two criticisms have some validity; but it should also be recognized that the story has merits. It is strikingly different in tone and theme from any of Turgenev's first five tales: in his fiction no less than in his plays, he persists in experimenting and innovating, so playing a leading part in extending the range of Russian literature to bring it abreast of the richest of Western literatures.

Granted that the love-story is in itself fairly ordinary, it is all the more surprising that the image of a woman happily in love is communicated to the reader with such force and vividness, and doubly surprising when it has to be conveyed solely through the sense-impressions of the narrator, without any direct access to her thoughts and feelings. Yet surely we do see and feel and believe we are present with the narrator.

No less of a *tour de force* – no less evocative and 'infectious' – is the portrayal of the two summer nights, at Sorrento and in the province of Orël. Botkin, known for his aesthetic discernment, wrote to Turgenev of the excitement aroused in him by the reading of such pages.[22] A reader of today might be put in mind of the verses of an Italian poet of our century:

Tutto era silenzio, luce, forza, desio.
L'attesa del prodigio gonfiava questo mio
Cuore come il cuor del mondo . . .[23]

(There all was stillness, power, light, desire.
In expectation of the miracle
My heart had swelled, become the whole world's heart).

Although the Italian night is alight with colours and perfumes, it is, as we might expect, the Russian night that reveals the longer and subtler spectrum of hues and modulations. It is in the Russian night that the tension reaches its highest intensity. In both nights the tension finds sudden and magical release in a song of triumphant love sung to the night by a woman who, believing herself to be alone, feels free to pour all her soul into the incantation.

It is for these hymns to night and for the picture of the woman riding hand in hand with her lover through the early morning silences that 'Three Meetings' deserves to be read and remembered.

4

Serfs and serf-owners: *A Sportsman's Sketches*

In August 1852 Turgenev's first major work, *A Sportsman's Sketches*,[1] was published in book form. It comprised twenty-two sketches, of which all but one ('Two Landowners') had appeared, singly or in groups, in the journal *The Contemporary*[2] between January 1847 and March 1851.

Just before he left Russia for what was to be a three-and-a-half-year absence in the West, Turgenev delivered to the editors of *The Contemporary* two short stories or sketches, which were published in the January and February issues of that journal. The first was a study of two peasants, Khor' and Kalinych; the second, a portrait of a ruined landowner, Pëtr Petrovich Karataev. The editors provided the former with a sub-title of their own devising: 'From a Sportsman's Notebook'. So far as the evidence goes, Turgenev saw no connection between the two tales and had no idea of using either or both as part of a series. But, encouraged by the enthusiastic approval of 'Khor' and Kalinych' by the public, the editors and, in particular, Belinsky, he quickly decided to capitalize on his success, envisaging first a 'cycle' of twelve, then fifteen, and, by September 1847, of twenty or twenty-one such sketches. The inclusion of 'Pëtr Petrovich Karataev' in the collection was decided, apparently, as late as the autumn of 1850.

Thirteen further sketches were written in that first year (1847),[3] three more in 1848,[4] two in 1850[5] and two in 1851.[6] In the 1860s Turgenev tentatively added a couple of stories, but in subsequent editions removed them. However, in the early 1870s he wrote three sketches, based on plans or drafts of the 1840s, expressly for inclusion in *A Sportsman's Sketches*, so that the total number in the 1874 and all later editions was brought up to, and has remained at, twenty-five.

For Turgenev and his contemporaries and for several generations of Russians after him *A Sportsman's Sketches* was not just a work of literature but equally, if not primarily, a doughty blow struck at the institution of serfdom. Twenty years after, at a time when he was concerned to defend himself against charges of having abandoned and turned against his country, Turgenev, who was as apt as any of us to mythologize his past, persuaded himself that he had gone and stayed abroad in order to be free to wage war on serfdom and that *A Sportsman's Sketches* was the fulfilment of his 'Hannibalic oath' to wage that war to the bitter end. Now, it is true that he had long hated serfdom and he may well have sworn to himself that he would never be reconciled to it; but it is certainly not true that he went abroad to fight it. He went abroad to be near Pauline Viardot, with no plans to fight serfdom nor any idea of how that could be done; 'Khor' and Kalinych' was written in Russia, to provide material for his friends' new journal, and not as one of a series, let alone the first move in a campaign; and there was no need for him to expatriate himself to write *A Sportsman's Sketches*: all twenty-two sketches were published there, with no more harassment and mutilation at the hands of the censors than was the lot of every awakened writer at that time.

Of all modes of indictment the most subtle is that which consists in simply holding up a mirror and letting the reflected image speak for itself. And the subtlety of Turgenev's indictment of serfdom may be measured by the amazing fact that in those years of so-called 'censorship Terror', twenty-one of his sketches were approved for publication in a journal and all twenty-two for inclusion in the book, although there the original text had almost everywhere been restored, in defiance of the deletions and alterations of the earlier censors. It is true that, shortly after publication, when the St Petersburg censors submitted a report on the book, the Emperor was so incensed that he ordered the dismissal, with no pension, of the Moscow censor who had passed it, and that for the remainder of Nicholas's reign no second edition could appear;[7] but no further action was taken against the author or his publishers.

In order to understand this course of events, one must take a closer look at the composition of *A Sportsman's Sketches*. The last of the twenty-two (as of the eventual twenty-five) sketches is a hymn to the beauties of nature as experienced by the sportsman, in all its variety of season and weather. Of the other twenty-one, one, 'Death', is a cross-class study of how Russians die, with no definable relation to serfdom; seven are portraits of gentry,[8] six are portraits of serfs,[9] and only seven focus directly on the negative aspects of serfdom.[10] In the gentry portraits the subjects of the portraits appear not as serf-owners but as country gentlemen or ladies; if serfs make an appearance in some of them, it is as domestic servants, not strikingly different from the domestics of Western countries at that time; in the serf portraits, the subjects appear not as serfs but as human beings. (The above analysis is as valid for the eventual twenty-five as for the original twenty-two: of the three 1870s sketches, one is a gentry portrait, one a serf portrait, in the third, Filofei is probably a freedman; serfs appear in all three, but serfdom is not an issue). In other words, censors could have read fourteen or fifteen of the original twenty-two sketches without discerning in them any attack on serfdom; the other seven or eight could have been read by different censors, so that no cumulative impression need have resulted. That the book should have passed muster is much more surprising; but, after all, the stories had already passed one censorship and the Moscow censor who approved the book, Prince V. V. L'vov, was a man of liberal views.

Readers today should bear in mind that in the context of the book a number of sketches have an impact and carry a message significantly different from what they are likely to have meant to their original readers, and perhaps even to their author before the idea of the book took shape in his mind. This applies particularly to the gentry portraits. To the modern reader and the traditional critic those portraits, however free from any direct or explicit reference to serfdom, yet constitute an implicit indictment of the class which was, by definition, that of the serf-owners. Whereas read separately when first published, they may well have seemed no more than a continuation of the line of Turgenev's earlier stories, in which he had set out to expose or 'debunk' two types of Romantic hero: the Schillerian idealist and the would-be Byronic hero. 'Andrei Kolosov', 'Three Portraits' and 'The Duellist' were obviously written without any thought of attacking serfdom; what was there to prevent 'Pëtr Petrovich Karataev', 'My Neighbour Radilov' and 'The District Doctor' from being read as psychological rather than as social studies?[11]

Like the three earlier stories, these three sketches – the first of the gentry portraits to appear – seemingly hinge on Romantic love and star-crossed lovers. Seemingly – because on further reflection one may wonder whether the love is here more than incidental to the fate of the protagonists. Karataev is ruined; but was he not the sort of man who was bound to ruin himself anyhow, with his combination of expensive tastes and utter unpracticalness? The love between Radilov and Ol'ga is engendered by their situation and condemned by their situation: if they had not fallen in love, they would have withered without having flowered; if they had not gone away together they would have pined away singly like Browning's frustrate ghosts;[12] going away together, they made themselves pariahs, social outcasts forever. Similarly, the love between Aleksandra and her doctor was created by their situation and doomed by their situation: love could neither defer her death nor alter the course of his life.

In fact, not only in these three sketches, but in five of the seven gentry portraits,[13] the protagonists are distinctly likeable, in spite of faults and foibles which are not inconspicuous, but which have nothing to do with serfdom. If for the unwary reader of the book these ladies and gentlemen take on the colour of serf-owners from the context, that is analogous to guilt by association, arguably to be avoided in literature as well as in life.

Karataev is a man of heady passions, reckless and feckless, incapable of running his estate, spending more than he can afford on dogs and horses and hunting. His passion for his neighbour's serf-girl probably begins in much the same key, but the obstacles raised between them refines and deepens it. At first he is prepared to give money, but when that proves useless, he is ready to risk serious trouble with the law and gradually to sacrifice fortune and health to keep her with him. Passion had grown into the love that breathes from the words he finds to describe, in retrospect, the delight he took in her while they were together. Finally, she refuses to let him make further sacrifices; but her departure only precipitates him on the downard course which must have begun before he met her. At the time of his first encounter with the Sportsman, he is already drinking; a year later, in Moscow, he is maudlin, befuddled, and living off his new acquaintances.

The district doctor is not a landowner, not a member of the gentry, but a *raznochinets*, that is, a man who has raised himself by education above the class – priesthood or merchants or free peasantry – into which he was born and who has not earned promotion into the gentry by military or civil service. Unlike

Karataev, with his extravagance and passion for display and responsiveness to beauty or excellence – in animals, in humans, in Mochalov's acting and Shakespeare's poetry – the doctor is a very ordinary, decent, plodding member of society. For Karataev love was a rapture of a few months; for the doctor it was a dream of a week or two. In both cases there was a social chasm between the lovers which neither could completely ignore or lose sight of; in one case it was the girl who had to look up to the man, in the second it was the other way about. Each love remained a memory for life; but the doctor's memories lack both the richness and the certainty of Karataev's: Karataev has known happiness and knows that he was loved; the doctor's love was darkened by anxiety and frustration at his own helplessness, and he is forever unsure what he had really meant to the dying girl.

Karataev's – and the doctor's – love is simple and straightforward; Radilov's is tangled and inhibited. Though his culture is not much less limited than Karataev's,[14] he is richer in experience, has seen more of the world, has served in the war against Turkey and come within inches of death, has seen death carry off his wife and child. The Sportsman is struck by his failure to discover any subject that interests his host and perceptively attributes this to an obsession with some one idea or passion. A modern psychologist might prefer to say that Radilov is obsessed by an inner conflict between his love and his duties which has absorbed all his vital energies. He has to choose between forswearing love and happiness for himself and the girl he loves or breaking the laws of his church and his country, forfeiting his place in society and abandoning his old mother to grief and loneliness. We do not know how long this deadlock has lasted, but evidently the opposing forces were so evenly matched that the balance could be tipped by a straw: the narrator's chance visit stirs up Radilov's memories and emotions and the guest's insistence that 'however nasty a situation, there is always a way out of it' suffices to free his host's paralysed will.

The next two gentry portraits – 'Lebedyan'' and 'Tat'yana Borisovna and Her Nephew' – are set apart from the other five by their tone and their technique. In tone they are distinctly Gogolian,[15] a characteristic they share with several of the sketches that hinge on serfdom but not with any of the other portraits, either of gentry or of serfs. The fair which serves as backdrop to 'Lebedyan'' will remind readers of 'The Fair at Sorochintsy', the first of Gogol's

Evenings on a Farm near Dikan'ka; 'Tat'yana Borisovna and Her Nephew' will recall his 'Ivan Fëdorovich Shpon'ka and His Auntie' by its title and 'The Old-World Landowners' by the atmosphere of the house and the warm-hearted hospitality of its mistress.

It is of the nature of portraiture that the subject must be seen frozen in a moment of time; since the present contains the sum of the past, his (or her) history should be limned in the face, occasionally a glance or gesture may hold a hint of the future; and this is generally the technique of Turgenev's portraits. They pivot on a single meeting with the Sportsman, in which the subject recounts his past, or narrates the past of a second subject, while the Sportsman observes his present. But writing is less limiting than painting in regard to time and place, so that the data of the single meeting are supplemented, as required, by reports of outside informants and/or, in two or three cases,[16] by a second meeting.

Both the Gogolian sketches deviate in a number of respects from the basic pattern of the portraits (and from each other). 'Lebedyan'' looks like a conflation of two stories originally planned as distinct:[17] two exhibitions of *poshlost'*, linked only by the common background of the fair, both too superficial and limited to justify the designation 'portrait'. Prince N. and his parasite do not even meet the Sportsman: they are merely seen by him; not a word is exchanged; he (and the reader) learns no more about the Prince than he can see. With the gentleman horsedealer there is interaction, if of the most trivial kind. Yet in one sense it may be considered noteworthy, as marking perhaps the lowest point to which Turgenev degrades his gentry. For the hallmark and watchword of a gentleman is everywhere *honour*: a dishonourable gentleman is a contradiction in terms. The emptiness and inhumanity which characterize so many of the gentry in the sketches that pivot on serfdom, are no doubt graver defects, but they are defects that attach to human beings as such; honour and dishonour are gentry (nobiliary) concepts and values, and here Turgenev is stripping his gentry of its specific claim to superiority and ground for pride.

'Tat'yana Borisovna', on the other hand, does contain two genuine portraits, but differs even more strikingly from the basic pattern of the other portraits. First, we have a continuous narrative covering a number of years (at least eight); and secondly, although the descriptions of some persons and scenes can only derive from a series of visits by the Sportsman, no such visit is ever referred to.

The two portraits, of aunt and nephew, are in stridently contrasting styles: the one idyllic, in pastel shades, the other satiric, in the loud colours of poster art. And one may doubt whether the two styles are truly harmonized when one measures the lack of emotional impact in the *dénouement*: do we feel a real pang when we see the good, candid woman battened on, befooled, separated from her friends by the graceless young loafer and sponger? Belovzorov (the nephew) is a phony bohemian (as Luchkov was a phony hero), but too crudely drawn to be interesting.

His aunt is interesting firstly, but by no means solely, as a rare phenomenon in Turgenev's work: a middle-aged woman delineated *con amore*. Would it be too fanciful to see in her a distant precursor of Chekhov's Olen'ka,[18] that is, Olen'ka as she ends up in middle age, with all her urges to give herself transmuted into maternal feeling? Tat'yana Borisovna is neither beautiful nor witty nor cultured: in fact, she is plain and simple-minded and uneducated; yet it is entirely without irony that her young visitors, whom she spoils and advises and comforts like a mother, think her 'a wonderful woman' (*slavnaya zhenshchina*) and that the Sportsman himself judges her 'an extraordinary being'. What makes her extraordinary is that she is herself – simple, unaffected, contented; that she cares about and for other people; that she gives all she has to give and asks for nothing. She loves flowers and animals and young people. Like Olen'ka, she identifies (but only emotionally, not ideologically) with those who engage her sympathies. And it is, naturally, these very virtues that threaten to destroy her when she lets her nephew invade and overrun her life.

The last of the gentry portraits, 'A Hamlet of the Shchigry District' and the Chertopkhanov stories (the second of which was written in 1872), are the most impressive. They present themes and psychological types that will evolve and hold an important place in Turgenev's later work: those of the 'superfluous man' and those he named after Hamlet and Don Quixote.

The original title of what became 'A Hamlet of the Shchigry District' was 'The Dinner': so presumably it was to comprise no more than the reception and dinner with which the present sketch begins. We may well have here, as in the case of 'Lebedyan'', a conjunction of two studies, with a fairly perfunctory connection. It has been argued[19] that the reception and dinner show us the kind of society that has reduced the Hamlet and his ilk to impotence, but, if this is accepted, the question remains: doesn't the relation between the opening pages and the rest have to be read into them? Be that as it may, the satiric picture of the vacuity and snobbery of the provincial gentry at the reception and dinner, like other predominantly satiric matter (Tat'yana Borisovna's nephew, 'Lebedyan'', 'Two Landowners') is comparatively flat and uninspired.

The protagonist of the bedroom scene, on the other hand, is the most complex and one of the two most engaging gentry figures in the book. A typical 'man of the forties' and 'superfluous man' (to use two formulas that came into use only later),[20] he depicts himself as a Westerner, brought up on German idealist philosophy, his adolescence prolonged in the smothering atmosphere of the *kruzhok*,[21] his mind extended and disturbed, but not ripened or energized, by three years of foreign travel, his will and emotions pitifully undeveloped. In a rare burst of communicativeness he unburdens himself to the Sportsman, a perfect stranger, whom he counts on never seeing again but in whom he divines a kindred spirit (*ya vashego polya yagoda*), analysing his own character with relentless honesty and outlining his history sufficiently to explain the formation of that character. He is shy of human contacts (*robok*) because he is 'a terribly proud[22] man'; he is emotionally inhibited (*neposredstvennogo net vo mne nichego*) because he is 'consumed by introspection'. These are two of the stigmata of the 'superfluous man' type, with which he shares a number of others, including that of being a failure and that of rejecting and being rejected by his society. We will examine the type more closely in connection with 'Diary of a Superfluous Man'.

If this Hamlet can be regarded as the progenitor of the line of Turgenevan Hamlets, Chertopkhanov, the protagonist of the remaining two gentry portraits, embodies not a little of Don Quixote.[23] Like his Spanish prototype, he is poor, fanatically devoted to the ideal of honour of a past age which he insists on extrapolating into the present, and unable to see the world around him as it is because determined to see it in terms of a world which has ceased to exist (if it ever did). Like Don Quixote, Chertopkhanov is ready to rush to the rescue of any victim against any odds: he rescues Nedopyuskin from the bullying landowners as later he will rescue the Jew from the infuriated peasants. His Dulcinea is a gypsy girl who abandons him, his Rosinante is stolen, his Sancho Panza dies before him. He loses the girl before whom alone he would humble himself in entreaty; he loses the friend who alone stood between him and utter isolation; he loses the horse on which he had concentrated his last affections and his ultimate pride. And more tragically obdurate – or should one say 'more fortunate'? – than the Spaniard, he dies without having seen his illusions for what they are. He is innocent of Western culture – perhaps, of any culture – but his passions are strong, his will is unbending. He represents the antithesis of the superfluous man.

The two Chertopkhanov sketches, written a quarter of a century apart, diverge from the typical pattern of other portraits – the second more radically than the first. In 'Chertopkhanov and Nedopyuskin', though the Sportsman has two meetings with the two friends, he derives his account of their histories and relationship not from them (neither of them could realistically have been credited with such an account), but from unnamed outside informants. In 'The End of Chertopkhanov' this technique is taken a step further: the Sportsman disappears completely, to be replaced by an unidentified omniscient narrator. In this respect it is unique among the sketches (though closely approached by 'Tat'yana Borisovna and Her Nephew'), as also in its length and in its approximation to a short story (rather than merely a sketch).

Five of the gentry portraits are complemented by the all too common appendage of the 'parasite', whom we have already encountered in the play of that name. In Karataev's case, it is the subject of the portrait who ends up reduced to that status, though this is only implied and we do not see him with his patrons. The other four parasites in the *Sketches* represent two different species. Belovzorov (the nephew) and Khlopakov (in 'Lebedyan'') are both healthy young men, both quite capable of earning a living, but both prefer to sponge: Belovzorov on his doting aunt, Khlopakov on a succession of casually met 'benefactors' who support him just as long as he amuses them. Both lead a comfortable and comparatively easy life, for the time being. Both are empty, thick-skinned, self-infatuated nullities, who evoke only contempt in the Sportsman (and in the reader).

Fëdor Mikheich and Nedopyuskin, on the other hand, evoke pity and some sympathy. Fëdor Mikheich (like Karataev) has ruined himself by living beyond his means; in his time he had been regarded as the most dashing fellow in his province, had abducted two of his neighbours' wives, and had been an excellent singer and dancer: in other words, a man of more than average vitality and energy and perhaps some potential talent.

The reader is surely a little disconcerted by Radilov's treatment of his 70-year-old dependant: surely a man unhappily in love should be more sensitive to other people's misfortunes? Is Turgenev indicating that Radilov is so unhappy that he can find relief only in adding to somebody else's unhappiness? Or is he making the point that serfdom inevitably callouses even the 'best' and most likeable of serf-owners? (Note that this second interpretation can occur only to those who read the sketch in the book; it could not have occurred to the original readers of *The Contemporary*.)

Fëdor Mikheich's life is far from easy, but it is not nearly as hard as Nedopyuskin's before he (like Kuzovkin) comes into his inheritance. In the tale of Nedopyuskin's tribulations we get a glimpse of what Kuzovkin's must have been while his 'benefactor' was alive. But, unlike Kuzovkin (and Fëdor Mikheich and Karataev), Nedopyuskin does not belong to the gentry class, and the poverty, the frantic struggle to survive, in which he had grown up had crushed his spirit and unfitted him for the rough-and-tumble of a working life. He drifted, like Khlopakov, from one 'benefactor' to another, but he could gain admittance only to lower social levels, where he was exploited in correspondingly more primitive style. Yet, however battered by life, he had not lost his capacity for devotion and love or the ability to appreciate a man as different from himself as Chertopkhanov and to make a Chertopkhanov his friend.

Before turning to the serfs and serfdom, it is worth noting that if the *Sketches* do not give us a complete cross-section of Russian society, they do include at least silhouettes of representatives of most of the classes intermediate between the gentry and the serfs: freedmen (Tuman in 'Raspberry Water', the hunter Vladimir in 'L'gov', Morgach in 'The Singing Match'); freeholders (Ovsyanikov and Nedopyuskin's grandfather); priests (barely glanced at for censorship reasons, in 'Two Landowners' and 'Death'); small traders (Gavrila Antonych in 'The Estate Office', the horse-dealer Sitnikov in 'Lebedyan'');[24] *raznochintsy* (the district doctor, Ovsyanikov's nephew Mitya, the student-tutor in 'Death'); a gypsy (Masha in the two Chertopkhanov stories); Jews, in 'The Jew' and the 1872 'The End of Chertopkhanov'. And high officialdom takes a bow in the person of Benevolenski (in 'Tat'yana Borisovna and her Nephew'); even the magnates of a bygone age (Count Pëtr Il'ich in 'Raspberry Water', Count Orlov-Chesmensky in 'The Freeholder

Ovsyanikov') make a fleeting appearance in the reminiscences of survivors from those times.

It has been remarked often enough that in turning his attention to the peasantry, Turgenev was following a fashion already current in France, Germany and Switzerland, and attempted even in Russia, notably in Grigorovich's 'A Village' (*Derevnya*), 1846. But in order to be true to his artistic creed (of realism) and to exert a positive influence on his readers, he had to aim at striking a balance between the predominantly idyllic presentation in Western writings and the more grimly 'physiological' treatment of the lower classes by his Russian predecessors. In the gentry portraits, as we have seen, the majority of subjects were likeable; but in the two 'Gogolian' gentry portraits and in the sketches focussed on serfdom, the portrayal of the serf-owners is, in varying degree, satirical and the types presented to us are more or less unprepossessing. Having thus perforce incensed numbers of his readers, Turgenev, if he was not to alienate their sympathies completely, had to make his portrayal of the serfs broadly convincing.

That was certainly his endeavour; and it seems fair to claim that even in the more lyrical of the serf portraits he has achieved a minimum of idealization. However, one need not equate realism with impartiality. All the subjects portrayed, both gentry and serfs, may well be drawn from life. But it is clear that Turgenev has ignored the finest type of landowner: there must have been at least a few as liberal and cultured as he, but we are not introduced to any. Whereas in regard to the serfs, his selectiveness operates the other way: in the portraits we meet some of the most attractive types (as represented by the boys in 'Bezhin Meadow', Kas'yan, Yakov the Turk in 'The Singing Match', Akulina in 'The Tryst', Luker'ya in the 1874 'Living Relics' and several more); and though in the sketches hinging on serfdom we do meet some quite repulsive specimens (the Bailiff Sofron, Khvostov, head of the Estate Office, Viktor in 'The Tryst'), besides such flotsam as Stëpushka in 'Raspberry Water' and Suchok in 'L'gov', nowhere are we allowed to see anything of the darkest sides of serf life: the alcoholism, wife-beating, *snokhachestvo*,[25] depicted by Turgenev's contemporaries and successors.

Admittedly, those were features mainly of peasant life, and we need to realize the paradox that hardly any of the serfs in *A Sportsman's Sketches* are peasants, and those that are are either

untypical (Khor') or uprooted (Kalinych, arguably Kas'yan) or
have walking-on parts (Vlas in 'Raspberry Water', the father and
son who come to appeal for justice against the Bailiff, Sidor who
comes to bribe the head of the Estate Office, the nameless poacher
in 'The Lone Wolf' and the similarly nameless dying peasant in
'Death'). There is not a single picture of a peasant living and
working in interaction with his family and the village community.
About a score are domestic serfs – the most miserable class of serf –
or former domestic serfs; a further dozen or so defy classification.

The main point made in Turgenev's serf portraits is the full
humanity of his subjects. In Luker'ya he shows us a saint (but an
unmistakably peasant saint in terms of her intellectual limitations);
in Kas'yan we have a *pravednik*, a seeker after righteousness, with
a touch of mysticism;[26] in the children of 'Bezhin Meadow' the
unspoilt freshness and freedom of spirit and the curiosity of their
age, and in 12-year-old Pavlusha the quiet courage of an adult; in
'The Singing Match', two artists and the response to art and eager
sense of beauty of their simple audience; in 'The Lone Wolf' a
strong sense of duty wrestling with compassion. In 'The Tryst' and
'Kas'yan from Krasivaya Mecha' and one or two other stories we
glimpse the delicacy and strength of the affections – here of a girl,
there of a man; in Khor' are imaged the intellectual virtues (and
limitations) and the practical efficiency and enterprise of one who
has attained as great a measure of independence as a serf could
aspire to.

Turgenev resisted the temptation of facile contrapositions: his
serfs are not presented as antitheses of the gentry. Nor does he
attempt to contrast cognate characters as they might be embodied
in members of the two classes, although in one or two cases he may
seem to approach that effect: Pavlusha and Chertopkhanov are
both Don Quixote types (in Turgenev's sense); the pseudo-artist
Belovzorov challenges comparison with the true artist Yakov the
Turk; the Hamlet of Shchigry and Kas'yan are both eccentrics not
made for this base world. In such cases the superiority of the serf
avatar is evident, though no parallels are drawn.

As regards serfdom – the relations between serfs and serf-owners
– *A Sportsman's Sketches* might almost serve as a textbook or
manual of the system and its abuses. It may be as well to recall
briefly the salient features.

The serf had no rights. His village was run not by an elected head but by the master's appointee. Absentee landlords often entrusted the administration of their estates to a foreign steward; but the tyranny and exploitation were likely to be much the same when the headman was a promoted peasant, as we see in 'The Bailiff' and 'The Estate Office'. The individual peasant was secure neither in his tenure of land, nor in his mode of life, nor in his family circle. The master could seize any piece of land that caught his fancy: witness Bespandin (in 'The Freeholder Ovsyanikov') and the anecdote about Turgenev's (great-)grandfather, who had not hesitated to wrest land away from a *free* peasant. In fact, the master could take away anything else 'belonging' to the serf. The master could take a man off his land and send him away to the city to earn quit-rent (Vlas's son in 'Raspberry Water') or to learn a trade or profession (Suchok in 'L'gov'). He could claim the man for personal services, regardless of how that might disrupt his husbandry (Kalinych), or for domestic service (Suchok again). He could send the man into the army not only to meet the draft but at any time as a punishment (Stegunov in 'Two Landowners', the Bailiff, as his master's deputy), or merely to raise money (as did Pushkin's friend Chaadaev during his youthful travels abroad). The master could break up the family by selling one or more of its members (this was forbidden by laws passed as late as 1827 and 1833; but the fact that the law had to be reissued so soon strongly suggests that it was not strictly enforced) or by claiming one or more for special services: the daughter(s) to wait on his wife (Arina in 'Ermolai and the Miller's Wife') or for his harem (Akulina in 'Raspberry Water'),[27] children of either sex to act or sing or play in his domestic theatre (Suchok again). Not to mention that the peasantry bore virtually the entire burden of taxation and of compulsory military service – a 25-year stint.

The most important distinction between serf and serf was the way in which each discharged his (or her) obligations to the master: obligations which, in practice, were limited only by the master's demands: he decided both in what manner and in what measure they should be discharged. The two basic modes of meeting these obligations were by quit-rent, that is, payment in money and/or in kind (Khor', Vlas) or by service: agricultural, industrial (i.e., working in the master's mill or factory: Il'yusha and his friends in 'Bezhin Meadow'), domestic or personal. It was the serfs on quit-rent who had the best chance of prospering: in favourable circumstances one member of the family could earn enough for two or more, so that the others could concentrate on working their land (like Vlas) or branch out into trade (like Khor').

The most wretched plight was that of the domestic serfs, in spite of the surprisingly wide range of activities opened up to some of the more gifted of them: as actors, musicians and even lawyers or doctors (of course, in the service of their master and dependent on his good pleasure, or whim). In any case, these gifted few, like the rest of the domestic serfs, suffered from the closer contact with their owners in two ways: they were far more constantly exposed than the peasants to those owners' caprices and moods, and they were immersed in an alien and empty way of life which was only too apt to disorientate and demoralize them (Akulina in 'Raspberry Water', Viktor in 'The Tryst'), and in those respects it was the most attractive personalities and the most talented who stood to suffer most.

As Turgenev makes Ovsyanikov say, the serf-owners were only too prone to regard their serfs as toys, playing with them and their lives in utterly irresponsible fashion, only to throw them aside or smash them when they tired of the game. They might ban a marriage between two who wanted and needed to marry or command the marriage of two who had no desire to marry (Arina, Petrushka and the miller in 'Ermolai and the Miller's Wife'); they might even impose celibacy on their whole household (Suchok). And as they played havoc with their servants' affections, so they might play havoc with their talents or their careers by refusing to let the most gifted practise the professions for which they had trained or buy their freedom (there were tragic cases of such serfs taking to drink or committing suicide); imposing a kind of work for which the individual in question had no talent or inclination (Kupriyan in 'The Estate Office'), or switching him or her arbitrarily from one employment to another, as in the ghastly case of Suchok (in 'L'gov'), who under six different owners had been put through ten different occupations and forbidden ever to marry.

Although many, perhaps most, landowners found sufficient scope for the exercise of their fantasy among their domestic serfs, the most whimsical were free to extend their attentions to their peasants: we have a ruinous example of this in Chertopkhanov's father. The inclusion in the group of sketches hinging on relations between serfs and their masters of a number of eighteenth-century landowners may have been prompted by several motives: by Turgenev's own lively (and enduring) interest in the life and art and culture of that century; by a desire to mollify or distract the censors, who were likely to be less alarmed by abuses of a bygone era than by those of their own day; perhaps above all by the wish to provide a glimpse of the nobility and gentry in their heyday, contrasting that vanished magnificence with the grey, impoverished existence of too many of their descendants, a condition that was to make the emancipation of the serfs both possible and necessary little more than a decade later.

As we have seen, the *Sketches* include several figures of such ruined landowners: pitifully silhouetted in Fëdor Mikheich, only half shown in Karataev (later, powerfully and poignantly drawn in the end of Chertopkhanov). Even more ominous is the fact that the gentry in *A Sportsman's Sketches* appears as a dying race: we meet not a single instance of a complete family of parents and children. There are one or two married couples, though we see only one of the pair; some are widowers or widows; most of the younger ones are unwed and childless.

Two more characteristics of this (third) group of sketches deserve attention. First, the ordinariness of the landowners who figure in them. There is not a single villain here: not a single type comparable to such historical figures as Kuroedov (depicted as 'Kurolesov' in S. T. Aksakov's *Family Chronicle*) or Count Kamensky (preserved for posterity in Leskov's 'The Toupée Artist'). Here there are not even any such eccentrics as Turgenev himself presents in the gentry portraits – not a single 'Hamlet' or Chertopkhanov. Secondly, this ordinariness of the serf-owners is thrown into relief by their serfs' attitude towards them. Remember the admiration and pride with which Tuman (in 'Raspberry Water') speaks of the deceased Count Pëtr Il'ich (and compare this with the somewhat surprising paean of Ovsyanikov – not a serf, nor a freedman, but a freeholder – to the equally dead Count Orlov). Remember Vasya's apologia (at the end of 'Two Landowners') for his petty sadist of a master who has just had him whipped: 'It served me right, sir, it served me right. We are not punished for trifles . . . That's not how our master is: our master – why, you wouldn't find another like him anywhere in our province.' The peasants are sometimes not quite so docile as the domestic serfs; but their resentment is commonly directed at the master's agents (as in 'The Bailiff', 'The Estate

Office', 'The Lone Wolf'); where the masters are themselves criticized, it is implicitly and either with condescension (Khor') or, at worst, without bitterness (Vlas).

These two devices, the presentation of quite ordinary land-owners and of their acceptance by their serfs, imply a scorching condemnation of the system: within such a system one did not have to be wicked or perverted to treat one's serfs with quite monstrous inhumanity. Ordinary people – people who would behave with ordinary decency in other contexts – did so because the system made it almost inevitable that they should. The twin bases of the abuses were, on the one hand, the serf-owner's virtually unlimited power and, on the other, his conviction – the sort of rationalization with which almost anyone in such a position is impelled to salve his conscience – that the serfs were not fully human, or, as Kropotkin puts it:[28] 'Human feelings were not recognized, not even suspected in the serfs.' Hence, of course, Turgenev's concern to demonstrate the falseness of this conception in his masterly portrayal of the full range of his serfs' imaginative and emotional resources.

As a landscape painter Turgenev must be unsurpassed among nineteenth-century writers. The whole 'action' of *A Sportsman's Sketches* is framed in the landscapes of his native Orël and the neighbouring provinces to north and south (Kaluga, Tula, Kursk). Woods, meadows and fields; rivers and streams; hills and gullies and glades; trees and birds – the hunter's eye is keen to note them all and the artist's pen to record them, with love. What he dwells on mostly is not the shapes of things but their colours and, constantly, the changes of light, the variations of weather and season and the sounds and scents of the wild. These colours and sounds he feels and renders as a poet. In an 1852 book review he writes: 'I love nature passionately';[29] and it is this passionate love of nature's beauties which quickens his observation and matches the music of his phrases and the shimmer of his rhythms to the play of sounds and light around and over him.

In that same review he writes: 'Man cannot fail to be interested in nature, he is bound to her by a thousand unbreakable threads: he is her child . . .' But he hastens to warn against the selfish forms such love is prone to assume: the Romantic reduction of nature to a 'pedestal for ourselves', since such an attitude is 'entirely at odds with the true meaning of nature'. What he preaches there, he has practised in his book: the richness of his response to all he sees and hears and smells is conveyed primarily by the instrumentation of his metaphors and his rhythms. This does not exclude occasional references to the narrator's response to a particular scene; but these are brief, often depersonalized (such a scene is apt to call forth such feelings) and nature neither frames nor shows any awareness of the narrator.

'Woodland and Steppe', the sketch placed at the end of the book,[30] takes leave of the reader by way of outlining some of the beauties of nature typically enjoyed by a sportsman in the course of pursuing his sport. These are described in the form of a dozen of the commonest experiences – several of which comprise a succession of shorter scenes – such as setting out before dawn on a spring day, vicissitudes of a day in July, the silence and peace of a forest arousing memory and imagination, a frosty autumn morning under a sun that shines without power to warm, summer mists, a journey into the steppe.

These vignettes vary or supplement the pictures of nature scattered among the preceding sketches; pictures which vary in length from one paragraph (or less) to nearly two pages; it is perhaps noteworthy that none occurs in any of the gentry portraits and that the only one to occur in close proximity to a landowner – the woods at Chaplygino as the Sportsman remembers them from his childhood contrasted with their present ruined condition[31] – barely disguises an object-lesson in gentry neglect and mismanagement.

Perhaps the most striking descriptions are of nightfall while waiting for the woodcock to take flight,[32] of the skyscapes and colour changes of a fine July day,[33] of lying in a wood looking up into the sky[34] and of the changes of weather and light inside an autumn birch grove.[35] Admire the acuteness and precision of the observation: the order in which the different birds fall silent in the twilight;[36] the modulations of the light and of shapes and colours of the clouds in the course of the day;[37] the definition of the time of year in terms of the different sounds made by the foliage in different seasons.[38] Note the cunning interweaving of adjectives (and adverbs) of bare and exact description with adjectives (and adverbs) redolent of living beings. On the one hand: 'it is still light in the wood'; 'the air is pure and transparent'; 'warm dampness'; 'the sonorous voice of the chiff-chaff'. On the other, 'the young grass gleams with the gay sparkle of emeralds'; 'the treetops . . .

are falling asleep';[39] 'the first little stars make a timid appearance'. And this vivification of the inanimate is reinforced by dynamic verbs: 'the crimson light ... glides ... rises ... passes'.

The landscapes are not introduced as ends in themselves: they have a number of functions. They constantly serve to define the time and place and to frame the action. They serve to define, implicitly, another dimension of the Sportsman's personality: they express his love of beauty, as his reactions to the serfs, and to their owners' treatment of them, express his humanity. Thirdly, they may serve as keynotes to the sketches in which they appear, variously foreshadowing or symbolizing: as the autumn day that opens and concludes 'The Tryst' foreshadows with its sunshine chequered by rain and its threat of winter in the offing the end of Akulina's love and dreams of happiness.[40]

As regards structure – *A Sportsman's Sketches* is a unitary work in a way in which neither Pushkin's *Tales of Belkin* nor Gogol's *Mirgorod* or *Petersburg Tales* is unitary. This unity, which is rather surprising in view of the genesis and evolution of the work, is generally felt and conceded. Russian critics have seen it as based on three principal factors. First, there is the thematic unity imparted by the orientation against serfdom; this is the most often adduced and emphasized, but presumably the one that weighs least with foreign readers and in the long run should become secondary for all who read the *Sketches* as literature.

The second factor is the unity of the world portrayed. Whereas the *Tales of Belkin* are not even firmly fixed in space or time and the *Petersburg Tales*, though fixed in space and arguably, though not unquestionably, in time, neither form nor are intended to form any sort of panorama: *A Sportsman's Sketches* does obviously take us on a conducted tour of a definite world. The third, and perhaps most fundamental, unifying factor is the persona and rôle of the narrator, the Sportsman: most fundamental, because it is his outlook, interests and values which delimit and body forth that world.

The narrator comes before us not as a rounded personage, but as a semi-transparent observer and catalyst of other people's views, attitudes, personalities. He is always ready to efface himself in order to display to the best advantage the person(s) he is observing, and in those sketches in which he is drawn into the foreground of the scene he is presented in quite unheroic guise, even as something

of a simpleton or sentimentalist (as towards the end of 'Lebedyan''
and 'The Lone Wolf' respectively). The assumed simplicity is often
a device for throwing into relief the qualities or attitudes of the
serfs; *vis-à-vis* his social peers his tone is neutral in most of the
gentry portraits, ironic in the two Gogolian ones and in the sketches
pivoting on serfdom.[41] But on one issue he is quite staunch and
coherent: his human values in general and his reactions to serfdom
in particular. Not that he obtrudes them: as often as not, we are left
to infer them from the way other characters react to his disapproval
or recoil.

In terms of viewpoint, the sketches fall into two groups according
to whether they are mainly told by the Sportsman or to him;[42] there
are a few which combine the two approaches (e.g., 'Ermolai and
the Miller's Wife' and 'The Freeholder Ovsyanikov'). Turgenev
takes care to preserve and convey to us the individual idioms of
each of the secondary characters who are all variously remote –
psychologically and culturally and in most cases socially – from the
Sportsman: he reacts to them with astonishment. It has been
remarked of these idioms that they are all lively and colloquial, that
is, addressed to a listener rather than to a reader, and this too sets
them off from the more literary idiom of the Sportsman.[43]

Much of Turgenev's later work is prefigured in the types and
structures of *A Sportsman's Sketches*. This is his first attempt at
presenting a social panorama, and he succeeds here by dispensing
with plot, protagonists and a cast of interacting characters. In the
short stories which he was writing before, during and after the
Sketches, he was experimenting with just these missing elements;
when he succeeded in combining the two sets of elements, the
result was *Rudin* and the series of novels that followed *Rudin*. For
his novels Turgenev was to adopt the viewpoint of an omniscient
author (or, at any rate, an anonymous third-person narrator); but
for most of his short stories and novellas, including most of the best
of them, he retains the device of indirect narrative, usually by a
first-person narrator who is one of the personages.

The order in which the *Sketches* appear in the book is quite
independent of the order in which they were written and first
published and tends to disguise, whether deliberately or not, both
the ideological shifts of emphasis and the artistic evolution of
Turgenev in those five years. The fifteen *Sketches* written in
Belinsky's lifetime (i.e. before June 1848) comprised all the seven

hinging on serfdom, the two Gogolian gentry portraits, a couple of
the serf portraits and the three 'love stories' (besides 'Death'); the
seven (in the 1852 volume) written after Belinsky's death comprise
four of the best serf portraits[44] and the two best gentry portraits[45]
(besides 'Woodland and Steppe'). Belinsky was scathing about
'The District Doctor'[46] and enthusiastic about the ones attacking
serfdom roughly in proportion to the directness and force of the
attack, so it was natural for Turgenev to hew mainly to that line.
With Belinsky gone, it was equally natural for Turgenev to broaden
his purview, to follow his bent as portraitist and psychologist and to
admit more of his natural lyricism into the sketches. It may be
significant that the sketch which was begun, around the time of
Belinsky's death, as 'The Dinner' blossomed out that summer as
'The Hamlet of the Shchigry District'.

Turgenev had begun with the intention of limiting the sketches to
twelve (later fifteen); he went on producing more until his friends
told him it was time to stop, time to turn to something different. He
had realized that himself, but it was easier said than done, and for
several years he struggled to disentangle himself from the limitations, thematic and formal, of *A Sportsman's Sketches*. There is a
good deal in his letters of the period about his need and desire to
slough off his 'old manner'; but it is far from clear what he means by
this term. Perhaps he and his critical friends were not too sure
themselves what needed to be changed.[47] Sometimes it seems to be
the treatment of character, sometimes the style: a phrase in which
he defends a later story as a step forward might apply to either: 'I
am not coquetting [here], not playing clever',[48] the implication
being that these were his besetting sins in the *Sketches*.

If the chief charge brought by his friends against the *Sketches* was
that of straining after effect, whether in language or in choice of
materials, there was a much more fundamental weakness, at any
rate, from the point of view of what Turgenev hoped and planned
to achieve in literature: namely, the static character of the tales.
They consist of portraits and landscapes: no plots, often not even a
story; no drama; no psychological complexities. Turgenev looks at
nature primarily with a painter's eye; and that is almost how he
looks at many or most of the personages. This general approach is
correlated with the rôle of the Sportsman as essentially an outside
observer of scenes and events, with the result that the objects of his
observation are distanced, if not somewhat flattened; at least, in all

but the post-Belinsky portraits. In his later stories Turgenev will aim to involve his first-person narrator more closely and deeply in the action, with a corresponding gain in dynamism and dramatic impact.

His attitude to this, his first important work, was characteristic-ally modest. While humbly accepting the strictures of his friends, or even capping them with his own – 'there is a great deal that has come out colourless, fragmentary; a great deal is only hinted at, some things ring false – overspiced or half-baked . . .' – he decided nevertheless that there is in the work enough that rings true to redeem it as a whole: he is glad that he has written it; it will be his mite cast into the treasure-house of Russian literature.[49]

5

Transition: the end of serfdom; the 'superfluous man'

By the beginning of 1851 Turgenev had written the last of the sketches,[1] just as his involvement with the theatre, which had run parallel[2] with his writing of the *Sketches*, was about to end. He felt a need to pause, to take stock, to wait for new 'impressions',[3] to advance along new paths. He knew he did not want to write any more sketches or any more plays. He wanted to write stories, but stories that would earn the critical attention and commendation which had been virtually denied to his earlier ones;[4] and he wanted to produce a novel.

Thus the first half of the 1850s was, even while the last of the sketches were being written, a period of transition and questing. Apart from 'Three Meetings', which in tone and theme had little in common with any of the stories of the 1840s or early 1850s, we can recognize in this period two thematic lines, both emerging from *A Sportsman's Sketches*, only one of them destined to be 'productive' in the grammarian's sense.[5] The productive line was that of the portrait of the gentleman, or, more specifically, of the type adumbrated in 'A Hamlet of the Shchigry District'; the other, which virtually came to an end within a year of the publication of the *Sketches* as a book, was that of serfdom.[6]

'Mumu', 'The Inn', 'The Mistress's Own Office'

In 'Mumu', written 1852, published 1854, we have another victim of serfdom and a fresh instance of man's inhumanity to man, already variously illustrated in the persons of Matrëna, Arina, Suchok, Akulina and the rest. But here the technique is quite different: not mainly because the story is told by an omniscient author, as nowhere in the 1852 *Sketches*, but because we have a piling-on of the agony, a Jamesian 'turn of the screw'.

First, Gerasim is torn from the familiar context of village life and transferred, without rhyme or reason, to the alien and unappealing setting of the city; then his first love, Tanya, is not only snatched from him with equal arbitrariness but thrown to a man for whom she doesn't care and who is only too likely to drag her down with him; finally, his last love, Mumu, is sentenced to destruction.

Thomas Carlyle is supposed to have said that 'Mumu' was the most moving story he had ever read;[7] but here too Turgenev takes care to stop well short of tragedy. His villainess is selfish and obtuse rather than wicked; his hero suffers perforce in silence: we can only guess what he feels, we can hardly guess what he thinks. Yet this very restraint adds edge to the poignancy.

Gerasim not only loses his Tanya: he is robbed of his image of her by the trick of her feigned drunkenness. He not only loses his dog: he is driven to kill her himself, to betray – as it must have seemed to her – her love and trust, with his own hands to tear out of his life the only source in it of warmth and comfort. The reader experiences not a catharsis, but something of the mixture of horror with impotent rage which Turgenev must have felt often enough in witnessing his mother's acts of malicious despotism.

Gerasim accepts them. Gerasim obeys. He settles in the city. He gives up Tanya. He drowns Mumu. We want to cry with the poet:

> Do not go gentle into that good night.
> Rage, rage against the dying of the light.

Gerasim does not rage. But his cup is full. He turns his back on the city. He turns his back on his mistress and her house.

The city is the negation of solitude and independence: it enforces contact with one's fellows; yet it is a soil in which opportunity flourishes: it offers chances of love and happiness. But love and happiness can never ripen in the shadow of the mistress: she spreads her blight as far as her eye can reach.

And so Gerasim departs from her and from the city, to return to the independence and solitude of the village. He marches through the darkness, nerved by desperation and joy, till he reaches home – a home unlit and unwarmed by any human presence. There he resumes the mode of life and work in which he had grown up, as though he had never left it. Or not quite: he has not forgotten. He will never forget. Never again will he look at a woman; never again will he own a dog: never again will he seek or suffer the companionship of man or beast. Existence continues; life is finished.

'Mumu' is a true story; in the lady Turgenev depicted his mother. But there are only a few of her traits in the lady in 'The Inn', another true story, written in the same year as 'Mumu', though not published till 1855.

In spite of appearances, here (as in 'Pëtr Petrovich Karataev') serfdom is not the real hinge of the story. It is true that the catastrophe – Akim's loss of 'his' inn – was made possible by the fact that the serf-owner owned not only the serf but also the serf's 'property' and that Akim's owner (like the gentleman-horsedealer in 'Lebedyan'') allowed greed to subvert her sense of honour: yet in fact Akim is ruined not by his owner but by his wife and her lover. In a Western society the same catastrophe could have been brought about if the inn had been rented under a gentleman's agreement, or without a properly drawn contract, and the landlord had decided to sell the property over his tenant's head.

Essentially, 'The Inn' is the story of Akim. It is another serf portrait; but it differs from such portrait-sketches as those of Khor' or Kas'yan as a motion picture differs from a photograph: it presents Akim dynamically, dramatically, through the story of his life.

Unlike Gerasim, who was an extraordinary being, morally no less than physically – in his devotion to duty, his sense of honour, his unselfish love: evidenced by the scrupulousness with which he carried out his household tasks, by his unfailing fulfilment of his promises and by his taking on himself the killing of Mumu to ensure that she suffer as little as possible – Akim is a quite ordinary man: goodhearted, easygoing and weak (whereas Gerasim was strong). Gerasim was young, Akim is old (by Turgenev's standard, but also, no doubt, in terms of the Russian peasant's life-expectancy at that time). And Turgenev eschews the turn of the screw: Gerasim lost his treasures – his rural peace, his Tanya, his Mumu – one by one, with years between the losses; Akim learns that he has lost his all – his wife, inn, savings – within the few hours prescribed by classical tragedy. Both men rebel. But Gerasim, as befits his strength, rebels against the all-powerful mistress (who could have had him brought back to the city, flogged, banished to some remote estate or buried alive in the army); Akim turns against his wife, then her lover, but only with an abortive gesture.

Akim, starting with nothing, has made his way in the world by his energy, shrewdness and uprightness; people like and respect him. He is a peasant, with his roots in the country. Naum, the spoiler, is a townsman,[8] an outsider: he not only has no roots, but in the fifteen years when he runs the inn after Akim, is unable to put down any. His whole life seems to pivot on cold calculation, yet this is occasionally swayed by a paradoxical instinct or intuition through which he senses some great opportunity or danger:[9] as when he divines in Dunyasha a stepping-stone or key to the fortune he is determined to make or when he is impelled, suddenly and for no reason, to sell his inn. Turgenev does not direct our attention to the incongruity of such intuition in such a calculating-machine, any more than he suggests a correlation between the contrasting ethos of Akim and Naum and their different social origins; it is for the reader to descry such straws in the wind: his enjoyment, not to say his understanding, of Turgenev will vary with his willingness to do so.

The vain lady's maid, Dunyasha, represents another example of the demoralization of house serfs by too close contact with their owners: she is a feminine analogue of Viktor in 'The Tryst'. Under a veneer of 'ladylike' ways she has lost, or failed to develop, the self-respect or moral backbone that is so evidently at the centre of Akim. In her marriage the veneer flakes away, she goes to pieces morally, and surrenders without reserve or scruple to her seducer.

Kirillovna is another stock figure of the gentry household: a house serf who, mostly by unlimited subservience and flattery, has become the owner's favourite and so, to some degree and in some fields at least, the power behind the throne. (A similar rôle could be played by a parasite, a decayed gentlewoman, as in the household of Matrëna's mistress in 'Pëtr Petrovich Karataev'.) We met a male analogue in Khvostov, the head of the Estate Office, whom his mistress deemed 'indispensable' while he was making a fortune at her expense. Kirillovna is doing the same on a more modest scale, but she does accumulate enough to buy her freedom and a husband. By pandering to her mistress's less avowable inclinations and screening the lady from the petty annoyances of every day, she too has made herself indispensable. Obviously, the precariousness of such a position, wholly dependent on the owner's mood or whim, would call for qualities of foresight, quick-wittedness and decisiveness in which the serf might well need to excel the mistress or master.[10]

Whereas religion seemed to permeate Kas'yan's whole life – a religion in which ethical principles were irradiated by a poetic cult of nature – in Akim, until the catastrophe, religion had played a more limited and much more conventional part. It needed the successive shocks of his loss of inn, wife and money, of his near-lapse into despair and crime, and of his narrow escape from prison or Siberia, to drive him in upon himself, burn up his attachments to the world in which he had lived and worked for more than half a century and turn his thoughts to the values and objectives of another world.

But in this too he remained conventional. Whereas Kas'yan journeyed by himself from region to region in quest of ever new delight from the beauties of nature, Akim made his way, just as indefatigably, from shrine to shrine, together with hundreds or thousands of similar pilgrims, seeking in prayer to make his peace with God. The people he meets are impressed by his piety and by the blend of humility and wisdom to which he has attained. The reader may be no less struck by the fact that it not only never occurs to him to blame his mistress but that, after the first moment, he refuses to blame his wife. It was his own fault – first for marrying a young wife in his old age, and then for failing to detect what was going on; so he had been punished justly: God Himself has made him understand that. Thus Akim and Kas'yan may be said to embody two contrasting facets of popular religion: the orthodox-ritual and the sectarian-mystical, both equally remote from the religion of active love, of selfless service (exemplified by such a figure as Pashen'ka in Tolstoy's 'Father Sergius').

Akim had turned his back on his old life because he could not bear to be pointed at in scorn or in pity by those who had known him in prosperity: so his piety and humility stem from a quite mundane pride, and are none the less genuine for that.[11] Turgenev, as usual, leaves it to the reader to notice (or miss) the paradox. And the fate of the other characters may deserve a second thought: that the greedy lady and the unscrupulous exploiter continue to flourish may be in accord with the requirements of realism; but why did poor, vain, silly Dunyasha have to be brought so low?

'The Mistress's Own Office' is the only surviving fragment of a long novel.[12] The main setting would have been based on Spasskoe, and Turgenev's mother and uncle would have been represented among the personages of the older generation. Varvara Turgeneva in fact had two offices at Spasskoe for the administration of her estates: the estate office, of which we were given a picture in *A*

Sportsman's Sketches, and her own office, which is the subject of this vignette. We see this office (like the other) organized and run on the model of government offices: the proliferation of paperwork and red tape; the favourites, corresponding to ministers, constantly tense and fearful in the presence of their 'sovereign', all too conscious of the precariousness of their positions and intent on shifting the blame for every mishap from their own shoulders onto others; the tug-of-war between the sovereign and her too-independent vizier, her steward Vasili Vasil'evich.[13] We read of the grandiose schemes for improvements, which will evidently come to nothing, and recognize the petty greed *à la* Kuntse (the lady in 'The Inn'): the fuss about the amounts of oats and hay lavished on a visitor's horses and the threat to serf actresses working away from the estate that unless they can quickly earn enough money to buy their freedom, they will be summoned home to more menial labours.

As it stands, this fragment would have fitted neatly into *A Sportsman's Sketches*, but for the fact that (like 'The Dinner') it would seem too slight to stand on its own. Anyhow, it forms an illuminating supplement to 'Two Landowners', 'The Bailiff' and, in particular, 'The Estate Office'. Here the thematic line of serfdom comes to an end, although we do meet portraits of serfs – as distinct from studies of relations between serfs and owners – in two or three later writings.[14]

'Diary of a Superfluous Man'

It would be unkind and untrue, though not so far from the truth as not to be worth hazarding, to say that the most memorable thing about 'Diary of a Superfluous Man'[15] is its title. ('Most memorable' must, in any case, not be taken to imply 'only memorable': though the 'Diary' is hardly one of Turgenev's best stories, it is arguably the best and most important of his stories up to that point.)

Critics seized upon the designation 'superfluous man' and proceeded to apply it, in course of time, to various personages in the writings of Turgenev's predecessors, to later personages of Turgenev himself and of other nineteenth-century and even twentieth-century Russian writers. In other words, 'superfluous man' became a label for a recognizable literary, and social, type, whose prominence and significance varied from period to period, but whose characteristics and rôles showed sufficient continuity to justify the same title. Summarily it may be said that the superfluous man is a type of 'outsider' created by Russian social conditions: an individual generally superior to his society in culture and sensitivity, but more or less crippled or warped, emotionally and/or in capacity for action, by social pressures; an individual who can find no place in his society; who is impelled to reject it, and is rejected by it rather in virtue of his positive than of his negative qualities.

The type that was to be surnamed 'the superfluous man' began to take shape in Turgenev's mind no later than 1844. It may be debated whether the narrator of 'Andrei Kolosov' is in the direct line of ascent, but there can scarcely be any question as regards the younger of the two speakers in the poem *A Conversation*. Four years later, in 1848, Turgenev returns to the portrayal of the type in the Hamlet of the Shchigry District and in Gorski, the 'hero' of the play *A Chain is as Strong as its Weakest Link*. And after another two years of work on the type, he offers us two more embodiments, full-fledged, if not yet fully matured: Rakitin in *A Month in the Country* and Chulkaturin, the author of the 'Diary'; and the type receives its name.

In setting the scene of the 'Diary' on a deathbed and putting the story into the mouth of the dying man, Turgenev is skirting the whole elegiac tradition, beloved of Pre-romantics and Romantics, of the unfulfilled life and the premature death; this is often presented in the guise of a 'dying poet',[16] but Turgenev adds to the difficulties of his task by not making his protagonist a professional writer. So, from one point of view, the 'Diary' is another exercise in deglamorization – and specifically the deglamorization of Romantic stereotypes – already attempted in *Parasha* and *Andrei* and pressed home in 'Andrei Kolosov' and 'The Duellist'. From another point of view, it is his most subtle psychological study so far, with the exception of the simultaneous *A Month in the Country*.

There is something intrinsically pitiful in the situation of anyone dying without having lived. In telling his own story Chulkaturin needs to capitalize on that natural sympathy in the reader and to steer clear of what is likely to alienate him: above all, self-pity; but also all attempts to justify his own failure and any Romantic indictment of society or life or the order of the universe. And he does just that: he takes all the blame on himself and he holds self-pity at bay by the tone of his narration, which ranges from the matter-of-fact, through a forced jauntiness (the forced note is, in the circumstances, an added touch of realism) and a wry irony, to Gogolian grotesquerie (for example, in the description of his partner in the mazurka). And he concentrates our interest by limiting the account of his life to three periods (two of them, short): his childhood, his love for Liza, and the twelve days preceding his death during which he sets down these reminiscences.

'Diary of a Superfluous Man' represents, as was said earlier, a reworking of the theme of 'A Hamlet of the Shchigry District'. That Hamlet was ruined by his Western education: Hegelian philosophy, the strains and stresses of his *kruzhok*, his travels abroad; Chulkaturin would seem to have been ruined by his home upbringing. The prim, unloving virtue of his mother and the affection, cut short by death, of his demoralized father evidently led to an emotional split in the child, comparable to the split produced in the Hamlet of Shchigry by the chasm separating the ideas and ideals of the West from the realities of Russian life. The result in both men is very similar: an emotional dislocation which unfits them for love and friendship.

The Hamlet of Shchigry was physically tougher: he managed to survive, if only by the skin of his teeth. Perhaps he was also tougher intellectually: he defined himself as 'an empty, insignificant and useless, unoriginal fellow';[17] and there is more substance to this than to the perhaps more glamorous but surely less meaningful 'superfluous man'. 'Unoriginal': that means he lacks personality, individuality, 'a smell of his own', as he says; and for a man imbued with Western values what greater humiliation could there be? 'Useless': that means he lacks a function in life, he is of no use to his fellows or to society; and for such a man what greater tragedy could there be? The other two epithets, 'empty' and 'insignificant' could be interpreted as mere doublets of 'useless' and 'unoriginal'; but might it not help to fill in the picture if they were referred respectively to his feeling and thinking: the emotional emptiness and the intellectual insignificance which made up his lack of individuality and his uselessness?

Chulkaturin analyses himself on a different level. He cannot fit in anywhere because he cannot relate to people because he is trapped inside himself. To understand how and why, we must consider the emotional development of the two heroes.

The Hamlet of Shchigry grew up malleable as wax: perhaps his mother's beatings had made him so. On this soft wax was stamped the culture of the West. The imprint remained, but the boy had never learned to love; so there was no vital emotion to set the seal of these values on his actions or personal relations.

With Chulkaturin the case was different. He had learned to love, but in head-on opposition to his values: 'Yes, I fought shy of my virtuous mother and passionately loved my wicked father.' The child was repelled by what he believed he should have loved and loved with all his heart what he believed he should have rejected. If both parents had lived, this split between heart and conscience would most likely have generated acute psychological conflicts, but what happened was perhaps even worse: the father died dramatically. His death not only marked the end of the boy's childhood and the loss of his home and his accustomed way of life; it not only left him without any source or object of love; but it branded on his consciousness the correlation: the object of love is not only unworthy, it is simply not viable.

At this point he abandoned the attempt to identify with his father (who had been a man of outgoing affections and strong impulses, so that the boy's passionate love had reflected his father's disposition) and fell back on an identification with his mother: not in her surface attitudes and activity, but in the self-love which formed the core of her being. So patterning himself on her, he grew up incapable of spontaneity and of disinterested love. Not only so; but because his later character resulted from a trauma which had arrested him in one line of development and violently switched him to a quite different direction he was equally incapable of taking up an integrated and honest attitude to his own self-love.

Thus it is that he finds himself the odd man out in the quartet that occupies the central period of the story. Two of the four characters are emotionally whole and adult: they are more concerned to give than to take; their love is single-hearted and unafraid, and so – though it is not mutual – they can unite to comfort each other. The third person in the imbroglio, the Prince, is as self-centred as Chulkaturin, but his self-love is simple and honest, and so he can take his fill of pleasure and move on, unscathed, 'to fresh fields and pastures new'. But Chulkaturin is equally incapable of selfless love, such as Bizmënkov's (or Liza's), and of coming to terms with his own egoism, and so – alone of the four – he emerges from the drama shamed and shattered.

What distinguishes Chulkaturin's egoism from that of the Prince is not merely his tortuous attitude to himself. The boy who had loved his father passionately was not dead in him, but only repressed. It was not inconceivable that in favourable circumstances that boy might have re-emerged and re-established himself, as is evident from the way Chulkaturin thaws into happiness in the three sunny weeks preceding the Prince's appearance. And when the Prince departs, Chulkaturin is in no doubt that he wants to marry Liza and make her happy: which, in that day and age, bespeaks a strong attachment.

But whereas Bizmënkov wants to marry Liza because for him love means giving and doing whatever the beloved needs – so that to propose to her is the obvious and only thing to do – Chulkaturin looks at the situation with a divided vision, his own and the world's (or his father's and his mother's), and from the latter point of view he admires himself, and expects admiration, for ignoring the scandal and flouting convention. For both men, marrying Liza represents, not happiness, since her heart is given to another and may remain so indefinitely, but the next best thing to happiness, the nearest they are likely to come. Bizmënkov recognizes this and, because he loves her, accepts it with gratitude; Chulkaturin too recognizes it but, because he loves himself also, expects her gratitude.

Of course, by this time he had already lost her in any case. The duel had made him hateful to her and, as he learns at the last, had actually broken down her reserve and given her to the Prince. Again it is left to the reader to feel the full force of this poetic irony: Chulkaturin seems hardly to have taken it in at the time, or even later, when he came to write down his story.

What he has grasped – what he does understand and feel with shuddering immediacy – is that he is dying, that his hours are counted, that life is over and that he has proved incapable of winning any of its gifts or enriching it by any contribution of his own. He can only look around him with yearning: what he can still see but will soon be lost to his sight for ever has become dear to him, now, when it is too late. Still divided against himself to the end, he can neither accept nor rebel. In fact, he is not even left with the last word. That is given to some unknown illiterate, who rounds off the melancholy record with his solemn disapproval.

'Journey into the Woodland'

In the summer of 1853 Turgenev wrote to a friend: 'It is time to
retire the peasants (*pora muzhikov v otstavku*)';[18] and that actually
marks the end of his literary involvement with serfdom. But four
years later, after four more studies of the superfluous man and his
first novel with its superfluous hero, Turgenev wrote 'Journey into
the Woodland',[19] in which he appears to combine the two distinct
lines of his stories of the early 1850s: portraits of peasants and
studies of the superfluous man. Indeed, at first glance, we might
fancy ourselves even farther back: in the world of *A Sportsman's
Sketches*. The scale of the story is the same; the incidents appear to
match those of earlier sporting expeditions; and the contrasting
portraits of the two peasants, Egor and Efrem, might recall those
of, for instance, Khor' and Kalinych. Turgenev himself succumbed
briefly to this illusion and included 'Journey' in the 1860 edition of
A Sportsman's Sketches; but he removed it from the later editions.
Why?

Because this is in fact a different world, with denizens of a different sort, viewed by a different eye. The narrator of the *Sketches* was
a semi-transparent observer and catalyst of other people's attitudes
and views. The narrator of 'Journey' has assumed the opacity and
the shape of a recognizable superfluous man. Then, among the serfs
of the *Sketches* there *was* room for individuality and even singularity,[20] but hardly for the kind of individualism that, like Efrem's,
tramples on law and preys upon society. Some readers may object,
'What about the Bailiff?' Sofron *is* an individualist (of sorts), but
hardly an individual; and he certainly preys on his fellows; but he
does so under the cloak of his master's authority, not as his own
man. Thirdly, and above all, nature, which, in the *Sketches*, framed
the lives of men in beauty and formed a source of lyric inspiration
for the narrator, has, in 'Journey', become a problem: an awe-
inspiring and terrifying problem.

The loveliness and endless variety of nature gives place in the
Woodland to a vast, sombre uniformity. In face of this immense,
voiceless, changeless gloom Man is dwarfed, frozen, overwhelmed
by the sense of his isolation, his impotence, his insignificance. His
past rises before him, futile and null, arousing only regret and bewilderment. It is too late for love and joy and hope. All that remains
for the heart is to disown them and forget.

That, at any rate, is how the problem of Man's relation to nature, to the order of the universe, presents itself to the narrator on the second[21] day. On the following, the final, day, he receives a revelation which he interprets as an answer to that problem. It is an answer that re-echoes the ancient Greek precept μηδὲν ἄγαν: Nothing in excess! There is a norm of health, characterized by balance and restraint; whatever exceeds or falls short of that golden mean is cast out by nature as unfit, worthless. Death is the price the insect pays for the ecstasy of its nuptial flight. The sick beast hides away from light and life, recognizing that it has lost the right to live. When humans suffer, the least they can do is keep silent.

Because this 'philosophy' is symbolized in the story by the mild and temperate forest fire, critics have been tempted to equate it with the author's own philosophy and/or to present it as his 'message' to the reader. But this is to overlook both the ambivalences of Turgenev – as man and as artist – and the intellectual inadequacies of the 'philosophy'.

As a man, Turgenev was averse to all systems;[22] and the indecisiveness that characterized his life is matched by the scepticism and ambiguity that informs the best of his art. The 'philosophy' that is revealed to the narrator is valid for him. But for Turgenev it can be valid, at most, only conditionally and partially. It represents an attitude to which he was prone in his phases of melancholy, an attitude corresponding to one basic aspect of his temperament; but it does not represent a creed embodying, or compatible with, all his ultimate values. To look no farther, it is incompatible with the cult of Don Quixote. More generally, love and art, human personality and dignity and freedom, which are among Turgenev's major values, are irreconcilable with passive resignation or inert surrender to the flow of time and change. The spirit of Chertopkhanov, the music of Lemm, the hearts of his most cherished heroines know nothing of any golden mean. And the limitations of the doctrine's validity are to be found within the story itself.

Not to mention that intellectually it leaves a good deal to be desired. Leaving aside its unargued assumption that man is on a level with all nature's other creatures – that his mind and skills do not differentiate him from other forms of life in kind rather than merely in degree – it is evident that the aspect of nature here presented as normative is only one among conflicting and contradictory others. Even forest fires may lay waste vast areas: like other such operations of nature as earthquakes, floods, hurricanes and volcanic eruptions, they do not appear to have heard of Aristotle. And on top of her physical cataclysms come her biological excesses: monsters and plagues.

Turgenev seems to ignore such intellectual objections; but for the attentive reader he redresses the balance artistically. 'Journey into the Woodland' introduces to us not one personage but four. The four can be seen as two doubly contrasted pairs: that is, the contrasts obtain not only between the two pairs but within each pair. On the one hand we have a pair of average or ordinary men, Kondrat and the narrator, set over against an extraordinary pair, Egor and Efrem. Yet what, except ordinariness, has young, carefree, cheerful Kondrat in common with the much older, anxious, dejected narrator? And what, except extraordinariness, has Egor, the virtuous stoic, in common with Efrem, the predatory epicurean? It might well be contended that a more fundamental affinity links Kondrat to Egor, as whole men, over against the split natures of the narrator and Efrem.

We can confirm this in their respective attitudes to life (or nature). Kondrat, as an average healthy young man, has been treated kindly by life and so has no reason not to be satisfied with nature, enjoying all she offers him. Egor has set himself apart from his fellow peasants and courted ruin in embracing a hunter's life, and has been punished accordingly: by the sickness of his wife, the death of his children, the dwindling of his prosperity. But as a whole man, an unflawed spirit, he accepts his lot without repining.

The sportsman-narrator has also been punished by life (or nature): not for being extraordinary but for being divided against himself. He had had a heart and mind capable of generous dreams, but had lacked the energy and courage to translate them into realities. And, being split, he cannot take his punishment as Egor does: he is as divided in his reaction to it as in everything else. One part of him admires, and would wish to emulate, Egor's acceptance (' "This man has learned not to complain", I thought'); the other part gives itself up to such tearful lamentations as he pours forth when left by himself on the second day. And from his anguished sense of wasted time and waiting death he seeks escape: immediately, by abandoning himself to the guidance of a stronger spirit (' "Let's go, you lead me" '), later by excogitating a 'philosophy' as fragile as the life of the ephemeral insect to which he owes it. A mere change of landscape and of light has sufficed to convert his dread and self-condemnation into a sense of ease and self-satisfaction at having 'solved' the sphinx's riddle. One might think that such infantile mutability would, by itself, suffice to disqualify the narrator for the rôle of sage or dispenser of wisdom.

The split in Efrem is of a quite different kind: not emotional or volitive, but perhaps intellectual. He is integrated in relation to himself and to nature, divided in relation to his society, towards which he takes it upon himself to play what to most minds would seem conflicting parts. As a member of the village community, he compels liking by his genial hospitality and respect or admiration by his wisdom in council; as a prowling outsider, he provokes resentment by his depredations at the same time as he inspires awe verging on terror by his overpowering personality and his singular abilities, which are believed to include a quota of magic. It is noteworthy that this duality of rôles and objectives has not impaired Efrem's judgment in the slightest: he knows exactly how far he can go in the exploitation of his fellows without tipping the balance of their fear and resentment to danger point. Thus, he respects their superstitions about wild bees' honey, while raiding their guarded hives, and, in general, he makes free with their property while refraining from violence against their persons. His primary urge is to excel or dominate in every field: so, instead of submitting meekly to nature, he harnesses her to his needs – as when he teaches Kondrat how to keep dry in the rain or when, with a word, he stops Kondrat's horses in defiance of their driver.

The rôles which these four men play in life differ in correlation with their differing attitudes to life. Kondrat has uncritically accepted a simply conventional part and has, so far, filled it adequately. The narrator has dreamed up for himself a part, or parts, which he has proved incapable of filling. Egor has *chosen* an *un*conventional rôle and sustains it with dignity in spite of reverses and tribulations. Efrem has cast himself in two singular, and contradictory, rôles, and contrives to distinguish himself in both.

How each man plays out his rôle is a measure of his spirit or courage. Kondrat's has not yet been tested, but he will probably stand up to everyday trials with ordinary patience. Egor has endured 'the whips and scorns of time' with stoic fortitude and has remained true to himself. But the narrator's heart has failed him; and the root of his defeat, as of Efrem's triumphs, is epitomized in the four words of Efrem's challenging motto: '*orobel – propal, smel – s"el*' (approximately: 'scared – you're dead, dare – you've won').[23]

So the 'philosophy' propounded by the narrator, and practised by Egor, is irrelevant to Kondrat and invalid for Efrem.[24] Nor, surely, does the narrator represent the highest of the four human types in the story. Does it even make sense to attempt to *grade* the four on a scale of higher and lower? Wouldn't Turgenev want us free to identify with any, or none, of them, or perhaps, better still, to some extent with all?

Traditional readings of 'Journey' have tended to concentrate on the narrator and his 'message': this involves missing many of the story's most interesting elements.

6

Love and the superfluous man

In the decade from 1843 to 1852, superfluous men, or forerunners of the type, appear in only six of Turgenev's literary works (poems, plays, sketches and stories). In only two of the six is the superfluous man indisputably a protagonist, and only in the last of them does the type receive a name. It was only gradually that the type took shape: the earlier specimens are sketched rather than portrayed; but by 1850 we have two portraits in depth: of Rakitin and Chulkaturin. In Turgenev's second creative decade (1853–62) we have a series of studies of superfluous men and their unavailing struggles to make good in life and in love (love being the key to life, a necessary condition for living in any significant sense). This forms the main theme of all the stories of these years; in the novels (to be considered in later chapters), which occupy the greater part of the decade, the superfluous man soon surrenders the centre of the stage to figures more capable of keeping their heads above water or even of making a mark on their immediate surroundings. It may be doubted whether such greater effectiveness was due to the emergence of stronger characters on the social scene in the wake of Nicholas I's death in 1855, or whether former superfluous men, no longer paralysed by the incubus of 'censorship Terror' and intensified repression, now found themselves able to breathe and move and even work. Probably, in the run-up to the Emancipation of the Serfs and the reforms that followed it, both things happened.

It will be recalled that this decade, which was to culminate in the realization of Turgenev's dream of ending serfdom, was also the unhappiest in his relation with Pauline Viardot. The unhappiness was channelled chiefly into the stories; the growing hope and relief and final exultation found modulated expression in the novels.

'Two Friends'

It is a far cry from the painful, probing self-portrayal of Chulkaturin to the light-hearted sketch of Vyazovnin in 'Two Friends'.[1] The critical reader might even be inclined to question whether Vyazovnin deserves the title of – justifies classification as a – superfluous man. Admittedly, he is one who can find no place in his society; he is superior to it at least in culture; and he appears to be crippled both emotionally and in capacity for action. But what has become of the sensibility and self-consciousness, the sense of being a misfit and the accompanying unease that characterize most avatars of the superfluous man? Doesn't this young man show an unmistakable streak of self-satisfaction which should set him apart from the rest of the fraternity?

Such objections deserve serious consideration, but may not be decisive. First, there is something of the dandy in Vyazovnin; and the dandies of the 1820s – the Chatskis and the Onegins – were still able to direct their critical faculties outward rather than inward; perhaps Vyazovnin is a throwback in that respect. Secondly, Vyazovnin is seen largely, if not entirely, from the outside: which is why 'Two Friends' may properly be called a sketch rather than a portrait; but that means that our view of what goes on inside him must miss a great deal. Thirdly, his boredom and restlessness are obvious symptoms of *malaise*. And if he has no inkling of the causes of this condition – what else could be expected of a man who is so strikingly incapable of understanding himself?

Chulkaturin had defined himself as 'a superfluous man with a little lock inside him [*chelovek lishni i s zamochkom vnutri*]'. That 'little lock' blocks his communicating his thoughts and feelings to other people; it does not hinder his access to those thoughts and feelings; he has no difficulty in confiding them to his diary. Whereas Vyazovnin doesn't know what to do with himself – because he doesn't know either what he is or even what he wants.

Left to himself, he might have continued to kill time on his estate to the end of his days. But his well-intentioned friend sees him as too good to be wasted so, as needing to be saved from himself and given an interest and an occupation, and, since Vyazovnin rules out a return to State service, prescribes marriage. Vyazovnin is not aware of any need or desire to be married, but he is willing to marry, to gratify his friend ('I am doing this only for you': dramatic irony indeed), provided his friend will shoulder the task of finding him a suitable wife.

If Vyazovnin almost never knows what he wants (he thinks he wants to marry Vera, but that turns out to have been a mistake or an illusion), he does usually know what he doesn't want: he is determined not to re-enter State service; he will marry to please his friend Krupitsyn, but he will not accept Krupitsyn's choice of bride; and ultimately he will not remain married to Vera. That is, his negative inclinations are strong enough to impinge on his consciousness, while his positive inclinations or velleities are not: that he actually had an unconscious wish to be married is revealed by his insistence that the search for a bride shall go on when Krupitsyn, discouraged by the results of their first two visits, wants to give it up; and he recognizes that he 'loves' Vera only when Krupitsyn demonstrates that he must be in love because he is jealous.

Vyazovnin no more knows what he is than he knows what he wants, as is shown in the dialogue with Vera's father when he asks for her hand in marriage: 'I am a man of honour, Stepan Petrovich, [. . .] I can vouch for that – and I love your daughter [. . .] I love her and I will do my best to deserve her love.' In fact Vyazovnin makes no effort to deserve his wife's love; he is bored with his marriage, though he had assured the old man that that would never happen; and his dallying in Paris proves that he is not a man of honour.

The portrait of Vyazovnin is inset in a good-humoured, only mildly satirical picture of gentry life in the wilds of Central Russia. Turgenev finds it difficult not to be spiteful in his depiction of widows and old maids, and the friends' first two visits have a faintly Gogolian tinge, but Vera and her father are delightful and their visitors are sheer fun. Krupitsyn, the rough diamond with a heart of gold, who inherits the happiness that Vyazovnin has thrown away, is an intriguing mixture of clearsightedness and obtuseness. It turns out that he was the man made for marriage and he was evidently wrong to urge marriage on his friend: marriage had almost killed the Hamlet of Shchigry and it kills – the attempt to escape from it kills – Vyazovnin. And if Vyazovnin could not be happy with Vera, with what sort of wife could he have been happy? Krupitsyn was probably right in deciding that the widow would not do, and wrong to be taken in by the old maids. He was right in opposing a marriage between Vyazovnin and Vera, but his acumen there may be due to his being already in love with her himself, without realizing it.

A cynic might say that 'Two Friends' has the nearest approach to a happy ending of any of Turgenev's stories so far. Nor would this be mere cynicism. Vyazovnin was no more viable than Chulkaturin. No doubt, he would not have chosen to die far from home, in a senseless quarrel, at the hands of a foreign duellist; but he had gone seeking adventure, if not trouble, and if he had lived, he would have destroyed Vera (as the Hamlet of Shchigry destroyed his wife), and quite possibly himself too, in a protracted and more painful, perhaps degrading, struggle.

'A Backwater'

In 'A Backwater',[2] written a few months after 'Two Friends', Turgenev attempts a fresh approach to the superfluous man, to his inability to enter into or maintain close personal relationships and the consequences of this for the women with whom he became involved.

The social setting is the same as in 'Two Friends' and viewed with the same humorous, or only mildly satirical, eye. Veret'ev, like his fictional predecessors, is the odd man out, but he differs from them in temperament, attitudes and circumstances. He is apparently younger than the Hamlet of Shchigry (though we are not told the Hamlet's age), and certainly older than Vyazovnin and Chulkaturin. Unlike those three, who are alone in the world, he has a sister to whom he is deeply attached. There is nothing in Veret'ev of the embittered exasperation of the Hamlet or the timid awkwardness of Chulkaturin or the prim complacency of Vyazovnin. Unlike any of them, he is a social being – outgoing, good-humoured, popular – the centre, if not the leader, in any group. Hamlet and Chulkaturin scrutinize themselves unsparingly and know themselves well; Vyazovnin is not introspective, yet imagines he knows himself – and is mistaken; Veret'ev does not want to know himself: he refuses to recognize his drinking problem or discuss its causes.

Unfortunately, these remain an enigma not only to him and to those around him, but to the reader too. Why has a man like Veret'ev taken to drink so young? Why do his capitulation to the habit and his abandonment of Masha coincide with his sister's marriage? Why does he let his attractive and intelligent sister throw herself away on a man like Stel'chinski? These are questions which readers can hardly fail to ask; but the author provides no clue to any answers.

One might suspect that the story is broken-backed because Turgenev failed to choose a viable viewpoint. On the face of it, 'A Backwater' may appear to be told by an omniscient author; actually, it was constructed to pivot on Astakhov: he is not the narrator, but the story starts with him, moves with him, and tells us only what falls within his purview – with one exception. The exception is chapter IV, which describes the dawn tryst of Veret'ev and Masha; but that chapter – incredible though this must seem – formed no part of the story as originally published in *The Contemporary*: it was added only when, in the light of the initial critical reactions, Turgenev came to rework the story for the 1856 edition of his fiction.

Even so, not much less than before is left to the reader's imagination. The fourth chapter has no bearing on the puzzles of Veret'ev's drinking or his sister's marriage or the relation (if any) between these happenings. All it does supply is a glimpse of the relationship between Veret'ev and Masha – which could only be inferred from the rest of the text.

'A Backwater' is the first Turgenev story in which the superfluous man shares the reader's (and author's) interest with the heroine and her feelings. In 'The Hamlet of the Shchigry District' the wife is a pale shadow, stricken by some wasting disease of the emotions, who dies just in time to save her husband from committing suicide: he cannot decide whether he ever loved her; she believed she loved him and he thinks that may have been true; but neither could find response or fulfilment in the other. In 'The Diary of a Superfluous Man', the protagonist is not loved by the heroine and her love (for the Prince) is told of, not shown. In 'Two Friends' it is not clear that Vera ever loves Vyazovnin, though she likes him and marries him willingly. But Masha is in love – passionately in love – with her superfluous man.

Masha is a rather 'unfeminine' girl (that is, unfeminine as perceived by the original readers), and her love is of a kind that Turgenev more often depicts in men. It is a love that enslaves and/or destroys the lover; 'destroys' may mean 'kills', or it may mean – particularly in reference to a man – 'degrades': as we saw in Petushkov and heard from Rakitin.

Love opens Masha's heart to poetry, to which it had always been closed. She had rejected it as 'untrue'; but Pushkin's lyric reveals her to herself, opens her eyes to the truth about her love, shows it to her as enslavement.

She makes a supreme effort to arrest Veret'ev's downward drift, to save him from himself – even at the cost of letting him understand that she loves him and will be his slave – if he will free himself from his bondage to drink. But she finds it is too late. Veret'ev's natural vitality has been sapped or frittered away, and drink has become the substitute which alone enables him to maintain as a façade the semblance of what he had once been. What she encounters now is not love, but a yearning for love – and emotional impotence: he will try to do anything she wants – except give up his vodka.

And so she kills herself. Veret'ev remarks during their last meeting that he loves the way she continually flushes while speaking, as her pride struggles with her modesty.[3] Both that pride and that modesty must have been outraged by the realization that she had been reduced to becoming the slave of a man who did not deserve her respect. She thought she could not live with herself in that condition – only to find out as she drew her last breath that in that belief too she had been mistaken.

Veret'ev lives on, having lost everything – his love, his sister, his health, no doubt his self-respect – everything except his clearsightedness and his memories. Fallen as he is, he can still look down on and jeer at Astakhov; coarsened as he is, he can still shudder at an allusion to Masha's suicide. He had fulfilled her prophecy: he had 'jested his life away'. But it was a very bitter jest.

'A Correspondence'

'A Correspondence'[4] presents a new variation on the now familiar theme of the collapse of a superfluous man and the tragedy of the woman with whom he seeks a relationship. This is one of Turgenev's more admirable stories, even if the artistry of the construction is not quite matched in subtlety by the exposition. There is a beautiful economy in the fifteen letters, where even the dates are used to cast light on the state of mind of the correspondents (except in the last two letters, dated years after the others and forming a sort of epilogue): the longer intervals – fifteen to eighteen days –

imply hesitation or conflicts of feeling; the normal interval is about eight days; and the one letter written after only four days (no. x) marks the breaking of the emotional ice, as Aleksei Petrovich is carried away to the point of assuming the part of consoler and guide. And the spotlighting of the two correspondents, who form the whole cast – no other person is more than mentioned – achieves a concentration of interest and allows a range of self-revelation remarkable in so short a story. If in contrast with this delicacy of touch, the generalizations about the nature of the Russian man and the predicament of the Russian girl – meaning the better-educated and more thoughtful men and women of Turgenev's class and generation – seem a little heavy, this can be defended as being in character: it is not for nothing that the protagonists are labelled or label themselves 'philosophers'.

The story took ten years to write. It was begun in 1844, in the aftermath of Turgenev's involvement with Tat'yana Bakunina; the letters remain dated 1840–2, that is, they overlap the period of that involvement; Mar'ya Aleksandrovna is 26, which was Bakunina's age when Turgenev first met her; and the central letters (vii–x) might be seen as an act of reparation, whether or not intentional. If she falls in love with her correspondent, the responsibility for that is placed squarely on him.

There is a recognizable difference in the language of the two self-portraits. A man can describe his feelings directly; maiden modesty forbids a woman to simply imitate him. She begins by generalizing her experience: not this or that happened to her, but this is what happens to Russian girls. In the following letter she offers an account – not of her feelings but of her situation, the circumstances in which she lives and her attitude towards them. Only in a third letter, after he has shown signs of a warmly personal feeling for her, does she venture one or two allusions to feelings of her own.

Mar'ya Aleksandrovna is a romantic dreamer marooned in a world of grey prose, of petty obtuseness. Her neighbours deride her artistic and intellectual interests; her mother resents her failure to marry; her uncle preaches domesticity and motherhood as woman's manifest destiny. But though she envies the dull married happiness of her elder sister, she cannot bring herself to renounce her ideals: she will not marry without love and she cannot love a man unless she can respect him.

However, if we compare her theory with her practice, must we not feel a certain uneasiness? She had fallen in love with Aleksei's cousin whom she had known long and well, and she is evidently ready to fall in love with Aleksei when their correspondence is cut short. Though we hear very little about cousin 'Théodore' – does that little inspire us with respect (he had behaved much like Turgenev with Bakunina)? Aleksei we come to know intimately; how much respect does that intimacy engender?

Of the local suitors we get only glimpses through the prejudiced eyes of the young lady: is it evident that neither of those men could have made a better husband than the two men to whom she is attracted? But in that case, are we not entitled to wonder if Mar'ya is the kind of girl who will repeatedly fall in love with men who cannot or will not marry her while repeatedly rejecting men who want to marry her and seem to have the makings of a good husband? Is she debarred from marrying, as she thinks, by a system of living values – or by an unconscious incapacity for real and lasting emotional intimacy? Turgenev does not pose the question in those terms – either to us or, probably (at the conscious level), to himself; but, as usual, he shows us enough to prevent the reflective reader from seeing Mar'ya as she sees herself – or as she makes Aleksei see her. Not to mention that Aleksei's later history can be seen as an answer – not necessarily the only one or the best – to her questions about life.

The case of Aleksei is in some respects clearer, in others, more intriguing. Here is a man simultaneously self-absorbed (as he himself stresses in letters III and VI) and self-alienated – to a point where he completely misunderstands himself. To measure how completely, it is only necessary to compare his self-characterization in the third letter with his relation to his dancer as depicted in the fifteenth. In letter III he credits himself with a capacity for, and love of, fantasy, with cool blood, indolence and pride; in his relation with his dancer we see him incapable of even a momentary illusion in her favour and reduced by his passion to a spate of activity and the swallowing of every kind of humiliation.

His incapacity for personal relations is manifested successively in three contexts. A couple of years before the first of these letters, he had become involved with Mar'ya's sister (at the same time as his cousin was courting Mar'ya), but had quickly broken with her. From the evidently conventional yet promising marriage on which she embarks during the correspondence (letter XIII) one might infer that she was a more 'ordinary' – or less uncompromising – girl than Mar'ya.

Having recovered from that first experiment, he seeks to involve himself with Mar'ya, a romantic idealist, such as he believes himself to be. He is (again it is he who tells us so) lonely and bored and very sorry for himself. Boredom and self-pity may seem a fragile foundation for an enduring love; but here is a sensitive, unhappy young woman prepared to confide in him and believe in him and be guided by him – and insensibly he gravitates towards her. Yet so sluggish is the pull of the spirit that it needs the jolt of his friend's letter from Naples, with its picture of earthy love and joy, to screw him to the sticking-point of deciding to revisit Mar'ya.

If he had gone to her – what would have happened? Most probably, another summer like the earlier one: long walks and talks, verses and sighs, perhaps another engagement – which might (or might not) have lasted as long as the first.

But what supervenes in fact is the love that enslaves and destroys. It is not a feeling rooted in any shared values, whether moral, aesthetic or intellectual: indeed, it is not rooted in any conscious layer of the victim's personality. It is redolent of the fatality of tragedy, of the philtres and spells of romance. We are put in mind of Phaedra, of Tannhäuser.

Generalizing from his own experience, Aleksei defines love – not a certain sort of love but all love – as a disease rather than a feeling: though it may wear various aspects, it admits of neither doubt nor evasion, but takes possession of a man – suddenly, against his will, like a fever, like cholera (of which Turgenev had a particular dread all his life), or as a kite swoops down on a chick and carries it off in its claws in spite of all the victim's struggles. There is no equality in love, no free union of souls – none of the ideal attitudes excogitated by German philosophers for want of anything better to do. In love the lover is a slave, the beloved his master: love is the most crushing kind of bondage. [Contrary to the teachings of Idealist philosophy], life cannot be directed, nor predicted, nor understood; and no man can know himself.

Such a creed would seem, surely, to leave no room for philosophy of any kind – yet more than one-quarter of Aleksei's last, long letter is filled with philosophizing; and in his very last paragraph, he, who had succeeded in nothing, achieved nothing, produced nothing – has no hesitation about instructing Mar'ya how to live the rest of her life. As might be expected, his directions are neither original nor cheerful: ask nothing of life, accept what it offers; go forward while you may; when your legs give way, sit down by the roadside and watch others go by – without envy or resentment, for they will not go much farther. Inconsistent to the last, he grafts an injunction to go forward upon a philosophy of resignation; if one is to ask nothing of life, why go anywhere? He had striven to understand himself – only to stagger from illusion to illusion; he had struggled to understand life (instead of living it), and life had turned him into an incarnate refutation of his thesis that 'the chief purpose in life is human dignity'.

'Yakov Pasynkov'

Turgenev's next story, 'Yakov Pasynkov'[5] has for its hero an idealist – a Schillerian idealist in the tradition of Stankevich's circle. Many features of the portrait are said to be borrowed from Belinsky; but Pasynkov is a 'mute, inglorious' Belinsky, with no new word to speak to his generation.

The story is, as so often in Turgenev, a wry comment on the absurdity of life. Love is in every case misdirected: at best to an unresponsive, at worst to an unworthy object. Pasynkov and the narrator both love Sof'ya, who loves Asanov, who is seen at first as a hollow man – vain, indiscreet, incontinent – and at last as a vicious one. Pasynkov is loved by Varvara, whom he doesn't notice, and by Masha, who would probably always have remained a child in his sight and whom, in any case, he doesn't live long enough to marry.

A subdued symbolism can be detected in some aspects of the story. Pasynkov's difficulties in obtaining regular documents could be symbolic of his struggles to secure a foothold in life and in society. He dies of an arrow-wound: arrows are the traditional weapons of Eros, the god of love. Several of the names too have symbolic overtones. Probably not Asanov: although *ásán* in Persian means 'easy' and Asanov was assuredly one who tended to take the easy course or way of least resistance, there is no evidence that Turgenev knew any Persian. It is known, however, that in general he gave considerable thought to the naming of his characters and he was bound to know that Sof'ya (Sophia) meant 'wisdom'. Wisdom can hardly be predicated of Sof'ya's choice of a

mate, but we may believe that Turgenev saw a fundamental wisdom
in the way she accepted all the consequences of her choice: in her
loyalty to her husband, her obviously warm and good relation with
her child, and the philosophy of duty which she has evolved to
shape and direct her married life. As a young girl, she had taken her
own desires and purposes as the law of her being; in her maturity
she has come to see salvation in submitting her desires and
purposes to a higher law. The constant through both the earlier and
the later part of the story is her strength of character, of will; but
there has been a dramatic *peripeteia* (reversal) in the direction of
that will.

Both the protagonist's names can be interpreted as symbolic.
Yakov (Jacob) was the hero who wrestled all night with the angel
and remained lame for life; so Pasynkov wrestles with his love and
carries the mark to his grave. As the poet says:

> Quiconque aima jamais porte une cicatrice;
> Chacun l'a dans le sein, toujours prête à s'ouvrir:
> Chacun la garde en soi, cher et secret supplice,
> Et mieux il est frappé, moins il en veut guérir.[6]

'Pasynkov' derives from *pasynok* – stepson; and surely Pasynkov
has reason to regard life as a stepmother. Not for nothing has he
chosen resignation as his watchword. Motherless, abandoned by
his father, brought up on charity, looked down on by his school-
fellows, he grows up without losing his native sweetness of disposition, but withdrawing the best of himself into the ideal world of
poetry. He lives for and by the ideals of that world – above all, for
love and friendship. In their service he thinks nothing of himself: he
saves his friend from a duel and the girl whom he secretly loves
from scandal; he undertakes the education of the waif Masha and
for a time transforms her world with his affection.

For himself Pasynkov may have achieved nothing in life; but he
diffuses warmth and light, and leaves a grateful memory in the
hearts of the few people who have meant most to him or to whom
he has meant most. If he dreamed his life away, his dreams
enriched the lives of others.

It may be questioned whether Pasynkov can properly be
numbered among the superfluous men. The narrator repeatedly
defines him as a Romantic – the last Romantic – and he does appear
to lack what many would regard as a basic characteristic of the

superfluous man: egoism. It is a distinction worth making: Schillerian idealists are not to be simply equated with superfluous men, though there are certainly close affinities between the two types. They are perhaps equally ill-adapted to life in their society and so cannot fit in; they live largely in an ideal world of their own, which is tantamount to rejecting the everyday world; they are generally superior to most of their social peers in culture and sensitivity. Sociologists may dispute whether all this adds up to a sub-type of superfluous man or to a separate species.

As one illustration of the gradation, we see the resignation, preached as mere practical wisdom by Aleksei Petrovich in the last letter of 'A Correspondence' – developed into a moral philosophy by Pasynkov: the protagonist of Schiller's poem 'Resignation' had renounced earthly happiness in the hope of bliss hereafter, only to learn that that hope had been its own reward – there would be no other. But the 'practical wisdom' and the 'philosophy' appear almost equally nebulous: Aleksei never explains – no doubt he doesn't know – what he means by 'go forward'; and it is never clear what Pasynkov has renounced that he could have had.

'Faust'

Later in that year, 1855, Turgenev completed his first novel, *Rudin*, but the novels will be considered in subsequent chapters. His next story, 'Faust', was composed and published in 1856. In his student days in Berlin he had been exposed to the cult of Goethe, and it is quite possible that at that time he, like the protagonist of this story, had known the masterpiece by heart. He had translated into Russian the last scene of the first part of *Faust*; and it will be recalled that in 1845 he had reviewed at length a Russian translation of *Faust*, defending Goethe as a great poet against the extra-literary strictures of his radical contemporaries.

Turgenev's utilization in his works of great figures from foreign literatures such as Hamlet and Faust, Don Quixote and Lear has yet to be studied in depth. He himself was, of course, not a specialist in English or Spanish or even German literature; he drew on works he had read and reread and loved, but as one great writer can draw on another: for his own purposes. The primary justification of the title of this story is that its catastrophe hinges on a reading of Goethe's *Faust*. There are also situational analogies. But to seek to see in the protagonists of 'Faust' Goethe's Faust and Gretchen is like seeking to see in the superfluous man the Renaissance Prince Hamlet. If 'there is nothing new under the sun' and if 'all things are in thoroughgoing interaction', no doubt there must be some connections; the question is: at what level of abstraction?

Although the story is told in letters, it is not another correspondence but an *Ich-Erzählung*: the letters are all written by the protagonist; the responses of the addressee are only occasionally alluded to.

Pavel Aleksandrovich is prematurely old at 35. He has obviously never been young. He has obviously never lived or loved (though he has, no doubt, imagined himself in love on occasion). But he loves nature: the trees and flowers with their colours and scents and, above all, the birds and their songs. In contrast with ever-youthful nature, his house is old and falling to pieces, and his servants have aged no less shockingly than he himself during the nine years' absence from which he has just returned.

His love of nature and his love of literature are compensations for his inability to relate to people. His ineptitude in personal relations is hinted in the allusion to his metropolitan valet, whom he had to get rid of because the knowing fellow made him feel inferior, and again when he reacts with fear to a carriage driving towards his home and the possibility of a visitor. His feelings are at best tepid, at worst bookish. He cannot record the death of a favourite dog in a letter to a friend without referring to Ulysses' faithful dog Argos; even at the age of 23, when he first met Vera, he could not fall in love with the girl – he could only entertain the hypothesis that it might be a good thing to marry her.

Like Onegin, Pavel Aleksandrovich 'was unable to fall in love when he should have and [. . .] hastened to fall in love when that had become a crime'.[7] Why so? He fails because of his basic half-heartedness, his emotional indeterminacy or asthenia; but with this there goes (as so often in life) what might be called an emotional curiosity, an urge towards fresh emotional experiences – or experiments. His return home has brought him face to face with all his past. It has made him poignantly aware how much of his life lies behind him – and how little it all amounts to. He senses that he has missed something – and that something, the most important thing in life.

Of course, he does not set out to fall in love with Vera at their second meeting, any more than at the earlier time. Indeed, the reader realizes what has happened (at latest when our hero starts resenting the too-frequent presence of the old German) well before Pavel Aleksandrovich does. But when Pavel Aleksandrovich does realize the truth, he makes just the same kind of mistake as he had made twelve years earlier. Then – at 23 – he had not had the strength of feeling or the firmness of purpose to stay and marry the girl; now he has neither the maturity of feeling nor the clarity of purpose to leave the woman in time.

Admittedly, to play Pygmalion – to awaken a sleeping heart or mind – is a tremendous temptation. It is an act of creation, to be ranged – like other creative acts – among the greatest joys man can aspire to. What if the dangers are commensurate with the joys, so that the case for self-denial ('*Entbehren sollst du, sollst entbehren*') is commensurate in strength with the temptation? None but a real hero will deny himself this – or any other – act of creation merely because he cannot be sure of his ability to shoulder the consequences and pay the price.[8]

But this hero's first blunder is crowned by a second. After Vera has told him she loves him, she asks what he intends to do, and he replies that he intends to do his duty as a man of honour – to go away. This, though less candid, is just as definite a petition in moral bankruptcy as Rudin's 'Submit, of course' in answer to a similar challenge.[9] At this point, the only honourable response would have been to start by finding out what Vera wanted him to do. No doubt, at an earlier stage, when he first found out he was in love, it would have been his duty as a man of honour to remove himself. But he had let that moment pass, he had failed to heed the voice of honour then; now he has no right to conjure up the phantom of an already flouted honour, to ward off Vera's needs and possible demands.

Needless to say, his reaction is appallingly in character. He is a man whose instinct before any trial is always to take refuge. From the prospect of marrying he had taken refuge in Germany and philosophy, from human relations he had sought refuge in nature, from life he had found refuge in literature. Now, from the challenge of Vera's love he seeks refuge in the word 'honour', just as, after the catastrophe, he will seek refuge from his guilt and regret in the preaching of duty – a purely abstract and notional duty, since he is evidently performing none and in the two years since Vera's death has not discovered any which it might be incumbent on him to perform.[10]

Vera is clearly an unusual girl – as unusual as her family history and her upbringing. The case of a girl growing up insulated from all stimuli to imagination and passion was apparently less singular then than it might seem today;[11] but the characters of Vera's grandparents and mother and the legacy of violent deaths and tragically disrupted lives must have set their special mark on her.

According to the narrator, she possesses no particular talents: perhaps because talent presupposes passion and/or imagination; that would seem to be confirmed by the discovery of her fine singing voice after her initiation. But she has grown up intelligent, candid and fearless. Intelligent enough to see through our hero at 16: 'I have the impression that B. is a good man but not to be relied on.' Candid enough to think aloud, whether waking or sleeping. Fearless enough to venture out belatedly into the world of imagination and passion which her mother had barred to her. And it is again the narrator who credits her with bright common sense, a penetration that belies her childlike inexperience, an instinct for truth and beauty and an understanding even of evil and absurdity.

It is usually difficult to understand why Turgenev's heroines should fall in love with his heroes. This is partly due to the fact that his heroes are so often his narrators and, as such, unable to give us a complete or unduly attractive picture of themselves. But Turgenev would presumably not have clung to this narrative technique if he had regarded falling in love as an intelligible phenomenon. It isn't and he doesn't. He has us exclaiming again and again, as we do in real life: 'What ever does she see in him?' Vera's falling in love is perhaps less startling than some other cases, since it is an immemorial tradition of myth and fairy-tale that the Sleeping Beauty must fall in love with the Prince whose kiss has awakened her.

Anyhow, we may suspect that Vera's love would have been doomed no less if Pavel Aleksandrovich had been a fairy-tale prince and not a superfluous man. For it was not for nothing that at 28 she had kept the face and body she had had at 16. It was not for nothing that her very daydreams were of arduous achievement amid the perilous wastes of the Sahara or the Arctic – typical adolescent daydreams – in stark contrast to her friend's banal fantasies of happiness in the guise of honeymooning in Venice. It was not for nothing that at home she continued to sit under her dead mother's portrait, so expressing symbolically, as well as acknowledging verbally, her desire to remain for ever under her mother's wing. And it was not for nothing that Pavel Aleksandrovich, gazing at that portrait, recognized that in attempting to 'emancipate' Vera he was challenging the dead woman to a duel.

We have here, in effect, a quite unusual triangle, in which the rival is not the husband (a mere lay figure) but the adored mother. Actually Vera is not so much her mother's daughter as her mother's creation. The gradual awakening of her own personality beneath the cold crust of her mother's indoctrination is traced out with delicate and precise brush-strokes: her tears after the reading of *Faust*, her sudden upsurge of tenderness towards her little girl next day (breaking the tradition in which she had been brought up and which she must have continued till then); her swings of mood and periodic attempts to plunge back into her former tenor of life; her singing to herself – and that song in particular: 'Rejoice in life'.

Vera believed in phantoms – evidently from experience: that is, she thought she had been visited by her mother's ghost even before Pavel Aleksandrovich re-entered her life. And as she had always blindly believed her mother's every word, she cannot but have believed her mother's definition of her: 'You are like ice: so long as you don't melt – solid[12] as stone; but melt – and there will be nothing left of you.' Yet this, surely, was a half-truth. Ice is not what Vera is – ice is the shell of her mother's teaching superimposed on her real personality. So when the ice began to melt, it was not Vera's personality that was breaking up; rather we might suppose that Vera's personality was being flooded by the melting ice in virtue of her belief in her mother's prophecy.

But the outcome was the same. Goethe's Gretchen, intending to put her mother to sleep, unwittingly kills her and dies to expiate her involuntary crime; Vera, seeking likewise to enjoy her love and evade her mother's interference, finds her way barred by her dead mother and dies to expiate her abortive rebellion.

Yet perhaps the balance between her thirst for life and her self-doubt was ultimately tipped not by the mother but by the lover. At 16, Vera had perceived that the man 'was not to be relied on'. That latent perception must have been revived, at least unconsciously, by his conduct in their last two meetings: first, he says he is leaving her (without consulting her wishes), next, he is

carried away by his excitement (without thought of the consequences for her). This explains why she identifies herself with
Gretchen – innocence betrayed – and him with Faust, the selfish
seducer: he too has profaned 'the holy place'.

'Asya'

'Asya',[13] though somewhat longer than 'Faust', is a lighter and
slighter tale. The narrator is young and flighty. The setting is
charming: Turgenev had enjoyed his stay at Sinzig, where he began
writing the story – and it flows, clear and sparkling as any woodland
stream on the neighbouring hills.

Asya's predicament as an illegitimate child was of painful interest
to Turgenev, since it was that of his own daughter, Paulinette. The
name, Asya, and some basic elements in the character of the
heroine are said to be drawn from a cousin of his, the illegitimate
daughter of his uncle Nikolai, who had been taken in charge and
brought up by Varvara Turgeneva. At the time the story was
written she was about 12; a couple of years later she married an
ex-serf, whose freedom had been bought by Turgenev not long
before. Some features of the heroine's biography are owed to
Paulinette, who in 1857 was 15: for instance, Gagin's conviction
that his half-sister could have no future in Russia and his con-
sequent decision to have her live abroad.

The Asya of the story is endowed with the essential moral
qualities of the 'Turgenev heroines' – honesty and courage in the
highest sense – and with the emotional disposition on which these
rest: singleheartedness. Such secondary characteristics as her 'unladylike' behaviour are attributable to the insecurity and resentments implanted in her by her birth and upbringing. The behaviour
is only an affectation designed to shock or intrigue or impress
strangers; it has no place in her relations with people who care for
her. But the insecurity is deep-rooted.

The narrator assumes that, but for this insecurity, his blunders at
their last meeting would not have proved irreparable. In this he
may be flattering himself: he is dodging the issue whether a girl like
Asya could possibly have remained satisfied with such a man as he
is. Gagin says that she needs an extraordinary man: either a hero or
a rustic shepherd: N. N. is obviously neither the one nor the other.
If Gagin is right in this, the heroic streak in Asya must be less

uncompromising than the heroic streak in Vera with her dreams of Arctic and Saharan adventure.

The narrator of 'Asya' may be seen as Pavel Aleksandrovich ten years younger than in 'Faust'. Several of Turgenev's love-stories, including 'Faust', 'Asya' and 'First Love', include a considerable amount of autobiographical material and their narrator-protagonist embodies some aspects of Turgenev's own personality at the ages, in these three stories, of 35, 25 and 16 respectively.

N. N. is, he tells us, healthy, young and cheerful, with plenty of money and no cares as yet, living for his own enjoyment. What he enjoys most is nature, in her less Romantic aspects, and human beings – human beings approached and regarded primarily as 'new faces'. The outward semblance of people is what interests him, but he tires of them quickly and keeps moving from place to place in quest of still newer faces.

He takes at once to Gagin, who is a young man rather like himself but warmer, less selfish, probably less well educated: although his admission that he had 'not studied properly' refers proximately to his art, it is reasonable, in view of his military schooling and career, to give it a wider meaning. He represents the type of happy-natured artist to which Turgenev will return in *On the Eve* (Shubin) and 'Song of Triumphant Love' (Fabio). What distinguishes him from those later figures is his dilettantism: they have it in them to become great masters, and do; Gagin has the gift but not the patience and self-discipline to develop and perfect it.[14] But, whatever his short-comings in culture and professionalism, Gagin as a human being – in his relations with other people – puts the narrator to shame, combining a shrewd eye for realities with a generous indulgence and showing a special considerateness and delicacy to those he is fond of: to his new friend no less than to his sister.

The narrator's first reaction to Asya is irritation. One might have expected his vanity to be tickled by her so obviously 'putting on an act' for his benefit. Instead, her pranksomeness alarms his timid conventionality; even later, when he has learned what lies behind it, he will say to himself: 'Marry a 17-year-old with her tempera-ment – how could I!' Gagin (rightly) assumes that N. N. will regard Asya's illegitimacy as an absolute bar to marriage; as Pisarev points out,[15] the tone and terms in which he explains and excuses his sister express not his own attitude but what he divines his new friend's attitude to be.

Once the narrator has understood Asya (as he thinks), he discards his disapproval; she is able to feel at ease and behave naturally; and he is, quite understandably, enchanted. That night, on the river, tears rise to his eyes and he defines the feeling behind them: 'a thirst for happiness flamed up in me'. Turgenev's heroes rarely know or understand themselves very well. N. N. does not suspect – even much later when he tells the story – that he may be constitutionally incapable of happiness.

Asya's first instinct, when she recognizes the nature of her feelings and that N. N. is not indifferent to her, is to run away. In terms of the prejudices and conventions of the time, that would have been reasonable; but her courage revolts against such a tame escape. Rather than let the chance of happiness go by default, she will face the risk of humiliation or worse: she summons N. N. to a tryst (as other Turgenev heroines had done and will do).

The tryst in 'Asya' provoked a good deal of controversy. Nekrasov and others felt that the hero's crassness was out of character; Annenkov and Chernyshevsky, from their very different points of view, contended that it was not.[16] They were certainly right. A weak man forced into a corner – forced to make choices or assume responsibilities – is quite likely to work himself into a rage, trying to shift the burden of blame from his own shoulders.

Pavel Aleksandrovich soon realized he was in love but took no appropriate action while there was time. N. N. took no appropriate action while there was time, and pleaded in his defence that he had not realized he was in love until it was too late. Rather than question whether N. N. was ever really in love – which would hinge on one's definition of 'in love' – it might be more useful to ask whether N. N. could ever have come to believe himself in love so long as there remained a possibility of having to prove it? Asya thought not – as her farewell note shows – and vanished from his life. She had grown the wings about which he could only babble; he had thrown away the momentary chance for which she had been ready to hazard her reputation and honour.

'First Love'

'First Love',[17] the culmination and crown of this series of love-stories, is, on Turgenev's own testimony, the most directly auto-biographical and goes back to an earlier period of his life than any

of the others. But 'autobiographical' does not mean it can be taken
as raw fact. We know that Turgenev was not an only child, and that
at the time of the story he was not 16 but 15; we do not know how
many other facts have been modified or adapted to the purposes of
art.

There is a piquant reversal of the Asya–N. N. theme in the
Vladimir–Zinaida theme. Vladimir is 16 to Asya's 17, Zinaida is 21
to N. N.'s 25; but in both stories – how rich and colourful are the
personalities of the girls, how wan and bloodless, in comparison,
those of the young men. Zinaida is, in the last resort, no kinder to
Vladimir than was N. N. to Asya; but her unkindness results from
the interaction of circumstances with her natural high spirits and
her deep-lying unhappiness; N. N.'s unkindness issues from
emotional shallowness and selfish timidity. Asya is no less carried
away by love, no less devoted, no less ready to sacrifice herself than
is Vladimir, but the backbone of her love is a self-respect that
demands an answering love and, failing to find that, she tears
herself away proudly and bravely from whatever substitute N. N.
might have sought to foist on her; Vladimir not only submits to
Zinaida's cat-and-mouse game, but abandons himself to it with all
the zest of an inveterate masochist, serves her blindly, and surrenders her without a murmur. Asya loves as a woman, Vladimir as a
child: he himself comes to recognize this after his glimpse of a
relationship between adults.

Admittedly, Vladimir has for readers one advantage over Asya:
we are told about her love by others, so that we catch only glimpses
and gleams of its ardour and poetry, whereas the awakening of his
love is revealed to us moment by moment with an art that matches
in sureness and delicacy the emotions stirred in Turgenev by these
memories of his far-off adolescence.

Zinaida's affinities with Asya go deep. Both girls are basically
insecure: Asya because of her illegitimacy, Zinaida because of her
poverty and (even more) because of her unworthy parents: her
mother is vulgar and slatternly, her father had been 'empty and
foolish': neither can have given her any affection or deserved any
respect from her. Both girls compensate for this insecurity by
playing a part: Asya romps, Zinaida coquettes. No doubt Asya's
'act' is comparatively harmless; but then, she is four years younger
and enjoys a much easier life, shielded and warmed by her
brother's indulgent affection (and if she has had more than her fair

share of hardships in the past, she has never lacked for affection). Zinaida, with no one but herself to depend on and besieged by a very mixed bunch of adorers, has developed a taste for power and a streak of hardness verging on sadism (as when she humiliates the doctor – perhaps the most estimable member of her circle).

However, under the surface rowdiness, she reveals many or most of the virtues of the 'Turgenev heroine': the singleheartedness, and the courage and honesty that it generates. As in Asya, such honesty comprises both candour and self-knowledge. Usually it involves also an instinctive attraction to the genuine and aversion from the spurious; Zinaida's toleration of Malevski suggests that in her this faculty has become somewhat blunted. But her feeling for beauty is evidenced by her attitude to Pushkin; her intelligence – by her insight into the characters of her adorers; her imagination by the subject of the poem she proposes to Maidanov and by her fantasy of the young queen: both of these evidently symbolize her own emotions and circumstances, but she invests them with a vivid grace, with a touch of true poetry.

It may be asked: but where is the pride that nerved Asya to flee from N. N.? Are we not confronted here with the same pattern of passion as in 'A Backwater' and 'A Correspondence' – the pattern of lord and slave, of absolute ascendancy and absolute dependence? That is apparently how young Vladimir saw it – and so have many readers after him.

The balance of evidence seems against this view. Asya's flight is irrelevant: she was quite prepared to give herself to N. N. if he loved her; she runs away when she senses that he does not love her truly or adequately. Zinaida has no reason to run away from Pëtr Vasil'evich on that score.

Ah, but what of the blow that horrified Vladimir so? And what of her kissing the weal, which horrified him even more?

The blow was assuredly not struck by way of asserting or establishing the man's mastery over the woman. It was a crude flash of exasperation, a momentary eruption of the wild rage to which (we had already been told) Pëtr Vasil'evich was occasionally prone; and in this instance we see him immediately remorseful and seeking to repair the injury. And in the kiss there is nothing of slavish submission; its meaning surely is that she accepts even his faults, that she loves him even at his worst. That would seem implicit in all we know of Zinaida and is borne out by the gesture with which she holds out her arms to him when he comes rushing into the room: the 'young queen' pardoning and cleaving to her obscure lover.

Of course, she does not submit. The quarrel between them must have hinged on her refusal to desert her mother – perhaps with a view to having her follow him to St Petersburg. From her bearing before (and after) the blow and from the fact that she remained behind in Moscow – is it not clear that she kept to her chosen course?

If there was bondage, it was not one way: the passion was mutual. Why else would haughty, masterful, coolly self-controlled Pëtr Vasil'evich have stooped to implore his wife with tears to provide the money for Zinaida's confinement? Why else should his fatal stroke have followed so closely on his apparent failure to obtain that help for her? His love for Zinaida had driven him to flout his own creed (of will as the key to freedom and power) and at least hastened his death. Not for nothing did his last thought for his son take the form of a solemn warning against love as a deadly drug.[18]

Zinaida and Vladimir survived their first love. Paradoxically, it was the man who all his life had preached self-will and domination over others who succumbed: another indication perhaps that, like Asya, Zinaida was able to achieve what her lover could only aspire to. When she died, several years later, it was not of love. Her 'weak chest' had always threatened an early death, and a second confinement proved too much for her. Vladimir did not die: he just never learned to live; but it would be rash to blame that on the brief 'storm of a spring morning' that was his first love.

While that love – Vladimir's experience of it – forms the core and essence of the story, he himself – the narrator-protagonist – is, strangely enough, not its most interesting male character. That designation better fits his rival and father, of whom we see so much less.

If Vyazovnin was a pallid reflection of the dandies of the 1820s, Pëtr Vasil'evich is half-brother to the 'demons' of the 1830s – a flawed Pechorin. He shares Pechorin's will to power with its streak of cruelty, Pechorin's elegance, coolness, social graces and mastery of physical skills (such as riding), as well as some of Pechorin's emotional inhibition. But he lacks Pechorin's intensity, his doom-driven urge to court danger and his singular understanding of himself. Of course, Pechorin would never have married for money; but then, he had no need to – and he was afraid of marriage.

But perhaps even closer than his affinities with Pechorin are his affinities with one of Turgenev's own personages – a most unlikely one. Surely his philosophy of life – 'Take what you can yourself and don't let others get you into their hands; to belong to oneself – that is the whole thing in life'[19] – sounds like a gentlemanly gloss on Efrem's motto: 'Scared – you're dead; dare – you've won.' And it is not just a consonance of apophthegms: there is a case for recognizing in the two men an identical type at different social, and therefore cultural, levels. Both are loners. Each is married, with one son; but their real life is lived outside their home. Yet both are impelled to pass on to their sons the lessons they have learned from life; only, Efrem is blessed with a son in his own likeness, whereas Vladimir is cast in a quite different mould than his father.

Pëtr Vasil'evich dominates his world as Efrem dominates his. Both inspire mixed feelings of awe and fascination. Each flouts the conventions of his society; but Efrem is content to make free with his neighbours' property (their honey); Pëtr Vasil'evich extends his claims over their persons. Both men carry, under their veneer of cool superiority, a rage which is liable to burst out in sudden violence. For both men freedom is the supreme good, though only Pëtr Vasil'evich has the sophistication to formulate this as a philosophy of voluntarism ('Know how to will, and you'll be free, and you'll be master too').[20] So both men equate freedom for themselves with power over others.

But whereas Efrem succeeds in his contradictory rôles, Pëtr Vasil'evich finally fails. He succumbs to love, which involves the negation of dominance and of autarky. Here the social differences play a decisive part: at the primitive social level of the village Efrem is free to act out his contradictory rôles openly, whereas Pëtr Vasil'evich is driven by the more complex pressures of his 'civilized' society to dissimulate his transgressions and is in the end reduced by its trammels to helplessness. Thus Efrem is in truth his own man, Pëtr Vasil'evich only imagines that he is, or, at any rate, is so only up to a point. And it may be that, rather than love, it is the shattering of this delusion that breaks him.[21]

After 1860 the theme of love and the superfluous man is displaced by other preoccupations and interests and other themes. There is a long break in the line that had led from Chulkaturin and Rakitin, through Vyazovnin, Veret'ev, Aleksei Petrovich, Pasynkov, Pavel

Aleksandrovich, the nameless hero of 'Journey into the Woodland' and N. N., to Vladimir and his father. Later Turgenev will return occasionally to the theme and the type – notably in 'Spring Torrents', *Virgin Soil* and 'Klara Milich' – but it ceases to be central to his creation.

7

'Hamlet and Don Quixote' – *Rudin*

The decade 1853–62 saw Turgenev's fiction arrive at full artistic maturity. In the form of the story, it produced such gems as 'A Correspondence', 'Faust', 'Asya' and 'First Love'. The sketch is left behind, to be replaced by the novel, of which no less than four appear between 1856 and 1862. But before considering these, it may be well to deviate once more from chronology to examine the essay 'Hamlet and Don Quixote', which, though completed and published only after his first two novels (and simultaneously with the third),[1] was conceived before any of them[2] and is commonly viewed as containing one key to understanding the heroes of all four.

'Hamlet and Don Quixote'

In this essay Turgenev presents Hamlet and Don Quixote as exemplars of two antithetical archetypes of human nature. To the reader he appears to be trying to do three different things at the same time: delineate two psychological types; persuade us that Shakespeare's Hamlet and Cervantes' Don Quixote are perfect (or almost perfect) embodiments of those types; and estimate the relative value of Hamlets and Don Quixotes for the Russian society of the 1860s. Unfortunately, the second of these purposes gets sacrificed to the other two: the psychology of the two heroes is twisted to fit the political manifesto.

The main thesis, though never made explicit, is clear enough (at any rate, in hindsight: it may not have been equally clear to all his readers at the time): Hamlet was the superfluous man of his time and place: Russia has had enough of superfluous men and needs now leaders of a quite different kind – in fact, of the opposite kind – in all essentials, Don Quixotes. Such a prescription could hardly fail to alarm conservatives and moderate liberals, while evoking scorn among radicals.

How, then, does Turgenev see these leaders of the future: what, in his eyes, does the Don Quixote type represent? Above all, faith: faith in something eternal and unassailable, in a truth outside the individual, not easily attainable – requiring service and sacrifice – but yet attainable by dint of faithful service and great sacrifices. Don Quixote is steeped in devotion to an ideal for which he is ready to undergo all possible privations and lay down life itself. He lives entirely, so to speak, outside himself – for others, for the destruction of evil. There is no trace of egoism in him: that is why he is fearless, patient, content with the poorest of food and raiment. Humble in heart, he is great and bold in spirit; his touching piety does not cramp his freedom; he knows neither vanity nor any doubt – whether of himself, of his mission or even of his physical strength: his will is an inflexible will. Constant striving towards a single end does involve a certain uniformity in his thinking, a certain one-sidedness of mind; he knows little, but that little is enough: he knows what his business is on this earth, and that is the most important thing to know. Don Quixote is an enthusiast in the service of an idea, and its radiance is all around him (*W*, VIII, 173–4).

To Don Quixote Turgenev opposes Hamlet: as egoism to devotion, as critical irony to enthusiastic faith, as sceptical intelligence to heart and will. Hamlet 'lives wholly for himself', although he does not believe (even) in himself; he is concerned only to observe and analyse himself; 'he can find nothing in the whole world to which his soul could cleave'; and 'he himself loves no one'. He believes in nothing and nobody (including himself). He does inveigh against himself, even to excess, and he recognizes and despises his own pusillanimity; but he lives by, and feeds on, that very self-contempt. In spite of his self-contempt and self-doubt, he is vain; although he does not know what he wants or what to live for – he clings to life.

One wonders: if that is the kind of man Hamlet is – can he be a tragic hero? Can the play be a tragedy (even though Turgenev permits us to pity its protagonist, because he does suffer, and his self-lacerations are even more painful than the beatings and reverses suffered by Don Quixote)?

To round off the antithesis between the Spanish knight-errant and the Danish prince, Turgenev contrasts them in their attitudes and relation to women and to 'the masses' (the people). Don

Quixote is an ideal lover: he loves an inexistent woman, whose pre-eminence he is ready to champion at the risk of his life; his heart is pure and he himself free from the slightest taint of sensuality; his very dreams are innocent. So Hamlet must be a sensualist – even a secret voluptuary. On what evidence? On that of Rosencrantz's smile when Hamlet declares that man delights him not – 'no, nor woman neither'. Of course, Hamlet does not love Ophelia: his feeling for her is by turns cynical and bombastic. He is incapable of love.

To make his case that Don Quixote has all the qualities of a leader, Turgenev expatiates on the relation between him and Sancho Panza, who is 'representative of the masses', that is, who typifies the common people in its tendency to be carried away by disinterested enthusiasm for such fearless, selfless heroes and to follow them in their pursuit of lofty purposes which it may not even understand. Nor does it matter if Don Quixote's attempts to do good most often end in failure or result in harm to, or worsen the plight of, those he tries to rescue: for 'the main thing is the good faith and the strength of the conviction [prompting the action] ... and the result is in the hands of fate'.

To demonstrate that 'Hamlets are indeed useless to the masses; they have nothing to give them, they cannot lead them anywhere, for they themselves are not going anywhere'; that Hamlets despise the common people ('for who that does not respect himself can respect anything or anybody?'), Turgenev designates as 'representative of the masses *vis-à-vis* Hamlet' none other than – Polonius. 'For Polonius Hamlet is not so much a madman as a child, and if he were not a king's son, he [Polonius] would despise him for his utter helplessness, his inability to apply his mind to any positive or sensible purpose.' Turgenev does not trouble to add that Hamlet certainly despises Polonius, but presumably that is the justification for the statement that Hamlets despise the people.

Before commenting on these flights of fancy, it may be well to recall Turgenev's own, already quoted[3] admission from a later context: 'Whenever I am not dealing with images, I become quite confused and am at a loss how to proceed. I always feel as if one could equally well assert the opposite of all I am saying.' Cervantes' novel and Shakespeare's play were two of Turgenev's favourite works of literature, which he had read and reread and 'knew' well and intimately; but it can hardly be disputed that in this essay he has ignored, misinterpreted or contradicted his texts wherever they are at variance with his theses.

He ignores the fact that Don Quixote is mad. In extolling that hero's selflessness, he ignores the fact that the Don's pursuit of knight-errantry is a means to the end of winning eternal fame for himself. He ignores the part played in Sancho's allegiance to his knight by his (Sancho's) ambition to become governor of an island or attain other high office. Above all, he ignores the fact that, if Don Quixote had succeeded in imposing his ideal of chivalry upon his world, he would have been leading it – not forward, but back to the Middle Ages of Charlemagne and King Arthur. The claim that his hero is free from egoism is contradicted by the knight's uninhibited thirst for glory, as the claim that he is free from vanity is contradicted by his frequent bragging of his prowess.

While Don Quixote is idealized, Hamlet is disparaged. What has become of

> The courtier's, soldier's, scholar's eye, tongue, sword,
> Th'expectancy and rose of the fair state,
> The glass of fashion and the mould of form,
> Th'observed of all observers . . .

or of Fortinbras' sober estimate that 'he was likely, had he been put on, / To have proved most royal'? As Turgenev portrays Don Quixote in abstraction from his madness and his craving for fame, so he examines Hamlet in complete abstraction from his circumstances and predicament: that within a few weeks he has lost his father in one sense and his mother in another – the two people who evidently meant more to him than anyone else – and that he then discovers that his father may have been murdered, his mother may be guilty of adultery as well as incest ('may have been', 'may be' – because it is not till he has seen the effect on Claudius of *Gonzago's Murder* that he can be sure that the Ghost was not a demon sent to drive him to crime and perdition). Is it any wonder if he is in shock – stunned, paralysed, helpless in the turmoil of his thoughts and emotions? Is it any wonder if he 'believes in nothing and nobody'?

Turgenev proclaims that Hamlet 'loves no one'. But if he doesn't love his parents, why is he convulsed – to the point of having to struggle with thoughts of suicide – by his father's death and his mother's remarriage? If he doesn't love Horatio, what does he mean by saying that he wears him in his heart's core?

In contradiction of Turgenev's contention that Hamlet despises the people and can only be despised by them, Shakespeare shows us his prince's cordial relation with the Players and his easy, unaffected exchanges with the Gravedigger, while Claudius himself is driven to testify to 'the great love the general gender bear him' (Hamlet) – a love so great that the King dare not attack or even restrain him openly. As for Polonius, if he 'represents' anyone but himself, it is certainly not the people – perhaps the Court clique, the dominant minority.

And if it comes to comparing achievements: Don Quixote leaves La Mancha and Spain in much the same state as before his three sallies; Hamlet, as we have seen,[4] succeeds in cleaning out the Augean stables of Claudius' palace and so creating the possibility (though, of course, 'the outcome remains in the hands of fate') of new and better leadership.

But, not content with contradicting his texts, Turgenev, characteristically, goes on to contradict himself. After declaring that Hamlets make no discoveries, invent nothing, leave nothing behind them save traces of their own personality – they leave no deeds or achievements behind – he tells us that it is the Hamlets who develop the discoveries of the Don Quixotes. Leaving aside the question of what it is that Don Quixote invents (he invents his own myth – but it is hardly likely that Turgenev will have had that in mind) – one asks oneself: is 'development' any less important, any less of an achievement than 'invention'?

After defining Hamlet as an incarnation of the principle of negation earlier exemplified in (Goethe's) Mephistopheles, he may momentarily have turned his eyes away from the figure of the superfluous man, to attend to Shakespeare's prince, for he does distinguish Hamlet's negation from that of Mephistopheles. Although Hamlet does not believe in goodness (what Turgenev should have said is that Hamlet doubts the genuineness of everything that presents itself to him as good) – he unerringly discerns evil and falsehood and by his relentless hostility to falsehood proves to be a leading champion of that truth in which he does not believe. Thus, his scepticism, his doubt is not indifference or Laodiceanism. It is a destructive force; but because it is not properly focussed or limited (and this is Hamlet's tragedy) it cripples his powers of action.

After such capital admissions, one might have expected a

balance-sheet something like the following. Hamlet and Don Quixote are both equally enemies of evil; but Don Quixote, being mad, sees evil where there is none (mistakes windmills for giants, puppets for Moors, votaries of the Virgin for kidnappers) and fails to see it where it is most blatant (in the duke and duchess), while Hamlet, being in his right mind (though emotionally disturbed),[5] sees clearly where evil lies and destroys it, but only when his hand is forced, so contributing to the deaths of several people whom he had no wish to kill,[6] as well as losing his own life.

But Turgenev's attention seems to have wandered again: he repeats his claims that the Hamlets, for all their intelligence, are apt to be useless and doomed to inaction, whereas the 'half-mad' Don Quixotes are useful because they 'move men' (in the sense of leading them to great objectives which they – the Quixotes – can see, or imagine). Yet Hamlets have the saving grace of 'forming and developing' disciples like Horatio, of implanting seeds of thought in their hearts, which germinate there and are then disseminated through the world. This last antithesis – between Don Quixote's capacity to lead the masses and Hamlet's to enrich the world through single disciples – appears to have no more textual support than the preceding ones.

. The essay also contains some more orthodox literary criticism, in the form of a comparison between Shakespeare and Cervantes as writers; but its abiding interest resides in the depiction of the two psychological types which Turgenev paradoxically denominates 'Hamlet' and 'Don Quixote'; in his equation of the Hamlet type with the superfluous man and in his choice of the Don Quixote type to provide the future leadership of Russia.

In fairness to Turgenev, it should be mentioned that in his cavalier treatment of his texts he is in good company: not a few professional critics, past and present, seem to the humble non-specialist equally ready to stand Shakespeare or Cervantes on his head. Proximately, Turgenev's approach to both heroes has obvious affinities with those of the Romantics, from Schlegel onward.[7] It should also be borne in mind that Turgenev does recognize that in most men the characteristics of both types are combined in varying proportions; and what he says about the types would be unexceptionable if he were not constantly referring it to Shakespeare's and Cervantes' heroes.

Rudin

If Turgenev had not already been thinking of novel-writing, the events of 1852 must have turned his thoughts in that direction. The death of Gogol, Russia's leading fiction-writer, and the publication of *A Sportsman's Sketches*, which seemed to mark him out as Gogol's heir, combined to present an obvious challenge; his relegation to his country estate, remote from the distractions of metropolitan life, offered the added incentive of leisure – plenty of empty time crying to be filled. Gogol had excelled alike in the short story and in the novel (he had also been the leading playwright of his generation, but Turgenev had probably decided by now to leave the theatre to others); and it is to these two genres that Turgenev would, from now on, devote his writing.

We have already traced the course of his story-writing in the decade following Gogol's death. His first attempt at a novel occupied the winter of 1852/3. In spite of the diffidence and self-doubts that punctuate his letters to his friends after the completion of the *Sketches*, he produced between November 1852 and March 1853 the first twelve chapters – some 500 pages – of a novel to be entitled *Two Generations*; the title and first draft of the plan apparently go back to the end of the 1840s; the twelve chapters represent the first of three parts.

The panel of literary advisers to whom he read the draft (Annenkov, S. T. Aksakov and two or three others) responded with mixed comments, but all seemed to agree that the two young protagonists were artistically unsatisfactory. Turgenev at first undertook to rework them, but was evidently so discouraged that he laid the manuscript aside for a couple of years, briefly considered returning to it, but almost immediately jettisoned it when he turned to *Rudin*, and later destroyed it. All that survived was the fragment he published in 1859 under the title 'The Mistress's Own Office'[8] and possibly one or more passages thought to have been incorporated in later works.

Rudin was not conceived as a novel. The first draft, dashed off in about seven weeks in June and July of 1855, was referred to by Turgenev as 'a long novella' (*bol'shaya povest'*). But in the last few months of that year, in the wake of advice from his friends and certain events in his personal world, the novella underwent not only considerable amplification but significant modifications. What had begun as another study of a superfluous man's failure in love, pivoted on a distinctly uncharitable representation of his former friend Bakunin, was developed into a full-length portrait of a many-faceted and more impressive figure. The single episode of Rudin's stay on the Lasunski estate was extended backward in time to his student days (in the flashback in chapter vi) and forward over the remainder of his life (in chapter xii and the epilogue – which, however, did not include the account of his death till the second, 1860, edition). The critical and predominantly negative portrayal in chapters iv–xi was deepened, enriched, poeticized in the epilogue, and the fusion there of traits of Bakunin with aspects of other models[9] helps to make Rudin a more typical representative of his species. But although *Rudin* had now attained the dimensions and complexity of a novel, Turgenev continues to vacillate in his designation of it. He published it first in *The Contemporary* with the sub-title 'novella'; in the 1860 edition of his *Works* it appeared with his two subsequent novels; in three further editions of the *Works* – among the stories; and only in his last (1880) edition was it placed definitely at the head of the novels.

Looking back from the vantage-point of 1879 on his literary career, Turgenev was to say that in his six novels, spread over the twenty-one years from 1855 to 1876, he had striven 'to the limit of [his] powers and ability, to depict conscientiously and impartially and to embody in appropriate types both what Shakespeare calls "the body and pressure of time"[10] and the rapidly changing physiognomy of Russians of that cultured class[11] that has been the primary object of [his] observation'. In fact, if we regard Turgenev's novels as so many chapters in a social history of nineteenth-century Russia, we must recognize that they cover a period not of twenty-one years but of nearly twice as many – beginning not in 1855, when *Rudin* was written, but in Rudin's student days in the mid-1830s.

In *Rudin* Turgenev takes up, in the context and idiom of his own time, the theme of *Evgeni Onegin* and *A Hero of Our Time*: he contributes his chapter to the history of the superfluous man in the form and on the scale of a novel. What differentiates Rudin from the superfluous men in his poems, plays and stories (including those written after 1855) is that these are private individuals, whose lives impinge only on their small immediate circle, whereas

Rudin, like Onegin and Pechorin, is a socially significant figure, of wide-ranging influence.

As in *Evgeni Onegin* and 'Princess Mary' (the core of Pechorin's Journal in *A Hero of Our Time*), the central axis of *Rudin* is again the impact of a superfluous man on the life and heart of a young girl, who falls in love with him and is rejected. But the secondary pattern is in various ways more complicated, borrowing features from both Pushkin and Lermontov and developing them different-ly. As in 'Princess Mary', Turgenev's hero has a rival; but whereas Grushnitski is worsted and killed, Volyntsev fails to provoke a duel and survives to marry the heroine. As in *Evgeni Onegin*, there is a second couple – Lipina and Lezhnëv – but though Lezhnëv goes through his phase of jealousy of the hero, he too is content to vent it in words and ends up happily married to his Aleksandra, who is as charming and almost as 'stupid' as Pushkin's Ol'ga Larina; we leave them raising a family in the most placid and unromantic manner imaginable.

Critics who know the history of the composition of *Rudin* dispute as to whether the protagonist has emerged as an artistically integrated character. Granjard writes: 'Moreover, *Rudin* demon-strates by the complexity of its structure and the lack of unity in the character of its hero that Turgenev had difficulty rising to the serene heights of epic objectivity.'[12] On the other hand, Maurois, who was not a Slavist but had the advantage of being a novelist in his own right, expounds a contrary view in persuasive terms:

What is very fine is Turgenev's concern to be fair to his personage. Rudin, unlike the heroes of bad novels, is not a person of unchanging character. Our opinion of him changes, as it does in relation to real people. It is this process of discovery that makes [...] *Rudin* an entirely novel technical *tour de force*. Never before had one seen such a multiple illumination of the hero, revealed to us from different angles as he is seen by observers with differing reactions. Even at the end we remain in mysterious uncertainty about him, as about real people.[13]

If Maurois had known *A Hero of Our Time*, he would, of course, not have claimed novelty for the technique of *Rudin*; but he has seized on a point overlooked by many critics: *Rudin*'s superficially conventional lay-out masks something very like the multiple illumi-nation introduced and used so brilliantly in Lermontov's novel. Turgenev discards the separate sections with their different nar-rators, but in both novels we have three distinct views of the hero:

his own (Rudin's in his letter to Natal'ya and in his last colloquy
with Lezhnëv in the epilogue; Pechorin's in his Journal), that of his
friend (Lezhnëv, Maksim Maksimych) and that of the narrator (in
A Hero of Our Time, the narrator of 'Bela' and 'Maksim Maksimych' and 'editor' of the whole book).

But Turgenev varies and complicates Lermontov's scheme. In
the earlier novel, the most revealing view of the hero is his own, the
least important that of the 'editor', with that of the friend somewhere in between. In *Rudin* it is the other way round: it is the
narrator's view which takes up most space and is most important,
while the protagonist's view of himself takes up least space and is
least important; the viewpoint of the friend is again intermediate in
scope, but makes a much larger contribution to our understanding
in Turgenev than in Lermontov because Lezhnëv is a much more
intelligent and cultured observer than Maksim Maksimych, who is
too simple and too remote – intellectually and emotionally – from
Pechorin to penetrate or interpret him: so only the narration of
fairly plain facts can properly be entrusted to him and his rôle is
played out and he disappears one-third of the way through the
novel. Lezhnëv, on the other hand, is not only a man on Rudin's
own social level and sufficiently sophisticated to be able to shed a
critical light on the hero – he is a man capable of modifying and
enlarging his views with changing circumstances: in fact, in chapters VI and XII and in the epilogue we hear from Lezhnëv not one
but three perceptibly different assessments of his friend.

Lezhnëv doubles the rôles of friend and foil to Rudin as Lenski
doubles those rôles *vis-à-vis* Onegin, whereas Lermontov splits the
rôles between Maksim Maksimych (friend and part-biographer)
and Grushnitski (foil and rival). Lezhnëv is also part-biographer –
in his account of Rudin's student days – and rival (if only in his own
imagination), but as foil, he compares with Lenski rather than
Grushnitski, who is a phony imitation or caricature of Pechorin,
whereas Lenski is partly complement, partly antithesis to Onegin.

Lezhnëv is no superfluous man. Though he has shared in the
experience of the *kruzhok*, though he has been exposed not only to
Rudin in his heyday but to the radiant personality and serene
visions of Pokorski (an avatar of Stankevich), he has come to terms
with life – the life of Nicholas I's Russia. He has ceased to write
poetry or to break his head over the 'accursed questions' – the
eternal problems of human destiny. Instead, he concentrates on

doing the jobs that lie to hand – running his estate, raising a family – and these he does very competently. Beyond them he does not look. One might even say that by the time the novel opens he has lost all awareness of a beyond; and when Rudin drops out of that beyond into his cosy, humdrum world, his instinctive reaction is to recoil, to bristle, to growl...

Jealousy, fear of losing his Aleksandra to the charmer, makes his judgment of Rudin harsh and, as she senses, one-sided; it is not till he is well and truly married that he feels secure enough to strike a balance; finally, moved by the spectacle of his friend's decline and made aware of broader perspectives by the tale of that friend's struggles and ordeals, he reverses himself and defends Rudin against Rudin. Lezhnëv is easy to see through, to comprehend, to appraise: a decent landowner, a good friend, an excellent family man.

What is Rudin? Rudin is the major literary representative of the superfluous man in Turgenev's 'generation'[14] – the 'men of the forties' – as Pechorin had been his representative in Lermontov's generation (men of the thirties) and Onegin in Pushkin's (the twenties). In the brief period – between the last years of Alexander I's reign and the latter half of Nicholas's – there had been great changes in the condition of Russia and the Russian gentry, and those changes had been reflected in the evolution of the superfluous man.[15]

The affluence and elegance of the Onegins and Pechorins has given place to genteel poverty for many: Rudin is penniless, shabby, economically dependent; and this loss of control over his material environment has set its stamp upon the hero's character and career. High-handed action is no longer practicable for him: so, like the Hamlet of Shchigry and Chulkaturin, he takes refuge in cerebration, in ideas. But whereas the former was broken by his mother's beatings and/or by the collision of his Western culture with 'Russian reality' and the latter was emotionally paralysed by the internal conflict between his paternal and his maternal inheritance, Rudin had been brought up by an adoring and devoted mother and then steeped – in the company of Pokorski and his circle – in an idealism embodied in and lived by its votaries: hence his tough self-confidence, as compared with the brittleness of the Hamlet and the timidity of Chulkaturin.

If pride is still the backbone of all three men (as in the superfluous men of earlier generations), it is a pride that operates in very different ways. The Hamlet's pride impels him to expose himself to humiliation: he haunts the gatherings of his wealthier neighbours knowing he will be cold-shouldered or ignored, and courts further snubbing by baring his soul to his unknown room-mate. Chulkaturin withdraws into himself: between his seething thoughts and emotions and their expression there is 'the little lock' of pride, which cuts him off from communion with his fellow-humans. Rudin's pride incites him not only to communicate with others but to establish an ascendency over them – an intellectual ascendency, since that is the only kind within his means.

In Rudin (as in his predecessors of the twenties and thirties) this pride can degenerate into petty vanity, as we hear from Lezhnëv that a slight to his pride would drive him up the wall or as we ourselves observe when he hurls his schoolboy taunt, 'It's you who are funking, not I', at Natal'ya as she turns her back on him. But at its best, his pride is anchored in the exercise of intelligence. On his first appearance in Dar'ya Mikhailovna's *salon*, he equates belief in oneself and in one's powers with belief in knowledge, culture, science, which implies that the sanction of pride has been transferred outside the self. For Rudin (as for Pechorin before him) pride is still the 'lever of Archimedes' which can move worlds from their foundations; but he points forward, beyond the superfluous man, when he demands explicitly that personality shall, when necessary, be sacrificed to the general good; and it would not have occurred to any of his predecessors that his pride needed to be controlled as a horse needs to be controlled by its rider – and, still less, that 'selfishness is suicide' (III, 267). This may explain why he is, and remains, free from the rancour of the Hamlet of Shchigry and Chulkaturin; Lezhnëv, in their last meeting, is surprised to find still so little bitterness in him (Epilogue, 366).

However, it is not only – arguably, not even mainly – pride that debars Rudin from love and friendship. What destroys his relation with Natal'ya (and other women; he had deserted even his mother) is a striking emotional poverty coupled with a no less striking perceptual obtuseness. Freud wrote[16] of 'sexualization of thought': by which he meant not the concentration of thinking on sexual matters, but an intellectual activity so all-engrossing as to absorb in itself all the vital energies (libido) – and this seems to fit the character of Rudin's cerebration.

When he attempts to narrate his student days, he leaves his audience unsatisfied: 'his descriptions lacked colour' (III, 268). Colour involves, and may here be taken to stand for, sensation and perception. Similarly, he remains unperturbed by Dar'ya Mikhailovna's adulteration and misuse of the Russian language – his language – because, we are told (IV, 272), he is probably incapable of noticing it. This is a fateful finding, inasmuch as it links his perceptual limitations to the estrangement from Russia and things Russian with which Lezhnëv charges him ('Rudin's misfortune is that he doesn't know Russia', XII, 349).

And as he is 'deaf' to his hostess' language, so he is 'blind' to the reactions of those around him and, all the more, to their quality as individuals: he mortifies and riles Volyntsev while seeking to gain his goodwill; he accepts Dar'ya Mikhailovna at her own valuation as 'a remarkable woman'; he grotesquely underestimates Natal'ya. And as he misjudges people – because he doesn't 'see' or 'hear' them – so he misjudges situations. These misjudgments, superadded to his incapacity for effective or sustained effort on the plane of action, owing to the submersion of his libido in cerebration – more than suffice to explain the failures of his successive 'projects': of agronomic reform, of making the river navigable, of teaching literature.

Rudin's thinking differs from that of the Hamlet of Shchigry and of Chulkaturin in that theirs is largely or entirely an internal process, whereas his is mainly addressed to others; and it differs from the thinking of the Pechorins and Onegins – which was also for public consumption – by being deadly serious: without a trace of humour or of the wit so characteristic of those heroes. 'He didn't know how to make people laugh', we are told (III, 268); he himself laughed only 'very seldom', and when he did, his laughter appeared to wrinkle and age him (IV, 274). He had read widely, but his reading had not endowed him with a solid body of knowledge because facts interest him only as stepping-stones to generalizations, so that his thought has remained both abstract and imprecise – neither truly philosophic nor truly scholarly, but rather an imaginative (even poetic) manipulation of ideas. It is worth noting, too, that although he spends much more time 'thinking' than Pechorin did, he has not, when we meet him, achieved any comparable understanding of himself. He cannot even make up his mind whether, at a given moment, he is or is not happy, whether he is or is not in love. His view of himself – as of much else – is constantly blurred by optimistic illusions.

This optimism, together with his material dependence and his cerebration, represent three major differences between Rudin and his predecessors of the twenties and thirties. 'All Rudin's thoughts seemed turned towards the future; that invested them with a quality of impetuosity and youthfulness' (III, 269). The cerebration marks an affinity with the Hamlet type of Turgenev's 1860 essay, while the optimism is characteristic of Don Quixote. The undertakings and failures recounted in the epilogue are obviously quixotic, and a culmination of quixotry is attained in his death: in a foreign land which means nothing to him, for a cause that is already lost, with a gesture whose symbolic defiance barely masks its tragic futility. To the question how the Hamlet type of chapters III–XI could have turned into the Don Quixote of the epilogue we will return.

Like Hamlet, Rudin casts a spell on the best of the people around him. The key to his charm is what Lezhnëv calls his 'enthusiasm': that is, the inspiration of his eloquence and the ideas and values which it proclaims. First and most fundamental among these values is the cult of thought itself – of thinking as the way to escape and transcend the petty particularities of everyday existence and to master the flux of impressions – the infinite details of reality – by reducing them to general principles and organizing those principles in an intelligible system. It is in such intellectual activity that he sees the foundation of all civilization or culture – it is this alone that can endue our transient existence with abiding meaning. Unfortunately, he is unequal to the preliminary labour of assembling the materials for such activity: that is, the facts from which to catalyse the general principles. And this may have been due not solely to indolence, but to something like an 'allergy' to the concrete, for we have seen how his account of his student days – about which he surely knew all the facts – lacked life and lustre.

Another of Rudin's major values is freedom; but we are left uncertain as to the scope of his conception of this freedom. It is obviously not the freedom of Dostoevsky's 'underground man' – to trample on logic – nor that of the modern existentialist – to remake himself – for on the evening of his arrival on the scene he declares that the highest joy of man ought to be the consciousness of serving as an instrument of higher powers (III, 270). Yet neither can it be the freedom to live and let live. In Pigasov's helpful classification of egoists – those who live and let live, those who live but won't let others live, and those unable either to live or to let live – Rudin presumably belongs in the third category. The practical results of his intellectual busybodying are exemplified in the wrecking of Lezhnëv's first love affair and the near-wrecking of Natal'ya's whole life. His quotation of Don Quixote as he leaves the Lasunski estate – 'happy is he to whom heaven has given a portion of bread for which he need not be beholden to any other man' – suggests that, at that moment, Rudin's freedom is primarily freedom from the material dependence on others, from which he is forever cutting loose, only to relapse into it again and again. But on the strength of his utterances of the first evening and of all we come to know about him before the end, surely he should be credited with a much wider and higher conception of freedom – as freedom to pursue truth and to proclaim it.

Rudin's other major values are beauty and love. Beauty means for him above all intellectual beauty – the beauty of ideas and systems, but to some extent also beauty of character, provided it can force itself on his notice. It might be thought that he is susceptible to sensuous beauty: after all, he calls for music and gazes out into the summer night. But his reaction to these is not to speak of music or nature, let alone Schubert or the scene before him, but to use them as prelude, by way of his private memories, for one of his flights of oratory into the empyrean of general ideas. So, too, he looks at an oak tree – but not with the eye of a painter or naturalist, nor even simply to delight in its shapes and colours, but to drag up some symbolic innuendo about the way it renews its leaves (as a great heart puts forth new love: IV, 292). In fine, he uses art and nature to frame his thought, as he uses Natal'ya or Basistov as receptacles for his thought – with no objective sense of what they are.

Love, likewise, is something that fires his thought or his imagination, not his blood: his love finds expression not in feeling, not in action, but in ideas and images – in words. His pronouncements on love are flagrantly contradictory, too: at one point he claims to have loved and suffered like everyone else (VII, 306), at another, he exclaims operatically: 'Anyhow, who loves in our day and age – who dares to love?' (VI, 291). And this is the conclusion of a speech which begins with an arresting paradox (that unhappy love represents not the tragic but the comic side of love) – only to fade away into Romantic clichés.

Needless to say, Rudin's ideas and values are not his inventions: they are the traditional ones of Idealist philosophy, and proximately of the German Idealist philosophy in which he had steeped himself. But in the context of Nicholas I's Russia, their exaltation of individual dignity, of intellectual independence, of faith in ideals – represented a clarion-call of protest. Rudin embodies the intellectual protest – as Onegin and Pechorin had embodied respectively the aesthetic and the volitive protest – against that *poshlost'* which Gogol's distorting mirror holds up for our horrified fascination. Each of these modes of protest had its moment of value, until it set into a stereotype – and so lapsed in its turn into *poshlost'*.

Readers who complain of a lack of unity in Rudin's character are, no doubt, disconcerted by the seeming discrepancy between the 'Hamletic' personage of chapters III–XI and the Quixote of the epilogue. They ought to recognize that the idealism of the Lasunski period is no less 'quixotic' than the undertakings or projects of the hero's latter years. If the demand is for an explanation of the transition from mere preaching to attempts to translate that preaching into action – need one look beyond the shock of his involvement with Natal'ya?

If he had had inklings before that of his inadequacies, glimpses of his weaknesses, they had amounted to little more than stimuli to flights of rhetoric: remember Pigasov's gleeful account (IV, 288) of Rudin's self-criticism: instead of depressing him, it seemed to cheer him up like strong drink.[17] But the ignominious rôle he had played in relation to Natal'ya made him see himself, if not quite as she saw him, certainly in a new, far more realistic perspective. His farewell letter to her, though not free from vaguenesses and touches of Romantic self-pity, does contain many lines of sober self-appraisal: 'I don't want to justify myself or to blame anyone but myself'; 'you were right: I didn't know you, though I thought I did'; 'how can I prove to you that I might have come to love you with real love – a love not of the imagination but of the heart – when I myself don't know whether I am capable of such love?'; 'Nature has given me much; but I shall die without having accomplished anything worthy of my powers'; 'I probably lack something essential for moving men's or possessing women's hearts – and domination over minds only is both precarious and useless'; 'I strive to give myself, eagerly, utterly – and I cannot'; 'I shall end up sacrificing myself for some nonsense in which I shall not even believe.'

The man capable of these insights (most of which would not have disgraced a Pechorin) could not sink back to the level of the mere preacher: he had to do something to validate the close of his penultimate paragraph: 'Perhaps I shall emerge from this trial purer and stronger.' And surely all those wanderings and enterprises, to which he devoted the years of his life and his more than slender material resources, were intended by him as service to a cause. Does it matter that he could not define the cause? Lezhnëv at the end, looking back over the whole odyssey, thought not: it is 'not a spirit of futile restlessness' that drives Rudin but a 'love of truth' (Epilogue, 366). And Lezhnëv, though not unerring, represents the highest standard of judgment in the book: he is dead right about Dar'ya Mikhailovna, whom he dislikes, and about Lipina, whom he loves; he understands and appreciates Natal'ya much better than her own mother does; and he has no illusions about his friend Volyntsev. If jealousy makes him unjust to Rudin in the middle reaches of the story, it is poetic justice that he is given a chance to redress the balance at the close.

If Rudin's ascent from the plane of words to that of action is really to be attributed to his encounter with Natal'ya, that would bespeak an exceptional position for her among Turgenev heroines. If love often adds a dimension to his girls and young women – precipitating a rapid realization of admirable potentialities – it seldom brings out the best in his men. Some are destroyed by it, like Aleksei Petrovich in 'A Correspondence'; most are emotionally frozen at the point or level at which love strikes them. To women love reveals what they are capable of; to men it is apt to reveal what they are incapable of.

Natal'ya's is an impressive personality – doubly so when we remember that she is only 17 and has not finished growing, either physically or psychologically. If we look back to Pushkin's Tat'yana, we can measure the evolution that has taken place – in literature as in life – from the girls and young women of the 1820s to those of the 1840s. The lines of development between women and men have remained parallel: there has been no convergence, much less any merging. In the men there has been a displacement of the psychological centre of gravity under increasing social pressures, in the women an intellectual maturation: from the practical heroism of the wives of the Decembrists, through the Romanticism of a Natalie Herzen[18] to the philosophizing of the Bakunin sisters,[19] and beyond – towards a Suslova and the Korvin-Krukovsky sisters.[20]

Pushkin's Tat'yana was a dreamer of dreams. Brought up on folklore and her nurse's tales, on love stories in the form of novels – the best of them dating from her grandparents' time[21] – she declares her love without any assurance that Onegin is even an honourable man: she had heard that he was unsociable and her novels had taught her to reckon with the possibility that he might be a professional Lovelace.[22] Her ideal of a lover is one who will save her from her spiritual solitude, from the maddening incomprehension of all around her, or, as she herself expresses it, 'a guardian angel'. It would not have occurred to her to expect that he should be the dedicated servant of some great cause or sublime idea.

Natal'ya, when we first meet her – and before Rudin does – is reading a history of the Crusades and already she 'knew the whole of Pushkin by heart'. Not fairy-tales and mid-eighteenth-century novels but history and contemporary literature (*Evgeni Onegin* was perhaps begun in the very year of her birth) are forming her mind. Lezhnëv, without knowing anything of what she has been learning from Rudin, says of her to his Aleksandra: 'And Natal'ya is no child; believe me, she thinks more, and more deeply, than you and I' (VI, 294). Interestingly, both girls receive a further or higher education through the man they fall in love with: Tat'yana is introduced, in Onegin's study, to Byron and Madame de Staël (and presumably to Sénancour and Constant); Natal'ya is not so much brought up to date as she has her horizons widened to embrace Goethe and German Romanticism. Though she is as little understood by her inner circle as Tat'yana, she refuses to take this tragically and is content to keep her own counsel. In love she is looking not for a saviour or guardian angel – not for a man to take care of her but, on the contrary, for a man she will support and serve and strengthen in some noble pursuit.

She is presented to us at the outset as a serious, intense girl who 'spoke little, listened and watched intently, as if anxious to understand everything'; reflective; studying hard; feeling deeply and strongly, but keeping her feelings closely to herself. She had to if she was not to fritter them away, for there was nobody in sight to evoke or share them.

Then Rudin appears and sweeps her away into his cherished

fields of German Romance and philosophy, of poetry and fantasy. Two months of close communion, indoctrination and feverish intellectual excitement were bound to spill over into emotion. But it is too easy to take Lezhnëv's charges of coquetry and acting at face value and blame Rudin for the emotional tangle that ensued; that is to misread both Rudin's character and the text. It is Natal'ya who reveals her feelings first, when she seizes on Rudin's fantasy of the apple-tree as a symbol of genius, to insist that the tree is breaking down for want of a prop. It is true that Rudin's next flight into symbolism (how the oak renews its foliage) has a reference to love; but for him that is merely an appendix to the immediately preceding conversation about the tragic in art and life (and love) – though Natal'ya may well connect it with her thoughts about the apple tree: that is implied by her tears when she is back in her room (VI, 290–2).

And it is again Natal'ya who next day challenges him to explain his simile of the oak leaves and, in response to his embarrassed prevarications, surprises him with the longest speech of her young life (though it consists of only four sentences) – on woman's capacity not only to appreciate self-sacrifice but to practise it. Yet even then Rudin is not convinced of her meaning. For this more than usual denseness there were no doubt two reasons. First, he was hoping to find an at least temporary 'haven' on the Lasunski estate and he was not unrealistic enough to suppose that the way to Dar'ya Mikhailovna's heart was by courting her daughter; it is true that he was later surprised by the vehemence of the lady's opposition to such a marriage – but that was after he had won the girl's love. Secondly (and mainly) he had persuaded himself that Natal'ya was in love with Volyntsev. Indeed it is not until his bungling quest for her confidences has wrung from her the avowal that she is in love but not with Volyntsev that his imagination at last catches fire and he starts to respond to her feeling (VII, 305–7).

The morning tryst near the remains of the haunted pond is obviously the most dramatic scene in the book; but it is also – and this is far from obvious – the most subtle, revealing to the attentive reader something in Natal'ya that she may take another two years to discover, and something else that she may never come to realize.

We see her approach, at the highest pitch of nervous and emotional tension, after defying her mother and bracing herself to give up her family, her home, the whole world in which she has spent her seventeen years – everything she has known. We could expect her to pour her heart out, to want to share all that is on her mind with this man to whom she is prepared to devote her life. Instead, we witness a prodigy of controlled reticence: first, in her carefully edited version of her colloquy with her mother, then as she succeeds in holding back her emotions and intentions until she has elicited his – until he has exposed himself completely. Yet this is not 'craftiness' (as Dar'ya Mikhailovna would doubtless have called it, had she been there): it is a vital instinct, and its intervention here betrays a deep unconscious distrust of this man to whom she had planned to entrust herself.

The other revelation comes after she has broken down in tears and Rudin adjures her (quite characteristically) to stop crying: 'for God's sake, don't tear my heart', and she replies, with eyes flashing through her tears: 'I'm not crying about what you think ... That's not what hurts: what hurts is that I've been mistaken in you ... So this is how you practise what you preach about freedom, about sacrifice' (IX, 324).

Surely this is a staggering confession. She is saying that what she finds unbearable is not that she is not to go away with him as his wife or lover – and not even that he doesn't love her truly – but that he has destroyed her vision of him: not that he is false to her, but that he is false to the ideals which he professed and which she has really made her own. And the tears are followed by bitter taunts: 'you are scared ... you didn't know me ... you don't love me.' It does not occur to her that if he has failed to understand her, she has failed no less to understand him. Perhaps she just assumes that at twice her age there is less excuse for him. And she is too young to realize that no one ever sees us as we see ourselves, so that whoever loves us loves perforce only his or her image of us, not our own.[23]

Anyhow, the point here is that Natal'ya's love is (like Rudin's) laced with fantasy – with an illusion too radically at odds with reality for any reconciliation to have been possible. An unconscious intuition of this is implicit in what she gives as the reason for her tears. But that intuition has to be brought into consciousness and confronted and assimilated before she can recover from the trauma. Over a period of two years she does recover: she marries Volyntsev. If she had truly loved Rudin, and not just her dream of him, she would surely have kept her word: that she would rather die than marry any other man. But the shattering of the dream shattered the love: there was nothing left to cling to, as Turgenev himself confirms when, in describing her anguish after Rudin's departure, he refers not to a loss of love, not to the loss of a beloved, but to 'a first disillusionment' (*pervoe razocharovanie*).

None of this, however, should disguise the capital differences between Natal'ya's fantasies and Rudin's. Rudin's embraced all the world, including himself; Natal'ya's concerned only Rudin: she was fully entitled to boast that she knew what love meant and that she knew what she meant when she said she loved him. Secondly, Rudin's illusions are substitutes for action and hindrances to action – opiate surrogates for living; Natal'ya's illusions are stimulants to action, and indeed extend the range of her aspirations and efforts. Above all: Rudin's fantasies have absorbed – drained off – his emotional resources; Natal'ya's have tapped new levels in the rich depths of her feelings. Turgenev shows us with equal artistry the first, unconscious stirrings of love in her, its brief, brave hour of expression, and the blank desolation of facing life without it.

However Rudin may have infected her momentarily with his illusions about himself, Natal'ya is basically a realist: intellectually honest, responsible, averse to self-deception and exaggeration (XI, 339: *dlya dushi iskrennei, ne zhelavshei obmanyvat' sebya, chuzhdoi legkomysliya i preuvelicheniya*). In this realism, as in the depth and strength of her feeling, Natal'ya is a true sister to Pushkin's Tat'yana. It is not so clear that Tat'yana shared Natal'ya's capacity for happiness, symbolized (somewhat whimsically) by her childhood habit of directing her evening walks always towards the still bright part of the sky. Tat'yana belonged to the age of elegiac poetry; she is at home in winter and under the moon rather than in spring and sunlight; she is pale, shy, sad, silent, a stranger in the midst of her own family.

Like so many girls of her own and the two previous 'generations', Natal'ya was born out of due season: there were as yet no fitting mates for them among the men of their age. Several decades more were to pass before Turgenev the novelist thought he could detect a significant change in that respect. Yet her marriage to Volyntsev does not appear to be a mere capitulation to convention. She rejects her mother's choice (Korchagin) and with him the values of her mother's world. She chooses 'a fine man' who 'loves her with all his heart', according to Lezhnëv (XII, 351), and whom she herself likes. He will look up to her and be ruled by her (Lezhnëv again); so

she will be free to live by her own values (as she would not have
been if she had insisted on pining away in her mother's shadow) and
to pass those on to her children. Her encounter with Rudin will not
have been for nothing: it has made a woman of her, and the ideals
he preached will live on in her and go to form the consciousness of
the next generation.

Within the microcosm of the novel, between its two poles – the
miniature court of Dar'ya Mikhailovna, with its phony glitter, its
veneer of French culture, its jester (Pigasov) and parasite (Pandalevski), and, over against it, the goodhearted and honourable but
dullish households of Lezhnëv and Volyntsev – the figures of Rudin
and Natal'ya stand out as vital, suffering human beings groping a
way through the fogs and bogs of Nicholas's Russia, with only
occasional glimpses of sunlight and with no firm ground under their
feet.

8

The 'Turgenev heroine': *A Nest of Gentry*

Turgenev's second novel, *A Nest of Gentry*,[1] was conceived and planned in the middle of 1856, a few months after the publication of *Rudin*. But he was abroad, unwell and unhappy, and he did not settle down to writing it till after his return to Russia in June 1858. He composed and completed it in the second half of that year; it was published in *The Contemporary* in January 1859 and in book form later that year. It was the most widely acclaimed, and in Russia remained the most popular and least controversial of his novels.

This second novel is considerably longer than the first. The difference cannot be measured by counting pages: 168 as against 132, so, roughly, a 27 per cent increase; but about 50,000 words compared with about 35,000: an increase of over 40 per cent. The discrepancy is due to a quasi-reversal in the proportions of narrative to dialogue: in *Rudin* narrative accounts for less than one-third of the text, in *A Nest of Gentry* for almost two-thirds. This results in a very different 'texture' for the two works. *Rudin* moves comparatively slowly but at a relatively high level of dramatic tension; *A Nest of Gentry* covers far more ground, but much of it at a lower level of tension.

No less significant are the differences in the lay-out of the two novels. *Rudin* consists of thirteen chapters, *A Nest of Gentry* of forty-six (in both works the last chapter is not numbered but entitled 'Epilogue'). That means that the average length of a chapter in *Rudin* is three times that of a chapter in *A Nest of Gentry*, and although the chapters in both works vary in length and some of the longer ones in *Rudin* comprise more than one scene, overall, we have the contrast between a short series of comparatively ample scenes and a much longer series of more concentrated vignettes. The multiplicity of scenes accommodates a larger cast of characters and a longer time-span: Lavretski's great-grandfather must have been born in the second quarter of the eighteenth century, but even if we disregard the times of his grandparents and great-grandparents as marginal figures, Lavretski himself was born in 1807 and the epilogue is dated 1850, so we have a bird's-eye view of nearly half a century, as compared with the twelve to fifteen years between Rudin's student days and his death.

A Nest of Gentry comprises four, very unequal, parts. The first – chapters I–VII – introduces us to all the principal characters except Lavretski's wife; this corresponds, as ravelling, to chapters I–III in *Rudin*. Part II, corresponding to the six-page flashback in chapter VI of *Rudin*, consists of chapters VIII–XVI: this gives us the history of Lavretski and the three preceding generations of his family. Part III, the birth and flowering of the love of Lavretski and Liza, occupies chapters XVII–XXXV, corresponding to chapters IV–XI in *Rudin*. The final part – the aftermath – makes up the last ten chapters and the epilogue; this corresponds to *Rudin's* chapter XII and epilogue.

In spite of such differences in technique, and differences we shall encounter in outlook and mood, both novels have their main action set in the same period – the beginning of the 1840s. It is not clear why Turgenev, writing at the end of the 1850s, in the stirring and hopeful years of a new reign, should have decided to plunge his characters back into the middle years of Nicholas I, far from any prospect of change and freedom; perhaps he felt a need, as in his early stories, to safeguard authorial perspective and balance by distancing his creation from his immediate circumstances.

This tampering with chronology creates some problems. Rudin was a Westerner, which was appropriate for the early forties, when Belinsky and Herzen were leaders of progressive thought and Turgenev was caricaturing Slavophils in *The Landowner*. Lavretski, though not a professed Slavophil, embraces a life that would have been approved by Slavophils and attacks or rejects the political and moral values of Westerners such as Panshin and Varvara Pavlovna; and this shift in authorial sympathies accords with the period when the novel was written rather than that which it purports to portray.[2]

That time-switch may account not only for the shift of sympathies or outlook but for the duality of tone or mood. Yarmolinsky contrasts our two novels in these terms: 'the atmosphere of *Rudin* is one of futility and frustration', whereas 'nostalgia pervades *A Nest of Gentry*'.[3] But perhaps there is a more important difference between the two worlds: in the second, Turgenev seems to have moved much closer to Existentialist positions – if we take the core of Existentialism to be the principle that man can make himself. Rudin had been fatally warped by his world, and though he comes to a limited understanding of his predicament, he barely begins to change himself or his style of life. Lavretski has been no less profoundly traumatized, by his education and his marriage, yet he does to a great extent remake himself and he does set a course for himself and hold to it. The long, dreary winter of Nicholas was over, the first years of Alexander hummed and vibrated with preparations for the ending of serfdom and, however personally unhappy Turgenev may have felt at the time of writing, it was almost inevitable that something of the new excitement and hope should get reflected in the book. And this finds expression not only in Lavretski's triumph over his past and in Liza's transcending the trammels of her world, but – more directly and unambiguously – in the glimpse of future happiness incarnated in the younger generation, hailed and blessed in Lavretski's farewell words in the epilogue.

One corollary of the lowered dramatic tension in *A Nest of Gentry* was the need to make the host of secondary characters more interesting. In *Rudin* most of the secondary characters are sketched in quite lightly. Apart from the hero and heroine, only Lezhnëv is developed in some depth. One indication of this is that we are shown something of his earlier life – and more vividly than the past of anyone except Rudin. In *A Nest of Gentry*, on the other hand, we have relatively detailed biographies for a surprising number of characters besides the protagonists: Lavretski's father, Liza's mother and nurse, Lemm and Panshin, to name only the most important.

But biographical detail is only one of the devices for investing these secondary characters with greater impact. They are also given more to do and to say. In *Rudin* the negative types – Pandalevski, Pigasov, even Dar'ya Mikhailovna – are not only 'flat',[4] that is, largely predictable, but essentially cogs in the machinery of the story. Pandalevski is a parasite on the make; he is needed chiefly to denounce Natal'ya's love for Rudin to his patroness. Pigasov is needed as a foil to Rudin and for comic relief. Some of the positive types are almost equally rôle-bound. Volyntsev is hardly anything more than (in theatre jargon) the 'second lover'. Lipina is essentially Lezhnëv's 'confidante'.

The chief secondary personages of *A Nest of Gentry* are surely far more vivid than any of those. Panshin, like Volyntsev, is the 'second lover', the hero's rival – but he is a three-dimensional figure. We are given his background, we are shown his talents at work. Volyntsev does scarcely anything but sigh or fume; Panshin draws, composes music and verse, sings, plays the piano, expounds his philosophy of life ('daring and a light touch'),[5] flirts with Liza's mother, teases Lemm, courts Liza, pits himself intellectually against Lavretski, emotionally against Lavretski's wife. We have his whole character and career unrolled before us.

Or compare the two 'confidantes', Lipina and old Marfa Timofeevna. What can we recall of Lipina beyond her chocolate-box prettiness and her kind heart? Marfa Timofeevna also has a heart of gold, but that is by no means all. She has character (which Lezhnëv explicitly denied to his Aleksandra). No doubt, she too is a type: the *bourru bienfaisant* in skirts; but we hardly recognize that as we read, only – if at all – on reflection. Her functions (no less than Panshin's) are manifold. She receives Lavretski's confidences and watches over Liza; she acts as a foil to her niece, Liza's mother, and she systematically punctures the pretensions and poses of those around her – her niece, Panshin, Gedeonovski continually squirm under her barbed comments. They are shams; she is genuine through and through. Yet she is not idealized – we are shown the limitations of her sympathies and understanding: in her attitude to Liza's religion, in her readiness to think the worst when she hears of Liza's night meeting with Lavretski in the garden, in her intolerance of Agaf'ya.

Similarly the two mothers, for all their basic affinities, are presented to us very differently. Both are middle-aged widows with children whose education they have left to other people and whom they hardly care for or understand; both are selfish, vain and indolent; both are interested only in men and have a particular weakness for young men. But Dar'ya Mikhailovna's rôle is almost purely functional: in the early chapters she is the lady of the house who provokes Pigasov into 'performing' and patronizes Rudin; in the later chapters she is Natal'ya's mother, who puts her foot down against any match between her daughter and a poor man and then tries to pick up the pieces of her relation with her daughter. Of Kalitina we see much more, beginning with her prehistory; her sentimental silliness is much more to the fore – and much livelier –

than Dar'ya Mikhailovna's series of 'great lady' poses. Kalitina actively supports Panshin as a suitor for her daughter's hand and intervenes actively, before our eyes, in the relations between Lavretski and his wife. Admittedly, this intervention is effective only in appearance – in reality Lavretski yields to Liza's plea, not to her mother's *coup de théâtre* – but we have been allowed to enjoy the comedy of Kalitina's seduction by the 'scarlet woman' and the comedy that she in her turn stages to bring Lavretski and his wife together.

Against their social background of eminently ordinary people Turgenev's heroes and young heroines – a Rudin, a Natal'ya, a Lavretski, a Liza – stand out in brave relief. They are the *raison d'être* of his novels: he writes novels not in order to indict his society – though he does that incidentally – but in order to discover the seed of the future, the new men and women to lead Russia out of her twilight of oppression and backwardness into the sunshine of freedom and culture.

The story of Lavretski is the story of a man uprooted in childhood, grotesquely mishandled in his formative years, groping his way back, through error, renunciation and sorrow, to strike roots in his native soil.

His father – like Herzen's father, like other Russians of that class and generation – had taken on a thick veneer of Western ways without assimilating much, if anything, of the spirit of the West. He was capable of marrying a serf-girl in deference to the teaching of Rousseau (or rather, really, to spite his father), but not capable of living with her or even of vindicating her position and dignity over against his family. He was capable of disrupting his son's whole psychological development with the eclectic eccentricity of an upbringing based on Rousseau's *Emile* and similar works – but capable too of lapsing into religious bigotry, abjuring his 'English' way of life, truckling to the authorities, and sinking finally into near-imbecility when the scare of the Decembrist Rising precipitated the descent of old age upon him.

At his father's death, Lavretski, aged 23, without a friend in the world, with little or no knowledge of Russian culture (his education had comprised, in addition to various forms of physical training, mathematics and the physical sciences, international law, heraldry and carpentry, but no Russian history or Russian literature) – Lavretski set out to re-educate himself and entered Moscow University.

There his age cut him off from his fellow students – all save one. Loneliness and inexperience led to the disaster of his marriage. It took him two years to discover the kind of woman he had married; after leaving her, it took him another four years abroad to get over the shock and face the claims of his country once more. He goes home with the idea of learning to administer his estates so as to ensure the prosperity of his peasants. But the meeting with Liza and the rumoured death of his wife tempt him into making a second bid for happiness. The reappearance of his wife (with a child in tow) snatches Liza from him almost immediately, and he goes back to the land and masters the task he had accepted as his objective in life.

Lavretski turns his back on his father's teaching to enter into the spiritual inheritance of his serf mother. We have here the apotheosis of the Slavophil virtues: toil, patience, humility, resignation: the virtues preached by Gogol – without much understanding of the underlying spirit – some ten years earlier, and by Dostoevsky ten years later.

We have seen how in Rudin the Hamlet-type elements of cerebration and egocentrism predominated, though with an admixture of 'Don Quixote' in the form of faith in his ideals and enthusiasm in proclaiming them. Lavretski, on the other hand, starts out and ends up as almost pure Don Quixote, in spite of his egocentric quest of personal happiness and the professed scepticism of his middle years. What he lacks of Don Quixote is, above all, the vitality: so that his faith is dogged rather than enthusiastic, his spirit is steadfast rather than 'great and bold'.

But there is a further, less obvious transmutation to be noted. Not only has the primarily Hamlet-type Western protagonist of the first novel given place to a near-Slavophil Don Quixote in the second, but one could say – simplifying slightly – that in *A Nest of Gentry* Rudin and Lezhnëv have exchanged places: Rudin has been stripped of his tragic attributes to contract into Mikhalevich; Lezhnëv has been invested with the attributes of a tragic hero to blossom out as Lavretski.[6]

Mikhalevich is a diminished and somewhat caricatural Rudin: he stands in much the same relation to Rudin as the personages of *An Evening in Sorrento* stand to those of *A Month in the Country*. Like Rudin, Mikhalevich is poor and shabby. Like Rudin, he is a product of the student *kruzhki* and the German Idealist philosophy of the 1830s and, more obviously than Rudin, he is an 'eternal student', who has remained fixated at that level. Like Rudin, he sets up to be the keeper of other people's consciences and, like him, seeks belatedly to apply his educational urges to schoolmastering. But as a comic character, and basically modest, he is unlikely to provoke anybody's jealousy or hostility, so that when we leave him, he appears, unlike Rudin, to have found himself a permanent niche.

Although a comic character, Mikhalevich is the – innocent – cause of a tragedy: Lavretski's marriage. His brief reappearance in Lavretski's life at a crucial moment – during Lemm's visit, on the eve of Liza's visit to Vasil'evskoe – may be compared and contrasted with Rudin's reappearance in Lezhnëv's life during his stay with Dar'ya Mikhailovna. Superficially, they were quite unlike: several weeks of embarrassed aloofness on neighbouring estates as against a few hours under the same roof in vehement, intimate debate. But though Rudin affected Lezhnëv then only indirectly – through the impression he was making on Aleksandra and Natal'ya – while Mikhalevich's impact on his host was direct (and vociferous), the effects in both men were very similar. In both, memories of their youth, their university days, are revived, to quicken sensibilities that had lain dormant: signalized in Lezhnëv by his growing ability to see Rudin in perspective and judge him with generosity, in Lavretski by the sense of mission he brings to the running of his estates (which he had, admittedly, taken up 'with diligence and care' even before his old comrade's visit; XXI, 191). What is achieved by the two visits is not any change in the course of Lezhnëv's or Lavretski's outward life, but a stimulation or enrichment of their inner life, and so, perhaps, some unconscious compensation for the harm they had caused at an earlier date.

Returning to his estate and rediscovering the ancestral way of life, the peasants and their traditions, Lavretski rediscovers the healing power of nature, in its immemorial slow drift, its drowsy silences. 'Always, at all times, life here is tranquil and unhurried', he thinks; 'whoever enters its confines must submit: here there is nothing to get excited for, nothing to be troubled by [. . .] And what vigour all around, how healthful this inactivity and quiet! [. . .] May the tedium here sober me, calm me, prepare me too to be able to carry out my task without haste' (XX, 190).

The implication is that the educated man, who has been torn

from the bosom of nature, has thereby become enfeebled, unhappy and spiritually deformed, while the people have remained close to nature and natural themselves, so that to return to nature is to return to the people and vice versa. For Lavretski, as for the Slavophils, returning to nature and to the people means renouncing one's personality in the Western sense – not only renouncing the Promethean, or Faustian, effort to dominate nature, to impose one's own patterns on reality, but renouncing personal happiness and the higher achievements of civilization in the realms of art and thought, in order to assimilate oneself to the rhythms of nature and to the needs and habits of one's peasants.

Rudin was an uprooted Faustian, who only late and dimly realized his lack of roots; and though he spoke of proving himself of service to the people, he could conceive such service only in terms of his own personality: that is, from outside and from above. In the light of Turgenev's thesis that the day of the superfluous men – the Hamlets – is over and that the future belongs to the Quixotes, it may be worth while to look a little more closely at how his heroes fare in the last resort.

Both men appear to us for the last time as already old – Lavretski at 43, Rudin evidently within a year or two of the same age. Of Lavretski we are told in so many words: 'he had aged not only in face and body, he had aged in soul' (Epilogue, 293). Rudin is described in more pathetic circumlocution: 'His features had changed little . . . but their expression was different. His eyes had a different look; his whole being – his movements, now dragging, now abruptly impetuous, his speech, which had lost its fire as if from exhaustion – expressed an ultimate weariness, a quiet, secret grief' (Epilogue, 356).

Lavretski, we are told, is entitled to feel satisfied because he has not lost his faith in goodness, his strength of purpose, his will to work; but it is plain that neither has Rudin lost his faith in goodness or his will to 'work' – in his very different way – and his death demonstrates that the faltering of his purpose at his last meeting with Lezhněv ('No, friend, now I am tired [. . .] I have had enough': Epilogue, 366) was only a temporary result of the fiasco that had immediately preceded it.

True, Lavretski can point to material success – to the productivity of his lands and the wellbeing of his peasants, whereas the seed sown by Rudin cannot be surveyed or measured. But was it not the Rudins of real life through whom, in that generation of the forties, the spirit of the future was taking root in Russia – the spirit which surely prepared and hastened the emancipation of the serfs?

As Lavretski looked back over his life, he felt sadness, but neither depression nor distress: he had things to regret, but none to be ashamed of (Epilogue, 293). Here he may have had some advantage over Rudin, who no doubt had reasons for shame in relation to his mother and, perhaps, to Natal'ya and others; but might it not be said that he had set his sights so much higher, that his activity had ranged so much more widely? 'He that is down need fear no fall', as the old song says; or, in Rudin's own words: 'I have never been able to build anything; but it is hard to build, old fellow, when you have no solid ground under your feet, when you have to create your own groundwork yourself' (Epilogue, 357).

Both men have remained movingly free from resentment or bitterness: Lezhnëv remarks with surprise on Rudin's freedom from rancour; and Lavretski welcomes 'though sorrowfully, yet without envy or any dark feeling' the onset of lonely old age (Epilogue, 293).

Is the pathos of Lavretski's end less or greater than that of Rudin's? Has the preacher Rudin deserved any less well of his country than the ploughman Lavretski? And which is more heroic: to accept the burdens and toil of customary rôles, like Lavretski (and Natal'ya) or to go out into the wilderness in pursuit of a vision of one's own, like Rudin, and Liza? These are the kinds of questions that readers of Turgenev must argue about.

Dostoevsky, who regarded Pushkin's Tat'yana as 'the apotheosis of Russian womanhood', declared that Liza was one of only two other heroines in Russian literature worthy to be named in the same breath.[7] But as a bearer of values largely alien to modern societies – values as remote from us as our own Middle Ages – Liza may seem a riddle to many readers, as she certainly has to not a few critics. And the difficulties are not diminished by the fact that Turgenev, who at the best of times had little use for psychological analysis, is more than usually sparing of it in relation to Liza. In fact, we might have had to give her up as an impenetrable mystery, if Turgenev had not been persuaded by his friends – very late – to write chapter xxxv (the story of her childhood and development up until the opening of the novel). It seems incredible now, in retrospect, that this should have been added as an afterthought –

doubly incredible when one considers the many pages devoted to the antecedents of sundry lesser personages, and trebly incredible when one recalls that Turgenev approved of the title *Liza* for the first English translation of the work.[8]

But even with chapter xxxv to refer to, critics have tended to ignore Liza, while expatiating on Natal'ya, Elena and Marianna (the heroines of *Rudin*, *On the Eve* and *Virgin Soil*), or to extol her in madrigals or hymns – which, however well deserved, make poor substitutes for explanations. A. I. Batyuto, in his substantial monograph, *Turgenev as Novelist*,[9] mentions Liza twice. First he adduces her as an example of Turgenev characters who embody a fusion of moral with aesthetic qualities. Later he speaks of her 'poetically brittle femininity and defencelessness in face of grim reality' which sets her 'apart from the whole of nineteenth-century Russian literature' and sees her as radiating 'a delicate poetry and inconspicuous but indubitable originality'. For Freeborn[10] Liza's 'image calls to mind not a face or a voice but the nostalgic residue of a love song or the compact and exactly phrased lines of an immaculate sonnet'. She herself is 'impervious to' the 'emotional needs' of those who love her, 'unmoved, almost impersonal, wrapped with a dedicated absorption in her nun-like calm'. Yarmolinsky[11] attributes to Liza 'a gossamery quality' and sums her up thus: 'For Liza, the Russian Gretchen, is less a flesh-and-blood woman than a symbol of unattainable happiness and irrecoverable youth.'

Two critics deserve more than honourable mention: Ovsyaniko-Kulikovsky, who devotes to Liza no less than two chapters of his book on Turgenev[12] and Gershenzon,[13] who in his brief mention of her makes two capital points about her attitude to life.

Ovsyaniko-Kulikovsky traces with fine critical insight the subtle build-up of our image of Liza: largely indirect, largely through the reactions to her of the other characters – Panshin and Marfa Timofeevna, but above all Lemm and Lavretski. He is particularly successful at bringing out the significance of Lemm and his music: it is through Lemm's admiration of Liza that we get our first inkling of how unusual and impressive a person she is; and it is through Lemm's canticle of triumphant love that we are given our crowning glimpse of what love meant (or better: what love might have come to mean) to her. As for Lavretski, he serves as the prism through which the reader discovers Liza: hero and reader meet her almost simultaneously and get to know her together.

But if this literary analysis is excellent, the same can hardly be said of the preceding psychological analysis. Ovsyaniko-Kulikovsky declares Liza 'a saint' – and evidently conceives a saint as an incarnation of the Kantian categorical imperative. This is, at best, unhelpful: whatever Liza is, it must include something to account for the love and devotion of generations of readers.

Gershenzon is not interested in Liza as an individual but only as an illustration of a particular facet of Turgenev's view of the world. But he observes, first, that Liza is characterized by a strong urge to repress personal will: to be a personality is a sin, and to assert one's personality in seeking happiness or in a love of one's own choosing is a still greater sin; and secondly, as a corollary of this conviction, she lives in fear of punishment, as witness her reactions to the news that Lavretski's wife had reappeared. To herself she says, 'It serves me right!' and to Lavretski, at their next meeting: 'Yes, we've been punished promptly': as if it could only have been a question of time anyway. But Gershenzon does not investigate further or deeper.

These two basic attitudes should not surprise the reader who remembers Liza's childhood. During the first four years of her life – the critical years – she had no one to love. Her father she feared; her feeling for her mother was 'indeterminate'. No wonder she was a serious, well-behaved child, little given to laughter and disinclined to play with dolls – that is, to play at parents and children.

Between the ages of 4 and 7 Liza came under the influence of Agaf'ya, a woman of peasant origin who, after leading a full life, including two marriages and a liaison with Liza's grandfather, had sought refuge from repeated reverses and misfortunes in religion. Liza developed a strong affection for this new nurse, who was probably the first adult to take her seriously and devote herself to the child; but the form taken by this affection is worth noting: it was not active or demonstrative, but passive – Liza listened to Agaf'ya and identified with her. In other words, she imbibed, without fully understanding, the attitudes and values of a woman who had known more sorrows than joys, who had been humbled by life and had bowed herself down in resignation. Those attitudes and values came to the child, at the conscious level, through the channel of her nurse's perpetual tales of saints and martyrs. These were as remote from everyday life as any fairy-tales could have been; but whereas children soon sense that fairy-tales are not unconditionally real, these religious stories were presented to the child Liza as the highest reality. And her feelings were further played upon by the mystery attending her visits to mass, which had to be made in secret in the very early morning, at hours when she would normally have been in bed and asleep: this must have reinforced her sense of the rift between the world around her and what Agaf'ya had accustomed her to regard as a better world.

The interlude with Mademoiselle Moreau, between the ages of 7 and 9, will not have affected her significantly, especially as Agaf'ya remained within reach – in the house. But at 9 she lost within a short period her father, who died, and Agaf'ya, who went away on pilgrimage. Marfa Timofeevna, who from that time on assumed the chief responsibility for her upbringing, loved her and did win her affection – but not without grave reservations, inasmuch as she took a view of religion very different from Agaf'ya's and accordingly sought to moderate the little girl's zeal and bring it within what she considered the bounds of reason.

The almost simultaneous loss of a father and a mother-surrogate was likely to be a great shock to any child, but in Liza's case we might suspect a major trauma. We know that she had feared her father, though she had had almost nothing to do with him – he was too busy to have time for his children. Unmotivated – or exaggerated – fear suggests a projection of repressed hate: that is, hatred of him for his failure to love her, driven from consciousness by religious or similar inhibitions, would have found expression in subconsciously ascribing to him her own hatred, which would then have resulted in – and justified – the fear of him that was her conscious attitude.

Nor is this mere abstract speculation. It receives confirmation from her diffuse sense of guilt and fear of happiness ('Happiness did not become me; even when I had hopes of happiness, there was something always clutching at my heart' XLV, 285–6). It receives further confirmation from her final resolve to devote her life to expiating her own (imaginary) sins and other people's real ones – specifically those of her father. And it is confirmed more subtly by two indications of frightening forces of repressed hostility or aggression that were apt to be unleashed in her by conflict. We are told (XXIX, 221): 'When she disagreed with someone she was talking to, she always lowered her voice, while at the same time experiencing great agitation': the lowering of her voice is by way of counteracting the violence of her feelings, and the great agitation is

a reaction to that same violence, of which she would not necessarily
– or, perhaps, in most cases – be conscious. The second indication is
less devious: when she received the news of the return of Lavretski's wife, there welled up in her 'certain bitter, malevolent
surges of feeling which frightened her' (XXXIX, 257) and which she
fought down only with difficulty.

Hence her fear of all conflict, her fear of giving offence to anyone
(XXXV, 243–4). Hence her reluctance to invest strong feeling in any
earthly object: 'she loved everyone, but nobody in particular'
(XXXV, 244). Hence her unwillingness not only to assert herself, but
to recognize her own qualities: 'I had thought that like my maid,
Nastya, I had no words *of my own*' (XXVI, 211).

From all these fears, conscious and subconscious, and the sense
of guilt she takes refuge in religion and in a pervasive sense of duty.
The sense of duty has the twofold function of regulating her
relations with other people while removing from her shoulders the
onus of responsibility: in other words, while eschewing all self-
assertion. The function of her religion is more complex. First,
obviously, it serves as the basis and validation of her sense of duty
and supplies that sense of duty with its content: that is, it tells her
what she is bound to do and why she is bound. Secondly, it is
related, in ways that are never made quite clear, to her sense of
guilt: that would appear to be the implication of her pronouncement: 'one needs to be a Christian [. . .] because every human being
has to die' (XXVI, 210): religion is to enable us to face or cope with
death; and death is a subject she thinks about 'often'. And it is to be
noted that fear (awe) is a basic element in her relation to God – in
fact, the first to be mentioned: 'the image of an ever-present,
omniscient God, invading her soul with a kind of sweet violence
(*siloi*) filled her [or it, i.e. her soul] with reverent fear' (XXXV, 242).
But Christ she came to feel as close, familiar, dear; and so, thirdly,
perhaps the most important function of her religion is that of
providing her with emotional scope – with a field in which she can
give free rein to the positive feelings of love, abandon, joy,
enthusiasm, to which she dares not give more than very limited
expression on the earthly plane. 'She . . . prayed with delight, with a
kind of controlled, shy surge of emotion . . . she loved only God –
ardently, timidly, tenderly' (*vostorzhenno, robko, nezhno*).

But all this does not entitle us to attribute to her a definite
religious 'vocation'. When we meet her, she is seriously considering

marrying Panshin. She thinks him a good man and admits that she likes him. That she probably likes him more than she realizes is implied in her breaking faith with Lemm – showing Panshin Lemm's cantata: a rather surprising lapse for a young lady with such an overwhelming sense of duty. She is drawn to Panshin, moreover, by the fact that she is not in love with him, so that in marrying him she would not be seeking her own happiness so much as gratifying her mother ('I am obeying, I am not taking anything on myself', xxix, 221).

That she does not marry him is due to the intervention of Lavretski, with whom she does then fall in love – much to her dismay (words like 'you frighten me' and 'I'm afraid' escape her more than once). However, this does not mean that if Lavretski's wife had actually died, Liza would not have married him and made him happy and achieved happiness herself, in spite of the load of fear and guilt under which she had grown up. This is made clear after her two painful scenes, with her mother and with Marfa Timofeevna:

She felt shame and bitterness and pain, but neither doubt nor fear – and Lavretski had become even dearer to her. She had hesitated as long as she had not understood herself; but after that tryst, that kiss, she could hesitate no longer: she knew that she loved – that she had fallen in love honestly, seriously, had committed herself firmly, for life – and she feared no threats: she felt that no force could break this bond. (xxxviii, 254)

Her fateful decision to take the veil – which has puzzled some critics and moved others to disappointment or scorn – would seem to follow naturally from this analysis. The fear of happiness, the sense of guilt, the dread of conflict would combine to point to withdrawal from the world in a crisis (only love could have kept her back – if love had not been, as here, forbidden). And those are actually the reasons which Liza herself adduces: 'This lesson was not [sent] for nothing [...] happiness did not become me [...] I know everything, my own sins, and those of others [...] All this must be expiated by prayer' (xlv, 285–6).

But in the days preceding her decision, emotions – mostly negative – had been intensified in her beyond endurance, and she adds yet another reason: 'I feel sickened, I want to shut myself away for good' (xlv, 286). And this also is relevant and true. A sense of duty such as hers implies a more than ordinary pride and fastidiousness, and the experiences she had just passed through must have excruciated the one and nauseated the other: the intrusion of so many vulgar eyes and tongues into her cherished intimacies, the scenes with her mother and Marfa Timofeevna, the meetings with Lavretski's wife and, perhaps worst of all, the upsurge in herself of inadmissible and hateful passions.

Moreover, her decision can be seen as a feminine counterpart to Lavretski's. Like him, she is dedicating herself to service: not only – most obviously – to the service of God, but to the service of the souls of sinners, whom she loves, or ought to love. Her prayers will atone for the sins of the father she had feared (and perhaps hated), for the frivolity and futility of the mother she had been unable to love, maybe for the lack of faith of the man she had loved and renounced. The 'missions' of both the lovers – both forms of service – involve the same 'Slavophil' virtues of patience, humility and resignation.

Liza's nature is not rich or fertile ('God had not bestowed on her particularly brilliant abilities or great cleverness; nothing came easily to her': xxxv, 243), but it makes up for this in strength and depth. Yet even this strength and depth are rooted in repression and inhibition. It is in saying no, in renunciation, that her strength is displayed. The deeps in her may kindle the dreams of such men as Lemm and Lavretski; but, in this base world, she can give them no more than dreams.

Does this mean that Liza is a feminine counterpart of the superfluous man? Certainly, she has more in common with such men than does Natal'ya, or Elena, or Marianna; but she differs from them at least as much as she resembles them. What she shares with them is chiefly her fear of life and of emotion and the inability to 'let go' of herself: the inability, to which Panshin refers, to sit still and do nothing (vi, 142) is symptomatic of a general inability to relax at deeper levels. What chiefly differentiates her from them is her strength of will and singlemindedness and the character of her faith. Not just the fact that she has a faith: although few of the superfluous men can claim as much, Rudin at least does have a faith; and if his is philosophical while hers is religious, that is of minor significance. What is important is that Liza's life is the expression or embodiment of her faith, whereas Rudin's life is a series of efforts to achieve a similar integration.

However, to elucidate the unconscious roots of Liza's behaviour, her unconscious emotional patterns, is not to explain – much less, explain away – the poetry of her personality. It is the poetry of a child who, having found no understanding or love in this world, has projected her need for love and understanding beyond the stars; who, hemmed in and stifled by the cloying vulgarity all around her, has withdrawn into the fastness of her own fantasy and there keeps herself unfalteringly clear of the lotus-eaters and their easy pleasures; who, too frail to transcend fear but too brave to succumb to it, has fashioned her fears into an armour of faith: which, like all armour, protects only at the price of constricting and excluding, of acting as barrier and limitation. It is the poetry of youth keeping faith with itself when life seems only to cheat and mock: without wishful thinking and without self-pity, refusing to capitulate and – which is more difficult – refusing to compromise.

All this poetry is symbolized in the song of the nightingale, to which she listens with Lavretski in the summer moonlight, and in the paean of heroic love which Lemm plays to Lavretski on the night when he and Liza first kiss.

It was a long time since Lavretski had heard anything like it. With its first note the sweet, impassioned melody took possession of the heart; it waxed and waned, filled with the radiance and yearning of inspiration, happiness, beauty; it evoked everything that is dear and mysterious and sacred on earth, and, breathing an immortal sadness, soared to die away in the heavens. (XXXIV, 238)

A Nest of Gentry is steeped in music, and music is Liza's element.

9

The New Man and the New Woman: *On the Eve*

Turgenev's next novel, *On the Eve*,[1] was written in the summer and autumn of 1859 and published in January 1860 – but not in *The Contemporary*, to which he had given virtually all his writings of the preceding twelve or thirteen years. His relations with that journal had been progressively strained by the growing influence on its policies of the radical critics Dobrolyubov and Chernyshevsky, and he broke with it when an article of Dobrolyubov, containing incisive criticism of *A Nest of Gentry*, appeared in its pages regardless of his pleas and protests.

On the Eve should be read with certain developments of the literary and political background in mind. First, there was the increasing clamour of radical critics for a new type of hero to replace the superfluous man, whom they regarded as out of date and out of place in the changing circumstances of the new reign. Secondly, Goncharov, arguably the most considerable of Russian novelists after Turgenev himself, had already attempted to respond to those demands: in the first half of 1859 he had published his second novel, *Oblomov*, in which he offered his version of not only the New Man but the New Woman as well.

His New Man, Stolz, a social hybrid, the product of a marriage between a cultured Russian lady and a practical German bourgeois, was supposed to have inherited the disparate virtues of his parents in roughly equal proportions. The radicals had dismissed Stolz as artistically unsatisfactory and socially (i.e., politically) irrelevant: so the challenge to portray a New Man had still to be met. Thirdly, though no date had yet been set for the Emancipation of the Serfs, it was evident that Russia was one year nearer to the blessed event and that it could not be delayed much longer. And fourthly, Turgenev was thrilled by the Italian struggle for national independence, which in 1859–60 was uniting the whole peninsula (except Rome), for the first time, into a modern nation-state. To his friend, Countess Lambert, he wrote[2] that, if he were only a little younger, he would throw aside all his work and go to Italy 'to breathe that now doubly blessed air. So there still is enthusiasm on this earth! [There are] people [who] know how to sacrifice themselves, are capable of joy, frenzy, hope! I would at least watch [all] that.'

Paradoxically, the first germ of *On the Eve* can be traced back to 1854 – before either *Rudin* or *A Nest of Gentry* had been conceived. In that year a neighbouring landowner, V. V. Karateev, about to leave for the Crimean Front and not expecting to return alive, entrusted to Turgenev a notebook in which he had set down the story of his love for a Russian girl, who at first responded but then fell in love with a Bulgarian student and went off with him to Bulgaria, where he soon died. The manuscript was to be published if possible; if not, Turgenev would be free to make use of it in any way he pleased. It was duly submitted to *The Contemporary* and turned down. The following year, while writing *Rudin*, he began to be haunted by the image of Elena, 'at that time still a new type in Russian life . . . but I needed a hero, a character to whom Elena, with her unfocussed yet powerful urge towards freedom, could give herself' (the image of a personage, of a 'new type' was usually the nucleus of a Turgenev work of fiction). Meanwhile, the writing of *Rudin* and then of *A Nest of Gentry* kept Elena at the back of his mind. When he was at last free to concentrate on her, he remembered his neighbour's notebook and, discerning no adequate Russian hero on the social scene, decided to conscript its Bulgarian.[3]

As compared to the two earlier novels, *On the Eve* is closer to *A Nest of Gentry* in length and roughly midway between the two in the proportion of narrative to dialogue; the cast of characters is even shorter than in *Rudin*; the chapters remain short as in *A Nest of Gentry*. The question addressed by *On the Eve* is again: 'What kind of leaders does Russia need and where are they?' But here for the first time the question is put explicitly. Shubin, who interprets Elena's choice of Insarov as implying that there are no Russian men worthy of her, twice asks cryptic old Uvar Ivanovich: 'When will our time come? When will men be born among us?' (xxx, 142 and xxxv, 167). On the first occasion he receives the oracular response that in time there will be such men; on the second, the old man contents himself with a vague gesture while staring into the distance – and we are left to guess whether that is because the second question has been asked by letter or whether it indicates that Uvar

Ivanovich (and his creator?) have lost faith in the interval between the two. Once more the story is a love story; but whereas hitherto the heroine's love has been frustrated, it now meets with an impassioned return: there is a period of happiness, however chequered and fleeting.

In his first attempt to create a positive hero Turgenev aimed to break away both from the Slavophil axiom that salvation must come from the people and from the radical demand for revolutionary leadership. He was firmly opposed to revolution in Russia (though not necessarily in Italy or elsewhere) and he considered the Russian masses not advanced enough to produce sufficiently enlightened leaders. Leadership *was* the key to progress, but the leaders must be enlightened, intelligent (like Hamlet) as well as heroic (like Don Quixote).[4] In the event, the hero of *On the Eve* appears to be significantly nearer to the radical than to the Slavophil ideal: he is an educated commoner and has revolutionary affiliations, though his revolution is not directed against Russia and we are not shown any of his revolutionary activities.

The difficulties of creating a new type of hero were compounded by the fact that here, for the first time, Turgenev had to rely on divination rather than observation, in which (as he well knew) his artistic mastery was rooted. The protagonist of Karateev's fifteen-page story cannot have been more than a silhouette or outline, and Turgenev had never met Katranov, the real-life prototype of that protagonist. No doubt he will have supplemented the data of Karateev's sketch by enquiries among Bulgarians and others who had known the man; but few if any of these will have been competent to supply the mass of live detail needed for literary creation.

Few critics, even among those most sympathetic to Turgenev's aims, have regarded Insarov, the Bulgarian hero of *On the Eve*, as an artistic success. Many have explained this as due to Turgenev's having had no live model to work from; but surely it is no less due to the idea from which he started, the conception of his hero in exemplary or (painful though it is to associate the epithet with Turgenev) didactic terms.

He had set out to depict a 'consciously heroic nature'; and he apparently assumed that such a nature must be endued with some of the attributes of a hero of classical tragedy. The tragic story of the murder of Insarov's parents by the Turks was not part of

Katranov's biography.[5] Katranov died at the age of 23 or 24; Turgenev makes Insarov two or three years older in order to interpolate a (mythical) return to Bulgaria before the novel opens, allowing time for him to mature from a simple student into a veteran nationalist leader carrying the scars of his clashes with the oppressors of his country. And whereas Insarov decides to return home for good after the outbreak of the Crimean War, when Russian troops had already occupied Moldavia and Wallachia (the future Romania) and would no doubt have gone on to drive the Turks out of Bulgaria, if France and Britain had not then intervened on the Turkish side, Katranov's last visit home was actually in the first half of 1853, before the outbreak of any war, so before there was any prospect of shaking off the Turkish yoke.

However, it is not the superimposition of a tragic biography that constitutes Insarov's heaviest handicap, but his characterization. When he comes to stay with Bersenev, Bersenev realizes that his guest 'never changes any of his decisions' (XI, 54). This is basically a Romantic attitude (deliciously guyed by Bernard Shaw in the dashing Bulgarian patriot of his *Arms and the Man*). Equally Romantic is the way Insarov deals with the drunken German on the excursion to Tsaritsyno. The feat needn't have been presented Romantically if all that was wanted was to contrast Insarov's effectiveness in action with Shubin's verbiage: Insarov was young and fit and had the initiative, the German was very drunk and over-confident, so it would have been quite in order for Insarov to have knocked him into the water. Instead, we are given to understand that Insarov picked him up – a man bigger and much heavier than himself – and, as he had threatened to do, threw him in.[6]

As if the Romantic attitudinizing were not enough, we have the Spartan or Boy Scout traits. Before settling down to work for the day, Insarov gets up at 4.0 a.m., runs round the whole of Kuntsevo, takes a dip in the river and downs a glass of cold milk. This may go some way towards accrediting his prowess at Tsaritsyno, but makes it all the harder to believe that he could later have had his health ruined by a mere downpour of rain.

His attitude to his recreations is no less strenuous. When he agrees to devote a whole day to relaxation, he sets himself to enjoy it with Anglo-Saxon earnestness: he 'walked without hurrying, looked, breathed, spoke and smiled serenely [...] and enjoyed himself thoroughly' (XI, 56). Shubin could not resist whispering to

Bersenev: 'That is just how good little boys go for their Sunday walks.'

His work was planned on a similarly heroic scale, comprising the study of Russian history, law and political economy; translation into Russian of Bulgarian songs and chronicles; collection of materials on the 'Eastern Question' (i.e., the problem situation of the ailing Ottoman Empire); and the writing of a Bulgarian grammar for Russians and a Russian grammar for Bulgarians. If such a programme was not calculated to lead to a nervous breakdown, it hardly inspires much confidence in our hero's realism (even had there been no such outside claims on his time as we see there were).

Perhaps it should be pleaded that the comic aspect of Insarov is required – to complete his resemblance to Don Quixote. Admittedly, the narrator appears to be totally unaware of it, as do all the characters save one; but that one exception, Shubin, while akin to Karateev in temperament and personality, certainly expresses some views of Turgenev himself. So is this an extreme example of Turgenev's devious subtlety or is it a breakthrough of the repressed? In other words, could Turgenev consciously identify with Shubin's gentle mockery of Insarov, or was he only impelled by his artist's instinct to show that that was how a person like Shubin was bound to react to a person like Insarov?

Insarov, like Liza in *A Nest of Gentry*, is revealed to the reader less by what he himself does and says than by the other characters' reactions to him. Bersenev is full of admiration for his Bulgarian friend; but though he supplies Elena with an outline of Insarov's biography, he is not very good at explaining just for what reasons or in what respects that friend deserves her admiration. She must find out for herself, he says, and by way of characterization can offer only the paradox: 'a man of iron. And at the same time, for all his intensity and even secretiveness, there is something childlike and candid in him' (x, 52).

Shubin, whose judgment is rarely warped by his prejudices, is critical, but, so far as we can check, just. His summing-up after a first encounter runs: no talents, no poetry, no charm; no intellectual complexity or depth; but a vast capacity for work, a good memory, a sound and lively intelligence; starkness;[7] and a real bond with his people (xii, 60). For Bersenev, Insarov's strength is awesome but, by implication, static ('iron'); Shubin conceives it as dynamic but potentially destructive: capable of demolishing walls and pulverizing people. It impresses and makes him uneasy at the same time. What he respects, admires and even envies in Insarov is his 'bond with his people' – in sharp contrast to the gulf separating the Russian educated classes from the masses – and his 'cause': that is, the liberation of his country.

To Elena, as to Bersenev and Shubin, Insarov is, first and foremost, an 'extraordinary' man. At one point, she cannot help being reminded by something about Insarov of the former butler, Vasili, who had saved an old man from a burning hut at the risk of his own life, who had had a simple, even stupid, face – and had ended up as a drunkard (xvi, 80). The point here, of course, is not that she expects Insarov to turn into a drunkard, nor even that she finds his face stupid, but that she has the impression that he is a hero, as Vasili was, and that perhaps there is not much to him beyond his heroism. Vasili's heroism had made her want to bow down before him; and Insarov, in the early stages of their acquaintance, inspires her with such awe that she dares not put to him the questions she is burning to ask.

What, then, is this 'heroism' which makes Bersenev appear to Elena 'a little man' in comparison with Insarov? It is, clearly, not a matter of anything he has done: so far, he has chiefly endured; and if he works hard, so does Bersenev. The core of Insarov's 'heroism' is perhaps his conviction – his faith, and his certainty and concentration of purpose – his 'inflexibility of will' (xi, 54). Both these are functions of his capacity to give himself unreservedly: to a cause in which he believes absolutely and which he serves with the whole of his will-power. The outward expression of this inner disposition is, firstly, a serenity which Elena contrasts, somewhat enviously, with her own unrest, and, secondly, the impressiveness, the suggestion of contained power to which such men as Bersenev and Shubin cannot but pay tribute, while his compatriots see in him a leader on whom they can rely unconditionally.

It is striking that for Elena the essence – and the essential virtue – of such heroism (i.e., self-dedication) is that it relieves the hero of sorrow and responsibility: 'Whoever has given himself wholly, wholly, wholly – has little to be anxious about, he no longer has anything to answer for. Then it is not what he wants, but what the cause demands' (xvi, 83).[8] In other words, individualism involves the stress of choosing and the pursuit of personal ends, and is bound up with unhappiness, whereas the hero sinks his self in his cause and all other ends are subordinated to its requirements.

This accords, too, with Bersenev's words in the first chapter of the novel, where its key motif is introduced. 'Is there really nothing higher than happiness?' he had asked. 'Is it not an egoistic word, a word which divides people?' And to Shubin's counter-question as to what words unite people, he replies: 'Why, art – you are an artist – country, learning, freedom, justice ... and love too ... but not the love you crave for now: not love-as-joy, but love-as-sacrifice' (I, 14).

These values are shared by Elena (though she might not be capable of formulating them in just such terms); yet it is Elena who brings Insarov down, through love, from the heroic to the everyday plane and, in so doing, destroys him. For her, it is true, their love involves some not inconsiderable sacrifices: it will cost her her home, her family, her country, not to mention the material comfort in which she has grown up. But for him it is almost entirely love-as-joy, and his first impulse – to run away from it – is a wise one: in relation to his mission and even to his integrity as a person. Baulked in his attempt at flight, he falls back on the traditionally fatal course of trying to serve two masters. The first result of this is that he gambles away his health. The second is that he loses his famous will-power: in the scene in which they become lovers, the part he plays is anything but heroic. So that it is symbolically appropriate that he is not allowed to do anything more for his Bulgaria, but dies prematurely and to no purpose in a far, foreign land.[9]

In fine, Insarov represents not an interesting character so much as an interesting history and situation. A basic weakness in his portrayal is that he is not made to 'act' – that is, to reveal character by words or deeds – except, in a very limited way, in his relation with Elena. In particular, we see nothing directly of his relations with his compatriots. That means that we never see his leadership in action, and the little we hear about it is so generic, so jejune, that it leaves hardly any impression with us.

Now, in a sense, the crux of the novel must be whether, or how far, Turgenev succeeds in making the reader share Elena's conviction of Insarov's superiority to his Russian contemporaries. Clearly, the question answers itself in regard to the windbag Lupoyarov.[10] Nor are we in danger of sharing Zoya's preference

for Kurnatovski, who is essentially another Panshin, brought up to
date by relieving him of Panshin's artistic velleities and lacing him
tight in a corset of sound business principles and bureaucratic
arrogance. But what of Bersenev and Shubin, who are evidently to
represent the spiritual élite of their generation?

Bersenev, though younger than Shubin, is both more mature
and, when the story opens, much nearer to realizing his aims in life:
he has taken his degree, and the road of his career stretches straight
and broad ahead of him. And, of the two, he is much easier to
appreciate.

First of all, he is as dedicated a man as Insarov (whereas Shubin's
capacity for devotion to a cause will not become evident for several
years more). For Bersenev teaching is a vocation, to which he looks
forward with a joy clouded only by a – surely unjustified – sense of
unworthiness. We see him immersed in his books, with a tenacity
equal to Insarov's. No doubt education as a 'cause' cannot compare
in glamour with art or with the liberation of one's country from
foreign tyranny. But Russia was not under a foreign yoke, and if
she was to be liberated from the yoke of her history, how more
effectively – how otherwise – than by education could that be
achieved? And Elena herself admits that Bersenev is probably
superior to Insarov intellectually – superior not just in learning but
in intelligence (xvi, 81–2).

Whereas Shubin is Latin is temperament and intellect, taking
after his French mother, and ends up as a sculptor in the French
tradition, Bersenev, formed by his father, is a product of German
Romanticism and Idealism. He is awkward in appearance and
movements and speech, shy and modest, something of a dreamer
and sentimentalist, unworldly and old for his years.

In his attitude to people Bersenev contrasts both with Insarov,
for whom people exist in function of their relation to his cause, and
Shubin, who regards them all with the eye and interest of an artist
and, though capable of generosity and devotion when necessary,
manages much of the time to enjoy life as it comes. Bersenev is
inspired by nature and by such arts as music rather than by people
in general, but he becomes deeply attached to a few people (his
father, Elena), and for them he is not so much prepared to make
sacrifices when necessary as eager to make great or multiple
sacrifices. Following Schopenhauer, he divides love into sacrificial
and joyous varieties and declares: 'To me it seems that the whole

purpose of our lives is to take second place' (or 'to behave as number two': I, 14); and that is the principle on which he acts, from first to last. He brings Insarov and Elena together, quite unnecessarily, in full knowledge of her craze for 'extraordinary' men, and once the inevitable has happened, he puts himself uncomplainingly and devoutly at the service of their love.

Bersenev has none of Shubin's sense of fun, nor of his understanding of people. He admires Insarov, but cannot explain why. Nowhere does he give evidence of anything like Shubin's powers of analysis and definition, in relation either to other people or to himself. If he is intellectually superior to Insarov, he has none of the Bulgarian's forcefulness and self-confidence.

Shubin is surely the most engaging male in the novel, although he is allowed to make his mark on the reader only partially and gradually: especially in the early chapters, Turgenev seems so anxious to leave a clear field for the merits of his principal hero that he is less than fair to Shubin (and even, though less obviously, to Bersenev). We see Shubin at first as a sort of weathercock, embodying all the defects of 'the artistic temperament'. He is shown as vain, idle, moody, a spoilt child, with claims to talent but nothing to support them. He is in love with Elena but cannot refrain from making a pass at every attractive girl within reach. As his policy in love, he lays it down that he is to be 'number one' (I, 14).

But as the novel develops, this is seen to be all surface froth: largely sheer pose, but partly, perhaps, effects of the frustration of his position as a mere hanger-on in the Stakhov household and of his failure to make any headway with Elena. She will not take him seriously, so he plays the fool with teasing ostentation.

When we take leave of him, in the last paragraph of the novel, we learn that 'Shubin is in Rome; he has given himself up wholly to his art and is regarded as one of the most remarkable and promising of the younger sculptors'. This tells us that not only has Shubin made good as an artist, but he is devoting himself entirely, unreservedly to his 'cause': in these terms, then, Shubin has as good a claim as Insarov to the title of 'hero'. Moreover, in the course of attaining this admirable position, Shubin has had occasion to reveal a number of qualities to which Insarov can lay no claim.

First, there is his sparkling sense of humour, which sets him apart not only from Insarov, but from all the other personages. There are some unexpected gleams of humour in Elena's depiction of Kurnatovski in her letter to Insarov (xxii, 106–8), and Bersenev once or twice sharpens his wit on Shubin in the early chapters; but Shubin is unique not only in the amount and quality of his humour, but in his readiness to exercise it at his own expense as zestfully as at other people's.

Then there is Shubin's interest in other people, combining a shrewd and penetrating eye for realities with a generous indulgence, as evidenced in his behaviour to Stakhov and to old Uvar Ivanovich. Insarov's interests are all wrapped up in his cause: even while he discusses some abstract question, such as Feuerbach's philosophy, his interlocutor can feel he is asking himself whether Feuerbach is or is not needed for his purposes. As for people – Shubin says of him: 'You will never be on intimate terms with him, and nobody ever has been on intimate terms with him' (xii, 60); and in fact, throughout the story, he remains aloof from everyone except Elena.

And thirdly, there is Shubin's considerateness and delicacy towards people he is fond of. His boast that in love he intends to be number one is not borne out by his conduct. When he thinks that Elena has fallen in love with Bersenev, he hastens to tell his friend and sends him to her as self-effacingly as Bersenev himself behaves between Elena and Insarov. On a more mundane plane, he carefully keeps to himself all he knows about Stakhov's extra-domestic goings-on and accepts the undeserved humiliation of apologizing to Stakhov rather than upset his aunt by forcing an explanation in front of her. Insarov, needless to say, never humbles himself before anyone: all his sacrifices are for his cause, and whoever would make any claim on his heart must serve that cause with him, and just as unreservedly.

Elena, though she is on the look-out for an 'extraordinary' man, notices none of these virtues in Shubin. He poses as self-centred and unserious, and she takes him at his word, without checking his sallies against his conduct. And when she catches him flirting with Zoya, it is the last straw: she writes him off.

So if we compare the three men – Elena's three suitors – in terms of their capacity for devotion to a cause, there is little, if anything, to choose between them on a long view, though in 1853 that is not yet evident in regard to Shubin. If they are compared in terms of their respective missions in life, Bersenev's will, no doubt, seem the humblest and most prosaic, but is arguably no less essential to the health of society than liberty or art; and we know that – contrary to appearances – it is Insarov, not Shubin, who is doomed to fail.

Humorously speaking, then, one might see Elena's choice of Insarov as a Judgment of Paris in reverse. Paris chose the wrong goddess, ran away with Helen (Elena) and unleashed a great war and the ruin of his country. Elena chooses the wrong man, runs away with him and ruins his chances of joining in the fight for the freedom of his country. No one had taught Elena that to be an extraordinary man is by no means the same as to be a better man: so she took that equation as her basic postulate: which proved unfortunate for the men as well as for her.

Elena was not intended to be the most important personage in *On the Eve*, but surely she has turned out to be the most interesting. We recall that the figure of such a heroine was soliciting Turgenev's imagination years before he could conceive a hero to match her; and there can be little doubt that Elena is based on observation, not invention. How does she compare with the heroines of the preceding novels?

She is the same age as Liza, a couple of years older than Natal'ya, but differs from both in the unusual degree of independence she enjoys and has been enjoying for several years before we meet her. She still lives under her parents' roof; but not only has she left behind her the governess and the prescribed reading that are still Natal'ya's lot, not only has she no Lemm or Marfa Timofeevna to live up to, but her parents, whose authority had never weighed on her very heavily, have virtually ceased to exercise any.

Liza's personality (and Natal'ya's) burns before us as a steady light, Elena's as a flickering flame. The narrator sees her as 'nervous' and 'electric' (VI, 32), meaning highly strung; just how highly strung we find out not only from the narrator but from her own accounts in her diary. The narrator's analysis suggests a periodic boiling up of emotions, which, finding no outlet, storm inside and leave her exhausted when they subside (VI, 35). In the diary there is a hand weighing her down and crushing her; she feels herself in a prison whose walls may collapse on her at any moment; her head is in a whirl and she is ready to kneel down and pray for mercy; she feels she is being murdered without knowing by whom or how, and she screams inwardly and cannot stop weeping (XVI, 79, 80–1).

All this implies the activity of strong destructive impulses in her:

she feels she is being murdered because at a deeper, unconscious level she feels murderous – in reaction to the frustrations of having no one who loves or understands her. As a child she had tried passionately to attach herself – first, to her father, then to her mother; both had failed her. Her father cared only for himself, and she has turned against him. Her kind-hearted mother no doubt felt for the girl, in her helpless, spineless way – not as a mother, but as a 'sick grandmother'.

Elena is both more articulate and much more introspective than either Natal'ya or Liza. She treats Shubin with a sharpness verging on arrogance, and, though she is always courteous with Bersenev, there is a touch of unconscious condescension in her interest: she cross-examines him about his plans, aspirations, and so on in a way that is evidently friendly in intention, but in which one doubts whether she would allow anybody to cross-examine her. And though she is at first restrained by awe from using the same tactics on Insarov, when he does give her an opening, her tone is not very different: on hearing that the quarrel he had gone away to compose had been about money, she exclaims: 'And for a trifle like that you travelled forty miles, you wasted three days?' – implying that she is at least as good a judge of his affairs as he is.

As for introspection – it wouldn't have occurred to Natal'ya or Liza to keep a diary; Elena has tried to do so some half a dozen times. The extracts from her latest effort (which form the sixteenth chapter of the novel) are largely a record of the progress of her relation with Insarov, including the revelations of her emotional turmoil, from which she gradually frees herself as that relation ripens into friendship. The record is cut short when she is startled by the discovery that she is in love with him.

Her earlier lamentations are studded with half-hearted attempts to clarify her own mental processes by asking herself such questions as: 'What do I want?', 'Why is my heart so heavy and so full of yearning?', 'Why do I watch the birds that fly by with envy?' But the questions had remained purely rhetorical: no attempt had been made at analysis, let alone at any sort of constructive answer.

Evidently, she had been tormented by the lack of any objective in which to invest her energies and of any object for her feelings. So it is easy to understand her admiration for anyone who is certain of his objectives and his course and who has succeeded in harnessing his emotions to something outside himself and greater than himself.

This, as we have seen, is the essence of heroism. She finds her own self such a burden – she is so anxious to relinquish responsibility for it – that she magnifies the achievement of this divestiture into achievement *par excellence*. And while her great ambition is to surrender herself to someone who has achieved such self-surrender (that is the basic meaning of her quest for an 'extraordinary' man), she is prepared, in moments of desperation, to toy with the idea of a very different sort of self-surrender: 'Truly, I would go away and work as a servant somewhere: it would be easier for me that way' (XVI, 81).

In all three heroines deep and strong feeling constitutes the core of their personalities, but in each the feelings are directed and tempered by a different motive power. In Natal'ya it is her mind: at 17 she already 'thinks more and more deeply' than the grown-ups; her heart is fired and she is initiated into womanhood by the intellectual feast that Rudin offers her; and she is surely the most 'reasonable'[11] of the three girls. In Liza it is a 'moral sense' that colours and canalizes both her thinking and her feeling. In Elena intellectual and moral concerns take second place to her practical urges.

We are left wondering just what she represents intellectually. In her diary, as we saw, questions are raised but never pursued. Her (long-vanished) governess is supposed to have implanted in her a love of reading, but we know nothing of what she reads or has read – only that she finds it impossible, for reasons not explained, to read the books which Bersenev brings her. Yet she is certainly far from stupid. In her portrait of Kurnatovski (XXII, 106–8) she displays, as we noted, not only keen powers of observation, but detachment, judgment and even humour, such as are conspicuously absent from her diary references to the men she knows. We may guess that here her thinking has been stimulated simultaneously by dislike of this new suitor and by a desire to please – or reassure – and entertain her fiancé. And in her last letter home (XXXV, 165) she claims to have learned Bulgarian and Serbian, evidently since her marriage; to have mastered two languages – even two with close affinities to her own – in about half a year bespeaks abilities that had been lying fallow but could bear a harvest at short notice when watered by practical needs.

The practical bent of her mind is underlined by making her indifferent to poetry (unlike Natal'ya) and to music (unlike Liza).

Here too she is on common ground with Insarov.[12] This impoverishment in culture – if not in personality – is no doubt part of the
price to be paid for their 'activism'; in real life Katranov did write
poetry – but then, he was less of a 'hero'. Their creator did not go so
far as to deny them all aesthetic sense: they share a love and
enjoyment of flowers.

 And then: what does Elena's religion amount to? We frequently
hear her asking herself whether this or that is a sin, whether she has
sinned, whether she is a sinner. But we never see religious
considerations operating in any decision on moral issues that she
has to make: whether it is a question of deceiving her parents or
giving herself to Insarov, she does what she wants to do, what she
feels like doing, without reference to any ethical or religious
principle. Unlike Natal'ya and Liza, who have their own high
standards but do not think of projecting them as demands on others
(with the exception, of course, of the man they love), Elena is an
intolerant and exacting girl. We are told that 'any weakness
[presumably, of will or character] aroused her indignation, stupidity angered her, and a falsehood she would not forgive in a
lifetime' (VI, 32). Nor was that all: 'her demands stopped at
nothing, her very prayers were often mixed with reproaches'.

 From the tone of her whole diary and from what else we know of
her we can infer that the essence of those protests was not
philosophical or indeed intellectual but emotional, and this accords
with the emotional disquiet or unrest which forms the keynote of
her character.

 It is true that she is impelled to succour the sick, hungry and
destitute; but that too is not a matter of principle but of feeling,
even of passion: such people 'disturbed her, were a torment to her',
and in this sphere her feelings are wedded to her practical urges. In
her diary she writes: 'To be good is not enough; to do good – yes,
that is the most important thing in life' and the narrator tells us that
this drive to do good goes back to her childhood. Doing good meant
relieving or forestalling suffering – whether of human beings or of
animals, where the range of her sympathy extends down to flies and
other insects.

 This may suggest that the root of 'doing good' is an over-
sensitiveness to pain rather than an excess of tenderness: it does not
lead to the formation of personal bonds or to any sharing of her
inner life with the objects of her charity.[13] But the alleviation of

suffering became perhaps a kind of 'cause', in which self and thought could be submerged – at least partially and for a time; when the story opens, it had already ceased to satisfy her. Incidentally, we are shown as little of Elena's beneficence as of Insarov's leadership; but this does not diminish her: she has been portrayed not only full-length but in depth (as Insarov has not).

In Elena, then, emotion – the need to love and be loved – fuses with a powerful urge to action in her (somewhat indiscriminate)[14] efforts to alleviate suffering, which finally find a focus in nursing the casualties of Serbian or Bulgarian struggles for freedom. So she ends up as a genuine heroine of a type emerging at just that time into history (in the Crimean War of 1853–6 women nurses distinguished themselves in the war zones on both the Russian and the Allied side), just as Insarov's type of activist (redentist) patriotism was, in the same period, common to multitudes of men in Italy and the Balkans. Thus Elena and Insarov claim attention not as mere fictional characters but as social portents (which can only doubtfully be said of Goncharov's New Man and New Woman).[15]

Of course, that is how they were meant to be seen – and how they actually were seen by many or most of Turgenev's contemporaries. For them Insarov's ultimate ineffectiveness, the derivation of Elena's protest and revolt from her private emotional frustrations, the cultural impoverishment and narrowing of personality common to both were not of major importance. Indeed, they are likely to have gone unrecognized by most readers. What Turgenev intended – and what his contemporaries generally felt as important – was that the protest and revolt which through three generations of superfluous men, from Onegin to Rudin, had remained on the plane of individual psychology had now at last been translated to the plane of action and, moreover, of concerted public action, action with a social purpose. That was made explicit in Insarov's words to Elena (XIV, 68): 'Mark this: the poorest peasant, the humblest beggar in Bulgaria and I – we all want the same thing. We all share the same purpose. You must realize what confidence and strength that gives us.' In these words he enunciates the principle for lack of which the Decembrists and so many of their successors went down to defeat – the principle that, in the nineteenth century, revolutions, to succeed, must involve the people, the masses.

Admittedly, there were critics even then who felt the artistic shortcomings in the presentation of Insarov, and there were critics who deplored his inaction for non-literary reasons. But to the young 'nihilists' of the 1860s Insarov and Elena were inspiring figures. They – the young readers – would have seen Insarov as Bersenev saw him: 'he is indeed an extraordinary man ... He is a man of iron.' They would have seen Elena as Shubin saw her: 'An amazing being ... a strange being' (I, 10). And the cause to which Insarov had dedicated himself (till Elena claimed him), the cause for which Elena was to strive and suffer after his death – they will have seen again through Shubin's eyes: 'Yes, it's youth and glory and courage. It's life and death, struggle, defeat and triumph, love, liberty and motherland! How fine, how fine! God grant everyone as much!' (XXX, 141).[16] And though it may not be as easy for the Western reader of today, this extra – this historical – dimension of the novel is worth keeping in mind.

10

The first nihilist: *Fathers and Children*

Fathers and Children[1] is by common consent Turgenev's best novel; it was also – and in Russian criticism has perhaps remained – the most controversial.

A number of the traditional misconceptions about the work and its hero must be blamed on Turgenev himself. The title implies that the central opposition is between two generations, but this is not so in any significant sense: Katya and Arkadi belong to Bazarov's generation in years, but in outlook Katya has remained with the older generation and Arkadi ends by rallying to their side. Insofar as there is a central conflict, it is Bazarov versus the Rest: Arkadi, Sitnikov and Kukshina are just camp-followers, the difference being that Arkadi is genuinely carried away for a few months, whereas the other two have nothing genuine about them but merely ape what they take for the latest fashions.

But, if it is Bazarov versus the Rest, it is not, in any simple sense, a class conflict – *raznochinets* against gentry – for Bazarov's ideas and attitudes are as remote from those of his own parents as from those of the Kirsanov brothers.

In fact, the word 'conflict' can only be used here in widely different senses. The opposition between Bazarov and his parents or even between Bazarov and Nikolai Kirsanov is muffled by mutual goodwill; it is essentially static and undramatic. The opposition between Bazarov and Katya never finds direct expression: his admiration of her is only confided to Arkadi and never reaches her; her semi-hostility to the 'alien' and 'predator' is rooted in unconscious jealousy – if she is to win Arkadi, she must wean him from his hero-worship of his friend – but it too goes no farther than Arkadi's ear. The only oppositions that involve dramatic conflict are those between Bazarov and Pavel Kirsanov and between Bazarov and Odintsova.

The storm of criticism provoked by the novel raged around the figure of Bazarov, and Turgenev's apologetics are of little help towards understanding that hero. The attacks had come from all sides, with the Right complaining that he had been glorified while the Left protested just as bitterly that he was a caricature. Turgenev continued for the rest of his life to deny both charges; but he was more disturbed by the alienation of the more youthful and radical part of his public, so that the main drift of his exegesis is to repel the accusations of caricature. Here are three specimens written within a ten-day period in April 1862:

To a representative and mouthpiece of the critical younger generation:

if the reader does not take Bazarov to his heart – with all his crudity, heartlessness, relentless dryness and brusqueness [. . .] the fault is mine and I shall have failed of my purpose [. . .] My vision was of a great wild crepuscular figure, half emerging from the soil, powerful, angry, honourable, yet doomed to destruction because it stood, after all, only on the threshold of the future – I envisioned a strange *pendant* to the Pugachëvs[2] and suchlike.[3]

To Herzen:

in creating Bazarov, I not only wasn't angry with him – what I felt for him was 'an attraction akin to disease'[4] [. . .] Of course, he overwhelms 'the man with the perfumed mustache' and the rest! It is the triumph of democracy over aristocracy. With my hand on my heart, I cannot feel that I have sinned against Bazarov [. . .] If people don't take him to their hearts as he is, with all his unseemliness – then, *I* am at fault and have failed to cope with the type I chose. It would have been easy to present him as an ideal [figure], but to make him a wolf and yet justify him – that was difficult [. . .] It seems to me that, on the contrary, a feeling quite the opposite of animosity shines through everywhere – in his death, etc.[5]

To his conservative friend Fet he had written ten days earlier, refuting his charges of bias:

Did I intend to abuse Bazarov or to extol him? *I myself don't know that*, for I don't know whether I love or hate him! So much for your [charge of] tendentiousness![6]

So for Sluchevsky Bazarov was to be seen as 'a tragic figure', for Herzen as 'a wolf', while to Fet Turgenev professes complete ambivalence towards his hero.

There is no need to impugn his sincerity. If he was only too apt to be swayed by the expectations of the person to whom he was writing, that was in great part because – like his personages – he had only a limited understanding of himself, and indeed only a limited intellectual understanding (as distinct from artistic intuition) of them.[7] There is some truth in each of those three passages; read together, they warn us not to take any of his pronouncements about the main characters or themes of this novel as authoritative definitions. His comments should be borne in mind but also constantly checked against the evidence of the text.

For example, in the same letter to Sluchevsky he declares: '*My whole tale is directed against the nobility as the leading class*' (i.e., against any claim that the gentry should provide the leadership for Russian society) and to Herzen he presents the superiority of Bazarov as 'the triumph of democracy over aristocracy'. Neither of these assertions can be taken at face value. Whatever superiority over the other personages we may allow to Bazarov, the novel shows clearly (and truthfully, in terms of history) that he is not yet a viable type, whereas Nikolai Kirsanov, Arkadi and Katya are all still viable.

Besides, in what sense can Bazarov be classified as a democrat? By origin he is, like Lavretski, the product of a cross-class marriage: his mother a gentlewoman, his father the son of a peasant. He is set as far apart from the peasants by his personal pride (and his education) as is Pavel Kirsanov by his pride of birth. Bazarov is the harbinger of a new élite – an élite based on personal merit. But one swallow does not make a summer: the day of the Bazarovs is still far off, and in the meantime the destinies of Russia remain in the hands of Arkadi Kirsanov and Odintsova's second husband. Admittedly, they are not leaders – they lack the vision and the creativity of leadership – but as caretakers or preservers of an inheritance they offer a respite, during which true leaders might have appeared.

Thematically and structurally *Fathers and Children* differs significantly from Turgenev's three preceding novels, although here again the hero is tested against a woman and against one or more other men. But in the earlier novels the contest between the men is secondary and episodic or muted: Rudin triumphs over Pigasov in a single evening and is hardly aware of Volyntsev's or Lezhnëv's jealousy; Lavretski routs Panshin in one brief debate; Insarov does not even clash with Bersenev or Shubin but is merely contrasted with them – whereas the testing of the man by the girl, by love, is central and crucial. In *Fathers and Children*, on the other hand, the conflict between the hero and the other man becomes central – so much so that many critics have treated this as the theme of the novel – and highly dramatic, though not crucial, while the testing of the hero by love remains crucial but ceases to be central.

As regards form, *Fathers and Children* is much the longest of the four works,[8] with twice as many chapters as *Rudin* and much greater variation in their length than in any of its predecessors. The proportion of dialogue to narrative is almost the same as in *Rudin*: that is, nearly two-thirds of the text is dialogue, which, like close-ups in film, slows the action, concentrates the field of view, and foregrounds and highlights the characters and their experiences. Indeed it is tempting to see *Fathers and Children* as a drama in four acts and an epilogue, with the first three acts of approximately equal length and the fourth shorter by slightly more than one-third. 'Act I', comprising chapters I–XI might be entitled 'Bazarov and the Kirsanovs'; 'Act II' – chapters XII–XIX – could be called 'Bazarov and Odintsova'; 'Acts III and IV' – chapters XX–XXIV and XXV–XXVII – might be styled respectively 'The Decline' and 'Fall of Bazarov'.

Who, then, and what is Bazarov? He represents Turgenev's third attempt to present in a novel a positive hero, a Don Quixote type in Turgenev's sense. As such, he should be (as Turgenev in his letters claims he was intended to be) both lovable and a tragic hero. Yet, paradoxically, he failed to win the heart of his creator: as Turgenev implicitly recognized in the already cited letter to Fet, and explicitly, seven years later, in an article, 'On the Subject of *Fathers and Children*', which left his critics as dissatisfied as before. Whether we regard Bazarov as a tragic hero is likely to hinge on what scale we posit as requisite for tragedy; but if we rank Pechorin and Rudin as tragic heroes, we can hardly refuse the same status to Bazarov.

Bazarov is introduced to the Kirsanov brothers – and so to the reader – as a nihilist. The word was not new, even in Russian, but Turgenev used it to designate what he took to be a new social type.

A nihilist, Arkadi explains to his uncle, is a man who does not bow before any authority, who takes no principle on trust, however widely respected it may be. Bazarov, in his first clash with Pavel Kirsanov, endorses this in slightly more aggressive terms: 'I have already informed you that I believe in nothing' (VI, 219). In a later argument he says, among other things: 'We act on the basis of what we recognize as useful [. . .] At the present time there is nothing more useful than negation [so] we negate [. . .] Everything' (x, 243). To Nikolai Kirsanov's objection: 'You negate everything, or, to put it more accurately, you destroy everything [. . .] But surely it is necessary to build too', Bazarov retorts: 'Indeed, that is not our business [. . .] The ground has to be cleared first.'

Among the values 'negated' by Bazarov are: art and literature and all aesthetic feeling, even for the world of nature; philosophy and other forms of abstract thought; and personal relations, in particular all forms of tender feeling. So he proclaims that 'a decent chemist is twenty times more useful than any poet' (vi, 219); that Pushkin is nonsense – no fit reading for a grown man (x, 238); that 'Raphael isn't worth a brass farthing' (x, 247). The idea of a man playing the 'cello makes him roar with laughter (ix, 236–7). He tells Arkadi that nature as Arkadi sees nature (i.e., as a source of aesthetic or emotional stimulation) is nonsense (ix, 236). Principles are an empty word – they don't exist (xxi, 325); philosophy is Romanticism (which in Bazarov's vocabulary is a term of unmitigated condemnation); love 'is an affectation' (xxv, 372). It is not worth while to study individual personalities, since human beings are as much alike, in soul as well as in body, as the trees in a forest.

Bazarov's own values are: utility (that is his criterion for action) and experience (that is his criterion for truth). In other words, he is a utilitarian and an empiricist – though he would certainly have protested against such terms as being foreign and abstract, and therefore superfluous.

In his initial definition of nihilism Arkadi avers that the nihilist 'regards everything from a critical point of view' (v, 216); so it is all the more striking that there is no sign of any such point of view either in Bazarov's rejection of traditional values or in his adoption of the newfangled ones. So Pisarev's conception of Bazarov as a sceptic[9] is untenable: our nihilist is just as dogmatic as Pavel Kirsanov both in his negations and in his axioms.

In the first 'act' of the novel, Arkadi implies, Pavel Kirsanov assumes and Bazarov at least acquiesces in the view that nihilism is the core of his (Bazarov's) being, nihilism being defined as the critical repudiation of all the traditions, conventions and values of the established order. The following three 'acts' reveal the fundamental falsity of these assumptions. That is a not uncommon pattern in Turgenev: we meet his protagonists full of illusions about themselves and are then shown how life explodes these illusions. But whereas in Jane Austen, for instance, the protagonists, starting from equally fundamental misconceptions, journey through self-discovery to self-knowledge and self-transformation, the Turgenev hero usually ends with no more understanding of himself than he began; and in the rare cases where he does achieve – like Rudin – a measure of insight into himself, remains incapable of living up to those insights.

So, abandoning the attempt to capture the essence of Bazarov in any such simple definition as 'nihilism', let us turn our attention to the drama which is to reveal him to himself.

In 'Act I' (chapters I–XI) Bazarov is surrounded by Kirsanovs – all alien to him in traditions and culture but differing in their attitudes and reactions to him. Arkadi is dazzled by him and appears as his devout disciple. Pavel is soon his implacable enemy. Nikolai is disconcerted and disturbed by him but anxious to understand him and do him justice. It is tempting to speculate that Nikolai's attitude represents the balance that Turgenev strove to maintain and which he claimed for himself in the letter to Fet cited above, and in the 1869 article 'On the Subject of *Fathers and Children*', while in fact he may at various times have felt much more strongly about his creation: both positively, like Arkadi, and negatively, like Pavel.

Arkadi is essentially a younger version of his father, as becomes clear by the end of the story; and Nikolai Kirsanov is not only a contemporary, but to a large extent a projection of his creator. Psychologically, he is invested with Turgenev's gentleness, his lack of drive, of self-assertion, of efficiency in practical matters. Ideologically, he shares Turgenev's liberalism: his measures to anticipate the Emancipation of the Serfs reflect Turgenev's own treatment of his peasants in those years, and the resulting difficulties and disappointments correspond to those that Turgenev himself had experienced. Common to both personage and author were the love of music and poetry – of Pushkin in particular – and the poetic feeling for landscape. It is less easy to gauge the amount of autobiography infused into Nikolai's relation with Fenechka; probably there was some.

In the light of all this and of Turgenev's insuperable ambivalence towards his hero, it was surely wise not to make Nikolai Bazarov's main antagonist in debate. Nikolai was temperamentally unfitted for effective polemics, irrespective of who the opponent might be. Not that Pavel Kirsanov, who is picked as Bazarov's adversary, is a truly impressive specimen of the superfluous man. It is hard to see in him more than a pallid epigone of a great line: Turgenev himself was ultimately driven to accuse himself of having 'sinned against artistic truth' by exaggerating Kirsanov's faults 'almost to the point of caricature' and 'making him ridiculous':[10] a not untypical Turgenev overstatement.

Though evidently a contemporary of Lermontov – born in the same year – Pavel Kirsanov shows no signs of 'demonism',[11] nor is he a dreamer like his brother: we are told that 'he was not born romantic, and his dandy's soul, dry, passionate and misanthropic in the French fashion, was incapable of dreaming' (XI, 252). He combines in himself traits of the superfluous men of the thirties and even the twenties (his 'spleen', his foible for the English, perhaps the Gallic 'misanthropy'): Bazarov has some grounds for labelling him 'an antique' (*arkhaicheskoe yavlen'e*: IV, 210), though his Slavophil inclinations may be of more recent date.

Bazarov has distinctly the better of his two clashes with Kirsanov in 'Act I' (chapters VI and X); and this is fair enough, for not only is the older man the aggressor on both occasions, but he rushes into battle head down, with a lamentable lack – lamentable in an ex-officer and a general's son – of foresight, let alone tactical finesse. Moreover, he attacks his enemy on that enemy's home ground with only limited knowledge of the terrain: that is, only a limited understanding of what he is up against, as he demonstrates, in the second encounter, when he is left breathless by Bazarov's cool negation of 'everything' – which should not have surprised him at all if he had paid any attention to Arkadi's original policy statement.

Now, it may be true to the facts of social life that a man of Kirsanov's station and culture would have been ill equipped to argue effectively with a Bazarov, but it is disappointing that the fight is so unequal and never comes near the bone of the contention. One sighs for just a little semantic sophistication: the gentleman has none, the nihilist shows barely an occasional glimmer. For instance, he is quite right when he points out that 'science' is a linguistic figment (VI, 219); yet when, immediately before that, he says, 'I believe in nothing' and, two minutes earlier, 'A decent chemist is twenty times more useful than any poet', he leaves himself wide open to a demand that he define 'belief' and 'usefulness' and explain just how he would propose to measure usefulness – but is not challenged.

The first clash is cut short, before it has properly got under way, by a diversion of Nikolai Kirsanov's. The second runs its course; but although it raises capital issues, the older man's clumsiness and excitement make it easy for Bazarov to dance away from them. Thus, Kirsanov tangles up the question of aristocracy and its claim to respect with the question of personality and the question of personality with his own personality and personal habits, so that Bazarov is free to riposte on the personal plane and avoid the general issues.

As soon as Bazarov goes over to the counter-offensive, he in turn becomes vulnerable – yet he is allowed to get away scot-free. First, he objects to the use of foreign abstract terms, such as 'liberalism', 'principles', 'progress'; then, when challenged to say what determines his actions, he declares: 'We act on the basis of what we recognize as useful.' Here he exposes himself to two devastating retorts. First, that most of the terms he uses in the physical sciences are no less foreign and some are no less abstract than liberalism, principles and progress. And secondly – and this would go to the root of his position – that his repudiation of principles is contradicted by his acting on the basis of what he considers useful, since that is obviously to act on a principle. However, in the latter part of this scene Kirsanov abandons argument for invective and so loses whatever chance he might have had of denting his opponent's armour.

Next day Arkadi and his friend leave the Kirsanov estate. In real life convictions are rarely changed by argument; if they change, that is likely to be the work of life itself; and so it is in *Fathers and Children*.

'Act II' (chapters XII–XIX) opens with a would-be Gogolian intermezzo in the capital of the province. These eleven pages (chapters XII and XIII) constitute a *pendant* and contrast to the first eleven pages of 'Act I' (chapters I–III): a *pendant* in that both sequences form only a prelude to the main business of the 'act' and in that each presents two foils to Bazarov; a contrast in that Bazarov has only a 'walking-on' part in the first, but a significant, though not dominant, rôle in the second, and in that the two foils in the first sequence (Arkadi and his father) are to play a far more important part in the story than the foils in the second (Sitnikov and Kukshina). There is a further contrast between the gentle, almost tender irony with which Turgenev introduces these Kirsanovs and the bald, uncharitable showing-up of the two city-dwellers. Gershenzon complains of the petty and superficial quality of Turgenev's satire; and so far as the portrayal of these two pseudo-radicals is concerned, it is hard to disagree with him. But at a deeper level – admittedly one that transcends the limits of the novel itself – there is a quite tragic irony in the contrasting quality of the disciples of Bazarov and of Rudin. To recall Natal'ya and Basistov while confronted with Arkadi and Sitnikov is perforce to ask oneself whether these differences in quality are to be correlated with the personalities of the two teachers or with the character of the two teachings.

However that may be, 'Act II' pivots on the 'duel' between Bazarov and Odintsova, as 'Act I' pivots on that between Bazarov and Pavel Kirsanov. In both cases it is not Bazarov but his opponent who takes the initiative – who forces or draws Bazarov into argument. In both cases Bazarov is allowed to have the last word, not to say the upper hand. His two colloquies with Odintsova (chapters XVII and XVIII) parallel his two disputes with Kirsanov (chapters VI and X): in both cases, the first is cut short (by Nikolai's intervention, by Bazarov's withdrawal though Odintsova tries to detain him), while the second works up to a climax of heated emotions and is followed by Bazarov's departure (from Mar'ino, from Nikol'skoe).

These parallelisms are on the surface and obvious. Less obvious is the fact that both Kirsanov and Odintsova are impelled to involve themselves with Bazarov – to come to grips with him – by what they have in common – by their affinities – with him. What all three have in common is, first, their anti-romanticism and dryness. All three fight shy of dreams and emotions, which implies not that they are unemotional but that they know or fear, at least unconsciously, the dangers of giving their emotions free play. In this sense, all three are chargeable with the 'misanthropy' which is imputed specifically to Pavel Kirsanov. They will not, they dare not, let anyone get too close to them. That is as true of Odintsova in relation to her sister as of Pavel in relation to his brother or of Bazarov in relation to his parents.

And in this 'misanthropy' there is another common element –

pride. That each of the men has an enormous regard for himself and considerable contempt for his fellow humans is evident. It may be less obtrusive in the woman; but she herself says to Bazarov: 'I [. . .] have been poor and proud like you' (xviii, 297); and Katya says of her to Arkadi: 'She is very proud . . . I didn't mean to say that . . . she sets great store by her independence' (xxv, 365). Of course the three, though equally proud, manifest their pride differently. Kirsanov's is a predominantly passive disposition, so that his pride holds him aloof from people; Bazarov's disposition is active, so that his impulse is to get involved with people, even if that means attacking them (xxi, 324); Odintsova's combination of curiosity with defensiveness leads her to welcome and explore new relationships, while refusing to commit herself too deeply.

Another trait shared by all three is that each is a law unto himself/herself: that is, they live as they think fit, without overmuch regard for conventions, public opinion or the susceptibilities of others. Pavel Kirsanov's dandyism is both out of date at the end of the fifties and out of place in such a rural backwater – a tacit challenge or provocation to his neighbours. Of Odintsova we are told that she ignored the gossip about her: 'she had an independent and pretty determined character' (xv, 271), and in her relation with Bazarov we see her not only playing with fire but imposing on him the 'order' of her domestic routine. Bazarov's pose of 'ungentle-manliness' is, like Kirsanov's dandyism, primarily a provocation; it is punctured by his agreement to fight in 'Act III', and in his relation with Odintsova it keeps breaking down. It is dropped in his dealings with his mother and with Fenechka, whom he has no desire to keep at a respectful distance – against whom, therefore, he has no need of armour, either defensive or offensive.

The two men are linked by a further characteristic which differentiates them both from Odintsova: their 'passionate and splenetic' temperament (to borrow Pisarev's apt definition). It is precisely this affinity of temperament which renders them intolerable to each other, though each of them tends to rationalize his aversion in terms of the other's pride. Pavel Kirsanov is more open and categorical: 'I hate that doctor fellow; in my opinion, he's just a quack [. . .] And his conceit is quite revolting' (x, 239). Bazarov is less ready, here as in other contexts, to admit or to recognize his own feelings; but after his first clash with Kirsanov, while justifying himself to Arkadi, he lets slip, 'Do you think I'm going to indulge these provincial aristocrats! It's all pride, the habits of a social lion, vanity' (VI, 200). And it is their common temperament that imbues the pride of both men with that aggressive arrogance from which Odintsova's equal pride is plainly free: which explains why Odintsova's 'duel' with Bazarov results from a mutual attraction, whereas that between Bazarov and Kirsanov issues from a mutual hostility.

So while the two men part with no harm done, Bazarov leaves Nikol'skoe carrying a deadly wound. In the mainly intellectual struggle against a hostile male Bazarov holds his own; in the mainly emotional struggle with an attractive woman he succumbs – though it takes another two 'acts' to finish him off.

Odintsova was not understood by Sluchevsky or his fellow students, and Turgenev, in his exasperated attempts to dispel their misconceptions, is less than fair to her:

Odintsova is just as far from *falling in love* with Arkadi as with *Bazarov* – how could you fail to see that! She is the very representative of our idle, daydreaming, curious and cold epicurean ladies, our noblewomen [...] First she would like to stroke the wolf's fur (Bazarov) – provided he won't bite – and then the boy's curls, and go on lying, all freshly bathed, on velvet.[12]

Most of this may fit; but the epithets 'idle' and 'epicurean' hardly correspond to the energy and courage with which she meets Bazarov's deathbed appeal. An epicurean would have stayed away – or, at best, stopped short on the threshold of the sickroom. She risked infection (we do not know how great the risk was, but, then, neither did she) by sitting close where he could see her, and by kissing him at the last. Bazarov himself says of her coming, 'This is a princely act' (*eto po-tsarski*) – so bracketing it with Napoleon's legendary visit to the plague hospital at Jaffa or Nicholas I's to the cholera victims.

Odintsova is fundamentally an unhappy person, like Pavel Kirsanov. Each of them is crippled by an emotional fixation: his for his lost princess, hers for her handsome scamp of a father, whom she had deeply loved, who had idolized her, joking with her, confiding in her and consulting her as an equal – in effect, allowing her to substitute for her dead mother. But whereas the man's fixation progresses towards virtually total social disablement (he ends, one may say, by bowing himself off the stage of life) – Odintsova not only succeeds in bringing up, providing for and marrying off her young sister, but herself achieves two relatively prosperous marriages, of the second of which the narrator is driven to admit, however venomously: 'they will live, perhaps, to attain happiness . . . perhaps [even] love' (xxviii, 399).[13]

Our third 'act' (chapters xx–xxiv) falls into two halves, with Bazarov's home the scene of the first two chapters, Mar'ino of the next two. At his home we witness the beginning of his breakdown, at the Kirsanovs' its crisis.

Bazarov's parents have more than a touch about them of Gogol's 'old-world landowners', though their decent poverty is far removed from the inexhaustible abundance of that Ukrainian estate; and whereas Gogol's old couple live for each other and their food, Turgenev's live for each other and for their son: which enlarges and enriches their humanity and invests their loss of him with a heart-wrenching poignancy. The portrait of the old doctor is etched with the same loving care as that of the other father, Nikolai Kirsanov. Both are good men and devoted fathers, struggling to keep abreast of developments in their society (both have put their peasants on quit-rent, at some sacrifice) and in science (in medicine and agriculture respectively) – in neither case very successfully. But they belong to different generations and cultures – classical and Romantic (the older man quotes Horace whereas Nikolai declaims Pushkin); the doctor flaunts his 'plebeian' origin, while Nikolai has feelings of discomfort, if not guilt, about his gentry status (*barstvo*: ix, 249); the old man has seen far more of Russia and of history in the making, has retained a physical energy surprising for his years, and displays a decisiveness in practical matters – whether extracting teeth without anaesthetics or in having a serf whipped for theft and drunkenness – that would have been quite beyond soft-hearted Nikolai Kirsanov.

These two chapters also give us a glimpse (often overlooked by critics) of Bazarov's past. We can see how and why he had become a loner: trailing his father's regiment from city to city, he had had no settled home, no regular schooling, no chance to strike roots or form friendships. He had inherited his father's physical energy and practical bent and had adopted his scientific interests and pride in his origins. But he had needed to distance himself from his parents too – and not only to escape being smothered by their love: to have grown up seeing his father always as a man under authority, and of authorities as overweening as, and much less urbane than, Pavel

Kirsanov, was enough to implant in him the seeds of his root-and-branch repudiation of the established order.

After three years of absence at university he returns to the home where he can remember spending only two continuous years of his childhood. Against the background of his parents' pathetic adoration, his inability now to come to terms with his friend, with himself or with life is thrown into painful relief. He tries to keep the old people at arm's length by joking, but after only two days gives up the attempt as too much for him and leaves them. During that time he does his best to pick a quarrel with Arkadi, deliberately exasperating him with paradoxes, with personal insults (which Arkadi lets pass), with mockery of Pushkin and finally with abuse of Pavel Kirsanov – till only the chance appearance of the old doctor prevents a quite serious fight.[14]

But it is Bazarov's new attitude to himself and to life that best enables us to measure the shocking changes wrought by Odintsova. He envies his parents their contentment in obscurity, when to him life now seems hideous and absurd; the prospect of universal prosperity in some remote future only moves him to hate those who will enjoy it when he is under the ground; it is impossible to slander any man, for the worst one can say of another will represent only one-twentieth of what he deserves; a proper man is one whom others can only either obey or hate (XXI, 323–7). The word 'hate' keeps recurring; and when Arkadi remarks that he does not hate anyone, Bazarov flings back: 'I do – so many people.' He complains that he can feel only boredom and rancour. His pristine self-respect is in abeyance, as he swings between bragging and self-abasement: one moment he is hinting that he is broken, the next, boasting that no mere woman shall break him; at one moment he implies that he has yet to meet a man who could stand up to him, at another he no longer knows – or, apparently, cares – where truth is to be found (in that case, what becomes of science?). Principles (that is, values) are nothing but subjective feelings,[15] and that applies equally to his own nihilism and to honour (or integrity: *chestnost'*). And we are about to see that this feeling has become as indeterminate and undependable in him as in the least heroic of mortals.

Bazarov's second stay at Mar'ino is marked by two climaxes: his kissing Fenechka and his pistol duel with Pavel Kirsanov. Each marks a stage in his continuing decline or demoralization. On his later – his last – visit to Odintsova, he was to boast that, although a poor man, he had never yet accepted alms. But alms are precisely what we hear him beg of Fenechka: the alms of her pity and affection, if no more. And when she fails to respond, he takes what she would not have given but has not the strength or the presence of mind to keep out of his reach.

This is doubly dishonourable. Fenechka regarded him as a doctor – had, in fact, at least once taken medicine from him; and even if this did not make her, technically, his patient, still, her infant was. Here he abuses the doctor–patient relationship. Besides, he was Nikolai Kirsanov's guest and was in no doubt about the relationship between Fenechka and his host. Clearly, he was violating the laws of hospitality as well as professional ethics – and without even the excuse of great love or overmastering passion: he was at the time passionately in love with another woman, and his approach to Fenechka was not impulsive but gradual and calculated: so that the lapse seems symptomatic of an at least temporary moral collapse resulting from a maudlin self-pity.

Nothing more was needed to put him in the power of Pavel Kirsanov, who at once seized the opportunity to turn the tables on him in the most humiliating way. During his first visit, Bazarov had not only worsted Kirsanov in argument, but had made him lose his temper and descend to undignified abuse so that he could be taunted with failure to live up to his vaunted sense of his own dignity. Now Kirsanov not only forces a fight on his enemy, but puts him in the position of having to go through a ritual that Bazarov considers absurd: that is, he makes him look ridiculous in his own eyes. Not having had the self-control to keep his hands off Fenechka, Bazarov now has not the self-control to bear the blow which his breach of honour deserves. He senses that his probable reaction would be a burst of fury in which he might well kill his frail, middle-aged adversary. So, after repudiating, on his first visit, 'all the socially established conventions', Bazarov is now compelled to eat his own words and bow to a convention of doubtful respectability even outside radical circles. Three chapters earlier he had been bragging to Arkadi: 'When I meet a man who can stand up to me ... I will change my estimate of myself' (xxi, 325); now he was facing a man who was not only standing up to him, but making him, Bazarov, dance to his tune.

Having accepted the duel, Bazarov has to accept all the traditional formalities and courtesies that go with it. He assumes for a day the manners of a gentleman – of the class which he so utterly despises. And so helplessly does he abandon himself to the current of events that, when the time comes to shoot, he neither aims to disable his opponent nor aims to spare his life, but leaves it to chance to decide the issue. Chance lets him down lightly, allowing him not to miss (which is what might have been expected from a complete tiro), nor yet to kill Kirsanov (which would have been too embarrassing all round), but to wound him slightly: which at once restores to the hero a part of his advantage by calling his medical skills into play.

Having settled this score (with the honours arguably even), in Act IV' (chapters XXV–XXVII) Bazarov returns to his parents' house – to die. On the way home he stops at Nikol'skoe for a last meeting (as he thinks) with the only two beings outside his family who, though in very different degrees, had meant something to him: for the purpose – admitted explicitly to Odintsova (XXV, 371) but only demonstrated to Arkadi – of making his peace with them.

We may grant that at the conscious level his death is not suicide. Though he had declared life now hideous and senseless in his sight (XXI, 323: *Chto za bezobrazie! Chto za pustyaki!*) and that he now felt nothing but weariness and rancour (*ibid.: ya chuvstvuyu tol'ko skuku da zlost'*), and though his behaviour at Mar'ino was an at least unconscious outrage to his self-respect – the core of his being: yet, if he had been asked whether he wanted to live or die, there is no doubt he would have opted for life. As for the unconscious, however, his four-hour delay in disinfecting the fatal cut tells a different tale: he knew very well the risk he was running and it is sheerly incredible that he could not have found on the spot some means of cautery, however crude and painful. What we see here is, at the least, another abdication of responsibility, as when he fired at Kirsanov without taking aim.

Rudin had gone to meet death. Insarov had been surprised by death. But we only see Rudin and Insarov die: we know nothing of what they thought or felt as the curtain fell. Bazarov faces death in a waiting game, armed with all the clearsightedness, courage and will-power of his earlier days. He brushes aside his father's comforting illusions, yet has sufficient feeling for his parents' suffering not to forbid the religious rites on which their hearts are set. He measures and economizes the remnant of his strength and keeps it in reserve for the only thing that is still important to him: the chance of a last meeting with Odintsova. With wry humour he tries to

console his parents and with gallant irony acknowledges that he
has met his match: 'But just you try to negate death! It negates
you, and that's all' (xxvII, 391).

When Odintsova comes, he is his old self, and something more.
With a delicacy of which he might not have been capable before,
he says not that he loves her but that he had loved her – though it
is obvious that all that now matters to him is these few minutes
with her. He pays tribute to her generosity of spirit and drinks in
her beauty for the last time. Free from self-pity and rancour now,
objectively, he looks at himself as he is and recalls how he
imagined he would be: 'And didn't I think too: I'm going to get so
much done, no question of dying! There's work to do, and I'm a
giant, aren't I! And now all there is for the giant to do is to die
decently, [even] though that's of no interest to anyone' (xxvII,
396). The unassuming stoicism is driven home by the homeliness
of the language. This is heroism without heroics. He has earned
his good death.

As later in Dostoevsky's novels, in *Fathers and Children* the
hero is matched against major aspects of his own personality
embodied in some of the other main characters. Bazarov hates
himself in Pavel Kirsanov and loves himself in Odintsova as Raskol'nikov will hate himself in Svidrigailov and love himself in
Sonya. As in Dostoevsky, the heroes cast themselves for rôles that
they are radically unfitted to play. What links Bazarov, Odintsova
and Kirsanov even more intimately than their 'misanthropy' and
pride is that all three miscast and misconceive themselves.

Odintsova imagines herself in search of love and happiness
when in fact she is terrified of both. Perhaps her father had spoilt
her for other men; at any rate, she takes care to choose husbands
as unlike him as possible. In intelligence and determination she is
Bazarov's peer; but her cool blood – or fear of her own repressed
feelings? – forbids her to give herself – either to a man or to a
cause.

In Kirsanov the contradiction between his image of himself and
the reality of his life is still more evident. He sees himself as a
bearer of time-hallowed traditions and values – the nobleman's
sense of personal honour and sense of duty to his society – while
his feud with Bazarov throws into cruel relief the indolence and
petulance, the personal vanity and caste prejudices at which
Bazarov gleefully rails. Kirsanov sees himself as the tragic victim

of a great romantic love; but he is no more able than Bazarov to bar his stricken heart against Fenechka.

But the split between ideal and reality, between self-image and self, assumes heroic and fatal dimensions only in Bazarov. There is the contradiction between his professed rejection of all principles and all received ideas and values and his blind acceptance of utility and experience as the criteria respectively for action and thought. There is the contradiction between his professed empiricism and his dogmatic negation of matters lying outside his own experience: for instance, his negation of art in spite of his acknowledged lack of aesthetic sensibility. There is the contradiction between his desperate approach to true scepticism – when he cries out that not only principles but all biases, including his own nihilism, are reducible to personal feelings and inclinations – and his failure to recognize the corollary: that in that case, other people's viewpoints and values may have as much validity as his own.

No less strident is the contradiction between Bazarov's pride and his anti-individualism. He contends that human individuals are not worth studying because they are as much alike as the trees in a forest, but at the same time he regards himself as a 'god' (XIX, 304) or a 'giant' (XXVII, 396) and accordingly despises the mass of mankind: specifically, women, peasants, poets, philosophers and gentry. This pride was based, of course, not on birth, looks or genius, but on his strength of character – his will-power; and the tragedy of Bazarov is the wrecking of this will. As in Greek tragedy, pride calls down retribution – *hubris* provokes nemesis.

It does so by way of the crucial contradiction between his intellect and his heart. While he presents to the world an appearance of extreme rationalism and toughness, Bazarov is in fact fundamentally emotional. The emotions that predominate on the surface are pride and aggressiveness: both are much in evidence already in the first half of the story – before his fiasco with Odintsova. After this reverse there emerges a quite romantic vein of self-pity, as in his colloquy with Arkadi (XXI, 322–7): he envies his parents' contentment, he envies the ant its immunity from pity, he feels nothing but 'tedium and malice'; to him life 'stinks'. A similar note is struck in his tempting of Fenechka (XXIII, 343): 'what use is my youth to me? I live alone, without home or kin (*bobylëm*) . . . If only someone would take pity on me.'

That his softer feelings are not entirely egoistic is suggested both by the liking children show to him and by the exaggerated anti-sentimentalism of his attitude to his parents. However, not too much should be read into either of these phenomena. Bazarov is a born leader, and children may respond to leadership, up to a point, on a non-sentimental basis. And though there can be no doubt of his affection for his parents, we see him ride roughshod over their feelings and subordinate their hopes and wishes to his whims without scruple: he has stayed away from them for three years and leaves them again after forty-eight hours because he is bored; he domineers over them and keeps them in constant uncertainty with the tacit threat that he will not stay unless everything is done just as he wants.

To recognize this soft core of Bazarov's character is to understand in great part how he could be crushed by Odintsova's rejection of him. Those who see him as a superman are driven to seek more recondite explanations. Thus, Ovsyaniko-Kulikovsky argues that Bazarov's love threatened his capacity for spiritual freedom and it was the need to defend that spiritual freedom which invested his struggle against his love with such tragic intensity.[16] Imagine what Bazarov himself would have said to anyone who had served up to him such a 'romantic philosophical abstraction' as 'spiritual freedom'.

Surely, the primary cause of Bazarov's misery is that he cannot get the woman out of his blood or out of his head. Hardly less torturing, though, was the wound to his pride – to his intellectual as well as his 'moral' pride. Not merely that he, Bazarov, had fallen hopelessly in love, that he had been rejected, and that he who set such store by his independence was independent no longer; but a deadly blow had been struck at his whole philosophy of personality and, more particularly, at his beliefs concerning women and romantic love.

He had been, we are told (XVII, 286–7), a great lover of women and their beauty; but romantic love he had called 'unforgivable silliness', and the proper place for people like Schiller's Ritter Toggenburg and the troubadours was, according to him, a lunatic asylum. 'If you like a woman', he would say, 'do your best to get your way, but if you can't, never mind, turn away – it isn't the end of the world.' Now he is finding out that it is the end of the world for him too.

Granjard[17] claims that in the first half of the novel – until his rejection by Odintsova – Bazarov is essentially a revolutionary, and that only after this does he turn from the politico-social to the cosmic plane and become a rebel. One capital difference between Bazarov and the real-life nihilists or revolutionaries of the later 1860s is that they were many and active, whereas Bazarov stands alone, and for that very reason (though not, perhaps, only for that reason) is debarred from action. And he is in no position to reveal his ideas and intentions either clearly or fully.

However, if we accept, for the sake of argument, that Bazarov in the first half of the novel can be seen as a potential revolutionary, or revolutionary in intention, surely the jeremiads about life in the second half do not amount even to an intellectually or morally coherent protest – let alone rebellion. It would seem truer to say that until his rejection by Odintsova Bazarov's pride and aggression have at their command enough energy to enable him to direct them towards practical objectives, so they remain orientated towards reality; but once this energy is dissipated – by the shock and pain of his rejection – they can operate only on the more rarefied and frictionless plane of fantasy (as in the quarrel with Arkadi and the tempting of Fenechka), while he falls back from active struggle into diffuse rancour and hate.

His death, if not simply a suicide, is still less, as Bazarov asserts, fortuitous. Turgenev tried, outside the novel, to explain it – like Insarov's death – as a historical necessity: both heroes had been born before their time. This is even less convincing in reference to Bazarov than it had been in reference to Insarov. We have seen why Insarov had to die in his bed in Venice rather than fighting the Turks in Serbia or in the Crimea (or even in some Bulgarian underground movement, later on). But to attribute Bazarov's death to historical necessity is to introduce a complete break between his death and the story of his life – it would make that story irrelevant. If his life is to be made relevant to his death, it is hard to find any convincing alternative to the view that Bazarov's tragedy is the wrecking of his will: *hubris* provoking nemesis.

The first warning note comes in his complacent condemnation of Pavel Kirsanov: 'But still I must say that a man who has staked his whole life on a woman's love and, when he loses, wilts and loses heart to the point of becoming good for nothing – such a fellow is not a man, not a male' (VII, 226). Then love comes to him too: as a foreign body,[18] as an infection against which he finds his boasted

will-power powerless. He stoops to solicit Fenechka's pity and steal
her kiss; he submits to fighting a duel against his convictions; he
loses his capacity to work; he becomes afraid to remain alone, yet –
symbolically – he loses his 'touch' with the people – his ability to
understand them and make himself understood by them. And
finally there supervenes that other foreign body, that other infection, which destroys him physically as the first had destroyed him
spiritually. He had sought to reduce the relations between men and
women to their physical components; but his relation to Odintsova
had poisoned his soul; it was left to a more material organism to
poison his body.

Pavel Kirsanov smoulders on, Bazarov is snuffed out. Why?
Does the contrasted outcome reflect the contrast between passive
and active spirit? Or is it that 'he whom the gods love dies young',
and should we, with Turgenev's closing chords of reconciliation in
our ears, echo the valediction of a somewhat older poet of love?[19]

> Meurs donc! Ta mort est douce et ta tâche est remplie.
> Ce que l'homme ici-bas appelle le génie,
> C'est le besoin d'aimer; hors de là tout est vain.
> Et, puisque tôt ou tard l'amour humain s'oublie,
> Il est d'une grande âme et d'un heureux destin
> D'expirer comme toi pour un amour divin!

The quotation will scandalize many – as a whole and, more
especially, for its final word. Malibran's love was for her art – for
music – and therefore, by definition, an ideal or 'romantic' love. So,
the quotation implies it is at least conceivable that Turgenev
wanted to 'ennoble' his hero at the end by allowing his love to rise
not only above his (Bazarov's) own callow philosophy of love but to
an ideal or heroic transcendence.[20]

Or was Bazarov shattered ultimately not by love but by the
gorgon face of truth? The Tolstoyan hero is ready for death when
he has seen through illusion to the truth of life; was Bazarov ripe for
death because he had seen through illusion to the truth about
himself?[21]

11

The legacy of nihilism: 'Enough';
Smoke

Fathers and Children marks a kind of climacteric in Turgenev's life and work. It is generally regarded as his best novel and far superior to either of his later ones. It was planned just before, and completed just after, the Emancipation of the Serfs – the great political objective on which Turgenev had set his heart and one of the main inspirations of his first great literary triumph, *A Sportsman's Sketches*. And the storm of criticism which it evoked was arguably one of the two major reasons for his removal abroad. In the six years from 1856 to 1861 Turgenev had spent some thirty months in Russia and kept his main base there; in the six years from 1862 to 1867 he spent about six months there and had his main base in Germany; and in the remaining fifteen and three-quarters years of his life he spent in Russia less than twenty-four months.

Although his 'German period' was one of domestic peace and happiness, marked by the *rapprochement* growing into closeness with Pauline Viardot and his blossoming love for the child Didie, the years immediately following the publication of *Fathers and Children* were for him years of political and literary crisis. His polemic with Herzen on the significance of the Emancipation, the problems confronting Russia and the policies required by them (which Turgenev conducted in private letters, while Herzen argued publicly in the pages of his journal) escalated into a quarrel and breach of relations that lasted several years. On top of this came Turgenev's implication in the government prosecution of 'the thirty-two' – Russians living or studying abroad who were suspected or accused of maintaining illicit relations with Herzen and his circle: to his surprise and dismay, he was summoned home to St Petersburg to appear before the Commission of Inquiry; and while the senators treated him with courtesy and exonerated him promptly, his former friends insinuated that he had cleared himself at their expense. And, as the years passed, he was coming to realize that the decree of Emancipation, to which he had looked forward,

which he had invoked for so long and which he had at first hailed as
the fulfilment of his hopes was, in fact, a half-measure, that had
ended serfdom without necessarily improving the life of the
peasantry.

But if he was depressed by the political and economic conditions
of Russia, it is probably not too much to say that he was traumatized by the defection of his readers. To have most of the critics
against him was hard enough (even if their attacks contradicted or
cancelled one another); but it was as nothing to having his readers
turn against him, and in particular 'the younger generation' with
what passed for its politically conscious vanguard. That was the part
of his public whose devotion had meant most to him, who had
looked up to him as their leader or teacher – and now, suddenly,
they had disowned and were anathematizing him as an apostate
from their cause.

This estrangement from a significant section of his readers and
the change of domicile which it helped to bring about had deep and
lasting effects on Turgenev's writing. In the seven years between
1855 and 1862 he had produced four novels; in the remaining
twenty-one years of his life he was to produce only two. On his
shorter prose works the effects were different: there was no
falling-off in output nor, arguably, in quality; but there was a flight
into the past: all but three of the twenty-one post-1862 stories and
sketches deal with the Russia of which he had the most intimate
knowledge – with pre-Emancipation Russia.[1]

For five years, in the aftermath of his disorientation, he seems to
be groping his way. He tries his hand at new kinds of prose writing:
first, in 'Phantoms', at what he himself denominated 'a fantasy';
next, in 'Enough', at a kind of Romantic prose elegy, half amatory,
half philosophical; then, after the uproar over *Smoke* (which was to
be his last novel for ten whole years), a retreat into the first half of
the century, into the reigns of Alexander I and Nicholas I, into
memories of his own boyhood and youth and early manhood and –
even farther back – into family history.

Thus the short fiction of those five years foreshadows the stories
and sketches of the remainder of his life in two respects: the scene is
laid (with one exception) in a pre-Emancipation world, and the
conception of 'realism' is widened to include tales of mystery or
fantasy: the first two of these appear in the mid-sixties, to be
followed by others of the same genre in the seventies and eighties.

If the breakaway into fantasy can be seen as reflecting to some extent the shock inflicted on Turgenev by the events of 1862–3,[2] the full measure of his depression and bitterness can be most directly felt in two other works of that quinquennium – 'Enough' and *Smoke*.

'Enough'

'Enough'[3] appeared between the two 'fantastic' tales, 'Phantoms' and 'The Dog', but the writing of its first half fell within the period of his work on 'Phantoms'. If 'Phantoms' is a repudiation of humanity, rooted in an elemental disgust which pierces the camouflage of dream or fantasy only towards the end, 'Enough' is a farewell to life and literature in fully human terms, free from mystery and disguise – in terms of feeling and reason.

'Phantoms' was a fantasy; 'Enough' is a lyric monologue. It falls into two virtually equal parts: the first half evokes the happiness of past love, the second laments the futility of human life everywhere. The memories have the virtue of their specificity: they present experience which is both personal and quickened by genuine feeling. The philosophizing is perforce unoriginal: its central theme goes back to Ecclesiastes, 'Vanity of vanities, all is vanity' – a theme treated since then by countless poets and thinkers, and never, perhaps, more often and more variously than in the nineteenth century.

Turgenev was keenly aware of the subjectivity of 'Enough', which constituted an infringement of his own artistic creed. Contrary to his usual practice, he did not submit it to the judgment of his friends before publication, nor did he publish it in any journal, but slipped it onto the last pages of the last volume of the 1865 edition of his *Works*, as if hoping that it would escape general attention. Much later he was to express regret that he had ever shared such intimate recollections and impressions with the public,[4] but he continued to rebut aspersions on its literary quality.

The dead artist whose jottings constitute 'Enough' (according to its sub-title) is a projection of Turgenev, as the narrator of 'Phantoms' is not. The places depicted in 'Phantoms' and perhaps one or two of the 'events' (for instance, the evocation of Caesar's ghost) derive from their author's experience, but the narrator remains almost as unsubstantial as the 'phantom', Ellis. The dead artist is a ghost of a different kind: we do not know who he was, where and when he lived, what he did – but we do get to know his perceptions, his feelings, his thoughts: not his outer but his inner life. The narrator in 'Phantoms' is primarily his social shell; the dead artist is a psyche without a social envelope. He sees nature with Turgenev's precise, painterly eye and describes it in Turgenev's lyric cadences: that is the best part of the first half. He recalls his love in the key of earlier Turgenev heroes: not for nothing did some critics reproach his creator with having produced another superfluous man. Indeed, his thinking has not a little in common with that of the narrator of 'Journey into the Woodland'.

The jottings open with a device beloved of the Romantics: two chapters or sections consisting of nothing but dots, to indicate omission – of what may never have been written. The first two chapters of text (numbered III and IV) announce that the artist has grown weary and old at heart, that the light of his spirit is burning low, that he has had enough of life, since there is nothing new under the sun.

This is implicitly contradicted in the following seven chapters where, addressing himself to the woman who has been and will remain the one great love of his life, whom he has left, for reasons he does not explain,[5] he evokes for the last time, in the face of death, the memories of their happy love. Its five stages, from recognition–revelation to perfect communion, are framed in five different settings – three of them, landscapes (one in early spring before the ice has melted, one in summer, one in autumn – the season of love's ripening) – climaxing in the hour of ecstasy in the temple and the reading of the good book in the little room with all the world shut out, with its echoes of Paolo and Francesca and its anticipation of Sonya and Raskol'nikov.[6]

The philosophizing is another matter. That is a tissue of inspiss-ated gloom, but riddled, as might be expected, with contradictions and *non sequiturs*. Hope is made possible only by illusion: to see life without illusion is to lose all hope – and not because life is terrible but because it is essentially so 'meanly uninteresting', so 'wretch-edly trivial' (XIII, 118). Macbeth was right: life 'is a tale/ Told by an idiot, full of sound and fury, / Signifying nothing'. To most of us this would seem to make nonsense of the immediately preceding paean to love.

Having thus proclaimed his solidarity with Macbeth, the artist proceeds to examine possible objections, that is, to consider experiences that might be adduced as making life worth living. First, the political in a broad sense: service to one's people, to the cause of freedom, to humanity. This is dismissed on the ground that humanity has made virtually no progress since Shakespeare's day or, indeed, in the course of recorded history: our life still pivots on the follies derided by Aristophanes. If Shakespeare were to return to earth, he would find that the modern tyrant lacks even the tragic grandeur of his Richard III.

Secondly: what of the creation of beauty in art? This admittedly ranks higher than political achievement: the Venus of Milo outshines Roman law and the principles of the French Revolution. But art is futile because it does not endure: the Zeus of Phidias has mouldered away, the masterpieces of Sophocles have been eaten by moths. True, there is beauty in nature and it is eternal, for though its individual embodiments are evanescent, they are infinitely repeatable. But such 'eternal' beauty is no substitute, and is scant consolation, for the fragility of art's creations, whose beauty is as unique as the personalities of their creators. The tragedy of man is that nature destroys as indiscriminately as she creates.

Thirdly: love – our supreme happiness – stands condemned by its littleness and transiency.

How much of this rhetoric carries conviction? However little human nature may change – would it not be worth while to organize one's society so as to promote health, education and welfare while minimizing sickness, suffering and oppression? To compare the Venus of Milo to Roman law or to the principles of the French Revolution is to compare the incommensurable, which is absurd. With the possible exception of architecture, there is no intrinsic reason why works of art should not survive indefinitely. That is most obviously true of literature and music: the loss of so much of ancient literature and other arts is to be attributed less to the destructiveness of nature than to human destructiveness. And the four lines in which love is written off in chapter XIII are refuted by the four chapters, in the first half of 'Enough', in which it has been glorified.

But, regardless of the brittleness of his arguments, the artist is determined to despair. For one who has shed illusion and faced reality, he proclaims, the only dignified course is to turn away, say,

'Enough!' and, 'folding his useless arms on his empty bosom', remain steadfastly conscious of his nothingness. To some this would-be tragic posture has seemed as wooden as the would-be tragic posture of Insarov:[7] all the more perhaps as, in his seventeenth chapter, Turgenev virtually drops the mask and speaks in what they recognized as his own voice: not as the fictional artist saying farewell to love and life, but as the disillusioned and embittered author laying down his pen and turning his back on literature. And however sincere his depression may have been at the time of writing, its effect on later readers must have been still further dampened by the knowledge that his next story would be written a few months after 'Enough' and his next novel would appear in print little more than a year later.

No one is likely to number 'Enough' among Turgenev's finest works; yet it is of interest: not only as self-revelation, as autobiography and as an experiment in form, but as another paradoxical attempt to come to terms with nature – very different from the narrator's creed in 'Journey into the Woodland' – and with life: diametrically opposed to the cult of duty professed (though not lived) by the protagonist of 'Faust'.

On the face of it, this might look like an evolution from Kant (duty) to Schopenhauer (all is vanity) by way of the Greeks (the golden mean); but it makes better sense to believe that he regarded creeds and systems as incompatible with true art.

Smoke

Smoke[8] did nothing to encourage a reconciliation between Turgenev, the critics and his readers. It was no less political than *Fathers and Children*, and this time the attacks on both Right and Left were overt and scathing. Bazarov had been treated by his author with considerable respect, Pavel Kirsanov with less – but still as by one gentleman to another. To the Gubarëv circle and to Russian high society Turgenev shows no respect at all.

This novel may be one of several Turgenev works formed by the combination of two originally separate plans.[9] Soviet scholars have conjectured that the love-story may derive from an 1862 idea vaguely alluded to in several letters of that year and that the political element may go back to the same period, when Turgenev, having been 'semi-officially advised' not to reply publicly to

Herzen's polemic in *The Bell*, may have decided in frustration to expound his views in fictional guise.[10]

Be that as it may, what is bound to strike readers of *Smoke* is the brutal juxtaposition of the two disparate themes – the political satire and sermonizing, on the one hand, the romance on the other – flowing side by side without mingling, like the different-coloured waters of the Rhone and Saône below Lyons. And the split between the themes is hardly more complete than the split within the political world: between high society and radicals – with Litvinov and Potugin as purely notional links, really outside both.

The duality of themes and classes – reflecting the increasing polarization of Russian society at the time – is matched by a duality of styles and modes of representation. The central characters – Litvinov and Irina – are 'round', are living people; if allowance is made for how much less we see of them, the same can be said of Potugin, and even of Tanya and her aunt; but the radicals and the representatives of high society are caricatures.

Like *Fathers and Children*, *Smoke* contrived to enrage or offend all the political camps. The tradition of treating it as primarily a political work persists to this day – and not only in the Soviet Union. Freeborn entitles his chapter on *Smoke* 'The Novel as Political Pamphlet'; the political aspects of the novel occupy roughly two-thirds of that chapter; and its author summarizes his position quite unambiguously as follows: 'For *Smoke* is not the portrait of a hero or heroine, but the portrait of a society, complemented by the history of the relationship between Litvinov and Irina during the ten days or so that they are together in Baden-Baden.'[11]

It seems to have gone unobserved that high society appears in only three of the novel's twenty-eight chapters; the radicals figure in six chapters, if we count one chapter in which they are only discussed and another in which ex-members of the defunct group separately make a last appearance: so radicals and high society together account for less than one-third of the book.

Statistics may be ambiguous indicators. What, then, if the political chapters and the love-story were published separately? The story of Irina and Litvinov could be read and enjoyed by anyone capable of appreciating a Turgenev love-story; the rest would be read only by specialists interested in Turgenev's view of Russian society in the mid-sixties. In other words, the love-story could stand on its own as literature, the politics could not.[12]

This does not mean that the political chapters were not important to Turgenev and to his readers, particularly at the time. It was important to him to answer Herzen publicly, and no less important to demarcate decisively his position over against the principal social groups which he regarded as obstacles to Russia's further progress: the reactionaries, the Slavophils and the lunatic fringe of the Left.

To define *Smoke* as a political pamphlet is, of course, to challenge comparison with Dostoevsky's *The Devils*,[13] and it might be argued that it is the political chapters – the pamphletic components – which 'raise' the Litvinov–Irina story from the plane of the novella to that of the novel. On the other hand, Dostoevsky succeeds, as Turgenev does not, in fusing his political with his non-political elements: so that it might equally well be contended that the politics in *Smoke* have converted a remarkable story into a structurally flawed novel.

The rage of the Left over *Smoke* was fuelled by the mistaken belief – based on some resemblances between Gubarëv and the poet Ogarëv, Herzen's lifelong friend and collaborator – that the satire on the Gubarëv group was aimed at Herzen and his circle. Turgenev disliked Ogarëv, but the portrait of Gubarëv is, in all probability, a composite, and his followers were certainly based on Sluchevsky and members of his Heidelberg circle of students; the prototypes of most of them have been identified, and the nicety of Turgenev's observation and judgment has been recognized in Soviet scholarship.[14]

His contempt for his radicals is mainly intellectual. They are windbags – all talk, with little understanding and no action. They are camp-followers (like Sitnikov and Kukshina in *Fathers and Children*) and nothing more: noisy, credulous and empty. One of their favourite pastimes is backbiting (Turgenev himself had been a victim of their prototypes). They are sheep blindly following a leader – till changes in fashion throw up some other leader, whom they will follow just as blindly. Like sheep, they are silly but harmless: Potugin affirms that 'they are . . . almost all of them, fine fellows'; even their backbiting is more absurd than malignant.

Their current leader, Gubarëv, is something worse. He is a man whose life belies his preaching, a man concerned not with ideas or values or useful action, but solely with personal power, a petty despot (as we see in the final chapter), but fit to be a leader only of sheep. The radical 'Tower of Babel' will crumble of its own accord, and Gubarëv will end up as a seedy landowner, bullying his servant (his former disciple) and, with his brother, preying on his peasants.

If the radicals are grotesque, high society is revolting. Turgenev's contempt for these people is mainly moral, though he has no illusions about their 'culture' either. Under the thinnest of veneers, under their expensive clothes and polished manners, there is an emotional and intellectual void. Snobs of the first water, their contempt for everything Russian matched by an undiscriminating cult of everything European, they kill time in continual quest of relief from their boredom and can find nothing better than laughing at superannuated French jokes or than the latest fashion in drawing-room superstition – 'magnetism', soothsaying, spiritualism.[15] The men are frozen in poses some of which date from the forties, while the women pursue their separate frivolities. Hollow people, most of them – but among the aimless, brainless, bloodless crew there is a small group that is potentially dangerous: the 'young generals' – the reactionaries who want to turn back the clock of history, annul the reforms of the sixties, including the Emancipation of the Serfs, and take Russia back to the conditions of Nicholas's reign, or even farther if possible.

The star of this clique is Ratmirov and, like Gubarëv among the radicals, he stands out by his odiousness. Superficially they are polar opposites: Gubarëv – heavy, coarse, pontifical; Ratmirov – elegant, smooth, diplomatic; but both men live a lie: the preacher professes radical views and battens on his peasants, the general professes a moderate liberalism and has other people's peasants flogged. And if Gubarëv is repulsive, Ratmirov is vile: the one makes his precarious way by exploiting the foolishness of those below him, the other makes his brilliant career by serving the vices of those above him.

To the uninstructed reader the relationship between Ratmirov and his wife must seem a riddle, to which the 'dark and dreadful story' of Eliza Bel'skaya, far from offering a clue, only adds more bewilderment. In fact, Turgenev, greatly daring, is here extending his moral condemnation to the very apex of the social pyramid. It is now generally agreed that the model for the Ratmirov marriage was that of the Albedinskys: General P. P. Albedinsky had married Princess Alexandra Dolgorukaya who had been the mistress of the Emperor Alexander II. Such cover-ups were *de rigueur* when the monarch had been indiscreet enough to compromise an unmarried girl;[16] the obliging husband could expect condign demonstrations of his sovereign's appreciation.

Evidently Bel'skaya had preceded Irina in the Emperor's favour. Irina, when she picked Potugin as a screen for her friend, had wanted to give her a good husband; but illness delayed the marriage; with the birth of a child the scandal became public and the young mother killed herself; a partial cover-up was still effected by getting Potugin to take charge of the child. For herself, when her turn came, Irina wanted not a good husband but one whose rank and prospects would enable her to continue to queen it in high society and who would agree to let the marriage remain a mere formality. So the Ratmirovs are locked together in an interdependence which is to both as hateful as it is indispensable.

Turgenev said that *Smoke* was written in a vein that was new for him,[17] but did not explain in what respect. Of course, the polemical depiction of whole sectors of society was an innovation, and that was perhaps what he had in mind. But there was one other novelty, at least equally fundamental, which puzzled and disoriented even the more perceptive critics and of which Turgenev himself seems not to have grasped the full significance: this was his first novel in which the protagonist of the love-story was not the 'bearer of the message'. For Pisarev, one of the most intelligent critics of the time, Litvinov was the hero of the novel – simply in virtue of his being the protagonist of the love-story. In reply to him, Turgenev makes it clear that the most important personage in the novel is Potugin; Litvinov is no more than a 'run-of-the-mill honest man' (*dyuzhinny chestny chelovek*).[18] To the reader approaching *Smoke* without political or other preconceptions it is clear that the traditional rôle of the hero of a Turgenev novel has been split: Potugin is the ideological centre of the work, Litvinov the centre of the story;[19] and though Potugin is not the most interesting of the characters, he is surpassed in psychological interest only by Litvinov and Irina.

Potugin is almost pure Don Quixote. His selfless and unrequited devotion to Irina challenges comparison with the Don's cult of Dulcinea (in fact, Potugin's love means much more to Irina – assuages some of the bitterness of her lot, whereas Dulcinea remains entirely insulated from and unaware of her knight). Potugin's single-minded dedication to the values of 'European civilization' matches Quixote's to the ideals of chivalry. The keynote of both personalities is faith:

faith in something eternal, unassailable, in a truth existing outside the individual, requiring service and sacrifice [...] He lives entirely outside himself, for others [...] There is no trace of egoism in him, that is why he is fearless, patient [...] Humble in heart, he is great and bold in spirit [...] Constant striving towards a single end [...] does involve a certain one-sidedness of mind [... He] is an enthusiast in the service of an idea.[20]

The coincidence between Turgenev's 1860 definition of Don Quixote and his 1867 portrayal of Potugin is impressive, though there is not a complete equivalence. First, as just observed, Potugin's love is of the heart, active and effective, while Don Quixote's is of the imagination, abstract and of no effect in the life of his lady. Secondly, Potugin's love is unsparingly clear-sighted, free from the illusions that reduce Dulcinea to little more than a wraith and a name. Thirdly – and most significantly – Don Quixote's 'love' is only one aspect or component of his faith (in chivalry), so that the sacrifices he makes are to his faith and only incidentally or notionally to his love, whereas in Potugin's life love and faith are independent and co-equal as movers – at the centre, respectively, of his emotional and his intellectual being – and his service and his sacrifices are primarily to his love, although his faith is an added factor in isolating him from his contemporaries.

Turgenev made no secret of the fact that he had put his own political views into Potugin's mouth, that Potugin was speaking for him. He will hardly have suspected how much more he might be thought to have in common with his hero. Potugin's position in the penumbra of Irina's domestic life must have reminded many of Turgenev's on the edge of the Viardot nest – both men, knights-errant sacrificing their personal life and private interests to follow the woman they love. Litvinov's first reaction to Potugin is 'respect and sympathy and a sort of involuntary pity' (v, 165): perhaps not very different from what some of Turgenev's friends would feel when they saw him acting in Pauline Viardot's operettas or running errands for her and her children.

We are left in no doubt that Potugin, in spite of his awkwardness and air of strangeness is immediately recognizable as 'no ordinary' man (v, 165). He is highly intelligent; the settled sadness discernible in his glance is relieved by a low-key sense of humour; his culture ranges from Latin poetry (Catullus), through Homer and

Shakespeare (at least in translation) to Russian folk-poetry; his judgments of his fellow humans is penetrating and equable, irrespective of his own feeling for the person: he is as just to Gubarëv as to Irina; and his intuition is as sure as his judgment: he appreciates Tat'yana immediately.

His philosophy of love (XIV, 239) is that of all Turgenev's unhappy lovers, from Rakitin on, but expressed with unprecedented pathos and hopelessness: man is weak, woman is strong; she is the warmth and light to which he runs as the child runs to its nurse – only to end up in outer darkness, unable to understand how it was possible to love and even how it is possible to live.

Potugin's (Turgenev's) political message is simple, if not fully spelled out. Russia must become civilized; that means learning from European achievements: adopting or adapting the best and avoiding the errors and defects. And learning involves study, involves hard work; woe betide those who preach or believe that there can be any easy substitute for such hard work: whether in the form of inspiration or individual talent or national characteristics.

Here Potugin is throwing down the gauntlet to every variety of conservative: from the reactionaries, through the Slavophils and the 'votaries of the soil' (*pochvenniki*)[21] to the 'moderate liberals' – all the groups turning their backs on Europe on the strength of an assumed special genius and/or special destiny of the Russian people, and so leading away from what Potugin–Turgenev saw as the only road to true progress, to civilization. In his insistence that that road led through education which involved effort – and time – Potugin was throwing down the gauntlet also to the radicals with their dreams of revolution or similar short cuts to the perfect society.

So much is clear. What is left indeterminate – perhaps, because it could not then be published – is the nature of this civilization which is declared to be the precondition of knowledge, art, aesthetic feeling and even the nobler forms of love (XIV, 236). To equate civilization with culture (or education in the highest sense: *obrazovannost'*) is a sketch-map rather than a blueprint, though it can, and no doubt should, be supplemented by reverse extrapolation from Potugin's strictures on the actual state of his world: for example, from his critique of the Gubarëv circle and their cult of personality one would deduce that the educated (civilized) man would be a thinker of independent mind and sound judgment, examining and discussing concrete problems on the basis of factual knowledge. But the political aspect, which was certainly of the essence of Turgenev's conception of civilization – that is, the rule of law and respect for the dignity of the individual – could barely be hinted at: in Potugin's strictures on the legacy of slavery in the Slav weakness of will and abject dependence on leaders or masters (v, 168–9).

Turgenev came tardily to recognize that there was an element of 'caricature' in Potugin's Westernism, and there are certainly exaggerations and contradictions in his diatribes. To see Western Europe as the spearhead of human progress and model for humanity was only to share the faith of millions – and not only Western Europeans – at that time; but to deny any Russian contribution to human culture – in literature after Pushkin, in science after Lomonosov – was less than just. Insistence on step-by-step education was reasonable as a general policy; but did that preclude short cuts always and everywhere, when Potugin himself had cited the Petrine linguistic revolution with approval (v, 171–2)?

While Potugin proclaims Turgenev's political creed, it is Litvinov – who disappointed so many readers of good will by not being the positive hero, the heir to Bazarov they were looking for – it is Litvinov who is destined to put it into practice, to find salvation in cultivating his garden: in the slow, patient application of Western knowledge and methods to the running of what remains of his estate.

Like Lavretski in *A Nest of Gentry*, he is a social hybrid, the offspring of a cross-class marriage: he is actually the third of such heroes, and Turgenev has rung the changes on the mixture: in Lavretski's case, gentleman married serf; in Bazarov's, gentlewoman married army doctor descended from peasant and ecclesiastic stock; in Litvinov's, gentlewoman married civil servant from a merchant family. In the first two of these unions it was the father, in the third, the mother who had the decisive influence on the formation of the son.

The handling of the love-story in *Smoke* can be seen as a reversal of the technique used in *A Nest of Gentry*. In the earlier work we are 'told about' the hero's unfortunate infatuation (his marriage) but 'shown' his true love (the abortive relation with Liza); in *Smoke* we are told of Litvinov's true love (his relation with Tat'yana which ultimately leads to marriage), but shown his unfortunate infatuation.

Not that the two infatuations have much in common. The men, the women, the circumstances – all are different. Lavretski, in spite of his years, is, at the time of his meeting with Varvara Pavlovna, still in many ways a child, with no experience of the world or even of a normal life and upbringing; Litvinov has grown up in a stable home and a united family and traditional setting, has been tempered by the stresses and perils of the Crimean War, has travelled widely in Western Europe and had a chance to observe different peoples and societies: he is a mature man with a settled purpose in life and emotionally committed.

Varvara Pavlovna is easy to understand. Pleasure-loving and vain but practical, cool and calculating, she is devoid of strong feelings and of moral sense. Irina, by contrast, is complex and enigmatic. The privations and humiliations of her early poverty had left her insecure and proud. Her beauty set her apart from her family and she grew up starved of affection. So her passionate nature is split between two needs: for love and for security – which to her pride presents itself as luxury and pre-eminence.

These characteristics are already developed in her when she first meets Litvinov in her parents' home. She is drawn to him by his adoration of her, by his integrity, perhaps by his sense of purpose, while she is repelled by his lack of elegance, of 'distinction' ('vous n'êtes pas distingué': VII, 185) and, no doubt, of prospects – though she could not admit that to herself. For all her intelligence, she understands herself no better than most people, and directs the sense of guilt, which often goes with a passionate temperament, against imaginary sins, while stoutly denying her real shortcomings. In this respect she seems to have changed somewhat between Moscow and Baden-Baden. There had been plenty of reasons for shame and remorse in the interval, and her bitter self-accusations now are nearer the mark, if still only in general terms. She has been corrupted and warped by the life she has led; she confesses and deplores this – without seeking to shift the blame onto society.

Potugin attests to her capacity for candour and generosity; and if he charges her with 'demonic pride' (XIV, 238), it is surely a pride untainted by vanity, as witness not only the confessions just cited but the unreserved humility of her appeal to Litvinov 'as a beggar' asking for alms (XIII, 227).

When she meets Litvinov in Baden-Baden, she is bored with her mode of existence, frustrated by the soullessness of the people who surround her, trapped in a loveless marriage, probably dissatisfied with herself. He appears to her as a figure out of her innocent girlhood, as 'a living man in the midst of all these lifeless mario-nettes', as a real Russian among so many Frenchified cosmopolites and (she knows from the past) as a man of intelligence and probity over against people who 'understand nothing, have no feeling (*sochuvstvie*) for anything'. She was bound to invite him to join the generals' picnic.

If he had been able to respond to her with cool indifference, she might have let it go at that, but his transparent avoidance of her showed that for him as for her their past was not dead. That may have quickened her sense of guilt for the unhappiness she had caused him originally as well as some of the old feeling, which had impelled her to keep informed of the developments in his life throughout the ten years of their separation – and the rest followed predictably.

There are parallels between Irina's passion for Litvinov and Natal'ya Petrovna's for Belyaev (in *A Month in the Country*). What Natal'ya Petrovna wanted from the young tutor was his youth, to restore hers which she felt slipping away; what Irina wants from Litvinov is his friendship or love, to restore the self-respect that she has gambled away in St Petersburg. In both cases there is a comparable social disparity between the woman and the man (aggravated in the play by the disparity in age). Both women brace themselves for a desperately rash breakaway, but Natal'ya Petrov-na is not given the chance to put her resolution to the test (Rakitin warns Belyaev off); Potugin's analogous attempt to save his lady from herself falls on deaf ears: Irina is tested, and her nerve fails her.

Readers for whom success is everything and failure the ultimate condemnation are apt to write off Irina's love as mere frivolity or self-deception. But this is to overlook two pieces of evidence. When she says to Litvinov (XXIII, 303): 'I know that I am a criminal and that *he* [Ratmirov] has the right to kill me', she is saying that to keep Litvinov with her as her lover, she is quite prepared to risk death; what she is unable to face is poverty, obscurity, humiliation. The same hardboiled readers may object that Ratmirov was not very likely to kill the goose that laid the golden eggs. 'Not very likely' is arguable; but, on the other hand, he was a man of brutal passions, Irina had already exasperated him with her teasing and taunts, and if his 'honour' had been publicly compromised, he might have 'had no choice'. And secondly, if we combine Irina's statement on that occasion, 'it was not so easy for me to trample on my conjugal duty [...] I know I am a criminal' with the narrator's assurance in the epilogue (XXVIII, 328) that she has crowds of adorers but no known favourite – it is clear, surely, that Litvinov was and would have remained her only lover, and that his doubts on that score, as well as Potugin's hints of past causes for jealousy on his part, were unfounded.

In Irina, then, we have a heroine as deeply divided in soul as any of Turgenev's superfluous men, and the label finally affixed to her by her society forms a further link with that type: 'an embittered mind' recalls Pushkin's characterization of Onegin's favourite heroes in poetry and fiction (i.e., of Western counterparts of the superfluous man) and/or Belinsky's commentary on that characterization.[22] Pushkin wrote of: 'contemporary man, with his immoral, selfish, arid heart [...] and his embittered mind, seething in vain activity'. Belinsky made the point that: 'An embittered mind is also a sign of a superior nature, for a man with an embittered mind is apt to be dissatisfied not only with others but with himself. Ordinary people are always self-satisfied.'

Cerebration, narcissism, infirmity of purpose, schism in the soul – all these Irina has in common with the superfluous man. What differentiates her from Turgenev's superfluous men (though not from some of earlier 'generations': of the twenties and thirties) is that, by the standards of her world, she achieves 'success': she succeeds in imposing herself on her world, in compelling the adoration, fear or attention of the various sectors of that world – even if at the price of inner devastation.

The keynotes of *Smoke* are demoralization and infatuation. The representatives of high society are infatuated with their own elegant selves and demoralized in the most basic sense – morally neutered. The radicals are infatuated with their vaporous 'ideas' and with 'the exuberance of [their] own verbosity' and demoralized by their alienation from 'Russian reality'. Irina is demoralized by her infatuation with 'security' (as she understands it). Litvinov is demoralized by his infatuation with Irina, and the 'love-story' that occupies roughly three-quarters of the novel is the story of that demoralization.

Litvinov's love for Irina in Moscow is not to be equated with his

'love' for her in Baden-Baden. At twenty he falls in love romantically, but naturally, healthily, wholeheartedly. At thirty the reacti-
vation of the earlier love splits him in two – not merely in the sense
that he is torn between his bond to his fiancée and his passion for
this bewitching simulacrum of his first beloved, but in the sense that
throughout the ordeal his mind remains uninvolved and clear-
sighted: at every stage he sees and knows what he should, or should
not, be doing but finds himself acting in the opposite way.

He is not, as some critics have suggested, a superfluous man; on
the contrary, he appears as a basically sound and whole character.
It is only in the less than two weeks of his stay in Baden that the
passion which lames his will, without clouding his mind, reduces
him to a state very like that of a superfluous man. Very like – but
still essentially different: if he had truly become one, he would have
stayed with Irina on her terms, like Aleksei Petrovich in 'A
Correspondence'.

The disabling of Litvinov's will is only momentary and partial.
Perhaps he senses that by staying he would destroy himself without
saving Irina; perhaps it is only his 'plebeian pride' (x, 207) and
honesty that lend him the strength to flee (like Belyaev). Irina did
not break him as Elena had broken Insarov and Odintsova –
Bazarov: lacking the obsessive streak in Insarov and the aggressive
element in Bazarov and the rigidity of both, he was able to bend
without breaking and was saved.

Contrary to his usual practice and, it would seem, to his theory
that 'psychology should be hidden within the artist as the skeleton is
hidden within the [. . .] body which it [. . .] sustains',[23] Turgenev
offers such a detailed account of his hero's thoughts and feelings
from first to last that any further commentary would be supererro-
gation. The insight and the exposition are alike masterly; much of
the material may have come directly from his own memories.
Tanya and her aunt are said to have been modelled on his young
kinswoman Ol'ga Turgeneva and her aunt: he had been briefly in
love with the girl in 1854 and disappointed her hopes (or her love).
As for Litvinov's struggles to escape from Irina's spell, these may
well reflect some of his dreams, between 1853 and 1862, of breaking
away from Pauline Viardot, as Potugin's thraldom suggests,
however unconsciously, elements of the post-1862 relationship.

In relation to their author Litvinov and Potugin complement
each other: Litvinov observes the aspects of Russian reality which

Potugin criticizes. Potugin is obviously Turgenev's principal spokesman; but on two key occasions that rôle is delegated to Litvinov. When that hero shocked readers by telling Gubarëv that he has no political views and considers it too soon for Russians to have any, he is expressing Turgenev's conviction that conditions in Russia not only ruled out any political initiative (from below) but made any attempt at long-term planning futile. And by changing the novel's title from the original *Two Lives* to *Smoke* Turgenev raises Litvinov's reduction of everything to smoke from an outburst of personal distress and self-disgust to a cry from his creator's heart climaxing those five years of authorial dismay and disorientation.

12

'There are more things in heaven and earth'

Turgenev's retreat into the past was seen as flouting Belinsky's demand for 'relevance'; but the 'fantastic' stories were condemned as violations of Belinsky's (and his own) creed of realism. He was accused – even by some of his friends – of 'mysticism', which he continued stoutly to deny. But for the rest of the sixties and throughout the seventies his short stories – whether mysterious or mundane – were ignored, derided, slighted or condemned as outdated by a majority of critics, left and right.

'Mysticism' in this context was often or usually intended as a metonym for 'religion', and the charge of mysticism had been levelled already at the concluding lines of *Fathers and Children*. To anyone familiar with Turgenev's thinking it should have been evident that those lines must express the thoughts and feelings of the two old people at the graveside, though transposed perhaps into a more sophisticated key – into terms general enough to strike answering chords in the hearts of his readers. Turgenev could never reconcile himself to the tragedy of life, and he did not believe in life eternal – only in the kind of immortality conferred by great works of art.

To the radicals (and some others) traditional religion appeared incompatible with reason and science, which were indispensable preconditions of social and political progress. But the simplistic image and cult of science embraced by the radicals – the assumption that all the phenomena of life are quantifiable and/or explicable and that all the problems of life can be resolved by reason – made no impression on Turgenev's rooted scepticism. For him as for Hamlet there were 'more things in heaven and earth than [were] dreamt of' in the philosophy of the schools. He made his Potugin extol reason, knowledge, education, which would, no doubt, have included such knowledge of science and technology as would be requisite for the infrastructure of a new society – the kind of education he had sent his Litvinov to seek in the West – but the infrastructure would be only the first step towards a fully human world, if that were possible.

It should be borne in mind too that 'science' at that time meant the physical sciences: so it was easy to scandalize the adepts of 'science' with studies of such mental phenomena as dreams, hypnosis, hallucinations and others which have since then become objects of scientific study. Turgenev's 'tales of mystery' are, of course, literary, not scientific presentations, but there is nothing anti-scientific about them: if anything can be called anti-scientific, it is the charges of 'mysticism' brought against him.

In recent decades attempts have been made to 'rehabilitate' Turgenev's late stories, including the tales of mystery, or to compensate for the misjudgments of his contemporaries and their followers. This has involved exploring connections and affinities between these stories and his earlier works and/or their relation to various aspects of his thought or life.[1] But for too long, too often the tone has seemed to imply that the late stories needed to be defended or justified, although even in his time, even by his ideological foes there had been general recognition that the telling was as masterly as ever.

There is still no consensus among critics as to how many of his stories should be classified as mysterious or fantastic. At least one critic[2] would have applied these epithets to no less than thirty (out of thirty-three); but most would probably limit themselves to between half a dozen and a dozen. 'Three Meetings' is not a mystery: it hinges on chance or coincidence – three chance encounters in widely separated places – and wideawake observers know that chance plays a much greater part in real life than it is supposed to do in 'realistic' literature. 'Faust' is not a mystery, in spite of Vera's visual and the narrator's aural hallucinations: these are not what the story is about. The same can be said of 'Lieutenant Ergunov's Story' (despite the eerie atmosphere in the scene of his drugging) and of 'Knock ... Knock ... Knock!', where the knocking is no mystery to the narrator and the hide-and-seek in the fog is grotesque rather than mysterious.

There is more room for argument about two other stories often listed among the fantastic. To readers of an earlier age there could well have been an element of the uncanny, not to say the supernatural, in the scene of the evocation of the dead tutor in 'A Strange Story', whereas today's reader will no doubt appreciate it as an, admittedly somewhat chilling, exercise in hypnotism. As for the watch, in the story of that name, which keeps turning up like the proverbial bad penny, there is nothing really mysterious about its disappearances or reappearances: it is only the boys who imagine there must be some occult influence at work: Davyd, because they seem unable to get rid of it, Aleksei, because of the inordinate excitement it generates in the members of his household.

So we are left with just six tales of mystery, in which the fantastic element is pervasive or pivotal or both: 'Phantoms', 'The Dog', 'The Dream', 'Father Aleksei's Story', 'Song of Triumphant Love' and 'Klara Milich', which fall chronologically into three groups: the first two written in the mid-sixties, the next two in the mid-seventies, the last two in the early eighties. Formally, too, we can distinguish three groups (though the pairing is not chronological): the dream stories – 'Phantoms' and 'The Dream' – are *Ich-Erzählungen*, that is, told in the first person by the protagonist; 'Song of Triumphant Love' and 'Klara Milich', in which hallucinations play a large part, are told in the third person by an omniscient author; 'The Dog' and 'Father Aleksei's Story', where the abnormal phenomena are more complex or less easy to define, are 'framed *Ich-Erzählungen*': the main story is told by the protagonist in the first person to the narrator of the introduction.

'Phantoms'

'Phantoms'[3] was defined as a 'fantasy' by Turgenev himself. His contemporaries were unable to make much of it – and it can hardly be said that posterity has done much better.

The germ of the work can be traced back at least to 1855. The original conception was apparently of a series or collection of pictures, sketches, landscapes being viewed in a picture gallery by an artist; but by the end of that year, a draft of the first chapter and the beginning of the second shows that Turgenev has exchanged the artist for a protagonist much more like the eventual narrator, has abandoned the pictures and the gallery and has introduced the mysterious female visitant.[4] It was, to say the least, a curious idea to have occurred to him in the period when he was writing *Rudin*; it is easier to understand why it was then laid aside for nearly six years while he was producing his next three novels; but though he thought himself ready to resume work on it in the last quarter of 1861, it did not actually get written till towards the middle of 1863.

The narrator is a young man who takes a not too serious interest in psychic phenomena. He proceeds to relate a series of experiences whose status is never clarified. Are they reducible to a dream or a series of dreams? On the basis of the first three chapters, that would seem the most likely explanation. It is compatible with the account of the flights in succeeding chapters, and it is never decisively contradicted, though it is evidently not the view of the narrator. If the accounts of the nights are dreams, the accounts of the days which separate them do in all probability refer to 'waking life'.

No less enigmatic than the status of the nocturnal experiences is the character of the flying visitant for any reader who does not realize, or will not accept the hypothesis, that they are dreams. The narrator enumerates various possibilities on the last page – apparition, wandering soul, evil spirit, sylph, vampire, or ghost of some woman he had known and forgotten – but is unable to decide between them. Of course, they are by no means mutually exclusive, except perhaps for 'sylph' and 'vampire'; the others overlap, if they do not coincide.

Another – admittedly, minor – mystery is the name of the fantastic she, Ellis. Why an English name? Why a man's name – and such an uncommon one? Is it possible that Turgenev had chanced upon the *Poems by Currer, Ellis and Acton Bell* (Charlotte, Emily and Anne Brontë) during his 1847 visit to London and later learned that the Ellis Bell, whose verses might well have appealed to him, was a woman? Or did he first stumble on the 1850 edition of Emily's and Anne's novels and poetry, containing Charlotte's brief memoir of her dead sisters, during one of his five trips to England between 1856 and 1861, when the name Ellis first appears in his manuscript? Or is this suggested connection – like 'Phantoms' itself – just a fantasy?

As indefinable as the nature of the narrated events and the nature of Ellis is the character of the relationship between her and the narrator. In the beginning and halfway through their association she says she loves him; for three nights she holds him in her arms, she kisses him more than once; yet on the third night she says she loves nothing, and when he asks, 'What about me?' she only concedes apathetically: 'Oh yes – you' (xx, 103). She refuses to tell him anything about herself beyond her name. The words which escape her (xviii, 98): 'I was detained. I was being watched', no doubt imply that she is part of a group and that her fugue with the narrator is an illicit escapade, but still reveal nothing of who or what she is.

There is something leech-like in her kisses; and as the intimacy proceeds, she appears to acquire substance and vitality while the narrator is gradually drained of colour and vigour. Her last words in chapter xxiv – 'I could have ... gained life ... but now ... Nothingness, nothingness!' – may, in this wider context, have a whiff of the vampire about them; yet she is evidently capable of such human emotions as jealousy (of the singer on Isola Bella).

The narrator reacts to her with a mixture of curiosity (attested by his pressing questions and his frustration in face of her unyielding reticence) and fear: most explicitly, in the second and third chapters, fear of the unknown, in the fifth, fear that he has fallen into a devil's clutches, and later, in chapter xvii, more concretely, fear of being drained or of losing his reason. Before their first flight he had felt that he had strayed into a charmed circle, that he had been caught up and was being swept away like a boat being drawn helplessly towards a cataract; and his disappointment when she is late for their third flight does bespeak a beginning of addiction – although earlier that day he had fancied himself sufficiently in control of his fate to decide that the coming night's flight would be the last. Appearances of tenderness and of eroticism are all on Ellis's side; he shows no signs of either: perhaps his fear inhibits both.

Lastly in our series of unanswerable questions: what is the significance of the thirteen or so (it is possible to arrive at different totals) pictures or scenes surveyed by the narrator – either singly or collectively? They comprise some half dozen pictures of nature and about as many scenes with figures; the sketch of the nameless Russian town in chapter viii approximates in tone, as well as in the absence of figures, to the former group. This consists of short descriptions, occupying between one-third and two-thirds of a page; it includes the peaceful Russian forest and river and the terrifying storm off the Isle of Wight on the first flight; the gloomy Pomptine Marshes and the ruined Roman *campagna* on the second; and, on the third, the legendary Black Forest and the heroic soaring of the cranes. The scenes with figures divide neatly into three pairs: scenes with unhistoric ghosts (Isola Bella and the beautiful singer, Schwetzingen and the eighteenth-century dancers), scenes with historic ghosts (Albano and Caesar with his legions, the Volga and Sten'ka Razin with his insurgent Cossacks) and scenes with living humans (Paris and St Petersburg). Only the first of these pairs is depicted *con amore*. The historic ghosts inspire horror, the live humans[5] – revulsion: all the genius and grace and terrors of the human past lead up to – culminate in – those twin fairgrounds of human *poshlost'* in the present, the capitals of the French and the Russian Empires.

Yet the very next chapter (xxiii) shows that the fault lies not in Paris and St Petersburg: that they are no more abominable than the rest of the world, the whole of mankind – reduced here to the insignificance of flies and engulfed in a loathing that spares nothing and no one, least of all the narrator himself. The monstrous vision of death that follows comes almost as an anticlimax.

In a typically helpless attempt to explain his 'fantasy' and dissipate a friend's misunderstanding, Turgenev insists that there is 'no allegory' involved and continues: 'I understand Ellis as little as you do. It ['Phantoms'] is a series of some kind of mental *dissolving views* projected from my present truly depressed and gloomy state of being.'[6] And he adds (prophetically, as we saw in the preceding chapter): 'There is no doubt that I shall either give up writing altogether or write differently, as regards both subject and manner, than I have written till now.'

Bearing this confession in mind, it might make sense to suggest that for the narrator the significance of the series of dreams was to foreshadow his approaching death, while for Turgenev the unconscious purpose of his 'fantasy' may have been to cast a veil of art over the effusion of Hamletic spleen that finds direct expression only in the twenty-third chapter.

'The Dog'

'The Dog'[7] was regarded by Turgenev himself as 'a trifle' (*bezdelka*) and, in deference to the disapproval of some of his friends, was omitted from the 1865 edition of his *Works* – only to appear in a St Petersburg newspaper the following year and in the *Works* in the 1869 and later editions. This serves to illustrate that he bowed to his friends' judgments only up to a point: in the last resort he would trust his own feeling. In fact, 'The Dog' is a brilliantly told little tale, based on an anecdote that he had heard several years earlier.[8]

Oddly enough, it is more believable than 'Phantoms', though it flies in the face of 'naïve commonsense' as 'Phantoms' does not. 'Phantoms' can easily be 'rationalized' by assuming it deals with a series of dreams: we don't for a moment believe it while we are reading it, but it can become believable in retrospect. Whereas we do believe 'The Dog' as long as we are reading it: we experience what the protagonist experienced, and the *elements* of his experience are clear and familiar to us, however little they may fit into the causal patterns of our everyday world. We have probably all been scared by mysterious noises in the dark; we have all heard about clairvoyance and predictions that come true: these things put no undue strain on our imagination – that is, no strain comparable to that imposed by the resurrection of Caesar and Sten'ka Razin.

If the sounds of a dog in the room are projections of some unconscious anxiety or terror in the mind of Porfiri Kapitonych, it is not surprising that they haunt him for weeks on end and even follow him to different places; what is extraordinary is that these sounds can be heard by other people sharing his room – people who have not been told what to expect. That is, in fact, the only 'inexplicable' point in the story, but even that is only one short step beyond the credible and familiar: if our hero were suffering from an unconscious terror, we should have no difficulty believing that his terror might be sensed by – communicated to – people close to him; here we need to entertain the possibility that the symptoms of his terror (the sounds) could be sensed by those others. And surely while we are reading we do believe. We believe because the narrator, knowing that his experience is 'incredible', is nevertheless utterly convinced that it really happened; because of the simple honesty that breathes from every syllable of his account; and because we see his hearers' incredulity gradually overpowered by that conviction and honesty.

The rest of the story, though no less mysterious to Porfiri Kapitonych and his audience, is comparatively straightforward. The Old Believer[9] Prokhorych is 'psychic' and readily divines that a man who has never had a dog and is haunted by the ghost of a dog in the night harbours an unconscious terror of dogs. His prescription is sheer commonsense: he bids his visitor buy himself a puppy and keep it by him, just as any parent will give his child a pet to forestall or cure its fear of animals. The prescription works: the hauntings cease.

Admittedly, Prokhorych says too that the hauntings were sent as a warning and that the dog to be bought will prove of use to – or meet a need of – its master; but this is so vague that it is bound to be defensible in some sense. Porfiri Kapitonych, of course, construes it, in the light of hindsight, as a prophecy of his adventure with the rabid dog; but there was no indication in the old man's words that he foresaw or knew any more than he said.

However, if more is to be read into the words 'prove of use' or 'meet a need', this would still require no belief in clairvoyance on the reader's part. It is common knowledge that many animals, including dogs, are prone to attack other animals and human beings who show fear of them or in whom they scent fear: so Porfiri Kapitonych with his repressed terror was more likely than most people to be attacked sooner or later by man's best friend, and then the dog which had already served, as pet and companion, to repress his phobia deeper into the unconscious, might indeed 'prove of use' as a bodyguard. Incidentally, this also explains the rabid dog's second attack. The first may have been 'pure chance' (of the kind we encountered in 'Three Meetings'), but it left our hero so disturbed and shaken that he could not sleep or even stay indoors, as elementary prudence could have been expected to counsel. In such emotional turmoil his terror of dogs must have been brought much nearer to the surface of consciousness: in fact, he now had reason to be terrified of at least one dog which, for all he knew, was still at large; and the rabid animal, roaming at random through the countryside, caught the scent of the man he had attacked and terrorized earlier in the day and turned aside to renew his attack.

In fine, the only mystery in this 'tale of mystery' – the only fantastic or seemingly inexplicable feature is the 'public' character of the ghostly sounds in the absence of any suggestion or prompting by Porfiri Kapitonych; and one wonders whether this detail was part of the anecdote as originally told to Turgenev or whether it was invented by him: after all, he is known to have altered at least the social status of the protagonist and the dates of the events and their narration (he transformed the *meshchanin* who first told him the story into an ex-officer and landowner and advanced the date of the narration from 1859 to post-Emancipation). And if it is an authorial interpolation – had Turgenev just not realized the difference in credibility between this detail and the rest of the story, or was he deliberately aiming to puncture the 'naïve commonsense' of his contemporaries, left and right?

For the modern reader, presumably, the fascination of 'The Dog' lies not in its 'fantastic' element, but in the characterization and the style. The personality of the protagonist is thrown into bold relief against its contrasting past and present settings: in the present, the colourless, spineless metropolitan gentlemen hanging on every word, echoing every pronouncement of the pontifical 'state councillor' in a room we do not even see; in the past – the loyal servants, the simple neighbours, lapped in the rural peace of small estates, and amid the squalor of the nearby towns the striking figures of the Old Believers.

Within the limits of the thumbnail sketches how those two old men come alive: the innkeeper with his vibrant faith, in the midst of his clutter and fug, the 'psychic' with his awe-inspiring authority. We can measure this authority by what we have seen of our hero's bearing towards Anton Stepanych, the oracle of the metropolitan gentlemen. Anton Stepanych is presented as a pompous ass, but he is a 'state councillor', an official of the fifth class, equivalent to a brigadier-general and, as such, an object of subservient deference to lesser mortals. Yet our little ex-hussar, though no doubt three or four ranks lower in the social scale, treats Anton Stepanych with a studied offhandedness verging on the offensive – whereas he is completely overawed by Prokhorych.

Over against the shadowy, anaemic gentlemen and the ascetic, rigid Old Believers, Porfiri Kapitonych is robust, earthy, vital. He takes life as it comes, instinctively confident that all is for the best and savouring with equal relish his winnings at cards, the scents and sounds and moonlight of the summer night outside his barn and – his rupture with his lady friend. Perhaps he owes that confidence to a peculiarity which sets him apart from most of Turgenev's personages: he is lucky. We learn this first in the introduction: short of means to run his estate, he comes to the capital to seek a livelihood – and in a matter of days is set up in a comfortable sinecure. Within the main story, too, he is lucky: first, at cards, then in his advisers, and climactically in his encounter with the rabid dog.

The 'lucky' characters in earlier works, such as Andrei Kolosov, the prince in 'Diary of a Superfluous Man' and, arguably, Efrem in 'Journey into the Woodland', were presented to us – and only sketched – by third parties; Porfiri Kapitonych is unique among them as not only a full-length portrait but a self-portrait. Indeed, what makes 'The Dog' so much more than an – according to its detractors, rather improbable – anecdote is that self-portrayal: above all, the language, which expresses the personality so immediately and so vividly. We hear the simple, unpolished fellow, without culture or imagination but also without a trace of affectation or vanity, bluffly honest, with his heart in the right place (as we see in his mourning for his dog), and not without a spice of humour (as appears notably in his account of the egregious Nimfodora) – we hear him tell his tale in his own uneducated and lively idiom, and surely we enjoy every minute of its conviction, raciness and verve?

Only at the beginning and the end are we aware of Turgenev slily hedging his bets as Anton Stepanych, after listening to this astounding slice of life, repeats with monumental imperturbability the challenge that had initially provoked the story: 'But if one admits the possibility of the supernatural – the possibility of its intervention in everyday life, so to say [. . .] what part is left for commonsense [*zdravy um*] to play?' A good question.

'The Dream'

'The Dream'[10] is far and away the most mysterious of the tales of mystery. But whereas in 'Phantoms' the title provides a key to the mystery – we can 'make sense' of the story only by interpreting it as a dream-sequence – and whereas the title of 'The Dog' throws no light on its fantastic elements, in the case of 'The Dream' it may be the title which constitutes the mystery.

In 'Phantoms' we have no difficulty – indeed, no choice – in determining the limits of the dream: the nights are all dream; in 'The Dream' there seem to be at least four different components or sections of the story that could conceivably be referred to or covered by the title.

First, the rape. Most readers will protest that that is a wild conjecture, without foundation and completely unnecessary. Why should the mother have imagined such a thing, when a real rape would have accounted so perfectly for her continuing sorrow and sense of guilt and for her alternations of feeling for her son? Surely, on any reasonable reading, the rape was real?

But stand that reasonable reading on its head: suppose that the real source of the mother's sense of guilt was her ambivalent feelings for the son who adored her. And remember that she had been obsessed by the sinister officer. True, she remembered the obsession as one of sheer terror; but surely the intensity of that feeling for a man who had not yet approached or spoken to her and about whom she knew nothing might imply unconscious feelings of a quite different kind. Hence a dream of being raped by that man, a dream which would have left behind not only horror, but shame and guilt for having betrayed her husband even if only in thought and involuntarily.[11] And later, when she found that she could not love her son as a good mother should and that it was perhaps her swings of feeling that had implanted in him that other, darker self – she might have sought to absolve herself of that guilt by fantasying that the dream-rape had been real. How many psychiatrists must have heard and had to unravel equally far-fetched screen-memories; and readers should not lightly assume that Turgenev could not vie with Dostoevsky in depth psychology. But – regardless of the status of the rape – how much of the rest of 'The Dream' is a dream?

There would seem to be three possible answers to this question. First, the title might be taken to cover the whole story except the first three chapters and the last paragraph of the last chapter. We know that the narrator is a solitary youth, highly strung, emotional, immersed in literature, in daydreams and in the dreams of sleep which actually play a crucial part in his life: he 'slept a great deal' and 'dreamed almost every night', remembering the dreams when awake and regarding them as significant, as prophetic (III, 271). He has a recurrent dream and two problems. The dream is of seeking and finding a father: very natural in a boy who lost a dearly loved father at the age of 7. The problems are: the reasons for his mother's intermittent hostility and the occasional welling up in himself of angry and wicked feelings: these do not appear to be correlated but just might be connected.

Since these darker passions cannot be inherited from either his mother or his mother's husband, he would have had cause to wonder (as many children do in various contexts) whether he might not have had a father other than the one he had known. Of course, this wondering will not have been conscious while it would have been a slur on his beloved mother's 'virtue'; but as evidence that it lurked in the wings even then, we have the father of his dreams – quite different from his mother's husband and, naturally, unprepossessing as the source of his own unamiable traits. At a certain age, if the stress of his two problems had grown with him, his reading would have shown him how he could have had another father while his mother's image remained unstained: she could have been 'forced', and that would have explained convincingly both his problems at once.

At this point all the essential elements of his dream would have been assembled in his mind; the accident of sighting in some café a stranger who appeared to him to resemble the father of his recurring dream would then have sufficed to trigger the dream which forms the substance of chapters IV–XVIII. This is a perfectly defensible reading. It eliminates all 'mystery', which may be a recommendation for some readers. Incidentally, it eliminates the question as to the status of the rape, since that has been reduced to a mere element of the narrator's dream.

The main objections that might be raised against this reading are that it is too long for a dream (but experts on dreams now assure us that events which seem to the dreamer to cover considerable periods are actually compressed by the dream into moments of waking time), and that it is too coherent and closely knit for a dream (but that is to discount the secondary elaboration to which dreams are subject when retold in the waking state).

Secondly, the dream of the title might be thought to cover only the last three sentences of chapter XI, the whole of chapters XII–XVII and the first half of chapter XVIII: in other words, the search for 'the baron', the chance discovery of his dead body and the disappearance of that body while the narrator returned home and brought his mother back to identify the corpse.

A strong case can be made for this reading. It reduces the dream to a much more 'acceptable' length (about one-third of the whole story); it provides a trigger more commensurate with the drama of the content (the mother's 'confession', followed by the witches' sabbath of the night storm); it even goes some way towards explaining the content: after learning of the outrage done to his mother, the narrator cannot but desire the death of the man who has ruined her life and burdened him with a fearful inheritance – and the dream fulfils his wish and even saves him from any temptation to parricide (such as may have lain at the root of his search).

A possible objection to this reading is that it does reintroduce an element of the fantastic – one reminiscent of the mystery in 'The Dog'. There we were left puzzled as to how the ghost noises (aural hallucinations) could have been heard by third parties; here we wonder how the image of the rapist, which had no doubt remained a torment in the mind of his victim (irrespective of whether the rape was real or imagined), could have passed from there into the dreams of the narrator (their son, if the rape was a fact).

Thirdly, one could hypothesize that the only dream in the story is the recurrent dream of the narrator about finding his father. This would make the whole of the story factual: that is, a succession of 'real' events – for dreams are real events, however the status of their contents may be conceived. Though some of the events related here are undoubtedly odd, they all seem susceptible of perfectly natural explanations.[12]

Turgenev's own comments concern not the scope of his title but the subject of his story; however, they only add to the mystery. He writes, in English:[13] 'I have only to say that in writing this small sketch, I did not feel any itching, *French* desire of touching a rather scandalous matter; I have tried to solve a physiological riddle – which I know to a certain extent from my own experience.' Clearly the 'scandalous matter' is the rape; but what is the physiological riddle? Some Soviet critics[14] reply, 'heredity'. Heredity was indeed much on the mind of writers, both in Russia and in France, in the seventies and after, as witness Zola's Rougon-Macquart cycle and Dostoevsky's last three novels. But what does 'The Dream' contribute to solving the riddles of heredity? And in what sense has heredity played any special part in Turgenev's life? He does not seem to have resembled either of his parents, physically or in temperament.

Surely, the riddle that is addressed in this story (though, needless to say, not solved) is the riddle of the nature of dreams. We know that he had long dreams which he remembered in extraordinary detail; in one letter there is a 700-word account of a dream in which he becomes a bird and is flying over a stormy sea[15] which some commentators point to as a first foreshadowing of 'Phantoms'. In fact, 'The Dream' does raise two questions about dreams. First, can dreams foreshow events? And second, how can an image in the mind of one person infiltrate the dreams of another? To the latter, the story offers no answer; to the former it implies an affirmative

answer if the story title is construed in either the second or third of
the ways suggested above.

One might note that in the background of these 'physiological'
riddles there are echoes of such ancient cosmic riddles as: 'Why is
innocence a helpless prey – and infected with the predator's guilt
into the bargain?' (in the mother's delirium: IX, 279–80); or, 'Why
are the sins of the fathers visited upon the souls of the children?'
(implicitly, *passim*). But whereas in the first dream story, 'Phantoms', the narrator's voice rises to tones of revolt and abhorrence,
here the protest dwindles to a murmur of piteous complaint.

'Father Aleksei's Story'

The next tale of mystery, 'Father Aleksei's Story'[16] approximates in
form to 'The Dog': both are framed *Ich-Erzählungen* and masterly
examples of what Russian critics call *skaz*: that is, a first-person
narration in a non-literary idiom (provincial, class-linked or otherwise idiosyncratic); but in subject, style and tone they could hardly
be more unlike.

On the other hand, 'Father Aleksei's Story' has thematic affinities with the immediately preceding 'The Dream': in both two
innocent lives are blighted – in the earlier work by an external,
adventitious evil (if the rape was a fact), in the later by a deep-
rooted inner conflict. In both stories the evil impinges directly on
only one of the protagonists, indirectly, but no less cripplingly, on
the other; and in both stories it is the indirect victim who figures as
narrator.

In style and tone, however, 'Father Aleksei's Story' is as different from 'The Dream' as from 'The Dog'. The narrator of 'The
Dream' is well educated and widely read, and he is writing; the
village priest's culture is of a more limited kind and he is speaking.
But far more striking than these obvious dissimilarities is the
contrast between the surprisingly matter-of-fact tone in which
the extraordinary events of 'The Dream' are narrated and the
emotional warmth which suffuses the old man's tale.

To a modern reader 'Father Aleksei's Story' is likely to appear
rather less fantastic than 'The Dream' or 'The Dog'. Yakov's
meeting with the wood-demon at the age of 10 seems to fall under
the heading of what psychologists today would call 'a visitation', on
which some remarks from an expert may not come amiss:

A number of people are able to recall an experience in their childhood in which they were visited by some special being [...] In a religious setting visitations may be regarded as a natural occurrence [...] In a secular setting, however, visitations have to be explained in psychological terms, as dialogues between the waking 'normal' self or ego and the wider Self speaking impersonally and authoritatively[,] occurring under conditions in which the subject is partly awake and partly asleep [...] Benign visitations seem to mark the achievement of a precocious self-awareness which sets the child apart from other children of his own age as possessing insight beyond his years, while malignant visitations seem to herald the onset of a severe neurosis.[17]

Converse with a demon or goblin must have seemed malignant in a priest's family, but Yakov himself seems not to have suspected the supernatural character of his visitor and in the following eight years the visitation appears to have left no trace.

However, at 18, he stuns his parents with a confession that he has developed doubts that unfit him for the priesthood and asks their permission to enter university and study medicine. At this point we might expect another Bazarov. But Bazarov had not grown up in a priestly family with its centuries-old tradition of continuity and commitment; he had grown up with his father's devotion to science before his eyes, and he had wandered about the world with little or no chance to strike roots anywhere. Yakov had lived his whole life in the Lilliput of his native village or between the cramping walls of the seminary, inhaling religion with every breath he drew. We can only guess who or what had jolted him into thinking his own thoughts, doubting all he had believed and lived for, surrendering his soul to the siren call of science. If the seed was sown by a friend who lent him books (and what other source of temptation could have come his way between home and seminary?), was the dream of science inspired by a girl, perhaps a member of the family that took him up as a protégé – a girl who first smiled on his hopes and then disappointed them? How else can one understand his praise of Marfa Savishna, the young widow who had found a way, in a few hours' talk, to soothe his troubled spirit: 'She is not like the rest of them'?

Yakov is torn between two opposed elements of his nature: the faith and submission in which he had been steeped since birth and the urge to independence, intellectual and practical ('I have begun to think a great deal': p. 293; he would not take a penny from his parents: p. 294 – both, Bazarovan traits). For a short time he

thought he could reconcile science with Christianity in a mission to
succour his fellow humans, as a doctor; but then his inspiration (a
girl?) failed him – and/or his nerve failed – and he fled to the refuge
of his home. To a devout Christian, brought up as he had been,
exchanging the vocation of the priesthood for the service of
materialistic, atheistic science was likely to seem a temptation of
the devil; and as the tug-of-war within him grew fiercer, he had
begun to hallucinate – project – his temptation in the figure of a
tempter.[18]

His two visits to the young widow brought a respite, due,
probably, just to the relief of being able to speak freely to a
sympathetic and understanding listener. But she could not provide
a solution: she was a god-fearing woman, and to have accepted her
as his comforter would have meant lapsing back into the bosom of
the Church and the village: he saw the devil laughing at him: that is,
the spirit of independence and knowledge mocking his backsliding
(as the girl masked by his formula 'the rest of them' may have
laughed at avowals of his continuing religious scruples). Yet the
forces of temptation were sufficiently weakened for him to agree to
the pilgrimage to Voronezh.

At Voronezh the struggle between religion and science came to a
head. Religion appeared to have won: during the whole seven days
of the journey there had been no sight of Satan, and buying the ring
for Marfa Savishna symbolized a readiness – not necessarily
conscious – to yield to her influence. If the spirit of independence
was not to be snuffed out for good, only desperate measures would
avail, only the raising of an insuperable barrier between him and his
past – nothing less than unforgivable sacrilege. The devil had
triumphed – but only at the cost of losing his disciple in this world
and – if the priest's intuition is to be trusted – with no assurance of
keeping his allegiance in the next.

We see Yakov only through his father's eyes, and the old man
knows all too little of what had gone on in the seminary and at the
university or even between his son and Marfa Savishna: hence the
need for the reader to fill in the gaps, catching at every subtle clue
or hint in the text. On the other hand, the figure of Father Aleksei
emerges, entire and evident, from his artless narration, with its
quiet dignity and candour informing the blend of churchly and
popular language. We see a man of simple goodness, of deep
feelings, of humble faith, who has lost the family he loved and lives

on only to minister to a flock whose respect and affection he has earned – a man who carries on in his desolate state without repining or thought of self.

13

The years that are no more

In the ten years between the publication of his fifth novel, *Smoke*, and that of his sixth and last novel, *Virgin Soil* (March 1867–January/February 1877), Turgenev produced almost exactly the same number of pages of fiction as in the preceding ten years, but distributed very differently between genres. The earlier decade brought forth four novels and six short stories (including two 'tales of mystery'), the later decade, one novel, four long stories (novellas), seven short stories (including two tales of mystery) and three *Sketches* (which went to round out the original twenty-two of *A Sportsman's Sketches*).

The zealous efforts to 'rehabilitate' the stories of this period or to justify their lack of 'relevance' all fail, for the simple reason that there is too much diversity – of themes, styles, form, settings and characters – to admit of generalizations that truly apply to more than a few. In fact, the only valid and significant generalization is one in which Turgenev himself defended his retreat into the past:

> but are you really so immersed in the 'immediate present' that you can't accept any types that are not *today's*? [...] Does every character really have to be some sort of exemplar [showing] just how one ought or ought not to behave? People like these [in 'A Strange Story'] have lived, so they have a right to be represented in art. That is the only immortality I acknowledge; but such immortality – the immortalization of human life in art and history – is at the root of all our activity.[1]

In other words, the justification of these stories (if they need any) is that they perpetuate the memory of human beings who have lived and loved and suffered and deserve to survive. One reason why they deserve to survive (though it cannot be said to what extent he recognized this) was that by their character or their history they had impressed themselves on his mind, had constituted themselves a living part of his past.

'Lieutenant Ergunov's Story'

'Lieutenant Ergunov's Story'[2] was Turgenev's nearest approach to an adventure story or thriller. It was begun during a lull in the writing of *Smoke* and completed immediately after the completion of that novel. The second half at least was written with exceptional zest and gusto – the last twenty-two pages[3] in a single eleven-hour sitting – though he later claimed, in rebuttal of a charge that it seemed to have been written hastily and carelessly, that it had cost him exceptional trouble and that he had written it three times. Of course, both accounts may be true.

The events of the story date back to 1826–7, at the very beginning of Nicholas I's reign (when Turgenev would have been 8 or 9 years old) in the Black Sea port of Nikolaev (which Turgenev had never seen). It is supposed to have been set down forty years later, shortly after Ergunov's death, by a member of his circle who had heard him retell it so often – once a month on average – that they all knew it almost by heart. But Turgenev does not here, as he had done in 'The Dog' and would do again in 'Father Aleksei's Story', give us the narrative in the protagonist's own words and style; instead, he entrusts it to a narrator whose attitude to Ergunov appears to be one of kindly condescension.

An irreverent reader might regard the story (though that can hardly have been the author's intention) as a parody of a more familiar kind of Turgenev love-story. It is certainly a love-story of sorts and, as in the typical Turgenev love-story, Ergunov's involvement with the two girls has proved to be not only the most significant but the sole significant event in his whole life. The split in the hero's affections conforms, too, to a recognizable pattern: as in 'A Correspondence' and *Smoke* (and, later, in 'Spring Torrents') an initial sentimental attraction – to Emilia – is thrust aside by a more powerful physical urge – towards Kolibri – and in each case it is the object of sensual passion who constitutes the threat to the hero's life or career.

In the true spirit, no doubt, of the adventure story, the criminal element is supplied by aliens: the virtuous, if slow-witted Russian hero is duped, robbed, all but murdered by foreigners. The procuress is a Jewess (shades of Hirschel in 'The Jew'!); the would-be murderer bears an Italian name but hails from Bucharest; the exotic young enchantress is apparently a gypsy: that she is not related to Luigi is indicated by Emilia's designation of her as his 'accomplice', and she is not Italian or she would not accent her name on the first syllable; even the flighty but good-hearted Emilia is German.

For the reader, excitement mounts as the warning signals succeed one another, but the obtuse young man goes blithely on his way, till he tumbles headlong into the villains' deadly trap. By a hair's breadth he survives, but for him as for more romantic lovers there is a grim price to be paid. Not only does it take him ten years to repay the stolen government money – ten years during which he was obviously in no position to think of marriage or a family; not only has the shock, which left that scar across his skull from ear to ear, apparently paralysed his romantic faculties; but forty years later our hero is still a humble lieutenant: his first step in love has spelled the last in his career.

The excitement approaches its climax in his two meetings with Kolibri and culminates in the masterly scene of the drugging, with its exquisite depiction of what Turgenev called 'the *imperceptibility* of the transition from reality to dream'.[4] Kolibri herself is a delicious creation, a kind of cross between Ellis and Asya: half vampire, half waif, all – seductive mystery. So naturally it is to warm-hearted Emilia, not to cold-blooded Kolibri, that Ergunov is quick to attribute his undoing: illusion springs eternal in the human breast.

All this gaiety, *brio* and observant irony was lost on a public, part of which was capable of condemning this story as 'immoral',[5] and Turgenev took heed of their reactions to the extent that no crime in his later stories was ever committed by professionals.

'The Brigadier-General'

'The Brigadier-General'[6] was written immediately after 'Lieutenant Ergunov's Story' and published the same month. Turgenev did not think too highly of it: he considered it 'one of the less important' of the stories to be included in a forthcoming collection in French translation – less important than 'Phantoms' or 'Ergunov'.[7] It received much higher appraisals from some of his literary friends – Annenkov, in particular, numbered it among Turgenev's best works of that period – and various critics detected affinities with *A Sportsman's Sketches*.[8]

It is indeed a sketch, deliberately designed by Turgenev as a frame for the protagonist's letter, which he regarded as a moving 'human document', worthy to be embalmed in art. He had discovered it in going through his mother's files after her death in 1850 and, then or later, had transferred it to his own, evidently with the intention of making some literary use of it. It was, in fact, to Varvara Turgeneva that the brigadier's appeal had been addressed; it was her aunts and uncle who had been his ruin. But we cannot identify the narrator with Turgenev: there is no evidence that he ever met Gus'kov.

Gus'kov does actually take us back to the eighteenth-century figures in Turgenev's earlier works: the personages of 'Three Portraits'; survivors like Ovsyanikov, ghosts like Count Orlov, Count Pëtr Il'ich and the narrator's grandfather in *A Sportsman's Sketches*. But what a contrast he presents alike to the magnates in their pomp and to the Lutovinovs (called 'Lomovs' here) in their lawless pride. A patriot, a hero of Suvorov's campaigns, he had fallen in love with the star of that violent and despotic family, had expended his fortune to rescue her from poverty and debt and then to maintain her in the style of life which she expected, had sacrificed his honour to save her from the consequences of her crime, and had continued to adore her memory through a destitute and miserable old age. To compare this love, as does the callow young narrator, to Werther's is to equate an immature if genuine passion, unable or unwilling to bear the pangs of unrequited love rather than cloud the happiness of the beloved, with a mature devotion ready to endure ignominy and penury so that its object might have life more abundant. Werther, admittedly, had no chance to live or die for Lotte, as Gus'kov did live and suffer for his Agrippina; that is no reflection on Werther, but it makes the comparison absurd.

Gus'kov is another Quixote – perhaps the most quixotic of Turgenev's creations. A simple man – free from Chertopkhanov's pride of race, lacking Potugin's intelligence and culture – he has distinguished himself on the battlefield and carried his cult of love to heroic lengths. But whereas Don Quixote constructed his abstract vision of an ideal Dulcinea on the basis of no more than rare glimpses of the model, Gus'kov had distilled his intimate experience of Agrippina into a memory of beauty and happiness, which can still rouse him from the semi-stupor of senility.

Prosper Mérimée, not understanding Turgenev's limited

purpose – of framing the letter – complained that the story was too short, that one wanted to see the heroine and the hero in his prime.[9] He is right in recognizing that Turgenev is here imposing a great, if not excessive, strain on his readers' imagination. We see, we are shocked by the old man's decrepitude and torpor – and we are expected, on the strength of no more than two momentary flashes of the pristine spirit (in the confrontation with the bull, on hearing his lady's name) to conjure up the hero and the lover in his heyday.

The letter, which Turgenev apparently edited only in some details, is a self-portrait that speaks for itself. Unfortunately, it is undated, and Turgenev has taken some liberties with the chronology, but it is evidently the letter of an old man. In spite of his rank, his military honours and his fortune, he evidently looks up to the Lomovs as to a superior breed: there is no sign of the hatred and contempt with which he will refer to them in 1837.

Like Turgenev's Quixote, he is a man of faith, who 'lives entirely [. . .] outside himself, for others [. . .] fearless, patient [. . . h]umble in heart [. . .] He knows little, but [. . .] he knows what his business is on this earth.' Even the sober references in the letter to his service and sacrifices, which might jar on a casual reading, aim to make it plain that he is not begging, but asking for a return of just enough of his own gifts to enable him to live out his life decently; the conditions in which the narrator finds him and shows him to us amount to a shattering indictment of his family's hardness of heart.

'A Strange Story'

In 'A Strange Story'[10] Turgenev advances from tales laid, or climaxing, in his childhood and adolescence to memories from his adulthood, from the years in which he was writing his first four novels, and, short though it is, this story seems closer to the formal and thematic complexities of the novels than to the linear simplicity of 'Ergunov' and 'The Brigadier'.

With an intuitive writer like Turgenev, who himself said that the starting-point of his writing was never an idea (but always a person, a character) and who sometimes read back into his works ideas that look like afterthoughts – it is pointless to speculate whether or how far the challenges in any given work were conscious or deliberate. 'A Strange Story' contains more than one challenge. Disciples of Belinsky must have disapproved the 'evocation of the dead' as

much as the Master had disapproved of Dostoevsky's 'The Land-
lady'; and some wealthy conservatives blamed Turgenev severely
for exposing such a phenomenon as the 'holy fool' to the civilized
eyes of Western Europe.[11] They seem to have missed the point that
the 'idiot' for whom they blushed had been invested with those very
'magnetic' (i.e., hypnotic) powers which were an object of their
own, often unintelligent curiosity (illustrated in the table-turning
seance referred to in the first chapter of 'Phantoms' and the attempt
to mesmerize the crayfish in chapter xv of *Smoke*). The radicals, on
their part, overlooked the bracketing (on the last page) of Sof'ya's
devotion to her 'idiot' with the devotion of a later generation of
Russian girls to the cause of revolution. By those radicals Sof'ya's
devotion would have been judged irrational, while self-immolation
to their cause would be seen as eminently reasonable; Turgenev's
narrator, while approving neither, tacitly implies an equal respect
for both.

The treatment of the idiot or holy fool[12] deserves notice. The
narrator obviously finds Vasili repulsive already at their first
encounter, when the young man is still fairly clean and tidy (except
for his matted hair): his eyes are terrifying, his presence is overpowering, under his gaze the narrator feels himself passive, helpless, completely subjugated. But the portrayal remains objective
and precise; in the second meeting – away from the effects of
alcohol, semi-darkness and suggestion – it becomes even more
matter-of-fact.

Vasili is an epileptic with hypnotic and perhaps 'psychic' powers;
although illiterate and inarticulate, he enjoys widespread respect
among the people for his piety – his praying and fasting – and in the
merchant class for his ability to evoke their dead. Sickly and unable
to take care of himself, he is 'mothered' and perhaps exploited by
the old woman Mastridia who takes the money she charges for
allowing access to him.

A few years later, Sof'ya has replaced Mastridia as his 'mother' –
and servant – as Vasili has exchanged his settled existence for
vagrancy and his rôle as a hypnotist for a rôle as a holy fool,
renouncing the comforts of sedentary 'work' – tea, clean clothes, a
roof over his head – for conspicuous mortification of the flesh –
rags, dirt, fetters, exposure to the elements – in bond to casual
charity.

The basic pattern of dominance-and-dependence has not

changed – dominance in relation to the world and a mixture of both in relation to the mother-figure – but we may conjecture that the proportions in his relation with Sof'ya are very different from what they had been *vis-à-vis* old Mastridia: as evidence of this, he has set his brand on Sof'ya by stripping her of her name and conferring, or imposing, on her a name from his own world – a distinctively plebeian name.

The disorder (dissociation) of his personality now finds overt expression in the pattern of utterance–guffaw–expectoration: the words in which he strives to convey the message of Heaven are constantly punctuated or interrupted by the laughter of the Devil, and the spitting signifies the victim's indignation at being thus made a vehicle for the forces of evil.

The events of 'A Strange Story' fall in the period when Turgenev was writing 'Yakov Pasynkov' and his first three novels,[13] and its heroine shows some striking affinities with the heroines of those works, her literary predecessors and 'historical' contemporaries. With her namesake, the heroine of 'Yakov Pasynkov', she has more in common than her name and age. Both girls are exceptionally strong-willed; both break away from their world to choose a life partner in defiance not only of the views and standards of that world but, arguably, of common sense too; each perseveres in her course and suffers the consequences of her choice without faltering or complaining.

What the new Sof'ya shares with Natal'ya (in *Rudin*) is the demand for a teacher who will not only preach but set an example of how to live. What she shares with Liza is religious fervour; the earlier Sof'ya had been summed up by her narrator as 'a Puritan', who lived by her sense of duty; Elena had called her God to account ('her very prayers were often mixed with reproaches'); but, like Liza, the later Sof'ya is driven by an unquestioning faith and an urge to self-sacrifice – specifically, to expiate the sins of an unloved father. What she shares with Elena is her activism: her urge 'to do good' – and, in particular, to do good in the world outside or in opposition to the established order.

There is a kind of emotional gradation which determines – or, at least, explains – the destinies of four of the five girls. Natal'ya is modest, and comes to terms with her world. Liza is humble – haunted by a sense of guilt – and withdraws from her world. Elena is proud – she wrestles with God and will not be content with less than a hero – and finds a field for heroic action outside her world.

For the Sof'ya of 'A Strange Story' humility is not enough; she thirsts for humiliation – which bespeaks a repressed pride more intense than Elena's overt pride – and she finds what she seeks: in service to a poor half-wit, whose coarseness and dirt must constantly outrage her delicacy as his rant and ignorance must outrage her intelligence.[14]

But it is not only pride that has been repressed in this Sof'ya – it is also the basic human need of love. Even if it were possible for Vasili's dependence to approximate to some form of animal attachment and for Sof'ya's mothering rôle to engender some semblance of maternal feeling, such feelings would undercut her need for humiliation, and so subvert her mission. It is these repressions – of love, pride, disgust and other feelings – which set this second Sof'ya apart from her four predecessors and make her lot appear so much more cheerless than theirs.

'Knock ... Knock ... Knock!'

Defending 'Knock ... Knock ... Knock!'[15] to an admirer six years after its publication, Turgenev defined it as 'a study of suicide, specifically – Russian, contemporary, self-centred, obtuse, superstitious and absurd, bombastic suicide', which 'constituted as interesting and important a subject as any social [. . .] question'.[16] The story is certainly a study – or, at any rate, an account – of a Russian suicide; since Turgenev held that human nature had hardly changed since the age of Shakespeare, or even of Aristophanes,[17] he was no doubt entitled to label a suicide of the 1830s 'contemporary' in 1870; and the five harsh epithets applied to the suicide are applicable at least to poor Teglev. In the same letter he judged this story to be 'one of the most serious I have ever written', while conceding that the execution might have fallen short of the conception. A less partial critic might consider it quite adequately described as 'a character study'. The character is one with which the author had little sympathy; but the effect of this is softened by letting the narrator tell his tale from the viewpoint of his teenage self: teenagers are not expected to be charitable.

Attempts have been made to discover some recondite social or political 'relevance' in the story – disregarding Turgenev's categorical denial of any such ramifications.[18] But that does leave open the question why he should have chosen to tie his 'study' to the cult of Marlinsky,[19] of whom he had himself been a votary in his mid-teens, but whose cult (unlike the Pechorin cult 'debunked' in 'The Duellist') had been dead and buried for decades. Is Marlinsky here just 'local colour'? Or is there here a confusion of purposes analogous to that which we found in 'Hamlet and Don Quixote': a current psychological type here wrongfully blamed on (there wrongly identified with) a definite literary character?

As well as a character study, 'Knock ... knock ... knock!' is a page of autobiography: during Turgenev's student years in St Petersburg, his brother Nikolai was in fact a junior officer in a Guards field artillery regiment. Turgenev will have visited him in camp, and Teglev no doubt derives from one of Nikolai's fellow officers.

The narrator's attitude to Teglev is artlessly ambivalent. While he claims to have felt affection (*polyubil ya ego*: IV, 271) and pity for his friend, he is merciless in pinpointing that friend's limitations: especially his intellectual and cultural limitations. Teglev reads nothing; his writing is riddled with spelling mistakes; his mind is full of superstitions. He dabbles in numerology to muster evidence – to feed his conviction – of his affinities with Napoleon.[20] His practical abilities are no better than mediocre. One wonders if all this really adds up to more than saying that Teglev was just an average officer of his time and place.

We see that he is good-hearted and physically courageous – ready to risk his life to save a puppy's – and capable of falling passionately in love (*lyubyat oni eë uzhastvenno*: XIV, 288). His undoing is the discrepancy between what he expects himself to be and what he is capable of being.

The narrator (followed by some critics) seems to see Teglev as simply the prisoner of a pose and his suicide as just the ultimate requirement of that pose. But that, surely, is to mistake the symptom for the malady: it would be more just to say that Teglev is a victim of the rôle imposed on him by his society; the 'pose' is nothing but the behaviour prescribed for the rôle, and it is not in acting out the rôle, but by his failure – his inability – to live up to the rôle that Teglev is impelled to suicide.

His oddity begins with his appearance: the asymmetrical eyes, which no doubt symbolize, if they do not actually involve, a skewed vision. By the time he attains officer's rank, he is already seen as weird, as fated, as under a special star: which (at that period) means as a hero in a Marlinskian mould. And that reputation is definitively fastened on him by his two 'exploits' – his rescue of the puppy and his guessing the three cards. It is worth noting that both those actions were totally disinterested and uncalculated; but once saddled with the status of hero, he makes the mistake of accepting and sinking himself in it. Lacking the clearsightedness and resolution of a Luchkov (in 'The Duellist'), who borrows from his 'model' – Pechorin – only the little he can understand and use, Teglev strives to see himself as a man of destiny and to act accordingly: he lets himself be convinced by the conviction of those around him.

But, however limited his intelligence and however inflated his vanity – the vanity that kept him aloof from his fellows, and indeed from all but those who would feed his sense of superiority like the young narrator and the enamoured Masha – the conviction in Teglev can never have been doubt-proof: at some level he must always have sensed that he was no Napoleon. That repressed inkling betrayed itself in his habitual expression, in which dissatisfaction was mingled with 'puzzlement: as though he were pursuing some discomforting thought within himself which he could never catch' (II, 268).

Yet the doubt remains repressed until his desertion of Masha, which – it is important to understand – bore no relation to his rôle or pose: on the contrary, as a man of destiny he was entitled to ride roughshod over social conventions and marry whom he pleased. The reader is offered two different reasons for the break. To the narrator Teglev hints, without altogether admitting, that he had jilted her for fear of offending his patron, his rich uncle; Teglev's servant, more kindly, ascribes it to his master's 'faintheartedness' (*malodushie*: XIV, 288), which may imply the same, but need not. If Teglev's semi-admission was the real motive, he stands convicted of *poshlost'*; if the servant had something else in mind, it cannot have been anything at all heroic.

In either case, the hero's faith in his vocation had been breached, was being eroded by doubt (hence the melancholy noted by the narrator) and could not long survive. The 'mysterious' rapping, the 'ghostly' calling of his name, and the death of the girl merely precipitated the process.

In the bizarre comings and goings amidst the fog of his last night, Teglev seems to be playing hide-and-seek not so much with his pursuers as with death itself. Obviously he remains, like Dostoevsky's Kirillov,[21] in two minds till the last moment: the natural, animal attachment to life at odds with the collapse of his faith in his mission compounded by remorse for his betrayal of Masha.

There is scant generosity in the narrator's response to the dead man's memorandum to Grand Duke Mikhail Pavlovich: proper little gentleman that he is, he is repelled by the spelling mistakes and the absence of style – by the bad form – rather than moved by the pathos of the little man's final, futile gesture of defiance to the Establishment.

So, yes, there is in this suicide, as Turgenev claimed, vanity and absurdity, obtuseness and superstition (in the refusal to believe the true explanations of the rappings, the whispered call, Masha's death); but is there not also a perverse loyalty to a false ideal and a determination to pay a supreme debt of honour – a life for a life?

'The Watch'

'The Watch',[22] the last short story to be published before *Virgin Soil*,[23] like 'Lieutenant Ergunov's Story', the first to be written after *Smoke*, was planned as something like an adventure story. That was before the introduction of the Latkins and the relationship between Davyd and Raisa, which now accounts for one-third of the whole; but even in its present form, this story and 'Ergunov' contain more 'action' on the adventure-story level than any other of Turgenev's short writings.

Both stories present the memories of sexagenarians[24] about events of their youth; 'Ergunov' took us back to the beginning of Nicholas I's reign, 'The Watch' takes us back a quarter-century farther, to the accession of Alexander I, a period of fresh starts and great hopes, following the terrifying uncertainties of Paul's five-year rule. As in 'Ergunov' (and several of his early stories) Turgenev chooses for 'The Watch' a social setting with which he is not intimately familiar,[25] but the characterization cannot be said to suffer for that in any of those works.

In this latest tale we have to do with a quasi-professional family living in genteel poverty in the small provincial city of Ryazan'. The father is a shady lawyer of sorts, but the focus is on the relationship between two teenage boys – the notary's son and nephew – and on the older boy's love for the daughter of a ruined former associate of his uncle.

The theme of two youthful friends is one on which Turgenev has rung the changes in a number of his writings: from 'Andrei Kolosov' through 'Yakov Pasynkov', *Rudin* (in the flashback to Lezhnëv's university friendships), *Fathers and Children*. In 'The Watch', as in all the preceding cases, the younger of the two is weak or unformed, the older is mature, with a strong personality: it is a relation of follower to leader, of disciple to teacher and model. The age of the couples varies: here Davyd and Aleksei are schoolboys, as were Pasynkov and his narrator when they became friends; two other pairs were university students; Bazarov and Arkadi had graduated when we meet them. Where the narration is in the first person (i.e., in all the cases except Arkadi–Bazarov) it is the younger friend who is the narrator: naturally enough, since the main purpose is the portrayal of the older boy, to whom the younger serves as a foil.

An unfriendly critic of the time saw Davyd as 'something like a cross between Bazarov and Baburin';[26] in fact Davyd is not an ideologue, let alone a nihilist: it takes a political critic to confuse principles with ideology. Even his cult of the stiff upper lip (tears are a luxury, an indulgence fit for the idle rich, and to show even joy too openly is to reveal a lack of spirit) expresses a naivety acceptable precisely in terms of his age.

Davyd had been brought up by a father whose values and principles had set him at odds with his society, who was paying the price for those values and principles in Siberia, and who would in the end triumph over the hardships and handicaps of exile. In the four years before the story opens, Davyd had had his principles and values tested, his will and courage tempered in an analogous, if lesser, ordeal: not only separated but cut off from his father and reduced to living in dependence on the man responsible for his father's exile, he had vindicated his freedom of thought and action against all family pressures and achieved a precocious maturity, rounded out by his emotional involvement with Raisa.

She had been formed in an even harder school. Within a mere two years, her father's ruin and rapid disintegration, her mother's death, the trauma that robbed her little sister of speech and hearing have thrust on her the rôles of mother, father, nurse and housekeeper all in one; and, young as she is, she has taken up this grievous load and carries it without wavering or repining.

Clearly, she and Davyd are made for each other: two heroic children standing out in shining relief against their backgrounds – of moral squalor in his case, of material squalor and physical decay in hers. And almost alone among Turgenev's young lovers, they not only triumph over their grim circumstances, but are actually allowed – if only off-stage – to find fulfilment and happiness in their love.

14

Down Memory Lane

In dealing with the stories written between *Smoke* and *Virgin Soil*, the sketches and the 'tales of mystery' might be said to group themselves, and it seems preferable to treat the novellas separately from the rest of the stories, but here the demarcation line is not quite as indisputable. Five tales running to less than 50 pages each were clearly short stories; three which range from 80 to 150 pages are certainly novellas; the problem case is 'Punin and Baburin' (63 pages), which falls between the two groups in length – and arguably in importance.

Turgenev sub-titles it 'a story' (*rasskaz*), not 'a novella' (*povest'*); but, seeing that for twenty-five years he classified *Rudin* as a novella, not as a novel (*roman*), he need hardly be taken as a final authority. In the latest commentary (*W*, xi, 494) 'Punin and Baburin' is referred to as a *povest'*; but that, again, need not be taken as settling the matter. It is included (not without hesitation) in this rather than the preceding chapter on the grounds that it *is* one of Turgenev's longest stories – exceeded in length by only five others in his entire *œuvre*;[1] that it includes at least one full-length portrait and covers a whole life; and that it offers glimpses of the evolution of Russian society through three decades.

'An Unhappy Girl'

It might be thought that in the construction of 'An Unhappy Girl',[2] Turgenev was multiplying rather than reducing difficulties for himself and his readers. He entrusts the story to two narrators: the events of 1835 are told by a 17-year-old observer (a perhaps fictionalized Turgenev); events of the preceding thirty-odd years are presented in a memoir by the protagonist, Susanna. The boy narrator is handicapped by the fewness and fragmentariness of his opportunities for observation: he chiefly enables us to *see* the actors in the events of 1835; Susanna is hampered by the lack of communication between her and her parents in the past and by her inability to see herself and to show – as distinct from telling about – her emotions, which she surmounts only in her account of her brief time with Mikhail.

So the story begins in mystery and ends in mystery – not of a kind involving any supernatural element, but in the sense that we are left in total ignorance both as to why Susanna's mother agreed to marry Johann-Dietrich Ratch and as to how Susanna met her death.

Of the two events the marriage is the more difficult to take in. However much Susanna's mother may once have loved her seducer, however meek and resigned to her own lot she may have become, how could she have suppressed the moral loathing she must have felt for a man like Ratch? Above all, how could she ever have put her beloved child in the clutches of such a man? It may be said that she was friendless and penniless in a strange land. But she was not a serf. She was free to seek employment as a governess or servant. She could have threatened suicide (as her daughter did later): her host might have been touched – or frightened. But she put up no resistance. She knew she was guilty – and her child knew that she knew it (XVII, 107).

For Susanna's death we have a choice between three explanations. Did she commit suicide, as she hinted, before she left the narrator's apartment, she was minded to do? Was she murdered, as the narrator, in his youthful detestation of Ratch, suspected? Or did she die, as Ratch asserted, of natural causes? While the romantic reader will prefer the first of these hypotheses and the moral reader – no doubt sharing the narrator's reactions to Ratch – will opt for the second, the most probable would appear to be the third.

The main objection to suicide is that the most natural time for her to kill herself would have been immediately upon her return from her visit to the narrator, when she had realized the full measure of her desperation and had braced herself mentally for the deed. Having let that moment pass, she could have been expected to wait at least a couple of days, to give Fustov a chance to repent: although we know that he returned to the city in time to find her alive, such promptitude was not to be counted on: the summons to return might have taken longer to reach him, his journey back might have been delayed by weather or otherwise. A second objection is that her expression in the coffin suggested that she had been surprised by death: this would be compatible with murder or natural causes but much less likely with suicide. Of course, neither objection is conclusive.

The objection to a hypothesis of murder is also twofold. First, although both narrators see Ratch as a villain of the most repulsive sort – servile, false, coarse, a bully, a crook, perhaps something of a sadist – nothing in their evidence suggests that he was capable of murder. Secondly, if he was, it would have had to be – in a man so mean-spirited – at a time of great need and/or of minimal risk; but Susanna's death occured at a moment when it served no immediate need of the Ratches and involved some significant risk. If Ratch had wanted to kill her for her pension, the time to do it was surely when Fustov was courting her, not when he had apparently abandoned her and when the young narrator, whose revulsion he must have sensed, might have conceived suspicions and even stirred up trouble.

The only objection to a diagnosis of natural causes would be that it has not been 'artistically prepared'; but we have been prepared for a sudden death in some form, and it is quite possible that medical science in 1835 would have found little or nothing to say on a demise of this kind.

Three of the principal rôles in Susanna's tragedy are filled by men of the eighteenth century – men of three different 'generations', and correspondingly different from one another: her father, born in 1760, his brother, born in 1770, and her stepfather, born in 1780: all three portrayed, if not *con amore*, in exquisite detail.

Ivan Koltovskoi represents a whole generation[3] of Russian nobles who had lived in France, mingled with French high society and/or steeped themselves in the culture of the French Enlightenment, and returned home with a veneer of courtly manners, scepticism (i.e., contempt for institutionalized religion), epicureanism (i.e., pursuit of instant gratification) and a disinclination for the burdens of state service and, often, of the cares and responsibilities of family life as well. The cult of good form and of appearances, evidenced in his gentleness of manner and elegance of attire, contrasts starkly with the emotional frigidity (he could marry the mother of his child to a Ratch and coolly exploit his young daughter, risking her voice and health, in the long hours of reading aloud that was the main alleviation of the tedium of his existence) and the lack of any real aesthetic discernment (he had no understanding or appreciation of music). Without interests or purpose, except to live out his life as comfortably as possible, he regarded his little world as destined to serve that purpose and no other.

Semën Koltovskoi is opposed to his elder brother as Slavophil *ante litteram* to Westernizer, as sanguine to phlegmatic, as active to passive egoism. Susanna's father has withdrawn early from his society and frozen the microcosm of his estate in the time of Catherine II; his agnosticism and gallomania are genuine – or, at least, the pose has fused with the man, the mask has become the face. The younger brother has plunged into the metropolitan macrocosm in quest of wealth and honours, and his religious zeal and 'patriotism' (epitomized in his speaking Russian rather than French) are patently rôles calculated to court favour and advancement in the last years of Alexander I and the beginning of Nicholas I's reign.

Ratch is a plebeian counterpart to Semën Koltovskoi, concerned only to make his fortune by any and every means and, to that end, ready not only to carry out his patron's orders but to adopt that patron's attitudes and comportment.

The portraits of the three men are masterly; but the story is, of course, the story of Susanna and of her sufferings at the hands of the men who successively dominate her life – the Koltovskoi brothers and Ratch – not to mention those who love or imagine they love her; and just this is left largely to our imagination. The trauma to the 8-year-old who discovers at one stroke that she is illegitimate, that her father has no feeling for her, and that her mother – the one person she loves and trusts – is a broken reed, unable to defend her own freedom and dignity, let alone to protect her child; the death of her mother which leaves the teenager to five long years of leaden loneliness in the shadow of a father who exploits and exhausts her and of a stepfather so malevolent that he denies her access to her little brother (his son by her mother); finally, after the brief interlude of love, happiness, hope – five more years of precarious survival under the pressure of constant hostility and humiliations[4] – all this (except the interlude) comes to us as history rather than drama, though, certainly, tragic history.

Wisely, Turgenev does not let Susanna tell us anything of her relationship with Fustov. He, surely, was easy to read: charming and shallow, essentially half-hearted; but no one blames a drowning person for clutching at a straw. Through two-thirds of her life she had had nobody on whom she could rely, nobody with whom she could share her thoughts and feelings; how, then, could she not respond blindly to any show of affection? Perhaps she had seen more in him than there was and committed more feeling to the relation than he could imagine, let alone return, or perhaps it had just been a gamble of desperation: anyhow, she had reached the end of her reserves of hope, vitality, endurance – and her heart broke.

'A King Lear of the Steppes'

'A King Lear of the Steppes'[5] is one of the most powerful stories of Turgenev's maturity; only in 'First Love', which is written in a very different key, do we meet with a male protagonist of comparable strength and fascination. The old man is seen through the awed and innocent eyes of a neighbour's teenage son, just as the father in 'First Love' was seen through the awed and innocent eyes of his own teenage son; in both stories the events are re-evoked and related several decades later by the man who had been that boy (namely, Turgenev). In both stories the hero's philosophy of life is shattered and he himself is destroyed by love.

Hostile critics were – or pretended to be – indignant at what they claimed was a trivialization or vulgarization of Shakespeare's masterpiece; they forgot that here was not only an established pattern in Turgenev's work (a pattern at which no one had carped before), but one arguably analogous to a standard procedure in classical literature.[6] From archetypal figures in foreign literatures Turgenev had regularly borrowed a single central characteristic as pivot for a work of his own: from Don Quixote the selfless dedication to his ideal; from Hamlet the crippling introspection; from Werther the self-destructive devotion. So now what he takes over from *Lear* is the towering pride – and the situation: the father who bestows all he has upon his daughters, thinking to govern them through their affection instead of their dependence, and the nemesis that overtakes this overweening.

Although the story is barely half as long as the average Turgenev novel, it is structured in the form of a full-scale five-act tragedy. 'Act I' comprises the first nine chapters: this is the 'ravelling' (*zavyazka*), in which we are introduced to the character and history of the protagonist and the rest of the cast; four of the nine chapters concentrate on the portrayal of Kharlov himself. 'Act II' consists of chapters x-xv and encompasses the first climax, which might be entitled 'The Abdication': in chapter x Kharlov announces his decision, chapters xi–xiv present the domestic and public ceremonies, in chapter xv we glimpse the shadow of things to come. 'Act III' – chapters xvi–xxi – represents the *peripeteia* (reversal): in terms of Kharlov's history it could be entitled 'Ordeal'; the other personages might prefer to designate it 'The New Order'. We are shown Kharlov's plight through the eyes of outsiders, of Kharlov's principal persecutor, Slëtkin, and through the narrator's; and, balancing the revolution in Kharlov's existence, the revolution in the lives of his household: the rise in material prosperity counterpointed by the moral decline into sadism, adultery and incest. In the 'fourth act' – chapters xxii–xxviii – we have the second climax or catastrophe. Finally the *dénouement* is crowded into the last three chapters – xxix–xxxi – or 'Act V': this contains the judgment of the people (the chorus) on Kharlov and his family and, in the aftermath of his death, the untimely demise of Slëtkin counterpointing the exaltation of Kharlov's daughters: Anna seen as a new Semiramis or Catherine the Great, Evlampiya as an incarnate goddess.

Kharlov is an uncouth Hercules – stentorian, smelly, uneducated. He is also a quite extraordinary compound of pride and fantasy. His pride is as enormous as his gigantic body. His tiny estate is his 'realm'; his family and few score peasants are his 'subjects'; he has come to consider other men as 'sub-adult' (*nedoroslyami*: I, 189); he fears no man: 'Where in the world is there a power that could thwart my will?' (xiv, 217); 'But the Lord God knows that sooner shall this globe of earth be shattered than I take back my word . . . or lose heart, or regret what I have done!' (xv, 221).

It is noteworthy that this pride is rooted not in realities but in fantasies. Kharlov is not at all proud of his prodigious bodily strength: that is just a gift of God. Nor is he proud of his manifest moral qualities – his disinterestedness and his fearless sense of honour: these are, he says, intrinsic attributes of gentle birth. On the other hand, he is so proud of his 'noble' ancestry that he does not hesitate to reinvent Russian history – a Golden Book and a Muscovite Grand Duke that never existed – and when admonished of his errors, retorts serenely: 'Babble away! If I say so, then it is so!' (I, 188). Nor does it occur to him that even if his lineage were all he claims, his family has come down in the world so far that, culturally and morally, it is now far closer to the peasants than to the actual aristocracy – intellectual or social – of his own day.

No less than of his 'nobility' he is proud of his intelligence. In fact, he is barely literate (it takes him a quarter of an hour to sign his name) and he does hardly anything to justify the narrator's assertion that he is not stupid; but, then, how does one assess the intelligence of anyone with so tenuous a hold on reality? Yet the man is monumental; his style is lapidary; his self-assurance is sublime – grotesquely sublime.

The turning-point in Kharlov's life and the origin of his tragedy is his decision to make over all his possessions to his daughters. He himself adduces two different motives for this – one immediately before and at the time of the transfer, the other in retrospect, just before the fatal *dénouement*.

The first alleged motive is his premonition of impending death (the dream of the black foal that kicked his left elbow and the persisting tremors in that arm may indicate a slight stroke during sleep); but this does not stand up to scrutiny – not even the scrutiny of the narrator's mother, let alone the reader's. If a man expects to die, he makes sure that his property will be disposed of as he intends, but there is no point in dispossessing himself of it beforehand – unless, perhaps, he wants to divest himself of his responsibilities in order to be free through the remainder of his days to seek his soul's salvation in prayer, fasting, pilgrimage or the like. Kharlov neither does, nor seriously plans to do, anything of the kind.

The second motive adduced by Kharlov, after his flight from home, is pride: he says – and this is, no doubt, true – that once he had conceived the idea, he was too proud of his intelligence to doubt that it was right. But that is to ignore the real puzzle: namely, what ever could have put such an idea into his head; and that he does not attempt to explain.

In other words: what purpose could such a transfer of property be expected to serve? The doubts and warnings of the narrator's mother when she first hears of the plan, of Bychkov (Kharlov's brother-in-law) and the lawyer after the signing of the deed, all imply that they regard it as an experiment, a test: specifically, a test of the relation between Kharlov and his family, that is, his daughters: whether in terms of his authority over them or in terms of their feelings for him.

Neither of these questions can have presented itself to Kharlov's consciousness. At the conscious level he was convinced of the absoluteness of his power and the boundlessness of their obedience, if not devotion. In relation to them he saw himself as God's vice-gerent on earth ('for I under God am their father and lord,[7] not answerable to any man, now or ever': XII, 213), while in relation to the rest of mankind he is an irresistible will. But the very exaggeration of this assurance implies an unconscious doubt.

All his life Kharlov has tyrannized over his household as a matter of course; it has never occurred to him to wonder with what feelings he has been obeyed, or whether he has been obeyed as Martyn Kharlov, father and head of his family or as the lord of the manor, with both economic sanctions and serfs at his disposal to enforce his will and, at need, subdue resistance. In his sixty-ninth year the repressed doubt emerges, if not into consciousness, then into that preconscious region from where it can trigger ideas and actions: this is hinted, however obscurely, in his penultimate speech to the narrator's mother towards the end of his visit in chapter X.[8] The expectation and fear of death, after plaguing him with dreams and fits of melancholy (X, 203–4) have made a tiny breach in his self-assurance, through which the long-buried doubt can creep out, to prompt the idea of his twofold test: will he still be obeyed when he can no longer enforce his will? And if so, will it be through fear – of his physical strength or his parental curse – or through love?

If love has no place in his vocabulary or in his conscious thoughts, there is one person in the world whose love he unconsciously needs: his younger daughter Evlampiya. That is implicit in the bitterness with which he inveighs against her 'ingratitude' and the half threat to kill her if she should fail him, which he utters as early as the day after his 'abdication' – so, before she has done anything to hurt him. She is his creation, his other self: he says of her, 'But Evlampiya, let me tell you, is just like me in disposition. Cossack blood – and her heart, a live coal' (XV, 221). She too knows this: in the verbal duel at the end she says to him: 'do trust me – you have always trusted me', and there are startlingly amorous overtones in the phrases with which she coaxes him to come down from the roof to her room, to her bed. And what is implicit in all this had become poignantly explicit earlier in six words that escaped him on the day after his abdication: 'Can she really not feel for me?' (lit. pity me: *Neuzhto zhe ei ne zhal' menya?*) (xv, 220). From what unplumbed depths of that seemingly power-drunk colossus must such a cry for compassion have forced its way?

Of course, the results of the test are the exact opposite of what Kharlov had wanted and hoped for. In relation to his daughters he had substituted fantasy for understanding, just as in relation to the facts of Russian history he had substituted fantasy for knowledge. The two young women make no sign, utter no word to defend him against the mean vindictiveness of his son-in-law, who is the husband of the one and the lover of the other. He is taught that his authority was never more than a function of his power: in giving away his power, he has stripped himself of all authority.

Faced with this trio of enemies, Kharlov submits, humbles himself, drains the cup of disgrace to the dregs. He flees only when his exasperated pride, bursting its bonds, makes him afraid it might explode into murder.

Why did he endure so long? Partly from pride: he could not bear to admit to the world that he had been so utterly wrong about himself and about his children; partly from religious sentiment: in the expectation of death and under the pressure of his afflictions, his eyes were opened to the evil he had done and the good he had failed to do in his long life, and his sufferings seemed to offer a means of partial expiation. But besides these two, there may well have been another, unconfessed reason: as Caesar, when he saw Brutus among his murderers, lost all will to resist, so Evlampiya's defection must have been a paralysing blow to Kharlov.

The concern and sympathy of the narrator's mother reinforced this resignation momentarily: he declared himself ready to forgive his tormentors. But once more he had misjudged himself: the goading of Bychkov broke down those improvised defences, and the rage and shame choked back and swallowed through four long months erupted in desperation. He had been destroyed – his faith in himself and in others had been killed, as he tells Evlampiya when she asks his forgiveness – and he in turn will destroy.

But he will destroy only symbolically. He will not curse his daughters, he will not kill Slëtkin. His tearing down the house has a twofold significance: he is destroying what he himself had built, as he had destroyed the whole fabric of his life when he gave away his property to his heirs; and at the same time he is destroying that, on the strength of which and for the sake of which his heirs had turned against him. And behind these two more or less conscious purposes hides another: to end his suffering and his despair.

So he falls to his death. It is a heroic fall: not so much because he has gone berserk at the last, like some Norse hero of old (he traced his descent from a Swede), but because, primitive and excruciated though he is, he has directed his huge strength and his huge despair away from the authors of that despair, against insentient brick and timber – and against himself.

Such heroism should not go wholly unrewarded, nor does it: in his last moments he is allowed to realize that Evlampiya does love him. She turns against her lover and renounces her property; she is concerned and afraid for her father, sorry and ashamed for the way he has been treated, anxious to be forgiven by him and given a chance to make amends. And this is not a mere gesture, to avert calamity: when he is dead, she makes a complete break with her past – gives up her lover and her inheritance and disappears.

There are in Turgenev's stories often sub-plots which would appear to deserve a separate play or story to themselves.[9] Such is the sub-plot of Kharlov's daughters: Turgenev leaves them in a penumbra in which a good deal escapes us. Both girls have inherited their father's pride and imperiousness, though Anna has had to stoop and dissemble as long as she lived in his shadow, while Evlampiya, as his favourite and unmarried, is likely to have suffered far less. Anna is certainly better educated and more intelligent than Kharlov; we do not know how far this would be true of Evlampiya.

It is clear that Kharlov's death sets up profound repercussions in his daughters. It develops Anna into a model landowner and a model mother – a woman of whom her male neighbours say with reluctant admiration that she would be capable of governing a whole country. It is true they also suspect her of having poisoned her husband; but that was the kind of gossip that was only to be expected. If she had wanted to poison him, surely it would have been when he was carrying on the affair with her sister, not after her sister's departure when she, Anna, was conceiving and bearing Slëtkin's children? And if she had poisoned him, surely she would not have been the kind of woman who could have raised such children as the narrator extols to us?

We can assume that Evlampiya felt much more deeply than Anna about their father: not only in virtue of their kinship in temperament, not only as his favourite, but in the light of her reactions to his despair and death. In fact, she goes on to emulate and surpass her father: he had seen himself as God's deputy only in relation to his family; she has herself acknowledged as an incarnate deity by a much larger 'family'. Kharlov had been torn apart by his fantasy and his pride in conflict; Evlampiya contrives to unite her master-passions and run them as a team.

In her portrayal by the narrator her dominant traits are sensuality and pride. Her reaction to her father's last fugue and death requires us to add to these two traits a third: a complex of moral, if not religious feelings, which impelled her to renounce all that she had set store by and to turn her back on everything that had been her life till then – perhaps analogous to the complex which had impelled her father, first, to renounce all his possessions and then to accept his martyrdom. So if, before her father's death, she had indulged her senses in her affair with her brother-in-law and her power-lust in thereby trampling on the laws of the Church and of society – after that death she was able to synthesize sensuality, power-lust and moral complex in her rôle as goddess and absolute mistress of the sect she had entered.

The proud giant Kharlov challenges comparison with another of Turgenev's unforgettable figures – the meek giant, Gerasim. Kharlov is not deaf and dumb, but he is no less insulated from reality by his fantasy than Gerasim by his deafness. Both men are progressively stripped of all they hold dear, of all that makes life worth living for them; both limit the expression of their despair to a gesture, which shocks their tormentors into at least momentary compunction.

Obviously the parallelism of situation is modified by differences of temperament, class and age. Gerasim's sufferings were inflicted by others; Kharlov's were largely of his own making. Gerasim's gesture of revolt is non-violent; Kharlov's is spectacularly violent. Kharlov seeks and achieves death; Gerasim 'goes on living' – accepts what has become no more than a life-in-death. Both giants we see stretched out too long 'upon the rack of this rough world'.

'Spring Torrents'

Like stories of the early fifties but unlike the later ones, 'Spring Torrents'[10] – in spite of the misleading introduction to the main story: 'This is what he remembered' – is told by an omniscient author: this is clear not so much from the rare incidents which Sanin could not possibly have remembered because he had never perceived them in the first place[11] as from the tone of subtle irony that suffuses so much of the narration and is equally alien to Sanin at 22 and at 52.

'Spring Torrents' is far and away the longest of Turgenev's stories – in fact, longer than *Rudin*; but it is not a novel, at least according to Turgenev's conception of the novel: it lacks both a socially significant protagonist and any relevance to the problematics of Russian society in the 1870s (or in the 1840s, for that matter).

Whereas in 'An Unhappy Girl' and 'A King Lear of the Steppes' Turgenev had appeared as a semi-transparent observer of people and events, in 'Spring Torrents' we see, if not Turgenev, certainly a persona of Turgenev as male protagonist of the story interacting with people with whom he had actually been involved in his twenties. The prototypes of the Rozellis[12] were a German-Jewish family who ran a confectionery in Frankfurt; Turgenev did make their acquaintance in the circumstances described and did fall in love with the daughter (there were actually two) but fled before he had become too dangerously entangled; Mar'ya Nikolaevna Polozova was modelled (on Turgenev's own testimony) on a real-life Princess Trubetskaya, of gypsy origin; and the original of Pantaleone had been a member – half servant, half friend – of that princess's household.

But if the personages of the story are real, the events related are not historical. Turgenev's stay in Frankfurt in May 1840, on his way from Italy back to Berlin and the university, lasted less than a week; at that time he had no estate to sell and, therefore, no occasion to detour to Wiesbaden; his acquaintance with the Princess Trubetskaya must have belonged to a different period.

Presumably, the Rozellis were metamorphosed into Italians because Turgenev shrank from creating a German heroine during and after the Franco-Prussian War, which modified his warm feelings for Germany (though not towards his many German friends). There is little that is distinctively Italian about the family.

Turgenev admits that the mother had become almost completely germanized, and both children had been born and raised in Germany. If they have inherited their father's Italian patriotism, that has not prevented Gemma from engaging herself to Herr Klüber or from ending up married to an American counterpart of Herr Klüber.

Of course, Turgenev is not fair to Klüber, and some of the writer's German friends let him know that he had hurt their feelings; he defended himself by claiming that he had often dealt more harshly with his own compatriots. That was true; and certainly there are Klübers in the world, and not only in Germany. But the real unfairness was not that which contemporaries complained of: it lay in letting Gemma (and the modern reader) imagine that Klüber could, at Soden, have behaved as Sanin did. Actually that was not an option for him: von Dönhof, as an officer and a gentleman, wouldn't have dreamed of fighting a duel with a shop assistant. At best, he would have ignored the insolent fellow; more probably, he would have had him thrown off the premises: so poor Klüber was bound to cut a poor figure anyway. Sanin's bravado, though romantically chivalrous, served no practical purpose except to make him look glorious in Gemma's eyes.

Unlike the Rozellis, Pantaleone is Italian and based on observation. It need not matter that he is (puns apart) a stage Italian: there are stage Italians (as there are stage Germans or Englishmen) in real life, and they do very well as minor characters in fiction; what may irritate some readers are rather the linguistic and other gaffes with which his author burdens him, by way of 'local colour'.[13] He remains authentic not because but in spite of them.

Emilio and Gemma are delightful. He is still young enough not to show the stigmata of the future hero who, twenty years later, will fall fighting among Garibaldi's Redshirts for the liberation and unification of Italy. For all his devotion to his family, his strong sense of honour and his patriotic inheritance, he has kept (when we meet him) much of the ingenuous playfulness of childhood.

Gemma, at first sight, is something of a puzzle. She has seen her brother faint before, and more than once: so why does she lose her head, why has she not taken the elementary step of loosening his collar and unbuttoning his tight clothes? A little later, there is the piquant contrast between her classical beauty and her talent for comic impersonation. We wonder: are we about to face a new type of heroine? But no: as soon as she falls in love with Sanin, the German-Italian girl becomes Russian, or almost – becomes a Turgenev heroine, or almost: a true Turgenev heroine would never have found happiness in the arms of a Jeremiah Slocum.[14]

She loves Romantic music (Weber), but her reading talents do not extend to romantic rôles: she reveals an underlying scepticism in the faintly mocking tones in which she reads the love scenes (vii, 23), and her comments (xii, 34–5) on the one (misremembered) Hoffmann story that had appealed to her, while reflecting the good sense at the core of her character, prove eerily prophetic of the future of her relation with Sanin. She is charmed by the young stranger and then genuinely carried away, at least for a time, by his 'heroism' at Soden and after; but how long could such feelings have lasted once she had realized his basic weakness?

Sanin is a pale shadow of Turgenev at 22: with all his emotional indeterminacy (and his charm), but lacking his literary culture and his political convictions: all he has read of Goethe is *Werther* – in French – and he is quite prepared to sell his estate with its serfs to the highest bidder. He is so little in touch with his feelings that he is the last person to recognize that he has fallen in love – but as soon as he does so, convinces himself that he had loved her from the first moment he saw her – and that he always will (xvii, 86). Having thus piled the irony as high as it will go, Turgenev packs him off to Wiesbaden to face the test of these convictions.

In Frankfurt Sanin had been a Russian among foreigners; in Wiesbaden he is back among his own people, and the German idyll (even the duel, if viewed objectively, was quasi-idyllic) condenses into Russian drama. In this very different setting – of opulence and luxury, contrasting with the honest poverty he had left behind – confronted by such very different characters, Sanin remains much what he has been: he sees everything without understanding anything; his thinking is all wishful; he does not act or feel from within himself, but reacts. He is clay in the hands of Polozova.

Polozova is a remarkable woman (though it hardly needed a remarkable woman to turn Sanin's head). Her stage-management is masterly: from her first entrance, with her hair down her back to show off its beauty, through the series of colloquies – in her hotel suite, in the public gardens, at the theatre – to that last wild ride: through pools, over ditches, out into the hills, up into the woods, the realm of storm and 'freedom' (*wo die Freiheit thront*: xli, 143).

This is not the first time Turgenev has tackled the theme of sexual infatuation, which he sees as the ancients had done: as a disease, a form of madness, destroying the character and disrupting the life of the victim (i.e., the 'lover') and often injuring his (or her) intimates as well. The first exercise on this theme was 'Petushkov', written at the age of 28.[15]

Contrary to an assumption widespread among critics, Turgenev does not regard such infatuations as peculiar to men, though it is true that – whether out of 'chivalry' or in deference to the prudery of his readers or out of genuine doubt about the extent of his own insight – he is apt to understate or blur the physical aspect of infatuation in his women. His first infatuated heroine – and one in whom the physical urge is least disguised – is Natal'ya Petrovna in *A Month in the Country* (1850), who is saved from ruining her life and deserting her husband and child only by the devotion of one man and the honesty of another. A later infatuated heroine is Mar'ya Pavlovna in 'A Backwater' (1854), who commits suicide for love; we see too little of her love to speculate about its exact composition. The other women destroyed by passion are Vera, in 'Faust', and the eponymous heroine in 'Klara Milich' (1882/3), to whom we shall come in chapter 16.

Returning to the male line – which has enjoyed much more critical attention – after Petushkov we met Aleksei Petrovich in 'A Correspondence' (1856), then Litvinov, in *Smoke* (1867), who actually escaped the toils of his enchantress, and finally Sanin (unless we prolong the series to include Turgenev's last two stories in which the men's obsession costs them their lives).

Polozova is very different from her predecessors: that is, the women who bewitched Petushkov, Aleksei Petrovich and (for a few days) Litvinov. Neither Vasilisa nor the unnamed dancer did anything to allure the men; neither did anything to keep her adorer in bondage; both tolerated rather than welcomed the adoration. And the men had come to them heart-free (Aleksei Petrovich's incipient interest in Mar'ya Aleksandrovna could not be considered a tie and would, in any case, have been unknown to his dancer).

But because Polozova's situation resembles Irina's – both have marriages that are purely notional, both seek to attach to themselves a man already engaged – some attempts have been made to liken their characters, which are in fact as unlike as those of the men they seek to captivate.

Polozova is simple, Irina is complex; Polozova is sensual, Irina is passionate; Polozova is clear-sighted and honest with herself, Irina is unable or unwilling to face the truth about herself; Polozova wants men as slaves, to feed her sense of power, Irina wants a man to have faith in her, to shore up her crippled self-respect. There is not a trace in Irina of the masculine streak in Polozova, who presents herself as a 'good fellow' (XXXVI, 120), takes the initiative in pressing Sanin's hand between hers and kissing him in the carriage, in bidding him 'almost roughly' follow her to the hut where they will make love. Where Irina is reticent, aloof, mocking, Polozova is frank about herself, amusing, tells a good story without mincing her expressions. Polozova is strong and self-confident while Irina is vulnerable and insecure; she is completely free from Irina's need of love and sense of guilt.

Irina is a prisoner of her society – its conventions and constraints – which condemns her to frustration and sterility; Polozova is, as she boasts, 'a free Cossack', that is, a free spirit, pursuing her own ends without fear of consequences, perhaps in virtue of her fatalism ('what will be, will be': XXXIX, 131), contemptuous of superstition (though she does believe in love charms). She has bought herself a husband in order to be able to laugh at conventions and do as she pleases, find her own happiness, satisfy her dominant passion.

The object of that passion she defines variously as freedom (XXXIX, 134-5) and power (there is no pleasure in the world to compare with that of commanding and being obeyed: XXXVI, 121). But these are not alternative objectives: the freedom she demands is for herself, and it is the freedom to enslave men; if she claims (XXXIX, 136) that she will no more put chains on others than she will let anyone put chains on her, that can be true only in the sense that she requires her slaves to be willing slaves (as her husband obviously is and as Sanin will be). Once a man is in her power, she will be ruthless in exploiting that power, as she obliquely warns Sanin on the first evening (XXXV, 116), and we see, in return for her favours – the joys of the sybarite for the former, of the lover for the latter – each must drain the cup of humiliation to the dregs. If Sanin's lot seems the crueller, that is because his ordeal is only beginning and because he is so much more sensitive than Polozov.

Polozova does not despise easy victories, such as von Dönhof, but what she needs to fire her blood and muster all her energies – to 'make life worth living' – is to achieve a purpose 'which seemed impossible' (XLI, 141). Sanin is not just another good-looking young man: he is a thoroughly decent young man – a Romantic, an idealist, 'a knight in shining armour', as she remarks, not altogether ironically (XXV, 114) – genuinely and (within the limits of his nature) deeply in love with a woman as beautiful as herself. To overcome that love, to take him from that woman and make him her own, her thrall, reduced to fawning on his fellow favourites[16] – all in the space of less than two days – is a feat calling into play all her resources of daring, wit, seductiveness, including those reserves of 'tenderness and modesty' from her girlhood, on which she draws only when she must appeal to a man's heart and imagination as well as his senses and which make her 'dangerous' (XL, 137) even to knights in shining armour.

If one considers this survival in her of a pristine innocence in the light of her confession the previous evening (XXXIX, 135) that in her childhood she had seen and suffered her fill of slavery (her father had no doubt been a serf originally: XXXV, 113), it is hard not to suspect her drive to enslave and humiliate men of the serf-owning class is, at least unconsciously, in revenge for some childhood martyrdom.

With Sanin she not only plays fair, she deliberately increases the odds against herself (and so, of course, the value of the eventual victory) by constantly reminding him of Gemma and his engagement: it is as if she were saying, 'Since I cannot defeat her face to face, I will keep her image before your eyes and defeat it there – I want to take as little advantage as possible of her not being with you.' Her challenge to Sanin is not to forget Gemma, to expel her from his mind and heart but, on the contrary, with his heart and mind full of Gemma to give himself, wholly and unreservedly, to her, Mar'ya Nikolaevna Polozova. Turgenev has anticipated by nearly a decade the dilemma of Dmitri Karamazov: the co-existence in the hearts (even of good men) of 'the ideal of the Madonna' with the 'ideal of Sodom'.[17]

And Turgenev the artist rose to the challenge of that extra-ordinary personality. However morally horrified he may have been by her destructive power-lust, he had in him too much of the Romantic not to respond to the fascination of elemental evil,[18] he had in him too much of the masochist[19] not to be thrilled to the marrow of his bones by this young Circe of the steppe, half animal, half goddess, as he himself blurts out in a climactic moment of the story. To a friend he was later to admit: 'That devil of a woman seduced me as she seduced that ninny Sanin.'[20]

The epithet 'devil' may turn our attention to the affinities between Polozova and the 'demonic' avatars of the superfluous man in the 1830s.[21] She shares with Pechorin the passion for power and the streak of sadism that permeates it. Pechorin defines happiness as 'sated pride', and we see Polozova in her hour of triumph wearing the pitiless, dull look of satiety (XLII, 148). She shares Pechorin's egoism and his contempt for his fellow humans, but also such virtues as the reckless courage, the lively intelligence laced with wit, the skilled energy with which he pursues his immediate objectives. What seems to differentiate them most sharply is their attitude to themselves and to life. Pechorin is deeply unhappy, deeply dissatisfied with himself and with life: this invests him with a heroic dimension – of thwarted aspirations, blighted potentialities, unplumbed depths – which, on the face of it and according to the traditional reading, is totally lacking in Polozova. She appears to be completely satisfied with life and with herself – limited and shallow – no more than the sum of her drives. He bears the sword and scars of the hero; she glitters in the silks and diamonds of *poshlost'* – unless we choose to assemble those hints about her childhood, take her cult of freedom seriously and see her preying on serf-owners as her battle against serfdom. In any case, she remains, artistically, a brilliant and impressive creation.

Sanin's latter end is of a piece with his beginnings. He sells his estate and sails off to America without pausing to ask himself whether Jeremiah Slocum will want a Sanin perched on the edge of his family nest or whether he will be welcome even to Gemma as a permanent guest or neighbour. He gravitates to her as Irina clutches at Litvinov – as a last hope of finding a meaning in his (her) life or, at least, of being washed clean of his (her) self-contempt and existential nausea.

In the 'frame' as well as in the main story Sanin is tinged with autobiography. In 1870, when he began to write it, Turgenev was, like Sanin, 52; and while he wrote, his world was turned upside-down by the Franco-Prussian War. He did not sell his estates, but he did broach the possibility of selling them[22] and he lost his home and his stable base in Baden-Baden. He did not end up in America; but the post-Napoleonic republican France, where he decided to rejoin the Viardots and settle for the rest of his life, must have seemed to him in many respects a 'new world'.

'Punin and Baburin'

'Punin and Baburin'[23] is another page of autobiography: the grandmother is Turgenev's mother; the garden is the garden at Spasskoe; the 12-year-old boy is Turgenev in 1830; and Baburin and Punin are based on persons from Turgenev's real life in that period.

Hostile critics, their memories refreshed by the publication, two years earlier, of 'The End of Chertopkhanov' reproached Turgenev with having plagiarized himself by duplicating the relation between Chertopkhanov and Nedopyuskin in that between the protagonists of his latest story. But if Punin does resemble Nedopyuskin physically and in his attitude to his 'benefactor', it is as a finished portrait in relation to a preliminary sketch or silhouette; and Baburin is – intellectually, temperamentally and socially – quite unlike Chertopkhanov: almost the only trait they have in common is the urge to protect victims and underdogs.

A much more intriguing parallel to a motif from an earlier story[24] is the narrator's attitude to his grandmother's guests: Baburin arouses in him hostility, fear and respect, while for Punin he feels not the slightest respect, but 'I came to love him with all my heart': just as Chulkaturin had 'fought shy of [his] virtuous mother' while he 'passionately loved [his] wicked father'.[25] The parallel is not perfect (Punin has no 'vice' corresponding to the father's gambling, though both men are equally feckless; the mother's puritan patience may have less appeal than Baburin's perseverance in protest) but the underlying pattern is the same: virtue is seen as not lovable and what is lovable is not respectable.

Punin is weak, unpractical, incapable of standing on his own feet; but he surrounds himself with bird-song, he intoxicates himself with poetry, he reveres Baburin and loves Muza; and he wins the heart of the narrator in childhood (as he won the heart of Turgenev's critics).

Baburin is an idealist. His idealism pivots on a stern sense of human dignity – not only his own, but that of other people equally – and because it is a militant idealism, it involves him in an endless series of clashes with those he serves – clashes in which the moral advantage remains with him, but always at the cost of his live-lihood. So he wanders over the face of Russia, poor, shabby, uncompromising: ever ready to raise his voice on behalf of the oppressed, to break a lance in defence of the defenceless. The years pass, his hair turns white, exile supervenes on poverty – but he persists and endures. He endures in expectation of a new order – of 'justice' for all – where human dignity may stand upright, washed clean of the taint and shame of serfdom; and having seen (he thinks) the advent of that order, he is ready to salute it with his *Nunc dimittis*.

And yet – Baburin's fate among critics was no happier than his fate in the story. Annenkov adjured Turgenev to create no more Baburins, no more 'respectable types' (meaning, characters who evoke no more than respect),[26] and the critics agreed with Annen-kov: they fumed over Baburin (and felt puzzled by Muza, whom Annenkov found boring). Why, then, is virtue unlovable, even when it is as genuine as it is in Baburin?

Baburin is imbued with the rationalism of the eighteenth century in which he was born. His idealism is rigid, narrow, compulsive. He provides for Punin, but it never occurs to him to avoid trouble out of consideration for his friend: however happy Punin may be in a place and however futile Baburin's intervention is bound to be, he must speak out. He has rescued and tried to educate Muza; but he has neither the imagination to ask himself what she wants of life, nor the sensitivity or flexibility to meet her on her own ground, nor the critical objectivity to recognize the enormous incongruity of his intended marriage: not mainly because of the difference in age – that could have been of minor significance – but because of the gulf in outlook and temperament between them. Punin captivates by being good-natured, innocent and funny (I, 162); Baburin is none of these things. He lacks charm; and he lacks both the endearing weaknesses and the spark of enthusiasm of a Don Quixote or even a Rudin.

Turgenev himself admitted that 'Muza deserved to be developed further',[27] meaning, presumably, that more might have been made of her, rather than implying that there is any mystery about her as she appears in the story. Allowing for the differences of setting and circumstances, she is likely to remind us of the Sof'ya of 'Yakov Pasynkov'. Both girls are determined to find their own way to love and happiness. Both are ready to dissimulate while that serves their purpose, but turn to open defiance when closely pressed. Both pick the wrong sort of man and, once their mistake has been brought home to them, courageously embrace its consequences, renouncing all further thought of personal happiness, to devote themselves unreservedly to the duties of their position. Only, Muza, being illegitimate and penniless, has to seek her happiness outside marriage.

When we first meet her, she is torn between her gratitude to, and awe of, Baburin, on the one hand, and on the other, her frustration, thirst for life and resentful pride. She has her fling and is abandoned by her lover; Baburin finds her again down and out. She has discovered, however, that she cannot go it alone and that she dares not kill herself: so she resigns herself to the only available alternative and, having accepted the rôle of Baburin's helpmeet, sustains it loyally to the last.

The story extends over more than thirty years and is told in a series of episodes separated by long intervals (seven, twelve and again twelve years) – a technique that Turgenev had explicitly deprecated in his 1852 review of the novel, *The Niece*.[28] That was before he had written any novels himself. He tried it first in 'Yakov Pasynkov', then, almost simultaneously, in *Rudin*, but only a couple of times after that.

15

Seeds of revolution: *Virgin Soil*

The 'nihilism' of the 1860s climaxed in the conspiratorial terrorism of Nechaev,[1] which fired the creative imagination of both Dostoevsky and Turgenev. Dostoevsky wrote *The Devils*,[2] embodying his conception of Nechaev in the figure of Pëtr Verkhovenski and basing the murder of his hero Shatov[3] on the real-life murder of the student Ivanov by Nechaev and his henchmen; the novel appeared in book form in the very year in which Nechaev was tried and imprisoned for life.

A little earlier – in July of 1870 – Turgenev conceived the idea of a novel with a 'political-revolutionary element', sketched out in some detail its three leading characters and several others more summarily, but had as yet no clear idea of the story as a whole. Eighteen months later he went back to the project and outlined the story (February 1872); three years after that, he went back and elaborated that summary: but, from first to last, it was to take him six years of brooding, reading, observing to produce his sixth, and last, novel, *Virgin Soil*.[4]

Dostoevsky's undertaking was easier than Turgenev's in several respects. Since his attitude to the nihilists was one of unreserved hostility, he could count on the indulgence of the censorship; Turgenev, who was bent on understanding and being fair to his personages and who obviously sympathized, in varying degrees, with his three central figures and respected all the sincere ones, had to tread far more warily: as it was, the censors allowed the second part of the work to appear after much debate and only because they had passed the first part. Above all, Dostoevsky, writing immediately after the Nechaev affair, could concentrate on a situation which had not changed substantially, while Turgenev, writing six years later, had to take account of important developments in the interval.

The Russian revolutionary scene, between 1862 and 1917, always comprised a variety of doctrines, trends and factions; but, simplifying for our purposes, one can say that in the second half of the sixties the dominant trend aimed at effecting quick and radical change by violent means, whereas in the first half of the seventies the centre of the stage was occupied by groups pursuing longer-term objectives by milder methods: seeking to share the life of the people and learn their language – their modes of thought – in order to be able to enlighten and lead them. Such groups concentrated their efforts at first in the cities, among the factory-workers and suchlike; these activities culminated in the summer of 1874 in a migration into the country of a mass – several thousands – of mainly young, educated, self-appointed missionaries determined to dedicate themselves utterly to the service of the people, however vague and various their conceptions of that service may have been.

By dating his story to 1868, Turgenev had anchored it firmly in the Nechaev period, yet it is tinged, whether or not intentionally, with hints of future attitudes and values: Marianna and Solomin, in particular, are more typical of the seventies than of the sixties. Meanwhile, Nechaev himself is represented by the shadowy Vasili Nikolaevich, whose surname is never uttered, who never appears, but periodically issues unexplained yet unchallengeable instructions, which send people in all directions, within Russia and beyond, threaten to liquidate a follower who is suspected of 'unreliability', or order 'action' – that is, insurrection – at the drop of a hat. The conspiratorial atmosphere, the authoritarian organization, the pervasive air of mystery, the expectation of imminent upheavals are all certainly characteristic of Nechaevism.

Critics who for years had routinely accused Turgenev of having lost touch with Russian realities suffered an unusually prompt and ignominious discomfiture on this occasion: the trial of 'the Fifty', which opened a couple of months after the publication of the novel, showed Turgenev right on so many points dismissed as fantasies by the reviewers that some of them were panicked into not only reversing themselves but suggesting that he must have had access to depositions in the police files.

Virgin Soil is the longest of Turgenev's novels, but in general shows no falling-off in the taut and deft handling of the story-line – though some critics have opined that the long nineteenth chapter (the visit to the two old relics of the previous century) was a piece of authorial self-indulgence. On the other hand, it might be suggested that they serve, like figures in a landscape, to show scale and give perspective: to convey how far Russian society had travelled in the course of a single lifetime.

The social structure, or grouping of the cast, in *Virgin Soil* resembles that of *Smoke* and contrasts with those of the earlier novels. In the first four novels the principal characters move within a relatively homogeneous framework of family, friends and neighbours, although, from the first, they are unlike and at odds with their society, and from novel to novel the opposition becomes sharper. Natal'ya can still marry within her world and Rudin can continue to proselytize, however unsuccessfully (but at long intervals still win a disciple such as Basistov); but Liza and Lavretski can only withdraw from their world – she, within the walls of a convent, he to a half life of lonely and joyless labour. Insarov is not only figuratively but literally an alien in Russia (and, no less, in the West); Elena is impelled not only to abandon her family, but to turn her back on her country. And Bazarov proves simply not viable.

But in *Virgin Soil*, as in *Smoke* ten years earlier, Russian society has become polarized into groups – a Right and a Left – and the principal characters now operate between or on the fringes of these groups. That is obvious as regards Litvinov and Potugin; Irina, if in, is not of, her world, and is momentarily almost swept out of it by passion. Similarly, in *Virgin Soil* Marianna finds herself in but not of the world of high society, does break away from it, then tries to integrate herself into the world of the revolutionaries, only to have it shatter around her. Nezhdanov and Solomin hover on the fringes of the revolutionary group – Nezhdanov unhappily, striving frantically to make a place for himself within it and failing miserably, Solomin as a sympathetic but sceptical observer, ready to advise and assist, without committing or imperilling himself.

Readers can hardly fail to notice how much better crafted the secondary figures are in this last novel than in its immediate predecessor. In *Smoke* the 'young generals' were mere silhouettes, the would-be revolutionaries rather jejune caricatures. In *Virgin Soil* both Left and Right are drawn in the round; the Left is treated with genuine respect and some sympathy (as Turgenev treated the young radicals who came to him for help or advice in real life); the Right is satirized, but with a contempt that often seems good-humoured: there is little of the loathing inspired by the generals. What little there is, is reserved for the arch-conservative Kallomeitsev. Unlike the generals, Kallomeitsev is not dangerous, though he is noxious. He does not want to take Russia back to the beginning of the century – he has no desire even to restore serfdom: he is too busy amassing a fortune by grinding the faces of the poor but free peasants, as he could never have exploited the serfs, who owned nothing. He is an upstart, a snob, a rapacious and completely callous moneylender, who has driven at least one of his peasant debtors to suicide; his terror of 'communism' would be comical if it were not so vindictive: at a time when radicals of all colours were probably to be numbered in hundreds rather than thousands, he is ready to see a Red under every bed.

The Sipyagins present themselves as moderate liberals, but might more fairly be classified as moderate conservatives. Turgenev, in his notes for the novel, defines the wife as a *poseuse*; in fact, attitudinizing is equally characteristic of both spouses, and liberalism is just one of their favourite poses, stopping well short of any conflict with their interests. The poses are designed to charm: in his case, as befits a man with political ambitions and prospects – a 'future minister' – to charm by impressing, in hers to charm by enticing, without coming anywhere near adultery. Both spouses are cool-blooded narcissists, who pose for each other with the same professional nicety as for the rest of the world. Turgenev puts them through their paces with an artist's appreciation of their artistry; his exposure of their seamy side may seem somewhat heavy-handed in comparison.

The governor is a different sort of narcissist: a dandy and 'epicurean' – easy-going but not without administrative ability, effortlessly charming (but not impressive). Turgenev nails him in a single sentence he addresses to Sipyagin: 'The law is not written for men like you' (xxxv, 267).

In contrast to the hollow people of the Right (and unlike the froth-blowers of the Left in *Smoke*), the revolutionaries in *Virgin Soil* are fully human. Turgenev does not disguise their intellectual limitations, which reduce them to passive instruments of unchallengeable leaders, but he sees and presents them as sincere, suffering men and women. It is impossible not to feel for Mashurina and Markelov, little as we see of them and peripheral as they are to the story of the main characters.

Mashurina – unlovely, graceless, inarticulate – is allowed to reveal the warmth and selflessness of her woman's feelings in her meeting with Marianna – the girl who had won the love of the man with whom she herself was in love – and again, in a minor key, when she sits through the hour of Paklin's jeremiads on the chance of obtaining a photograph of the dead Nezhdanov.

And Markelov – the failed soldier, the failed lover, the failed landlord, the failed insurgent – is also given two scenes in which to show his true mettle. First, the scene in which, tormented by jealousy, he insults Nezhdanov in the crudest and ugliest way, but then swallows his jealousy and his pride to humbly beg his rival's pardon, remembering that they are both fighters in the same cause; and the scene in which he outfaces Sipyagin and the governor with quiet dignity, justifying the peasants who had betrayed him, spurning the proposal to compromise with the authorities, brushing Kallomeitsev aside with a sneer and a smile and scornfully puncturing his brother-in-law's orotund phrase-making, while locked in a desperate inner struggle to preserve his faith in the cause at any cost. He had been abandoned and betrayed by the very men of whom he had felt surest: might his blind faith in the cause not have been equally misplaced? But no: rather than admit that he could have lived for an illusion, a lie, he must and will take all the blame. It was not the orders that were impossible of execution – it was he who had failed to carry them out.

Turgenev was reproached for not doing justice to the populist movement – for not conveying either the numbers involved or the variety of types – for implying that it consisted of a tiny clique of fanatical dullards and social misfits. As regards the numbers, that is to ignore the date of the events narrated: 1868 was not 1874. According to Venturi,[5] Karakozov's attempt in 1866 on the life of Alexander II unleashed such repression that between 1866 and 1868 'there was not a single group in Russia able to carry out clandestine activities or to make known its ideas by giving a more general significance to its internal debates'. Then came Nechaev; but what we know of his movement hardly involves significant numbers or outstanding individuals.

Besides confusing dates, critics overlook both the limitations of the novel (Turgenev did not intend, and was not equipped, to write a work on the scale of *War and Peace* or even of *Anna Karenina*) and the restrictions of the censorship. What he did contrive to include in his 296-page panorama of Russian society and to publish at that date was surely no mean achievement.

There is the uncompromising, withering indictment of the ruling hierarchy – both its reactionary and its pseudo-liberal wings. There are glimpses – striking even in their compression – of the wretched condition of the 'freed' peasantry: the squalor, the drunkenness, the crushing load of debt – with usurers of the gentry class as the chief villains, but not forgetting the merchants (Golushkin) and the kulaks. There is the promise for the future represented by Marianna and Solomin. And there is the representation of the rank-and-file activists – even in the small Nechaevist sector – as heroic: not in understanding or abilities or achievements, but in purity of intention and in selfless commitment to the liberation of their people.

If the split within the political world of *Virgin Soil* is as sharp as that in *Smoke*, the relation between the two themes – political picture and love-story – does here achieve a semblance of unity, while still falling short of fusion. This difference between the two novels can be attributed to three other changes: the author's attitude to the radicals has altered; these later radicals – the forerunners of the populists – are active as compared with Gubarëv's static group; and whereas Litvinov and Potugin were no more than observers in both political camps, no less than six of the personages in *Virgin Soil* have some involvement – and not merely as observers – with their ideological opposites.

For the love-story Turgenev has reverted to his original pattern, adapted from *Evgeni Onegin*: the hero appears as a stranger in the heroine's world and she falls in love with him; it turns out that he is 'not free' to commit himself or marry her; she marries a lesser man who truly loves her. As we saw, Turgenev experimented with this theme in his poems, *Parasha* (1843) and *Andrei* (1845) and in the play *A Chain is as Strong as its Weakest Link* (1848). In *Rudin* as in *Onegin*, the hero is psychologically not free to love and the heroine marries a surrogate; Lavretski is not free legally and Liza, in taking the veil, is wedded to Christ; Insarov is unfitted physically, and Elena embraces the cause to which he was pledged.

In the two novels of the sixties this pattern is discarded. In *Fathers and Children* it is the hero who falls in love; he is rejected and dies. In *Smoke* there is a pattern of interlocking triangles reminiscent, to some extent, of *A Month in the Country*.

But if the story pattern has come full circle in *Virgin Soil*, the 'message' has continued to evolve. In the first four novels, it is only by analogy or figuratively that one can speak of a message; what they actually do is to pose and seek to answer a question: 'Where are our leaders to come from?', or, more specifically: 'Which (if any) of the leading types in our actual social landscape is fitted to lead Russia towards a brighter future?' These novels successively examine and test a Westernizing, socially oriented intellectual – a 'superfluous man' of the most admirable kind; a landowner with Slavophil affinities, devoted to his land and his peasants; an educator and an artist measured against a foreign patriot and 'revolutionary'; and a scientifically trained radical with revolutionary potential. Each hero in turn fails the test; each has a mite to contribute to the immediate present; none has the combination of qualities to move or shake the frozen society of Nicholas I.[6] So the message, in all these cases, is simply: 'Not he! Not these!' – or, more positively, that a leader (and, by implication, a direction) has yet to be found.

In *Smoke* and *Virgin Soil* the problems addressed are basically different. The gentry and the intelligentsia have been written off as potential leaders; if great changes are to come – which seems unlikely – they can come only from above, from the autocracy. The most that literature can do is to point to the course which Russia ought to follow and to look for the kinds of men best qualified to show the way, that is, to take one small step facing in the right direction.

In *Smoke* the main emphasis is on defining the course: that is the 'message' as proclaimed by Potugin. Litvinov can hardly yet be seen as a rôle-model. Yet he has brought back with him the technological knowledge and skills of the West, and in the years to come he will have a chance to raise the level of agriculture and lay the foundations of local industry – a better chance than the Lezhnëvs, Lavretskis and Kirsanovs of the past, inasmuch as he will be operating with hired (free) labour and so be able to introduce, however gradually, and impose higher standards, rather than lose himself in the 'immemorial slow drift' of unchanging folk ways.

In *Virgin Soil* the emphasis has shifted from the message to the man – to the rôle-model; but there is still a message. It is twofold, negative and positive: an indictment of the sickness and sores of Russian society in the present, and a prescription for the future. The indictment is shared between Nezhdanov and Paklin, who tell us much that the author has not time or space to show; the prescription is entrusted to Paklin, who (as befits the Voice of Truth) is misshapen, shrill, pathetic, not immune to panic, yet so witty, clear-sighted and intelligent that we must believe not only his prescription but his indictment in spite of its occasional lapses into petty particulars.

The positive message can be reduced to the two words, '*Ecce homo!*': Solomin and his like are Russia's best, if not only, hope for eventual salvation. Again, as in *Smoke*, the chief character in the novel is, for its author, not the hero of the love-story, who is likely to be the chief character for the reader, but the embodiment (rather than, like Potugin, the bearer) of the message.

It is not known who was (were) the model(s) for Solomin, but he is clearly not a type with which Turgenev would have been on familiar terms, so that, as a creation, he may be comparable to Insarov and Bazarov. Readers will probably agree that he is artistically more alive than the former, less fully realized than the latter. He appears in only about half of the novel's chapters and, being a man of few words, plays little part in some of those in which he is present. Overall, he never emerges entirely from the shadows: there is a good deal about him that Turgenev is unable to show us, whether because he doesn't know or because of the censorship. We see nothing and are told very little about Solomin's work, his relations with his workmen and with his employer. His relations with the revolutionaries remain ambiguous: Mashurina is sent to ask him whether 'everything is ready', as if he were one of them; he answers that 'nothing is', as if it were no affair of his. And even his relations with Nezhdanov and Marianna are seen more from their side than from his.

He is represented (like Liza Kalitina) largely through the reactions of the other characters to him. The feeling he inspires in all of them is trust – an unhesitating, unshakeable confidence in his reliability, his competence, his integrity. The Sipyagins, like his employer and his workers, are impressed as much by his assurance as by his expertise. Kallomeitsev, who is rash enough to tangle with him, is effortlessly crushed. The revolutionaries accept him on his own terms. Nezhdanov, Marianna and Paklin regard him with profound admiration (mixed with various kinds of other feelings).

But he not only knows what he is doing – he knows where he is going. He knows that there is no chance of successful revolution in any foreseeable future. He predicts (XXIII, 179) that within thirty years – in his lifetime – the gentry will have lost possession of their land and, with it, most of their social (i.e., political) importance. And in answer to Markelov's rejection of gradualism, he distinguishes (xx, 145) the gradualism of the Establishment, which amounts only to a brake on all action, from (his sort of) 'gradualism from below', which will move forward in expectation of better things.

Solomin is neither genius nor hero; but he has health and strength, steady nerves and shrewd judgment, a good heart, honesty and, above all, as Nezhdanov remarks, 'balance'. In other words, his greatest asset is not any one outstanding faculty but the fact that all his faculties work in unison, are harnessed to the pursuit of his purposes, instead of pulling different ways and so neutralizing each other (as they do in Nezhdanov) or submitting to the tyranny of one extravagant emotion, which can only lead to trouble (as with Markelov).

Nezhdanov is in many ways the antithesis of Solomin. Solomin is extrovert; Nezhdanov is preoccupied with his own thoughts and emotions to the point of losing all capacity for action and for personal relations. Solomin is simple, calm, a man of action; Nezhdanov is complex, agitated, a creature of feeling. Solomin has faith in himself; Nezhdanov has none. Solomin is a democrat but no revolutionary; Nezhdanov is something of a revolutionary (perhaps rather, at bottom, a rebel), but, as Paklin tells him (II, 18), no democrat. Solomin is a sober realist; Nezhdanov a Romantic. Paklin's odd description of Nezhdanov (xxxviii, 294) as 'a Romantic of realism! [sic]' is explained by Turgenev in his first jottings towards the future novel (W, xii, 314): such people 'yearn and strive for reality as, earlier, Romantics did for *the ideal*. What they seek in reality is not poetry – which they scorn – but something great and significant; but that is absurd: real life is prosaic and ought to be prosaic.'

The flaw or rift in Nezhdanov can be traced in part to his illegitimacy, which has quickened the rebellious instincts in him and misled him into mistaking personal rebellion for revolutionary ardour. But his culture, tastes and interests are far removed from those of the revolutionaries to whom he has bound himself. Hence the constant struggle to repress his real self (exemplified in his attitude to his poetry) and to compel himself to feelings and actions at variance with his nature, till he comes to feel 'like a bad actor in a part which doesn't fit him' (xxx, 226) or, as he says elsewhere, 'there are two men inside me, and the one will not let the other live'. Hence the scepticism which, beginning as self-doubt, extends outward to the cause he is supposed to be serving and so to the accepted major values of his world, overlaying even his faith in his fellow humans, as when he questions whether kindness can exist in a woman except as a function of stupidity or whether it is possible for any man to be, as Paklin claims Solomin is, unaware of his own superiority. Hence the aching weariness, the sense of being only half alive – and the logic of the final suicide.

As compared with Rudin, his predecessor of the forties, Nezhdanov lacks the toughness and self-confidence that stemmed from and reflected an inner unity, however one-sided: in Rudin the primacy of the cerebral element engendered faith: in himself as thinker and in ideas as objects of thought, while in Nezhdanov feelings are at war with one another as well as with his thoughts, and no one element is powerful enough to impose a lasting synthesis upon the rest.

Marianna represents Turgenev's rediscovery of the lovableness of the heroines of his literary youth – from Parasha to Liza – in the young nihilists (he himself in his notes for the novel had defined Marianna as a 'girl-nihilist') of the sixties and seventies.

It is worth noting that, like her predecessors, Marianna is still a lady, a scion of the gentry: there has been no shift, corresponding to that for the heroes, towards the other end of the social spectrum. Like Elena, she begins as a proud, unhappy girl; but, unlike Elena, she feels free to direct her resentment and hostility against the older generation, since this is represented not by parents (hers are dead), but by an uncle and aunt who have done nothing to deserve her love. So, instead of repressing her resentments and frustrations into hysteria (such as we glimpse in passages of Elena's diary), instead of sterilizing them in the form of self-pity and/or personal hatred of her guardians, she is free to develop and generalize them in the form of indignation on behalf of all the suffering and oppressed of the world and to work off her everyday rebelliousness in such 'unfeminine' or 'unladylike' activities as smoking, cutting her hair short, dabbling in science and 'social questions'. Nor was her indignation as passive or abstract as the reproaches which Elena mingled with her prayers: it found expression in a passionate demand for justice and a readiness to devote her whole life to making that possible, flaunted in her 'socialist' views and attitudes and in such activities as teaching.

What is driving her wild when she meets Nezhdanov (she has found the teaching, under ecclesiastical supervision, not worth while) is that she does not know where or how to begin. They are drawn to each other as rebels in a hostile world, and she seizes the opportunity to escape to freedom and begin her mission.

She differs from Elena and resembles Liza Kalitina in that principles and goals take precedence with her over personal relations and feelings (though, of course, her principles and goals are unconnected with religion). She does not – and probably could not – lose herself in another human being, in love; but that does not mean that she is cold-hearted or emotionally self-sufficient: she is able and willing to make sacrifices in personal relations also, as is evident in her readiness to remain linked to Nezhdanov after she has seen through him. Moreover, she has a deep need for emotional security: that is what attracts her from the first to Solomin.

Yet there is in her 'a core of inner freedom', as has been recognized by a number of critics. Over against her own needs, as over against other people's claims on her, she remains 'captain of her soul'. Her order of priorities is stated most clearly and simply in a brief exchange with Solomin (XXIX, 221): '"You wanted to sacrifice yourself?" "Yes – yes – yes!" "What of Nezhdanov?" "What of him! We will go together – or else I will go by myself."'' She is committed to service – of the people or the cause – and if Nezhdanov will not or cannot share in that, she will not be held back.

The quality she values most in herself is 'honesty' (*chestnost'*), as witness her greeting to Solomin at their first meeting: 'Give me your hand, and know that you are facing an honest girl.' It is also a quality that draws her to both Solomin and Nezhdanov (being perhaps the only quality that the two men have in common). And it is worth noting that this is a quality predicated of, or claimed by, all the positive characters in the novel – and conspicuously missing in all the representatives of high society.

Marianna has a lively and delicate feeling for other people's dignity, which makes it easy for her to form friendly relations with all sorts of people. That is most charmingly demonstrated in her conquest of the peasant woman Tat'yana, but it is no less evident in her first encounters with prickly Mashurina and with reserved Solomin. Even her first approaches to Nezhdanov, in spite of some superficial clumsiness, are very quickly effective in thrusting aside the social barriers and establishing a bond between them.

She is also a penetrating – and objective – observer, as when she realizes in a flash not only that Mashurina is in love with Nezhdanov but that 'this woman loves him more than I do!'; and she is a discerning judge of character, as shown in her evaluations of Markelov and Solomin (and even her aunt). Among the heroines of the novels she is, with Liza, the most 'quixotic', in Turgenev's sense: that is, the most deeply imbued with 'faith' and the least emotionally dependent.

Turgenev's six-novel social chronicle – of the second half of Nicholas I's and the first half of Alexander II's reign – ends on a note of sober hope and of courage. Over the span of three or four decades he has traced out the destinies of the 'superfluous man': from the forties, when his voice crying in the wilderness was the voice of civilization, through twenty years of decline and disintegration to a final, not ungenerous, suicide. He has traced out the development, the flowering of Russian girlhood and womanhood, from the Romantic devotion of Natal'ya and Liza's rejection of her world, through the baffled questing of Elena and Irina, to the real New Woman: free and fulfilled in dedication to her self-chosen course. And he has shown us the struggles of the superfluous man's immediate successors, the rebels bent on upheaval and negation – Insarov and Bazarov – and the slow ascent of their 'rivals' and eventual heirs, the builders, striving with the resources available to them to preserve, to improve, to progress – Lezhnëv, Lavretski, Litvinov – till the bearers of the message – a Rudin, a Potugin – have fused with the builders to produce the whole man, the embodiment of the message, the man who foretells the future (XXIII, 179) and moves towards it smiling his 'guileless' smile (XVI, 113), his 'marvellous' smile (according to Paklin: XVIII, 125) of understanding and assurance – Solomin.

16

The last writings

After the publication of *Virgin Soil* in January and February 1877 there is a break of about three and a half years in Turgenev's fiction-writing.[1] That is by far the longest intermission in the thirty-three years since his first story; and although there may have been more than one contributing factor, the main cause is likely to have been discouragement: this was his third novel in a row to have been rejected by the radicals and the 'younger generation', and he must have known that it would be his last. It had taken him ten years to write, and he could not count on another ten years of life, let alone of creativity. And anyhow, what would be the use?

In those fictionless years he turned to another form of writing – the fragmentary self-communings to which he himself gave the title *Senilia* (Writings of Old Age), but which are more generally referred to as *Prose Poems* (*Stikhotvoreniya v proze*). All but half-a-dozen of these were composed between the summer of 1877 and the summer of 1880, so that they form a literary bridge across the gap in the fiction.

Their first designation, *Posthuma* (*sic*), implies that Turgenev had not intended to have them published in his lifetime; but about a year before his death he yielded to the solicitations of the editor of *The European Herald*, which published fifty-one (out of a total of eighty-three) in January 1883, substituting Turgenev's sub-title *Prose Poems*, for his title, *Senilia*. Thirty-one others were withheld, as too personal – too intimate – for publication and did not see the light till 1930 in France, 1931 in the Soviet Union.

The *Prose Poems* represented a new genre in Russian literature and were promptly, though apparently not widely, imitated. Critics have exercised their ingenuity in hunting for foreign models; but while the idea of 'prose poems' may well derive from Baudelaire's *Le Spleen de Paris*, also known as *Petits Poëmes en Prose* (1869), Turgenev's is a medley *sui generis*, in which portraits and anecdotes jostle dreams, lyrical landscapes alternate with psychological and philosophical aphorisms, records of the author's intimate feelings are punctuated by polemics, literary or personal. Most of the 'poems' are characterized by the concreteness and plasticity proper to the fiction-writer, and these attributes, together with the variety of tone, effectually differentiate them from other works to which they have been compared.

Turgenev explained to his editor that these were jottings analogous to the 'sketches' and 'studies' made by painters with a view to their utilization in larger and more important works, and there is no reason to call this in question. In fact, 'A Meeting' (one of the poems not published in 1883) was incorporated, with only minor modifications, four years after it was written, in 'Klara Milich' as Aratov's dream at the beginning of chapter XI. It is easy to believe that if Turgenev had lived to write other works, many more of those fragments might have found a place in them.

However, as it stands, *Senilia* is by far his most subjective work – approached, in this respect, only by the second part of 'Enough'. Through a transparent mask of flawless style he pours forth his literary and personal rancours, the bitter wisdom gleaned from disappointments, betrayals, denigration; the misery of lonely old age; the horror of approaching death. Yet it is not all gloom and hopelessness. While he can write he will not despair. There have been moments in life – moments of unfading beauty and inspiration – and with these he struggles to 'shore his ruins' against the blasts of fate. He evokes a summer day in an ideal Russian village; the martyrdom of a Russian Billy Budd; the mourning of a poor St Petersburg sleigh-driver for his young wife; the mysterious bond of life that makes comrades of man and animal (dog or marmoset) and of man and man across the barriers of class and age (the beggar, the puling infant); visions or dreams of happiness (on an azure sea or amid lofty hills); life transfigured by love and genius in an instant of ecstatic achievement; life sanctified by heroism, animal (the sparrow courting death to save its brood) or human (the girl ready to risk all for love, the sister of mercy at the front, the young revolutionary pledged to limitless sacrifice in the service of her cause).

It is significant that Turgenev's first attempt to return to fiction followed his 1879 visit home, where he had been surprised and moved to find himself hailed by progressives – members of that 'younger generation' that he had missed and mourned since *Fathers and Children*. In a period of dark repression, the frustrated and stifled young turned to him as the author of *A Sportsman's Sketches* – the champion of freedom for the serfs – as the creator of Liza and Elena and Marianna – those paragons of Russian girlhood and womanhood – and as the tireless advocate of those values of human dignity and spiritual freedom, the lack of which weighed on them so heavily. They turned to him as a symbol of humanism and honesty – and by way of a gesture of defiance to the Establishment. But it needed another year and a further, longer visit to Russia, which confirmed, though in less demonstrative fashion, the renewed bond between the writer and his younger readers to hearten him to the point of producing another story.

So in the last two years of his literary life, until writing became physically impossible[2] – between the summer of 1880 and the end of 1882 – Turgenev wrote four more stories,[3] keeping to the two genres he had adopted since the 'failure' of *Fathers and Children*: evocations of pre-Emancipation Russia, as observed by him or related to him, and 'tales of mystery': two final glimpses of the decline and fall of the Russian gentry and two strikingly innovative displays of creative fantasy.

'Old Portraits'

The first two stories to be written were conceived as part of a collection or 'cycle' under the general title *Memories – My Own and Other People's*; and when the first one met (like 'Khor' and Kalinych' thirty-four years earlier) with a friendly reception, Turgenev was quick to fantasize that this might be the start of another success like his first.

Like 'Khor' and Kalinych', 'Old Portraits'[4] forms a diptych – a pair of complementary portraits – or perhaps rather a triptych, with the secondary but significant figure of the serf corresponding to that of the serf-owner in the earlier story.

The Telegins, husband and wife, bring up the rear in the long line of eighteenth-century figures in Turgenev's fiction – from 'Three Portraits' (1845) through *A Sportsman's Sketches* (1846–51), 'The Brigadier-General' (1867), 'An Unhappy Girl' (1868), 'A King Lear of the Steppes' (1870), 'The Watch' (1875) to the old couple in *Virgin Soil* (1876) – not to mention Lavretski's ancestors, Bazarov's parents, various serfs and other, more shadowy forms. And the variety of types is noteworthy: they have generally as little in common as personages of Turgenev's own age or younger.

Aleksei Telegin was born in 1760, the same year as Susanna's father, Ivan Koltovskoi. But what a contrast between the frigid narcissist, self-insulated from his ex-mistress and little daughter, and the warm-hearted husband and host (although Telegin, when the narrator knew him, was years older than Koltovskoi when he died); between the would-be Voltairean, with his thick veneer of French culture and contempt for all things Russian including the Russian language, and the generous, pious old man, who was 'Russian in everything': loved Russian songs, the Russian steam bath and only Russian cooking, who in his youth had sung Russian songs and danced Russian dances, and spoke a wonderful – pure and racy – Russian; between the man with 'a soul of stone' and the man of 'no mean soul'. Perhaps the only trait they share is their perpetuation of the culture and outlook of Catherine's time several decades into the following century and their seclusion from the society of that new age. But Telegin remains 'open': to his wife, to his young kinsman, to his peasants – he remains inwardly alive, and so deserves to outlive his contemporary by more than twenty years.

As compared with the equally long-lived and equally good-hearted old couple in *Virgin Soil*, the Telegins belong to an earlier generation – were born a couple of decades earlier – are richer and have lived more variously and fully: they have had experience of the great world, have seen Catherine in her glory and enjoyed the favour of her favourite, Orlov, and they have had children (who broke away from them).

One should perhaps bear in mind the different ages at which the subjects were observed as well as the extent of the observation, not to mention the attitudes of the observers. The Telegins were in their 70s during the series of visits of their well-disposed young kinsman; Fomushka and Fimushka were in their late 80s at the time of the single brief visit by a younger generation bent on destroying all that they had stood for (Koltovskoi had been observed between his mid-50s and his mid-60s by an embittered child and adolescent).

Any suspicion that Turgenev might have allowed nostalgia to cloud his vision or soften his judgment of a serf-owning society is silenced by the introduction of the serf, Ivan Sukhikh. His story demonstrates again – perhaps even more directly and uncompromisingly than any of the *Sportsman's Sketches* – that, however humane the serf-owner and however happy the serf in his service, the system will inevitably wreck such happiness, drown idyll in tragedy.

'A Desperate Character'

'A Desperate Character'[5] stands in roughly the same relation to 'Old Portraits' as 'Pëtr Petrovich Karataev' to 'Khor' and Kalinych'. 'Khor' and Kalinych' was predominantly idyllic – although the master's exploitation of Kalinych, entailing the disruption of his peasant economy, and his solitary existence without wife or child, presumably due at least partly to that economic insecurity – make him an object of pity, in some measure, to the narrator, if not also to his friend Khor'. 'Karataev', like 'A Desperate Character', is a tragedy, and the protagonists of the two sketches, conceived and written thirty-five years apart, reveal a startling affinity, although the self-destructiveness, which in Karataev was no more than a drift, has become a drive in Misha Poltev.

We saw Karataev only twice, briefly, towards the age of 30. All that we learn about his past at the first meeting is that he has known a short spell of love and happiness and that he has ruined himself by his extravagance and unpracticalness; all that we learn about his future at the second meeting is that he is drinking himself to death. Whereas we have Misha's whole history, from childhood on. He too, in effect, drank himself to death by the age of 30 (or sooner); he too had his few months of love – though only at the end of his life and in a key very different from the exuberant paean of Karataev's.

Karataev is not an average landowner: his romance with Matrëna and his passion for Shakespeare set him above the mean; however, his gradual decline into debt and drink is not untypical. There is nothing in him of the desperation which makes Misha extraordinary.

And Misha's 'career' is as extraordinary as his character. He had been brought up by a highly-strung and sentimental mother and by a father (perhaps a contemporary of Fomushka and Fimushka)[6] who was convinced that thinking was not only dangerous but unnecessary, since all the problems of life had been solved and the rules of right living had been laid down once for all by the wisdom of former generations. Encased in this narrow and rigid mould, Misha had grown up with no outward indication of discomfort or disaffection except his 'wild' and 'almost brutal' laughter (II, 32); his parents' death releases the repressed, which bursts forth with a vehemence proportional to its 18-year-long constriction.

Like many of his real-life contemporaries,[7] Misha sets out to burn the candle at both ends: having sold his estate – dirt-cheap in his eagerness to be rid of his past – he tries 'wine, women and song'; he tries religion; he tries military service in the Caucasus, where he does his best to get himself killed and becomes a compulsive gambler, ready to stake his left hand on a game of cards and his life on a trifling bet.

If the riotous living and the soldiering were unconscious attempts to cut loose from his religious upbringing, they fail: at the front he thinks nothing of exposing himself, but cannot bring himself to kill or wound 'the enemy'; and the gypsy women were evidently only incidental to the wine and song: in his later years, however low he sinks in the world, he refuses to take advantage of the women who are attracted to him, will not risk hurting any of them.

After his discharge from the army he embarks on a course of strangely deliberate self-humiliation, operating as a beggar in his own social world; but just as his bodily vigour and health have remained undinted by his earlier excesses and the dangers he has courted, so now his spirit and his pride remain unchastened and unsubdued: he will raise money by offering his nose to be tweaked, but woe betide the man who dares to tweak a second time having paid only once.

Then his social world casts him out as the army had cast him out, and he is next seen as a beggar among beggars, though still a prince of beggars, to judge by our last glimpse of him. And not till he has squandered the last reserve of that seemingly inexhaustible health and energy does he escape from his despair: for he ends up not on a highway or under a bridge with a bottle in his hand, but reclaimed, socialized, repentant, in love.

What is the source and nature of the desperation that has dominated and shaped almost the whole of his adult life? According to the narrator, it was 'despair without an object', by which he evidently means 'without any objective cause' – in implicit contrast to the despair of the revolutionary youth of a later generation. If we accepted that diagnosis, we could explain poor Misha's ruin as the effect of a too-restrictive upbringing on a boisterous temperament, intensifying its natural ebullience to a point of complete intolerance of all restraints. There are people who cannot bear such social restraints as demands for punctuality or such physical restraints as the wearing of ties and belts, and we could see Misha as one of that family: something of the kind appears in his reaction to his 'uncle's' abortive attempt to save him from himself.

But although that clash between education and temperament was no doubt a factor, the story itself hints at other aspects or dimensions to Misha's problem. First, the narrator's facile assumption that the young man's despair has no objective – translate: social – causes is contradicted not only by the admittedly elliptic but nonetheless significant avowal (IV, 37) that the very thought of the poverty and injustice in Russia makes him feel suicidal, but by his earnest attempts after his marriage to make himself useful, to work, and his bitter self-reproaches for having wasted his life without doing anything useful. Misha differed from the youth of the sixties and seventies not in unawareness of or indifference to the sickness of his society, but in seeing no way to alleviate it.

Moreover, on the psychological plane there is much more than a revolt of temperament against socialization. Misha's temperament is at war not just with the behavioural constraints of his upbringing but with the religious feeling solidly implanted by that upbringing and attested by his phase as a lay brother, by his inability to hurt women or even enemies and most decisively by the attitudes and values of the personality that reveals itself fully only in the year before his death. If Misha Poltev is a rebel without a cause, it is not for want of social conscience or moral potential. But his father had instilled in him a horror of thinking and Nicholaian society, in the years of blackest reaction, offered him no opening for 'useful work'.

Misha's tragedy invites comparison with that of another 'desperate character': Yakov in 'Father Aleksei's Story'. In both we have a young man destroyed by a conflict between religious feeling and in the one case, temperament, in the other, intelligence. Yakov's mind is drawn to science as the key to social service (and, perhaps, happiness); his religious feeling condemns this as apostasy from his God and faith. Misha is debarred by his upbringing from thinking, from the use of his mind, and is thus precluded from discovering any way to social service; his religious feeling is unequal to controlling his temperament, but strong enough to make him a failure in all his undertakings: it may be the need to hold down that

feeling which drives him to more excessive actions than would be
called for by his temperament on its own.

'Song of Triumphant Love'

'Song of Triumphant Love'[8] is unique among Turgenev's works in
more ways than one. It purports to be a tale extracted from a
sixteenth-century Italian manuscript, though it probably owes
more to Flaubert's *contes* than to Bandello.[9] For a man with nearly
half a century of writing behind him and less than three years of life
ahead to venture into a strange world and fashion a new style to
match the norms of that world surely bespeaks a more than
common courage and enterprise. The epigraph, from Schiller,
'Dare to stray and to dream!', may well refer to the feat of mastering
this new genre as well as to the crisis of the heroine.

We start to read in some trepidation: for when have we seen the
hero of a Turgenev story actually winning and settling down in
happy marriage with the girl he loves? We have been told it
happens: mostly to secondary personages, such as Lezhnëv and
Volyntsev, but even, in one line of the last chapter, to Davyd.[10]
However, there is an abyss between telling and showing. Yet here
is Fabio not only marrying his Valeria, but preparing to live happily
with her 'ever after'. Is this a fairy-tale?

But no: even in a Turgenev fairyland such happiness could not
last. And it doesn't last – for more than three pages. Then: re-enter
the tempter – at which point fairyland gives place to the more
familiar world of Turgenevan psychology. Admittedly, some of the
fairy trappings remain. There is the charmed necklace which Muzio
presses on Valeria; there is the incantation over the Shirazi wine;
there are the shared dreams and the sleepwalkings; there is the
tongueless Malay with his protracted resuscitation of Muzio.

But these are all peripheral – or, more precisely, local colour: to
a sixteenth-century reader they would seem no more extraordinary
than the potion that lent Juliet the semblance of death or Pros-
pero's sorceries, not to mention Macbeth's witches or King
Hamlet's ghost. By sixteenth-century standards Turgenev must be
judged discreet; and surely it was not for the sake of these marvels
that he wrote this story, any more than it will have been for the sake
of the vampire Ellis that he had written 'Phantoms'.

What happens is that after four years of uneventful, happy

marriage Valeria's peace of mind is broken by the sudden re-entry into her life of the man she had nearly married. Her confessor speaks of her imagination being disturbed (VIII, 67), but it is far more than that. It looks as if emotions have been released or activated in her which had hitherto found no scope in her marriage. The evidence for this is fivefold.

First, an emotional barrier springs up between Valeria and her husband: she dares not tell him the truth about her dreams, she is impelled to lie about them (though he has already guessed their gist because his attitude to her has not changed, his love and trust have not faltered). Secondly, there is the disappearance of innocence from her expression when Fabio tries to resume work on her portrait. Thirdly, there is the epigraph, 'Dare to stray and to dream!' – and Valeria follows the prescription to the letter. Fourthly, if we assume that Muzio's power over her is, basically, hypnotic and accept the widely held view that hypnosis cannot make anyone act against the fundamental structure of his/her character or the deepest levels of his/her will – the implication is that if Valeria goes to Muzio, it is because there is some element in her which unconsciously wants to go. Fifthly, there is the desired result – her pregnancy.

It makes little difference whether we suppose that the child will be Muzio's according to the flesh or believe that Valeria has been set free by her experience with Muzio to conceive a child by her husband – as a married woman who has been childless for years quite often finds herself with child after she has adopted (or even only decided to adopt) someone else's child. In other words, if we ask what happened in the jasmine pergola on the second night of Muzio's stay, there are three possible answers: a rape; a quasi-rape, if Valeria's love for her husband and conscious horror of Muzio were unconsciously at grips with her craving for a child; 'nothing happened' – either because between two sleepwalkers nothing could or because her resistance was too wholehearted. But the emotional storm unleashed by these experiences was potent enough to wake her from her trance of saintly innocence and fit her for motherhood.

Thus, even in fairyland the problems and conflicts remain recognizably human, and indeed Turgenevan-human. What chiefly differentiates fairyland from real life is that there the problems and conflicts prove amenable to solutions and that the somewhat bizarre means invoked to produce those solutions are able to operate without negative after-effects – without leaving any unhappy traces behind.

The song which gives the story its title represents a second musical peak in Turgenev's work (saturated as it is with every kind of music, from bird-song to opera), as complement and antithesis to Lemm's canticle of triumphant love on the night when Lavretski first kissed Liza. What they have in common is passion; but Lemm's is a heroic hymn, a blend of earthly and heavenly, of joy and sorrow, comprising 'all that is dear in life'; Muzio's is a dithyramb of purely sensuous fulfilment and exultation, glittering and heady as his perfumed wine, sinuous and fascinating as the snake whose skin enwraps the scroll of his violin.

Muzio plays his song three times: at the first supper, as a challenge to Fabio and an invitation to Valeria; later that night, in triumph, after drawing her into his dream; and on the second night, to celebrate their meeting in the jasmine pergola. But Muzio will no more attain happiness than did Lavretski.

'Klara Milich'

With Turgenev's last Russian story[11] we return from Renaissance Italy (or fairyland) to Russia – in fact, for the first time since 1862, in a story or novella, to post-Emancipation Russia: the scene is laid in 1878. Turgenev himself called the story 'After Death',[12] but it is more commonly referred to by the title under which it was first published, as 'Klara Milich', the name of the heroine.

The starting-point of Turgenev's creative interest was gossip about a man who had fallen passionately in love with an actress who had committed suicide by taking poison on stage; this appeared to him to have the makings of a 'semi-fantastic story in the manner of ... Poe'.[13] Like the fictional Klara, E. P. Kadmina had been an opera singer before becoming a dramatic actress; she had shown considerable talent (Turgenev had actually once seen her singing). But she was a woman of 28, not a girl of 19, and she died without even knowing of the existence of her adorer, whose love became an obsession only after her death. He was 35 years old when she died and survived her by another twenty-eight years. So the story and Aratov's character are entirely Turgenev's invention.

The element of 'mystery' involved no real difficulty, even at that time, for his more intelligent readers:[14] it consists, evidently, of a series of hallucinations, as Aratov himself divines while he still has his wits about him. He is presented to us as an exceptionally impressionable, suggestible young man, brought up to believe in Schiller and 'the spirit world'; a single word or phrase is sometimes enough to trap and control his imagination. The singular circumstances of his three meetings with Klara; her tragic death; his fear that he may have been its cause and horror and remorse when it is demonstrated that he was; certain phrases, such as '[If] I meet – I'll take [him]' (*Vstrechu – voz'mu*) and 'undefiled' (*netronutaya*) lay hold of his mind – all this builds up into an obsession; he develops a fever which brings on hallucinations; and his weakened heart gives out. Turgenev's masterly orchestration makes his account of this process at once thrilling and soberly convincing.

Klara is a much more interesting personality than Aratov, even apart from her musical and acting talents. She is exasperatingly attractive in her passionate unreason. With a father whom she could only despise, a mother who deserved no more than a condescending benevolence, she concentrates all her love on her sister, who is, however, too unlike her in character and temperament to satisfy more than a part of her. By way of compensation she constructs her own world of romantic fantasies, to which she abandons herself with unreserved conviction. She sees the real world like Don Quixote – through the transforming medium of those fantasies: that is, she sees not what is in front of her but what she is determined to see. And when her illusions shatter themselves against the real being of her fellow humans, she lacks the flexibility to learn (it is typical that after hearing Aratov's criticism of her singing she abandons music) and the patience to work out alternatives for herself, but defiantly rings down the curtain.

Aratov asks himself at one point why she had chosen him. That is excess of modesty. He is a handsome young man (I, 77), as she could see, and she had no doubt ascertained from his friend, Kupfer, that he possessed the essential virtues of her ideal man – 'honesty, candour, purity – above all, purity' (XIII, 115). That he was unsociable yet tender-hearted were no doubt added attractions; his fragile health and lack of any clear purpose in life were evidently not deterrents.

The tryst was bound to be a fiasco, both parties being equally inexperienced, naïve, and therefore clumsy. Aratov came to it with no idea of what to expect, and so was uneasy, irritable and stiff. Klara, having failed to inform him beforehand of the purpose of the meeting, should have taken the initiative immediately, but her nerve fails her, she leaves him to flounder, and then condemns him out of hand for not being vain enough to have guessed or assumed her feelings and for not being able to reciprocate them while knowing virtually nothing about her. She had fallen in love with him: therefore he must – he ought to – have fallen in love with her: if he hasn't, that proves him unworthy of her. Aratov's later sense of guilt, while evidence of his 'tender heart', is, by any reasonable criterion, excessive.

In a sense, Klara appears to be more at home on stage than outside the theatre. The programme she had chosen for the concert at which she expected Aratov to be present was carefully planned. Her first song expressed the joy of a lover whose love is returned. For her second piece she had evidently chosen something neutral, in case he stayed away; seeing him in the hall, she substitutes a Russian version of Mignon's cry of yearning (from Goethe's *Wilhelm Meisters Lehrjahre*), and crowns that with perhaps the most compelling love declaration in Russian literature, Tat'yana's letter to Onegin.

Her suicide is similarly a work of art. She bides her time till she has won the hearts of Kazan's theatregoers and then poisons herself in full view of her fans, so ensuring for the act a resonance that was almost bound to reach Aratov sooner or later. Of course, she could not foresee just how he would react to the news; but, given his tender heart, he would at least never forget her, perhaps he would be unable to love any other woman – in any case, she would have done everything possible to make good her boast that if ever she met her ideal man, she would 'take' him.[15] And if we read the line in her diary, 'Must [start] all over again, if only . . .' (XIII, 116) in the light of Kupfer's statements, 'she was as proud as Satan himself' and 'she could not endure mortification' (IX, 102), may we not suspect that her suicide was due at least as much to injured pride as to love? If she could not have love and life on her own terms, she would destroy herself – and leave her mark on the man who had failed her.

Nor, surely, did Aratov die of love, even if the delirium of his last days was filled with delusions of love, happy and consummated. In his two meetings with Klara attraction had been at odds with repulsion, momentary compassion with recurrent irritation. After learning of her death, his predominant emotion is anxiety – the urge to make sure he had had no part in it. Once that hope was killed, he felt possessed, felt himself 'in her power', and the feeling has nothing of glad self-surrender – it is obsessive (her image is constantly before his eyes), oppressive, nightmarish (culminating in the dream of being in the boat with death).

Then the hallucinations begin – at first, auditory, finally visual; and it is only at that point that he declares he has fallen passionately in love with her; but it is in fear and trembling that he supplicates her ('if you don't want me to go mad'), saying the things which he knows she wants to hear. And surely it is not till the following moment – when he does 'go mad', that is, when he loses all sense of reality – that his remorse and terror are submerged in 'love'. As long as he was in his right mind, he was perceptive enough to realize that it was not Klara but her sister who represented the values he had dreamed of and looked for in a woman. The crowning irony of 'Klara Milich' is that, instead of choosing Anna to share his life, he is driven to throw himself away on a ghost whom, while she was alive, he had neither admired as an artist, nor desired as a woman, nor been able to communicate with as a human being.

So ends Turgenev's 38-year-long career as a writer of fiction – as author of six novels and more than sixty sketches, short stories and novellas that have taken a place of honour in the treasure-house of world literature.

17

Epilogue

Great writers do not lend themselves to conclusions. Turgenev lived in the same Russia as Dostoevsky and Tolstoy; the world which he envisioned and created – the world at which we have been looking from the 'vantage-point' of more than a century later – is as multifarious, as distinctive, as problematic as either of their worlds. Comparisons would seem not so much odious as pointless: the three had as little in common as three such great contemporaries could have – yet there are a few characteristics in which Turgenev stands opposed to the other two.

First, there is his classic sense of measure and form. Dostoevsky deplored his own lack of that grace and lamented that he was impelled to stuff each of his novels with material enough for several; Tolstoy asserted, balancing between defiance and satisfaction, that *War and Peace* could not be brought within the definition of any existing literary genre. On the other hand, when Turgenev errs, it is by giving the reader too little rather than too much (remember such 'afterthoughts' as chapter IV of 'A Backwater' or chapter XXXV of *A Nest of Gentry*); if Lavretski's genealogy seems slightly out of scale, if Fomushka and Fimushka seem somewhat less than germane to the themes of *Virgin Soil*, these are unique departures from his norm. And the concentration of interest, the economy and subtlety of detail, the instinct for structure and balance in his writings are unequalled, perhaps, in any other Russian writer of his generation.

Secondly, no one is likely to imagine Tolstoy or Dostoevsky as writers of anything but prose, whereas Turgenev in his prose remains a poet: his 'lyricism' is an established cliché in the critical literature, though it is a quality easier to recognize than to analyse. It is, in any case, not a matter of multiplying metaphors or other tropes, nor of lapsing into metric rhythms: Turgenev was as careful as his master, Pushkin, to eschew the surface attributes of verse.

If one says that his prose is 'beautiful', one means at least that it is simple, clear, precise, supple in its modulations and evocative. A Turgenev description – of a landscape, for instance – is not just a series of sense-impressions (not to mention that Turgenev would have seen, heard, smelt, understood much more than most of us could if we had been there) – it is a synthesis of these impressions permeated by his own emotional and artistic responses to them. Permeated – not coloured (and much less – blurred or distorted or sentimentalized): what he says is what is there, but how he says it sets the key of the reader's response. However, the reader needs to listen with a 'third ear'; some, who do not, have been shocked by that serenely honest vision, have even complained of 'a terrifying detachment'.

Thirdly, and most profoundly significant – whereas Dostoevsky and Tolstoy are, in their very different ways, religious writers – men wrestling in their own lives and in the persons of their heroes with the problems of religious belief and its rôle in their world – Turgenev is an unbeliever. Although he professes – whether as an expression of his basic scepticism or as a precaution against 'perlustration'[1] – to keep an open mind as regards the existence of God,[2] he had certainly closed it to the possibility of a personal afterlife.[3] Hence his life-long terror of death (though in his last long year of hopeless pain he faced it as bravely as his own Bazarov); hence the underlying melancholy that prompted Pauline Viardot to style him 'the saddest of men'; hence the elegiac note, the Vergilian *lacrimae rerum* at the root of his celebration of beauty, whether in nature or in persons; and hence his exaltation of quixotry – a compound of faith and love – as the prime mover in human history and the prime condition of human fulfilment.

Paradoxically, his unbelief did not prevent him – and this is some measure of the range and generosity of his sympathies – from creating a gallery of religious figures unsurpassed in variety and appeal by the Christian Tolstoy or the Christian Dostoevsky: a gallery comprising mainstream Orthodox, such as Akim (in 'The Inn'), Bazarov's parents, Father Aleksei, the Telegins (in 'Old Portraits'); such striking sectaries as Kas'yan, the Old Believers in 'The Dog' or Evlampiya Kharlova; a nonconformist as singular as Sof'ya in 'A Strange Story'; a would-be apostate (Father Aleksei's tormented son); and two saints – a peasant, Luker'ya, and a lady, Liza Kalitina – not to mention such aberrant or indeterminate types as the 'desperate character', Misha, or the 'idiot' ministered to by Sof'ya.

Turgenev is unique among his peers in his personal love–hate relationship with nature. She is the Great Mother, the creator of all living things, whose beauty enchants his senses and moves his heart; but she is also the mother who devours her own offspring, who destroys, without purpose and without pity, all that she brings forth – she is death and the horror of death. Crushed by the funereal gloom of the Woodland, he shudders and weeps; in the arms of Ellis he recoils from his bird's-eye view of the earth into Hamletic disgust, existential nausea. He 'cannot bear the sky' – 'that eternal ... empty immensity'.[4] But reason and philosophy cannot silence the voices of his heart: he 'adores' life 'with all its caprices, its hazards and habits, its fleeting loveliness'; he will spend hours lying somewhere out of doors, 'intent, absorbed and absorbing' – absorbing the acrid freshness of odours from the fields, the tinge of 'serene sadness' in the songs of the birds, glimpses of a duck or cow vignetted in a moment of time, the pathetic fragility of young leaves outlined against that sky which he cannot bear.[5] Two of the most touching 'Prose Poems' celebrate the solidarity of humans and animals: of man and marmoset in their common loneliness,[6] of man and dog in the shared sense of their mortality.[7] While, on the plane of life, this contradiction between heart and head is compounded by a twist of pure Turgenevan irony: that gentlest of men, that poet of nature is also the gleeful slaughterer of innocent birds.

Within the frame of two-faced nature Turgenev's personages live their little day – or wrestle with the problem of how to live – or try to live but fail. Failure means failure to make yourself, in the words of the prophet, to 'become who you are'.[8] The wrestlers, like Jacob of old,[9] remain lamed for life: whether they hitch themselves to the puritan ethic of toil and renunciation – *Entbehren sollst du, sollst entbehren* – or embrace its antithesis – *Wage du zu irren und zu träumen*.

The basic duality of nature is reflected in every major aspect of human life, including the author's apprehension of it. As a committed 'realist', Turgenev sets out to observe and understand; but as a poet he is constantly aware of phenomena not amenable to understanding, of realities that can be observed and reported but not explained, of an aura of mysteries ignored by the blinkered science of his day. His so-called tales of mystery represent only the tip of an iceberg – studies of mental processes such as dreams, hallucinations, hypnosis, perhaps extrasensory perception – and, incidentally, a snook cocked at the scientific fundamentalism of his radical contemporaries; the supreme mystery, of course, is that of human motivation as we meet it in character after character, from Andrei Kolosov and his friend to Klara Milich and Aratov.

The function assigned by Dostoevsky and Tolstoy to religion is by Turgenev assigned to love: he writes, 'in every man there is a beast, which can be tamed only by love'.[10] And love in all its protean variety is at the centre of Turgenev's work, because he sees it as the centre of human life, the testing-ground of human powers and potentialities, the measure of human worth. Love is the key to such happiness as men and women can hope for; it is the force that inspires genius to the creation of beauty and exalts faith to the heights of heroism. Of course, it is no less double, no less 'a power of opposites' than life or nature itself. Love could endow Asya (and her peers) with wings, set the seal of personality on a Gerasim, a Vera (in 'Faust'), free a Kharlov from the 'long littleness' of his life – but love could as well paralyse the narrators of 'Asya' and 'Faust', kill a Mar'ya Pavlovna (in 'A Backwater'), drive an Aratov mad, degrade and enslave a Petushkov, an Aleksei Petrovich, a Sanin.

The essence of love is the urge and capacity to give oneself. Rudin had lamented, 'I strive to give myself, eagerly, utterly – but I cannot'; this incapacity is the curse of the superfluous man, from the Hamlet of Shchigry to Nezhdanov: he is 'locked' into himself: by timidity or pride or conflicting emotions and values. Yet he keeps his eyes fixed on an ideal, striving to preserve at least his freedom and dignity, while the Aleksei Petroviches and Sanins throw themselves away, sell freedom and self-respect for a mess of pottage.

Not that those who were able to give themselves – the Quixotes – are any happier. Like the votaries of courtly love, like Don Quixote, like Turgenev himself, the Lavretskis and Potugins, the Pasynkovs and Bersenevs, above all, the Turgenev heroines are fated to love the forbidden or unattainable.[11]

Clearly, it is those heroines who embody 'quixotry' – that is, impassioned faith, love in the service of an ideal – in its purest form. The quintessence of that impassioned faith is distilled in a prose poem entitled 'The Threshold'.[12] A nameless Russian girl is standing outside the open door of a vast unlit building; a voice issuing from the darkness addresses to her a series of questions,

which she answers. Does she know what awaits her if she enters –
cold, hunger, hatred, derision, contempt, insults, prison, sickness,
even death? – Yes, she knows. – And total isolation, loneliness? –
She knows. She is prepared to bear every kind of suffering and
attack . . . and not only from enemies but from friends and kin. She
is ready to offer up her life, unknown, unremembered, anonymous;
she wants neither gratitude nor pity. – But what of crime? Is she
ready for that? – Her head droops: this is evidently the hardest
question so far. – But yes: she is ready even for crime. There is a
pause before the ultimate test. Does she know that she may lose her
faith, cease to believe what she believes now, see her young life as
ruined to no purpose? – Yes, she knows that too, and yet she wants
to enter. She is bidden to do so, and as she steps across the
threshold and is lost to view, two voices are heard in the outside
world. 'Fool!' snarls the first; 'Saint!' responds the other.

This revolutionary catechism takes us back to 'A Strange Story'
and its equation of Sof'ya's self-immolation to the 'fool in Christ'
with the self-immolation of the girl revolutionaries. Without
approving, Turgenev feels a deep respect for their sense of mission,
in spite – or, perhaps, rather because – of its extremism. Ten years
before 'A Strange Story' he had proclaimed that it didn't matter if
Don Quixote's attempts to do good most often end in failure or
worsen the plight of those he seeks to succour, for 'the main thing is
the good faith and strength of the conviction [prompting the action]
. . . and the result is in the hands of fate'. Nearly a decade after 'A
Strange Story' his creed is still the same: the value of action – and of
the agent – is to be measured not by results but by the intensity of
the love-and-faith that fuels the action. Folly or sainthood: the
distinction may be in the eye of the beholder.

In 1859 he had recognized revolution in Italy (and Insarov's
planned revolution in Bulgaria) as a holy war; between 1869 (the
date of 'A Strange Story') and 1878 (the date of 'The Threshold') he
is no longer sure that revolution in Russia might not be a holy war
too, even though all his instincts cry out against it and his reason
tells him that it would have no chance of succeeding in the present
or the foreseeable future.

In comparison with Tolstoy's 'archaism'[13] and Dostoevsky's
apocalypticism, readers of today may well find Turgenev's serene
and equitable view of Russian actuality and immediate prospects
convincingly 'modern'. They will surely be struck by the contrast

between his vision of society in the novels (with the partial exception of *Smoke*), where a long-term hopefulness prevails in varying degrees over scepticism, and his vision, mainly in the stories, of the individual – a tragic or, at least, elegiac vision, variously tempered by irony.

The crowning paradox of this tragicomic individual existence is that it finds its completest fulfilment in an impossible love, a love of the unattainable. Heroic in its self-transcendence, it is achievable even by simple souls, by the poor in spirit. Love is the justification of life; the only existence that justifies despair is that of the man who dies without ever having loved or been loved (as in the early poem 'The Old Landowner').

As a poet Turgenev presents to his readers what he himself has loved most: beauty, in nature and youth, in art and the human spirit; truth, that is, intellectual honesty; and freedom, above all from the inner shackles of prejudice, superstition, 'system' – within the frame of his Russian landscape and of the drama of a century of Russian history. While as a man and a 'hero of his time' he projects in his creation the antinomies of existence as he experiences – as he suffers – them: the antinomies of poetry vs civic obligation, of personality vs nature, of values vs facts, of love vs freedom, of 'fantasy' vs 'realism', of Don Quixote vs Hamlet.

Notes

INTRODUCTION: TURGENEV AND HIS ANTINOMIES

1 A. Dall'Aglio, '"Andrei Kolosov", opera di maturità', *Annali dell'Istituto Universitario Orientale (sezione slava)* (Naples, 1969), p. 167.
2 R. L. Jackson, 'The Root and the Flower, Dostoevsky and Turgenev: a Comparative Esthetic', *The Yale Review* (Winter 1974), 228–50 (232, 238).
3 Nina Brodiansky, 'Turgenev's Short Stories: a Revaluation', *Slavonic and East European Review* (December 1953), 70–91 (79).
4 L. 3569, to M. A. Milyutina, 6 Mar. 1875.
5 L. 76, to Pauline Viardot, 11 Jan. 1848. Admittedly, this is in a discussion of acting techniques: 'mais, en général, c'est le calme *provenant d'une forte conviction et d'un sentiment profond*, le calme qui enveloppe pour ainsi dire de tous côtés les élans désespérés de la passion, qui leur communique cette pureté de lignes, cette beauté idéale et réelle, la vraie, la seule beauté de l'art'.
6 'Faust, tragediya. Soch. Goethe. Perevod pervoi i izlozhenie vtoroi chasti.' M. Vronchenko, 1844. Sankt-Peterburg. *W.* I, 214–57 (223).
7 L. 499, to L. N. Tolstoy, 20 Dec. 1856. The letter is quoted by Henri Granjard, *Ivan Tourguénev et les courants politiques et sociaux de son temps* (Paris, 1954), p. 283. Granjard quotes from the 1949–50 edition of Turgenev's *Works*; oddly enough, the sentence cited here is missing from the latest (Academy, 1961–8) edition of the letters.
8 L. 2235, to Ludwig Pietsch, 24 Feb. 1869: 'Sobald ich nicht mit Gestalten zu thun habe, bin ich ganz verwirrt und weiss nicht – wo ein und aus. Es kommt mir immer vor, als ob man jedesmal mit gleichem Recht das Entgegengesetzte behaupten könne – von alledem, was ich sage.'
9 Boris Zaitsev, *Zhizn' Turgeneva* (Paris, 1949/1931), p. 200.
10 M. O. Gershenzon, *Mechta i mysl' I. S. Turgeneva* (Moscow, 1919), cited from Brown University Slavic Reprints 8 (Providence, 1970), pp. 83–4.

I LIFE AND REPUTATION

1 The letter begins in the third person – 'a fellow is galloping', etc. – but then switches to the first.

2 N. V. Stankevich, 1813–40: see p. 11 and portrait of Pokorski in ch. VI of *Rudin*.

3 L. 25, to M. A. Bakunin and A. P. Efremov, 8–10 Sept. 1840.

4 Dostoevsky, at 17, was writing in similar terms to his elder brother, Mikhail: 'philosophy is poetry, only in its highest degree' (31 Oct./12 Nov. 1838). The concepts and language of German Idealist philosophy were in the air.

5 L. 3569, to M. A. Milyutina, 6 Mar. 1875.

6 L. 646, to A. N. Apukhtin, 11 Oct. 1858.

7 This is the title of a work by Turgenev's friend, P. V. Annenkov, dealing with Russian literary history in the period 1838–48 – the period which saw the rise to significance of Turgenev, Goncharov, Dostoevsky, Herzen, Grigorovich, Saltykov, under the critical aegis of Belinsky.

8 Most biographers give the difference in age between Turgenev's parents as six years – a tradition that may well go back to Varvara Turgeneva herself. Turgenev, in a brief autobiography drafted at the end of 1871, published in 1872 and in a revised form in 1874 (*W*. xv, 204–5) wrote that his mother lived to the age of 70 and died in 1850. That would place her birth in 1780. The latest Soviet edition of Turgenev's *Works* adopts these dates, 1780–1850, presumably on more solid evidence than Turgenev's memory, which was quite unreliable for dates even in his own lifetime. Acceptance of the earlier dating carries with it the remarkable implication that Varvara Turgeneva gave birth to her illegitimate daughter at the age of 53.

9 The best and fullest account of the relationship between Turgenev and Pauline Viardot is still April Fitzlyon, *The Price of Genius: A Life of Pauline Viardot* (London and New York, 1964), although almost half of Turgenev's published letters to Pauline Viardot have appeared since it was written. Turgenev's beloved was much more than a great singer and actress. She was a great pianist, a gifted teacher, a composer and a remarkable personality who dazzled opera- and concert-goers in London, Paris, Madrid, Berlin, Vienna, Petersburg and Moscow, inspired Gounod and Massenet, was a friend of famous musicians, artists and poets, served as the prototype of George Sand's *Consuelo* – not to mention that she was an intelligent and cultured woman who read and spoke four or five languages.

10 L. 609, to P. V. Annenkov, 7 Apr. 1858: 'you know that it is nearly a year and a half since a demon entered into me in the shape of a bladder disorder and gnaws at me night and day'.

11 L. 582, to L. N. Tolstoy, 7 Dec. 1857: 'khot' vsë im otdam – a perestanu byt' "barinom"'.

12 L. 616, to D. Ya. Kolbasin, 20 Apr. 1858: '*ya gotov na vse zhertvy*'.

13 L. 1007, to Countess E. E. Lambert, 10 Dec. 1860.

14 L. 1011, to the same, 29 Dec. 1860.

15 André Mazon, *Manuscrits parisiens d'Ivan Tourguénev* (Paris, 1930), p. 61.

16 L. 2099, to Pauline Viardot, 2 July 1868 (in reference to Wagner's music which had finally won her approval): 'I feel it may be very fine [*beau*], but it is something different from what I have loved in the past and what I still love, and it will need some effort to uproot me from my position [*m'arracher à mon Standpunkt*]. I am not quite like Viardot, I can still do that, but not without effort [*l'effort est indispensable*], whereas *that other* art catches me up and carries me away like a wave.'

17 L. 4190, to Baroness Yuliya P. Vrevskaya, 7 Feb. 1877: 'Vy pishete, chto Vash "zhenski vek" proshël.' Vrevskaya had used the phrase in reference to herself.

18 Pelageya Turgeneva, known as Paulinette (little Pauline), was born of a brief liaison of Turgenev's with a seamstress in his mother's house, in 1842. He discovered or rediscovered the child's existence in 1850 and sent her to France to Pauline Viardot, who had offered to bring her up with her own daughter, Louise. In the event, the two girls did not get on together, so Paulinette had to be sent to boarding-school and Turgenev's hopes that she would serve to draw him and Pauline Viardot closer together were disappointed. When Turgenev returned to France in 1856, he found a tall, gawky girl of 14, 'absurdly' resembling him in features but unable to speak a word of Russian. When she had finished her schooling, he engaged an English widow – a Mrs Innis – as governess or chaperone and took a flat in Paris for them, which he shared with them at times. He also sent them travelling on the Continent to round off his girl's education. Paulinette apparently loved him (she kept all his letters, even the most unflattering, and brought up her daughter to revere his memory); but she and he had nothing in common, she was jealous of Pauline Viardot, and, although Turgenev in his letters (too often redolent of the Victorian father) kept assuring her of his affection, he ended up owning to himself that not love but only a sense of duty had been at the core of his relationship with her. From the time she left school his only thought was to marry her off; but she rejected a number of suitors before accepting Gaston Bruère, the manager of a provincial glass factory, in her twenty-third year. The marriage was happy at first and, after several miscarriages, she gave birth to a daughter, Jeanne, in 1872, and a son, Georges, in 1875.

19 L. 1419, to Pauline Viardot, 14, 15 Jan. 1864: 'Je me fais l'effet d'un homme qui rêve: je ne puis m'habituer à l'idée que je suis si loin de Bade, et les personnes et les objets passent devant moi, sans avoir l'air de me toucher.'

20 L. 2586, to the same, 5 Dec. 1870: 'votre absence me cause une anxiété physique – c'est comme si l'air me manquait...'; cf. L. 2682, to M. V. Avdeev: 'this attachment has grown to be a part of my life [*sroslas' s moeyu zhizn'yu*], and without it I should be as if without air'.

21 Z. 113, 22 July 1862.

22 Z. 42, to Pauline Viardot, 18 June 1862.

23 Z. 43, to the same, 9 Aug. 1862.

24 When she is sixteen, he writes to Pauline Viardot (L. 2097, 29 June
    1868): 'I positively worship that enchanting being [i.e., Didie] . . . ; I
    now have a little altar in my temple next to the great altar.'
25 GZ. 125, 29 Mar. 1869.
26 Z. 116, 19 Jan. 1870.
27 Z. 119, 24 June 1873 and Z. 120, 5(?) July 1873.
28 Now he can hug as well as kiss her (Z. 122, 25 May 1874 and *passim*),
    can kiss not only her hands and forehead and eyes and cheeks, but her
    feet (GZ. 133, 30 June 1877, GZ. 137, 9 Sept. 1877) and her mouth
    (Z. 137, 11 June 1880; GZ. 145, 19 June 1882). The kisses become big,
    fat kisses [*Schmatz*]: Z. 136, 6 May 1880. When he returns from Russia
    after her confinement, he must find her looking as pretty as a picture,
    and she must turn his head – enough to make her husband really jealous
    (GZ. 132, 13 June 1877).
29 By means of literary readings, at Pauline's parties and elsewhere. The
    Russian Reading Room founded and endowed by such activities lived
    on until closed by the Germans during the Second World War.
30 L. 5022, to P. L. Lavrov, 27 Nov. 1879.
31 L. 4911, to Gustave Flaubert, 7 Aug. 1879: he is 'very well', but his soul
    is a cesspool.
32 L. 2242, to A. A. Fet, 2 Mar. 1869.
33 L. 6079, to Dr L. B. Bertenson, 3 Jan. 1883: 'ya sovershenno spokoino
    smotryu chërtu v glaza [. . .] No povtoryayu, niskol'ko ne unyvayu.'
34 L. 6149, to P. V. Annenkov, 7 Apr. 1883.
35 Not counting the sketch, 'Une fin', dictated, mainly in French, to
    Pauline Viardot about a fortnight before his death.
36 Mariya Savina, a gifted young actress, who in 1879 revived *A Month in
    the Country*. Turgenev saw her in it, as Vera, and was enchanted by her
    rendering of the part – and by her. She represented the last of a series of
    amitiés amoureuses in which he had sought to supplement the deficien-
    cies of his relationship with Pauline: in the first half of the fifties – Ol'ga
    Turgeneva and Countess Mar'ya Tolstaya (sister of L. N. Tolstoy); in
    the second half of the fifties and first half of the sixties – M. A.
    Markovich (pen-name – Marko Vovchok) and Countess E. E.
    Lambert; Baroness Yuliya P. Vrevskaya in the mid-seventies; Mariya
    G. Savina 1879–83. None of these relationships was purely epistolary;
    Turgenev and Savina met both in Russia and in France.
37 But Dostoevsky, unlike Turgenev, died in the government's good
    graces.
38 Edmond and Jules de Goncourt, *Journal: Mémoires de la vie littéraire,
    1864–78* (Paris, 1956), under 28 Feb. 1863.
39 L. 3398, to Henry James, 7 Aug. 1874: 'Truth compels me to say [. . .]
    that I have large hands and feet, an ugly nose – and nothing of an
    "aristocratic" temperament – and I don't regret it.'
40 N. A. Ostrovskaya in *I. S. Turgenev v vospominaniyakh sovremenni-
    kov* (Moscow, 1969), vol. II, p. 63.

41 E. Ardov (= Elena Blaramberg), *ibid.* (1983), p. 165.
42 Edmond and Jules de Goncourt, *Journal*, under 2 Mar. 1872.
43 *Ibid.*, under 5 Mar. 1876.
44 Gustave Flaubert to Turgenev, 24 or 31 Mar. 1863, *Correspondance* in *Œuvres Complètes*, vol. xiv (Paris, 1975).
45 L. 1190, to Countess E. E. Lambert, 14 Mar. 1862.
46 L. 145, to Pauline Viardot, 29 Jan.–3 Feb. 1851 (under 30 Jan.) on his headlong flight from the ovation at the theatre after the staging of his play, *The Provincial Lady*; and L. 1785, to the same, 4 Apr. 1867; 'Je dois ajouter que faire une lecture est une vraie corvée pour moi. Je ne puis m'empêcher d'avoir un secret sentiment de honte.'
47 L. 1425, to Pauline Viardot, 28–29 Jan. 1864.
48 Ludwig Pietsch, *Wie ich Schriftsteller geworden bin* (Berlin, 1883). Pietsch was an artist as well as a man of letters, so his portrayal of Turgenev at their first meeting may be worth citing (as a Western view of Turgenev in the forties to complement the Russian views of Turgenev in the seventies): 'His head was particularly striking: it was a head such as I had never seen before and was never likely to forget. His face was unmistakably Russian. It had prominent cheekbones and was dominated by a nobly formed forehead and powerful nose. His head was covered with thick and rather long brown hair, parted on the right side. Thick, almost black eyebrows overshadowed his greenish-brown eyes, curiously melancholy and soft and set wide apart. A short brown mustache covered his slightly pouting upper lip. His cheeks and finely-chiselled chin were clean-shaven.'
49 D. V. Grigorovich, 'Literaturnye vospominaniya', 1892–3, ch. xiv in *I. S. Turgenev v vospominaniyakh sovremennikov*, vol. i.
50 L. 113, to Pauline Viardot, 11–14 Aug. 1849 (under 12 Aug).
51 For example, L. 42, to Aleksei Bakunin, 16 Feb. 1843. When Mikhail Bakunin, the friend of his youth, after more than twelve years of prison and exile, escaped from Siberia and turned up in London at the end of 1861, Turgenev not only contributed handsomely to a pension for him but exerted himself to secure the return of Bakunin's wife from Siberia to European Russia.
52 L. 6168, to L. N. Tolstoy, 11 July 1883.

2 POETRY, PLAYS, CRITICISM

1 L. 8, to A. V. Nikitenko, 7 Apr. 1837.
2 L. 3523, to M. V. Avdeev, 11 Jan. 1875.
3 M. Yu. Lermontov, 'Pervoe yanvarya', 1840: 'I derzko brosit' im v glaza zhelezny stikh, / Oblity gorech'yu i zlost'yu!'
4 'The Crowd' (Tolpa), 1844, lines 15–18, 23–8.
5 A. S. Pushkin, 'To the Poet' (Poetu), 1830: 'Ty tsar': zhivi odin.'
6 Pushkin, 'The Poet and the Crowd' (Poet i tolpa), 1828: 'Tebe by pol'zy vsë ... V razvrate kameneite smelo [. . .] Dlya vashei gluposti i zloby.'

Nor is there any contradiction between these two poems and God's admonition to the prophet, in 'The Prophet' (Prorok), 1826: 'And kindle with thy word the hearts of men.' Men are those who have hearts that can be kindled by his word; the crowd consists, by definition, of 'eunuchs in heart': *my serdtsem khladnye skoptsy.*

7 'The Crowd':
 Mne inogda smeshny zabavy ikh . . .
 Mne samomu smeshnei moi stradan'ya.

8 L. 2667, to M. A. Milyutina, 27 Apr. 1871.

9 Pushkin, e.g., 'The Beauty' (Krasavitsa), 1832; Lermontov, e.g., 'To M. A. Shcherbatova', 1840.

10 Pushkin, e.g., 'I loved you . . .' (Ya vas lyubil . . .), 1829; Lermontov, e.g., 'A Prayer' (Molitva), 1837.

11 'The Country' (Derevnya), VII, lines 17–18, published 1847.

12 It is traditional to say that the word *poshlost'* is untranslatable, combining in itself the associations of such English words as 'banality', 'triviality', 'mediocrity', 'vulgarity'. *Poshlost'* is the quintessence of the most banal and vulgar aspects of everyday life.

13 L. 141, to Pauline Viardot, 13–21 Dec. 1850 (under 20 Dec.).

14 Preface to the volume of his plays in the 1869 edition of his *Collected Works* (VII): *W.* III, 245.

15 *The Bachelor* (*Kholostyak*), written, published and staged 1849; *The Provincial Lady* (*Provintsialka*), written 1850, published and staged 1851.

16 *An Imprudence* (*Neostorozhnost'*), 1843; *Moneyless* (*Bezdenezh'e*), 1846; *A Chain is as Strong as its Weakest Link* (*Gde tonko, tam i rvëtsya*), 1848; *Conversation on a Highway* (*Razgovor na bol'shoi doroge*), written 1850, published 1851.

17 *The Parasite* (*Nakhlebnik*), 1848, published 1857.

18 *Breakfast with the Marshal of the Nobility* (*Zavtrak u predvoditelya*), 1849, published 1856.

19 *A Month in the Country* (*Mesyats v derevne*), 1850, published 1855.

20 *A Chain is as Strong as its Weakest Link*, 1848, staged 1851.

21 *Moneyless*, 1846, staged 1852.

22 *The Parasite*, 1848, staged 1862.

23 *A Month in the Country*, 1850, staged 1872.

24 L. P. Grossman, 'Teatr Turgeneva' (1924), in *Sobranie sochineni*, vol. III (Moscow, 1928), pp. 137–41 and 152–68, esp. 160–6.

25 Prosper Mérimée, *Théâtre de Clara Gazul* (Paris, 1825), enlarged edition, 1830, third edition, 1842.

26 Alfred de Musset, *Comédies et proverbes* (Paris, 1840); first published 1834 as the second instalment of *Spectacle dans un fauteuil*, with only six of the later ten titles.

27 Grossman ('Teatr Turgeneva', pp. 142–51) seeks to link them with the French *comédie-vaudeville*, but does not indicate what characteristics they share with that type of play that are not to be found in Gogol.

28 Grossman, *ibid.*, p. 191, n. 1 (cited *W.* III, 447, n. 1), points out that

the setting of a coach travelling on the highway had been used by Scribe in his vaudeville, *Le Tête-à-tête*.

29 The play was originally intended for an actress with a good singing voice, but as the part was later played by actresses who did not sing, the aria was sung by the Count and accompanied on the piano by the actress.

30 Female characters such as Kaurova, Odintsova (in *Fathers and Children*), Polozova (in 'Spring Torrents') are not 'Turgenev heroines' in the commonly accepted sense.

31 Grossman, 'Teatr Turgeneva', pp. 161–2, suggests an affinity between Gorski and Octave in Musset's *Les Caprices de Marianne*. This is tenuous, though not altogether fanciful. Octave is a projection of one aspect of his author, as is the protagonist – also called Octave – of Musset's novel, *Confession d'un enfant du siècle* (1836), which certainly influenced Lermontov's *A Hero of Our Time*. But there are quite profound differences between the Octave of the novel and Pechorin and between the Octave of the play and Gorski.

32 On Onegin and Pechorin see F. F. Seeley, 'The Heyday of the "Superfluous Man" in Russia', *Slavonic and East European Review* (December 1952), hereafter referred to as 'Seeley, 1952'.

33 Another 'untranslatable' term. The dictionary gives 'daily round', 'everyday life', 'mode of life'.

34 Cf. Balzac's 'La Femme de trente ans', 1828–44.

35 As the censors actually insisted on making the protagonist of *A Month in the Country*.

36 Written, published and staged in 1849.

37 Peter the Great had divided the civil service into fourteen ranks, corresponding to ranks in the armed forces (the fourteenth being the lowest). The Bachelor, Moshkin, is eighth rank, Vilitski, tenth, about to be promoted, and von Fonk ninth.

38 His name shows that he is of German descent and with pretensions to nobility. The Baltic (and other) Germans, who occupied a disproportionately high number of places in the Russian administration, were widely unpopular and figure frequently as a butt of Russian writers: e.g. Klüber in Turgenev's 'Spring Torrents', the general commanding Orenburg in Pushkin's *The Captain's Daughter* and, with unforgettable savagery, the German generals in Tolstoy's *War and Peace*.

39 This formula, derived from the title of Dostoevsky's 1861 novel, is traditionally translated 'the insulted and injured'.

40 Grossman, 'Teatr Turgeneva', pp. 179–81; V. V. Vinogradov, 'Turgenev i shkola molodogo Dostoevskogo', *Russkaya literatura*, no. 2 (1959), cited *W*. II, 605.

41 Written 1848, published 1857, staged 1862.

42 It would be interesting to know whether Pirandello ever saw *The Parasite* on the stage and was inspired by it in writing his early comedy *Tutto per bene*.

43 There is vagueness or contradiction concerning the age at which she left home. In the first exchanges between Kuzovkin and Ivanov it is said that she has been gone about six years and was then about 14. But not only is this hard to reconcile with Ol'ga's initial failure to recognize Kuzovkin and her having forgotten his patronymic but it is at variance with the rest of the chronology (Korin, her putative father, died before she was born, his widow survived him only a few years and after her death the child went to live with her aunt) and with the fact that Kuzovkin played at dolls with her and that Tropachëv remembers her as 'so high'. So, apart from the early mention of '6 years' and 'barely 14', the impression in the rest of the play is that Ol'ga left home as a young child.

44 Kuzovkin is only 50; but Turgenev considered himself old at 50 and in his letters constantly refers to 50 as the beginning of old age.

45 'Show' is to be read here in a purely neutral sense – with no implication of insincerity.

46 It would be unfair to criticize Turgenev for not exploring in Pirandellian fashion how she had reacted to the shock of the changed vision of herself in the world. But do we not deserve some indication of how she had come from her vision of Kuzovkin as a poor dependant to acceptance of him as her father?

47 The first version of the play was written in 1848–50, so antedates *An Evening in Sorrento*. But in 1855 it was published in a form radically mutilated by the censorship (with the protagonist forcibly transformed into a widow); when Turgenev prepared the play for inclusion in the 1869 edition of his *Works*, he restored the part of the husband and most (but not all) of the 1850 text: so that both the 1855 torso and the canonical 1869 restoration are later than *An Evening in Sorrento*.

48 'Teatr Turgeneva', pp. 169–81.

49 Honoré de Balzac, *La Marâtre*, written in the spring of 1848 and staged in the summer of that year. It was Balzac's first successful play and has been seen as blazing the trail for the 'theatre of Realism'. Turgenev was in Paris at the time and must have seen it.

50 This does not hold for the secondary characters: the doctor is a minor centre of activity.

51 The emotional *agōn* between Natal'ya Petrovna and her husband is kept in the background and never fully developed.

52 In his Act II colloquy with Rakitin. In the original version the reference to Belinsky, though covert, was unequivocal; by the late 1860s this had lost its 'actuality', so is slurred in the final version: what remains is that Belyaev is interested in progressive ideas (*W.* III, 408–9).

53 This exception is *An Evening in Sorrento* which, as has been suggested, is something like a skit on *A Month in the Country*. *The Parasite* might appear to be another exception; but although Ol'ga evidently loves her husband and believes he loves her, the reader (or spectator) is unlikely to think him capable of love.

54 *Turgenev i Savina* (Petrograd, 1918), p. 77: cited in *W.* III, 406.
55 'sam stanovish'sya melkim': Act II in the soliloquy following his colloquy with Natal'ya Petrovna.
56 'ya ne lovelas' ('I am no Lovelace').
57 Act V, just before the last entrance of Shpigel'ski.
58 Act I: 'sniskhoditel'ny, laskovy, postoyanny'.
59 *Ibid.*: 'ya khochu, chtoby *vy* khoteli'.
60 Act V, colloquy with Belyaev.
61 She and Rakitin are on stage, respectively, 64 per cent and 57 per cent of the playing time, as compared with 34 per cent for Belyaev, 27 per cent for Vera, 10 per cent for Islaev.
62 Act IV, near the end: den' ob''yasneni. Properly 'ob''yasnenie' means 'explanation', 'accounting', 'having things out', '(love) declaration'. 'Day of declarations' might be a more faithful rendering, if an inadequate one.
63 Act III: 'On eë ne lyubit. Ya spokoina!'
64 He might have taken as epigraph to the play Vergil's 'Improbe Amor, quid non mortalia pectora cogis!' (Unconscionable Love, / to what dire lengths you drive poor human hearts!, *Aeneid*, IV, 412). It is clear from 'Spring Torrents' that Book IV of the *Aeneid* remained fresh and productive in his memory even at a much later date.
65 L. 4195, to M. M. Stasyulevich, 9 Feb. 1877.
66 Gustave Flaubert, *Correspondance*, in *Œuvres complètes*, XIV (Paris, 1975), letter to George Sand, 28 Jan. 1872.
67 E.g., in the review article on N. Kukol'nik's five-act tragedy, *General-poruchik Patkul'* (Lieutenant-general Patkul') (1847), *W.* I, 272–98.
68 Review of F. Miller's translation of Schiller's *Wilhelm Tell*, *W.* I, 207.
69 Review of M. Vronchenko's translation of pt I and paraphrase of part II of Goethe's *Faust* (1845), *W.* I, 214–56.
70 L. 270, to S. A. Miller, 24 Oct. 1853: 'That youth and freshness, that life seemingly steeped in eternally laughing sunlight, all the enchantment of poetry at its first appearance on the lips of an immortal and happy breed.'
71 Johann Heinrich Voss, *Homers Ilias und Odyssee*, first published 1780. Turgenev owned the fifth, revised edition of 1833.
72 L. 3241, to Ya. P. Polonsky, 10 Dec. 1873.
73 Edmond and Jules de Goncourt, *Journal* (Paris, 1956) under 2 Mar. 1872: 'Tourguéneff, laissant échapper tout son enthousiasme pour ce comique, pour ce père du rire, pour cette faculté qu'il place si haut et qu'il n'accorde qu'à deux ou trois hommes dans l'humanité.'
74 L. 74, to Pauline Viardot, 25 Dec. 1847.
75 L. 112, to the same, 4–9 Aug. 1848, under 6 Aug.: 'factice et froide.'
76 L. 3180, to Julian Schmidt, 29 Aug. 1873.
77 L. 3183, to A. A. Fet, 2 Sept. 1873.
78 L. 3200, to the same, 25 Sept. 1873.
79 I have checked my impressions against the research of N. Kauchts-

chischwili, 'I. S. Turgenev e l'Italia', in *Miscellanea Turgeneviana* (Bergamo, 1877), and was glad to find we were in substantial agreement on the points just made.

80 LL. 73 and 74, to Pauline Viardot, 19 and 25 Dec. 1847: 'the greatest of Catholic poets, as Shakespeare is the greatest of [. . .] anti-Christian poets'.

81 L. 510, to L. N. Tolstoy, 15 Jan. 1857.

82 L. 6215/2187a, to Jacob Caro, 26 Dec. 1868.

83 L. 79, to Pauline Viardot, 29 Apr–2 May 1848, under 30 Apr. But Calderón may have made a deeper, if less lasting, impression.

84 L. 67, to Pauline Viardot, 19–20 Nov. 1847.

85 L. 3600, to P. V. Annenkov, 13 Apr. 1875, on the lack of poetry and fantasy, and L. 3779, to M. E. Saltykov, 7 Dec. 1875, on the 'stink of literariness'.

86 L. 6025, to M. M. Stasyulevich, 24 Nov. 1882.

87 L. 3078, to A. A. Fet, 5 Mar. 1873; L. 4629, to Julian Schmidt, 13 Oct. 1878.

88 L. 3302, to M. M. Stasyulevich, 27 Mar. 1874.

89 L. 169, to Pauline Viardot, 4–7 Mar. 1852.

90 L. 2700, to A. A. Fet, 14 July 1871.

91 L. 4924, to E. Ya. Kolbasin, 17, 26 Aug. 1879.

92 L. 2957, to P. V. Annenkov, 17 Oct 1872.

93 L. 2212, to the same, 24 Jan. 1869; L. 2218, to A. A. Fet, 25 Jan. 1869.

94 L. 5350, to P. V. Annenkov, 13 Jan. 1881.

95 L. 5204, to Vs. Garshin, 26 June 1880.

96 L. 5984, to L. N. Tolstoy, 31 Oct. 1882.

97 L. 1968, to Ya. P. Polonsky, 25 Jan. 1868.

98 L. 347, to A. A. Fet, 18 Apr. 1855. These should not be taken as empty compliments: Turgenev could be ruthlessly frank in criticizing particular works of these and other friends in his letters to them.

99 Although it is not usual to make this distinction, obviously over-estimation is as much a departure from 'justice' as under-estimation.

100 Novalis, Kleist, E. T. A. Hoffmann; Wordsworth, Coleridge, Shelley, Keats. But he continued to quote Byron, the hero of his youth; and there are occasional mentions of the German Romantics by characters in his fiction and plays.

101 There is a scathing reference (L. 2972, to Ya. P. Polonsky, 29 Oct. 1872) to a Russian translation of Musset's *Rolla*, but it is not clear how much of the condemnation refers to the translation, how much to the original.

102 Pen-name of Johann Paul Friedrich Richter, 1763–1825.

103 L. 270, to S. A. Miller, 24 Oct. 1853.

104 L. 3704, to V. V. Stasov, 5 Sept. 1875.

105 *Les Misérables* (1862): L. 1648, to P. V. Annenkov, 12 Mar. 1866; *William Shakespeare* (1864): LL. 1470 and 1490, to Valentine Deles-

sert, 14 May and 28 July 1864; *Les Travailleurs de la mer* (1866): L. 1661, to P. V. Annenkov, 24 Apr. 1866 and L. 1692, to I. P. Borisov, 7 Sept. 1866; *Quatrevingt-treize* (1874): L. 3299, to A. F. Onegin, 20 Mar. 1874 and L. 3320, to P. V. Annenkov, 16 Apr. 1874. If he had any comments on *L'Homme qui rit* (1869), the relevant letters have been lost.

106 *Chansons des rues et des bois* (1865): L. 1630, to Th. Storm, 30 Nov. 1865 and L. 1631, to P. V. Annenkov, 10–11 Dec. 1865; *La Légende des siècles*, second series (1877): L. 4217, to Henry James, 28 Feb. 1877 and L. 4220, to Ya. P. Polonsky, 2–5 Mar. 1877.

107 'sochinitel'stvo': see above, p. 78.

108 L. 5987, to P. I. Veinberg, 3 Nov. 1882.

109 L. 273, to P. V. Annenkov, 31 Oct. 1853; cf. L. 1623, to A. A. Fet, 22 Oct. 1865.

110 L. 506, to S. T. Aksakov, 8 Jan. 1857 and L. 3384, to Gustave Flaubert, 12 July 1874.

111 L. 5945, to M. E. Saltykov, 6 Oct. 1882 and L. 5946, to P. V. Annenkov, 7 Oct. 1882, building on N. K. Mikhailovsky's article 'A Cruel Talent'.

112 As a devout anti-Romantic, Turgenev religiously eschewed the term 'genius' in reference to living writers and regularly used 'talent' instead, differentiating genius from talent by qualifiers like 'of the first order' and similar phrases.

113 L. 3293, to A. A. Fet, 16 Mar. 1874.

114 L. 5565, to Ludwig Pietsch, 10 Nov. 1881.

115 L. 4259, to F. M. Dostoevsky, 9 Apr. 1877.

116 L. 3399, to Henry James (Sr.), 10 Aug. 1874.

117 As late as 1857 Turgenev was still accusing himself of dilettantism (the opposite of professionalism): L. 578, to Countess E. E. Lambert, 15 Nov. 1857.

118 L. 3978, to V. L. Kign, 28 June 1876.

119 L. 4174, to E. V. L'vova, 23 Jan. 1877: 'Scribitur ad narrandum, non ad probandum' (One writes to narrate, not to prove something); cf. the admonition to German writers in L. 4189, to Ludwig Pietsch, 4 Feb. 1877: 'Meidet den *Fingerzeig*' (Don't *point*).

120 L. 6199/1191a, to M. N. Zubova, 18 Mar. 1862.

121 Turgenev acknowledged with regret that he had occasionally lapsed into subjectivity, notably in 'Enough': L. 4560, to M. M. Stasyulevich, 20 May 1878.

122 L. 4171, to E. V. L'vova, 22 Jan. 1877: 'Beregite chistotu yazyka, kak svyatynyu.'

123 L. 3657, to S. A. Vengerov, 6 June 1875 and L. 5297, to Ludwig Pietsch, 21 Nov. 1880.

124 L. 4816, to M. Necheles, 16 Apr. 1879.

125 L. 2430, to P. V. Annenkov, 1 Jan. 1870.

126 L. 4816, to M. Necheles, 16 Apr. 1879.

127 L. 6037, to Sidney Jerrold, 2 Dec. 1882.
128 See the challenging article by A. P. Chudakov, 'O poetike Turgeneva-prozaika' in *I. S. Turgenev v sovremennon mire* (Moscow, 1987), pp. 240–66.

3 FIRST STORIES

1 'Andrei Kolosov' (1844); 'Three Portraits' (Tri portreta: 1845, published 1846); 'The Duellist' (Bretër: 1846, published 1847); 'The Jew' (Zhid: 1846, published 1847); 'Petushkov' (1847, published 1848).
2 'Mumu' (1852, published 1854); 'The Inn' (Postoyaly dvor: 1852, published 1855).
3 'Diary of a Superfluous Man' (Dnevnik lishnego cheloveka: 1850).
4 'A Hamlet of the Shchigry District' (Gamlet shchigrovskogo uezda: 1848, published 1849).
5 Pushkin in his *Tales of Belkin* (1831) and Gogol in his *Evenings on a Farm near Dikan'ka* (vol. I, 1831; vol. II, 1832) introduced 'editors' (Belkin, Pan'ko) who had heard the tales from different narrators and published or prepared to publish them. Belkin died suddenly before he could publish; his intention was carried out by an anonymous metropolitan man of letters. Lermontov took a further step by introducing the future editor of the stories that were later to evolve into the novel *A Hero of Our Time* as a character, who hears the first story from a narrator who had taken part in it and then, in the second story, witnesses the meeting between the narrator of the first story and its protagonist (Pechorin, the protagonist of the whole novel).
6 In two of the three, the narrator of the main story is one of its principal personages; in the third, he has taken no part in it.
7 See n. 54 to ch. 2 above.
8 N. K. Krupskaya, 'Detstvo i rannyaya yunost' Il'icha', first published in *Bol'shevik*, no. 12 (1938); cited from *W.* v, 548.
9 Written not later than 1845 and published at the beginning of 1846. So it antedates 'The Duellist', written in 1846 and published at the beginning of 1847, although in all editions of Turgenev's *Works* – both in his lifetime and since – it has appeared in third place, that is, after 'The Duellist'.
10 V. G. Belinsky, 'Peterburgski sbornik' in *Otechestvennye zapiski* (1846), no. 3: cited from Belinsky, *Sobranie sochineni v trëkh tomakh* (Moscow, 1948)), vol. III, p. 86.
11 Summarized in *W.* v, 563–4.
12 Of course, Kolosov differs from Luchinov in having 'a sense of honour': he does not seduce Varya; if her heart breaks, that is not his fault.
13 The 'Byronic hero' was first popularized in Pushkin's 'Southern' poems (*The Captive of the Caucasus*, 1822; *The Fountain of Bakhchisarai*, 1824; *The Gypsies*, 1827); but the somewhat tenuous heroes, especially of the first two, were soon overshadowed, if not eclipsed, by

the eponymous hero of *Evgeni Onegin*, 'a novel in verse' in eight chapters (1825–32), whose affinities are not with Byron's 'Eastern' poems but with his *Don Juan*. For the relationships between Onegin, Pechorin, Turgenev's Rudin, see Seeley, 1952, and for the continuation of the line in Goncharov's Oblomov, Seeley, 'Oblomov', *Slavonic and East European Review* (July, 1976).

14 As noted by several Russian critics: see *W.* v, 558, citing an allusion to Luchkov in a letter of Chekhov dated 6 Feb. 1898.

15 Vsë v komnate Fëdora Fëdorovicha dyshalo poryadkom i chistotoi (Everything in Kister's room was redolent of order and cleanness – or purity: 'chistota' means both).

16 Turgenev uses not the neutral term *evrei* but the derogatory *zhid*.

17 Cf. the references to Jews in Stankevich's letters to his family during his journey from his home to Berlin in 1837: N. V. Stankevich, *Perepiska 1830–40*, edited and published by Aleksei Stankevich (Moscow, 1914).

18 Nekrasov was the editor of the journal in which 'Petushkov' was to appear. Turgenev wrote from abroad (L. 68, to V. G. Belinsky, 26 Nov. 1847) requesting Belinsky to read the proofs, mark any feeble passages, and ask Nekrasov to improve them in a few words – 'for instance, to make it *clear* that Vasilisa became his lover, etc., etc.'

19 In this he is certainly mistaken: Vasilisa was not yet ready to give up enjoying herself and settle down.

20 Written December 1851 or January 1852, published February 1852.

21 See *W.* v, 590–3.

22 Quoted *W.* v, 591.

23 Gabriele D'Annunzio, *Laudi del cielo, del mare, della terra e degli eroi* (Milan, 1928), bk I, 'L'Annunzio', p. 11.

4 SERFS AND SERF-OWNERS: *A SPORTSMAN'S SKETCHES*

1 The title *Zapiski okhotnika* has been variously translated: 'zapiski' as 'notes', 'notebook', 'memoirs', or (more loosely) 'sketches'; 'okhotnika' as 'sportsman's/of a sportsman', 'huntsman's/of a huntsman', etc. So, too, the titles of some of the sketches have been englished in different ways: 'Bezhin Lea', 'Kasyan from Fair Strath', 'The Burgomaster' and 'The Steward' (*Burmistr*), 'The Werewolf', 'The Singers', 'The Meeting', 'Rattle of Wheels'.

2 *The Contemporary* was founded by Pushkin in 1836; on his death, at the beginning of 1837, it was taken over by his friend Pletnëv and eked out a comparatively undistinguished existence for a decade till it was acquired by Nekrasov and Panaev, who enlisted the services of Belinsky and made it Russia's foremost left-wing journal; it was closed down by the government in 1866.

3 Four published in May, two in October 1847, six more in February 1848; the thirteenth, 'Two Landowners', could not pass the censors and appeared only in 1852, in the book.

4 'Raspberry Water', 'The District Doctor', 'The Lone Wolf', published February 1849.

5 'The Singing Match' and 'The Tryst', published November 1850.

6 'Bezhin Meadow' and 'Kas'yan from Krasivaya Mecha', published in February and March of 1851.

7 The first edition sold out in the first quarter of 1853 (L. 246, to I. F. Minitsky, 24 May 1853, cited W. IV, 505).

8 'The District Doctor', 'My Neighbour Radilov', 'Lebedyan'', 'Tat'yana Borisovna and Her Nephew', 'Pëtr Petrovich Karataev', 'A Hamlet of the Shchigry District', 'Chertopkhanov and Nedopyuskin'. In 'The District Doctor' interest may be divided between the narrator (who is not a member of the gentry, but not a serf or peasant either) and the dying girl. In 'Karataev' it might be argued that the story pivots on the serf-owner's refusal to let Matrëna marry Karataev; in fact, events might have followed much the same course if the girl had been the old lady's daughter or ward.

9 'Khor' and Kalinych', 'Bezhin Meadow', 'Kas'yan from Krasivaya Mecha', 'The Lone Wolf', 'The Singing Match', 'The Tryst'. Only in the first of these does a landowner figure significantly. A stricter classification might assign this sketch, together with 'Karataev', to a separate category, in which serfdom does figure but the portraits (of the two serfs and of the landowner respectively) are the central components.

10 'Ermolai and the Miller's Wife', 'Raspberry Water', 'The Freeholder Ovsyanikov', 'L'gov', 'The Bailiff', 'The Estate Office', 'Two Land-owners'.

11 See no. 8 above.

12 Robert Browning, 'The Statue and the Bust'.

13 The exceptions are 'Lebedyan'' and (in respect of the nephew) 'Tat'yana Borisovna and Her Nephew'.

14 The differences in cultural level are signalled by differences in speech styles which will be blurred, if not lost, in translation. Radilov's limitations are conveyed, with Turgenev's usual discretion, by his mispronunciation of Voltaire's name. Karataev probably (at least, till he came to Moscow), and the doctor almost certainly, would not even have heard of Voltaire.

15 At the highest level of abstraction this might be translated as 'satirical', though Gogol's satire is as distinctive as Swift's or Voltaire's.

16 In 'Khor' and Kalinych', 'Pëtr Petrovich Karataev' and 'Chertopkha-nov and Nedopyuskin', which deviate from the norm in other ways too.

17 This is known to have been the case with a couple of other sketches: 'Raspberry Water' and 'A Hamlet of the Shchigry District'.

18 In 'Darling' (Dushechka), 1898 – a masterpiece of ambiguity such that Tolstoy could see her as an ideal of womanhood, a view probably shared by only a minority of readers. For a non-Tolstoyan appraisal see F. F. Seeley, 'On Interpersonal Relations in Chekhov's Fiction',

Annali dell'Istituto Universitario Orientale (sezione slava) (Naples, 1972), pp. 59–90 (65–6).

19 V. A. Kovalëv, *Zapiski okhotnika I. S. Turgeneva* (Leningrad, 1980), p. 51.

20 The 'men of the forties' – Turgenev's liberal generation – were to be counterposed later to 'the men of the sixties' – the generation of radicals and nihilists. On the genesis and evolution of the superfluous man, see Seeley, 1952.

21 *'Kruzhok'* (plural *'kruzhki'*), diminutive of *krug* = circle: a small circle or group of people united by common interests. In the 1830s and later, such *kruzhki* of (mainly) university students united in the pursuit of self-improvement through study of philosophy and political theory. The most famous *kruzhki* are those of Stankevich (which included Belinsky and Bakunin) and of Herzen and Ogarëv. For a very different view of the *kruzhok* (based on that of Stankevich) see ch. VI of *Rudin*.

22 The word here translated 'proud' is *samolyubivy*, the adjective corresponding to the noun *samolyubie*, which is a calque of the French *amour-propre* (which has no corresponding adjective). But *samolyubie* corresponds only loosely to 'pride' or *amour-propre*.

23 On Turgenev's idiosyncratic view of Don Quixote, expounded in his 1860 article 'Hamlet and Don Quixote', see Introduction and ch. 6 above.

24 And probably the contractors in 'Death' and 'The Singing Match'.

25 From *snokha* = daughter-in-law: denotes incestuous relationships between the head of the household and his sons' wives.

26 A *strannik* (wanderer) perhaps with leanings towards the Old Believer sect of *stranniki* or *beguny* (runners); see *W*. IV, 556, quoting N. L. Brodsky, *I. S. Turgenev i russkie sektanty* (Moscow, 1922). Compare with Kas'yan the *strannik* Makar in Dostoevsky's novel *The Adolescent* (*Podrostok*, also rendered as *The Raw Youth*).

27 Cf. Leskov's 'The Make-up Artist' (or 'The Toupée Artist': 'Tupeiny khudozhnik').

28 Peter Kropotkin, *Memoirs of a Revolutionist* (New York, 1971), ch. VIII, p. 57 (first published 1898–9).

29 Review of S. T. Aksakov's *Notes of an Orenburg Sportsman* (*Zapiski ruzheinogo okhotnika Orenburgskoi gubernii*), *W*. V, 414.

30 Though written in the last quarter of 1848 and first published February 1849.

31 In 'Death'.

32 At the beginning of 'Ermolai and the Miller's Wife'.

33 At the beginning of 'Bezhin Meadow'.

34 In 'Kas'yan from Krasivaya Mecha'.

35 At the beginning of 'The Tryst'.

36 At the beginning of 'Ermolai and the Miller's Wife'.

37 At the beginning of 'Bezhin Meadow'.

38 At the beginning of 'The Tryst'.

39 The Russian text here has a verbal adjective (participle): *k zasypayu-shchim verkhushkam*.

40 So N. Engel'gardt, 'Melodika Turgenevskoi prozy' in N. L. Brodsky (ed.), *Tvorcheski put' Turgeneva* (Petrograd, 1923).

41 See Brodsky, *ibid.*, the articles by A. S. Dolinin, 'Turgenev i Chekhov' and K. K. Istomin, 'Roman "Rudin": iz istorii turgenevskogo stilya'.

42 It will be recalled that in one sketch, 'The End of Chertopkhanov', the Sportsman is replaced by an anonymous omniscient narrator.

43 I owe some of the above points to A. M. Rybnikova, 'Odin iz priëmov kompozitsii u Turgeneva', in Brodsky (ed.), *Tvorcheski put' Turgeneva*.

44 'Bezhin Meadow', 'Kas'yan from Krasivaya Mecha', 'The Singing Match', 'The Tryst'.

45 'A Hamlet of the Shchigry District', 'Chertopkhanov and Nedo-pyuskin'.

46 In a letter to Annenkov dated 15 Feb. 1848: 'I couldn't understand a single word of "The District Doctor" and will therefore say nothing about it; my wife is crazy about it: that's women for you!' (cited *W.* IV, 545).

47 A passage such as the following can hardly be said to shed much light on the matter: 'For too long I have been endeavouring to extract the distilled essences – *triples extraits* – of human character, then pour them into little flasks and invite my respected readers to uncork and sniff them [on the plea]: "They do smell of Russian types, don't they?"' (L. 197, to P. V. Annenkov, 9 Nov. 1852).

48 Or, 'not subtilizing' (*ne koketnichayu i ne umnichayu*): L. 210, to I. S. Aksakov, 9 Jan. 1853.

49 L. 189, to P. V. Annenkov, 26, 30 Sept. 1852.

5 TRANSITION: THE END OF SERFDOM; THE 'SUPERFLUOUS MAN'

1 That is, of the 1852 volume, disregarding those added in the 1870s. Cf. L. 152, to E. M. Feoktistov, 14 Apr. 1851: 'I give you my word of honour that *A Sportsman's Sketches* have been terminated for ever.'

2 Parallel apart from the first (*An Imprudence*, published 1843, never staged) and the last (*An Evening in Sorrento*, written 1851–2, but neither published nor staged in his lifetime).

3 L. 161, to I. S. Aksakov, 16 Dec. 1851: 'the lack of any desire to write increases every day [...] It is not apathy, not tiredness – it is the waiting, the desire for real, substantive impressions.'

4 Belinsky had greeted most of his early stories with a kindly mention – but Belinsky was his friend. 'Three Portraits' had impressed Apollon Grigor'ev.

5 A 'productive' form is one which continues to generate fresh examples: in English the plural in -(e)s is productive, that in -en (children, oxen) unproductive.

6 The third of the thematic lines in *A Sportsman's Sketches*, namely, the portraits of serfs as individuals, survived only in 'Journey into the Woodland' (see pp. 132–6, above) and in 'Living Relics' (1874).

7 As reported by Turgenev's friend and translator, William Ralston, cited *W*. v, 505.

8 Specifically a *meshchanin* – a member of the class of small urban craftsmen and tradesmen.

9 On the later stories that hinge on a mystery apparently not reducible to chance, that is, unlike the mystery or chance underlying 'Three Meetings', see chapter 12, above.

10 Cf. Sofron, the Bailiff (admittedly, not a domestic serf, and so with much wider powers as a vizier or deputy of the master, to whom he too had made himself 'indispensable').

11 Compare the ending of 'Father Sergius', where the Prince is still elated at having been able to behave like – and indeed better than – a real beggar: neither he nor his author appears to suspect that pride is still at work in him.

12 See chapter 7.

13 Vasili Vasil'evich represents Nikolai Nikolaevich Turgenev, our author's uncle, Varvara Turgeneva's brother-in-law, who administered her estates for a number of years. Turgenev later made the mistake of reinstating him in that position and was shamelessly fleeced by him, yet very characteristically forgave him when he heard that his exploiter was blind and sick and alone.

14 See n. 6 above.

15 *Dnevnik lishnego cheloveka*, written 1848–50, published 1850.

16 An example from the last quarter of the eighteenth century, which could have been known to Turgenev, was Gilbert's* 'Adieux à la vie' which concludes:

Au banquet de la vie, infortuné convive,
    J'apparus un jour, et je meurs;
Je meurs, et sur ma tombe, où lentement j'arrive,
    Nul ne viendra verser des pleurs.

Salut, champs que j'aimais! et vous, douce verdure!
    Et vous, riant exil des bois!
Ciel, pavillon de l'homme, admirable nature,
    Salut pour la dernière fois!

Ah! puissent voir longtemps votre beauté sacrée
    Tant d'amis sourds à mes adieux!
Qu'ils meurent pleins de jours, que leur mort soit pleurée,
    Qu'un ami leur ferme les yeux!

*Nicolas-Laurent-Joseph Gilbert, 1751–80, a native of Lorraine. Note how he shares Chulkaturin's love of nature.

17 'pustoi, nichtozhny i nenuzhny, neoriginal'ny chelovek'.

18 L. 250, to P. V. Annenkov, 6 June 1853.

19 'Poezdka v Poles'e', 1857.

20 The individuality and singularity of many of the serfs in *A Sportsman's Sketches* was a critical commonplace and was often regarded as a defect rather than a virtue, on the ground that a documentary should concentrate on the typical.

21 Turgenev refers to it as 'the first day'. He divided this story into two chapters, entitled 'First Day' and 'Second Day'; but actually the first chapter covers two days. Day One – the journey into the forest and the arrival at Svyatoe – occupies almost four-and-a-half pages; Day Two – in quest of grouse – occupies five-and-a-half; Day Three (Turgenev's 'second day') covers nine pages. Oddly enough, this confusion seems to have escaped notice.

22 See quotation from L. 3569 on p. 2.

23 The formula is untranslatable in its conciseness and punch. S''el, past tense of s''est' = (1) eat (up); (2) destroy, wipe out.

24 For an aristocratic counterpart of Efrem, see chapter 6, p. 159.

6 LOVE AND THE SUPERFLUOUS MAN

1 'Dva priyatelya', written 1853, published 1854.

2 'Zatish'e', written in the first half of 1854, published in October of that year. Neither 'A Backwater' nor 'A Quiet Nook' (as the title is often translated) fully renders the sense and associations of *zatish'e*, which means primarily 'a calm' (as at sea), a suspension of noise, movement, activity, and only secondarily a place characterized by such a state.

3 These too are only approximate renderings: *stydlivost'* is closer to French *pudeur*, *samolyubie* to *amour-propre* than to *fierté* or *orgueil*.

4 'Perepiska', completed 1854, published 1856.

5 Written in twelve days, February–March 1855, published April 1855.

6 Alfred de Musset, 'Lettre à M. de Lamartine' (1836).

> (Who once in life has loved must thenceforth bear
> Within his breast a wound that heals no more.
> He keeps it close – a torment, secret, dear –
> And, reckless of his pain, rejects all cure.)

7 V. O. Klyuchevsky, 'Evgeni Onegin i ego predki', originally in the journal *Russkaya mysl'* (1887), republished as an appendix to vol. v of his *Kurs russkoi istorii* (Moscow, 1937). Klyuchevsky attributes both the failure and the crime to vanity or conceit (*iz chvanstva*); which is perhaps less than fair – even to Onegin.

8 The Pygmalion theme had already appeared in *Rudin*; but Vera, unlike Natal'ya, is a victim of two would-be Pygmalions – working at cross-purposes.

9 *Rudin*, ix, 323: 'razumeetsya, pokorit'sya'.

10 Researchers into Schopenhauer's influence in Russia have made a respectable case for dating its initial impact on Turgenev to the early or middle 1850s. Sigrid Maurer McLaughlin in her impressively researched *Schopenhauer in Russland: zur literarischen Rezeption bei*

Turgenev (Wiesbaden, 1984) sees 'Faust' as the first of Turgenev's works to show clear traces of 'an inner genetic contact' with Schopenhauer's philosophy and specifically with his *Transzendente Spekulationen über die anscheinende Absichtlichkeit im Schicksal des Einzelnen* in *Parerga und Paralipomena.* She sees 'Faust' as imbued with the 'transcendental fatalism' of that essay: i.e., she sees its protagonists as exemplifying and the story as expressing or working out that doctrine. Although a number of the traces of influence are interesting and plausible, the general thesis rests on what seems to me a misconception of the characters and events of 'Faust'. Resignation (*Entsagung*) is not achieved by either of its protagonists. Vera is torn apart and destroyed by the warring elements of her nature: the outer crust moulded by her mother and the inmost urges stirred to life by the poetry. Pavel Aleksandrovich has buried himself in solitude (as he had intended to do for the summer before he met Vera again), but he is not resigned: he is plagued (very properly) by grief and guilt – surely not what Schopenhauer intended for his sages? As for the puritanical pronouncements in his penultimate paragraph – about duty and toil as the essence of life – they may well be due to his having read Schopenhauer, but unfortunately they bear no discoverable relationship either to his feelings (which are as self-centred as ever) or to what he is doing with his life (evidently nothing).

11 According to A. I. Beletsky, 'Turgenev i russkie pisatel'nitsy 30–60-kh godov' in Brodsky (ed.), *Tvorcheski put' Turgeneva* (Petrograd, 1923) the theme had been handled by more than one of the minor women writers of that period.

12 'krepka' combines such meanings as 'strong', 'staunch', 'firm'.

13 Written 1857, published January 1858. Asya is an unusual hypocorisma for Anna.

14 In Gagin's self-indictment Turgenev – astonishing as that must seem at this date – is castigating himself. See his L. 578, to Countess E. E. Lambert, 15 Nov. 1857, in which he accuses himself of dilettantism and vows to sin no more in that way.

15 D. I. Pisarev, 'Zhenskie tipy v romanakh i povestyakh Pisemskogo, Turgeneva i Goncharova', sect. IV, in *Sochineniya* (Moscow, 1955), vol. I.

16 See *W.* VII, 423–4.

17 'Pervaya lyubov'', written at the beginning of 1860, published March 1860.

18 'etoi otravy', lit.: 'that poison' (XXI, 72).

19 Isaiah Berlin's translation: *First Love* (Harmondsworth, 1977), p. 50.

20 For Henri Granjard, *Ivan Tourguénev et les courants politiques et sociaux de son temps* (Paris, 1954), p. 219, Efrem is a mere 'thief and rogue' (*un voleur et un fripon*). If he had recognized in Efrem a plebeian Pëtr Vasil'evich, he might have studied the man more carefully. As a member of his village community, Efrem is nothing like a thief and rogue; and even as an outside predator, if he had been

nothing but a thief and rogue, he would long ago have been neutralized in gaol. Nor does 'his contempt for the social order and its constraints, his scorn of honesty and other civilized virtues' make of Efrem 'the true child of nature as Turgenev now sees nature'. Why should Efrem have any more claim to the title 'true child of nature' than Kondrat or Egor? And is Pëtr Vasil'evich any less contemptuous of the social order and its constraints than Efrem? Yet surely we view Pëtr Vasil'evich not as a child of nature but as a highly 'civilized' person?

21 Cf. the last paragraph of ch. 10, p. 234.

7 'HAMLET AND DON QUIXOTE' – *RUDIN*

1 Published January 1860, after *Rudin* and *A Nest of Gentry* and simultaneously with *On the Eve*.

2 Discussed with E. M. Feoktistov, if not before: see his letter of 17 Sept. 1851 to Turgenev, cited *W.* VIII, 553.

3 See Introduction, p. 3 and n. 8.

4 *Ibid.*

5 That surely is at the root of his treatment of Ophelia and perhaps explains his savage condemnation of Rosencrantz and Guildenstern – not just to death but to damnation. It is arguably those emotional conflicts – to which Hamlet refers variously as 'melancholy', 'conscience', 'thought' ('is sicklied o'er with the pale cast of thought') and which Turgenev calls 'egoism', 'scepticism' or 'unbelief' – that account for his fatal dilatoriness in carrying out the Ghost's command.

6 'Contributing', not 'causing'. If Hamlet had killed the King promptly, Polonius, Ophelia, Gertrude and Laertes would have remained alive; but: Polonius and Laertes brought about their deaths by their own treachery; the Queen was murdered, unintentionally, by Claudius; and Ophelia's madness, though precipitated by the death of her father, had surely been prepared by the loss of her lover, whom she had alienated by her half-heartedness (first cutting herself off from him, then conspiring to elicit the cause of his 'madness').

7 See Anthony Close, *The Romantic Approach to Don Quixote* (Cambridge, 1978), and Willi Erzgräber (ed.), *Hamlet-Interpretationen im 20.ten Jahrhundert* (Darmstadt, 1977).

8 *W.* v, 594–605.

9 M. N. Chernov, 'Rutsyn and Rudin', *Turgenevski sbornik*, vol. III (Moscow–Leningrad, 1967), pp. 72–6, suggests that at least Rudin's projects in the epilogue may owe not a little to those of Turgenev's neighbour, Nikolai Karlovich Ruttsen (1826–80), another quintessential superfluous man.

10 Hamlet's actual words to the players (III.ii.) are: 'to hold, as 'twere, a mirror up to nature; to show virtue her own features, scorn her own image, and the very age and body of the time his form and pressure'. Turgenev, as usual, quotes from memory.

11 The word here translated 'class' is *sloi*: lit., layer, stratum.

12 Henri Granjard, *Ivan Tourguénev et les courants politiques et sociaux de son temps* (Paris, 1954), p. 217.

13 André Maurois, *Tourguéniev* (Paris, 1931), ch. II, in *Œuvres complètes* (Paris, 1952), vol. VIII, p. 446.

14 The term 'generation' is used here and elsewhere not in a biological sense (Turgenev was only four years younger than Lermontov and nineteen years younger than Pushkin – though Lermontov was dead when Turgenev published *Parasha* and Pushkin was dead when Lermontov achieved celebrity with his ode *The Poet's Death – Smert' Poeta*), but in the sense in which Russians speak of 'men of the forties' (the 1840s), 'men of the sixties' (the 1860s) and in a sense analogous to, if not identical with, that in which Spaniards speak of 'the generation of '98'. Russian literature of the 1820s was dominated by Pushkin, the first half of the 1830s by Pushkin and Gogol, the second half by Gogol and Lermontov. The 1840s gave rise to a more numerous and diversified group, including such figures as Belinsky and Herzen, Turgenev and Dostoevsky (to name only the greatest).

15 See Seeley, 1952.

16 Sigmund Freud, 'Totem and Taboo', in *Standard Edition of the Complete Psychological Works* (London, 1955), vol. XVIII, p. 89.

17 The pun on 'gor'kaya vodka' (bitter vodka) is lost in translation.

18 Herzen's cousin and wife; see F. F. Seeley, 'Herzen's "Dantean" Period', *Slavonic and East European Review* (December 1954), 44–74.

19 One of whom had been in love with Turgenev, two others had been emotionally involved with Stankevich (the principal model for Pokorski in ch. VI), while all four were more or less in love with their brother Mikhail – the main prototype of Rudin.

20 A. P. Suslova, Dostoevsky's mistress in the early 1860s, an outstanding avatar of the 'emancipated young woman' of that decade; Anna Korvin-Krukovskaya (1843–77), writer and participant in the Paris Commune of 1871 as wife of the Communard, Victor Jaclard; her sister, Sof'ya Kovalevskaya (1850–91) earned a doctorate in mathematics from the University of Göttingen in 1874 and was appointed Professor of Mathematics at the University of Stockholm in 1884.

21 Richardson's *Clarissa* (1747–8) and *Sir Charles Grandison* (1753–4), and Rousseau's *Julie ou La Nouvelle Héloïse* (1761).

22 Her expression is 'a cunning seducer' (*kovarny iskusitel'*).

23 If anyone objects that seventy more years were to pass before Pirandello could dream up a husband desperately jealous of the man his wife loves in him (*Uno, nessuno e centomila*, 1926), let him or her reread Leopardi's 'Aspasia', written twenty years before *Rudin*. This is not to suggest that Turgenev ever read 'Aspasia' – only that the psychology was available.

8 THE 'TURGENEV HEROINE': *A NEST OF GENTRY*

1 *Dvoryanskoe gnezdo*: variously translated as 'Home of the Gentry', 'Liza or A Nest of Nobles', 'A House of Gentlefolk', 'A Nest of Gentlefolk', 'A Nest of Hereditary Legislators' (*sic*), 'A Noble Nest', 'A Nobleman's Nest': see Introduction to Richard Freeborn's translation, second edition (Harmondsworth, 1979). Written 1858, published January 1859.

2 T. P. Golovanova, '*Dvoryanskoe gnezdo*: Turgenev i Gertsen v period sozdaniya romana' in *Turgenevski sbornik*, vol. III (Moscow–Leningrad, 1867) traces the *rapprochement*, in and after 1857, of such (left-wing) writers as Herzen and Chernyshevsky to the more enlightened wing of the Slavophils and argues that Turgenev wrote *A Nest of Gentry* with the arguments of these writers – more particularly, of his friend Herzen – in mind.

3 Avrahm Yarmolinsky, *Turgenev: The Man, His Art and His Age* (New York, 1961), ch. 19, p. 171.

4 In E. M. Forster's sense: see his *Aspects of the Novel* (London, 1927), ch. 4. 'Flat' characters pivot on a single characteristic, or small number of compatible characteristics, as compared with 'round' characters, which are 'capable of surprising [the reader] in a convincing way'.

5 Ch. VI, 143: Turgenev has *lëgkost' i smelost'*. *Lëgkost'* is the abstract noun from the adjective *lëgki* which, like German *leicht*, means both 'light' and 'easy'. Freeborn, *A Nest of Gentry*, translates 'dexterity and daring'. The alliteration is appealing and Panshin is certainly dexterous (as a rider, a pianist, a draughtsman); but is that what he would be most inclined to boast of?

6 As recognized by Apollon Grigor'ev, 'I. S. Turgenev i ego deyatel'nost'', in *Russkoe Slovo*, 1859, nos. 4, 5, 6, 8.

7 In his speech at the unveiling of the Pushkin memorial, 8/20 June 1880, published in the August 1880 issue of *Dnevnik pisatelya* (*Diary of a Writer*). The other heroine, mentioned in the speech but not included in the printed text, was Natasha Rostova (in Tolstoy's *War and Peace*).

8 *Liza*, by Ivan Turgenief. Translated from the Russian by W. R. S. Ralston, 2 vols. (London, Chapman and Hall, 1869), in close consultation with the author.

9 *Turgenev-romanist* (Leningrad, 1972), pp. 149, 334.

10 Richard Freeborn, *Turgenev: The Novelist's Novelist* (London and New York), 1960, p. 113.

11 *Turgenev*, ch. 18, p. 161.

12 D. N. Ovsyaniko-Kulikovsky, *I. S. Turgenev, Sobranie sochineni*, third edition, vol. II, in *Slavistic Printings and Reprintings* (The Hague, 1969). See ch. VII, 'Liza (Heroine of *A Nest of Gentry*)'; ch. VIII, 'Analysis of *A Nest of Gentry* in General and of the Image of Liza in Particular in Terms of the Artistic Techniques'.

13 M. O. Gershenzon, *Mechta i mysl' I. S. Turgeneva* (Moscow, 1919), Brown University Slavic Reprints, VIII (Providence, 1970), pp. 59–60.

9 THE NEW MAN AND THE NEW WOMAN: *ON THE EVE*

1 *Nakanune*: begun in France, 28 June 1859, finished at Spasskoe, 6 Nov. 1859, published in *The Russian Herald* (*Russki vestnik*), January 1860.

2 L. 722, 24 June 1859: just four days before he started *On the Eve*.

3 Turgenev tells the story in 'Preface to the Novels', written for the 1880 edition of his *Collected Works* (*W.* XII, 304–7), but mistakenly dates his receipt of Karateev's Ms to 1855. L. 309, to N. A. Nekrasov, 10 Nov. 1854, shows that at that date he already had the Ms. Karateev did survive the Crimean War, but died young, in March 1859, just before the novel was begun. Turgenev was also mistaken in saying that Katranov died in Bulgaria. He contracted tuberculosis there, but returned to the West for medical treatment and died in Venice 'suddenly' in May 1853 (see *W.* VIII, 512–13).

4 L. 776, to I. S. Aksakov, 25 Nov. 1859: 'My novella [i.e., *On the Eve*] is based on the idea that what we must have is *consciously* heroic natures (o neobkhodimosti '*soznatel'no*' geroicheskikh natur) – so that there is here no question of the [common] people – if the cause [of progress] is to advance.' The adjective 'soznatel'ny', corresponding to the advert 'soznatel'no', means, first, 'conscious', then 'conscientious', then 'socially conscious'.

5 What is known of Katranov's life is summarized by L. I. Rovnyakova in sect. II of the commentary to *On the Eve*, *W.* VIII, 512–14.

6 The Tsaritsyno episode is alleged to come directly from Karateev's Ms.

7 *Sush'*: from *sukhoi* = dry, arid, dour.

8 Gilbert Gardiner's translation, *On the Eve* (Harmondsworth, 1979), p. 196, with modifications.

9 There is no merit in the argument that Insarov had to die of tuberculosis because that was how Katranov died. If Turgenev could invent tragic deaths for Insarov's parents and the hero's two-year return home – why not a different death for the hero? Could he not have been allowed to fall fighting in Serbia?

10 Introduced in ch. XXXIV – no doubt, to complete the gallery of educated male types (though it may be questioned whether the intrusion of such a caricature into the poetic sequence of Insarov's last days does not strike an artistic false note).

11 In the sort of sense in which one thinks of Turgenev as more 'reasonable' than Tolstoy or Dostoevsky.

12 They romp through the picture gallery; at the opera their reactions are not to the music (Turgenev did not care for Verdi) but to the sad fate of the heroine and to the singer's struggles to transcend her vocal limitations.

13 This cannot be said of her brief bond, at the age of ten, with the

beggar-girl Katya; but Katya won her heart and admiration not as a recipient of charity or victim of violence but as the rebel who dared to hate her tormentor, the adventurous spirit determined to break free – to live and revel in 'God's own freedom'.

14 Evidenced by the contrast between her concern for insects and her cool indifference to Shubin's love-pangs – not to mention her disregard for her mother's sorrow, not just when she left Russia but when she decided never to go back.

15 For a comparison of Goncharov's version of the New Man and the New Woman with Turgenev's, see F. F. Seeley, 'Oblomov', *Slavonic and East European Review* (July 1976), 335–54.

16 Gardiner's translation, *On the Eve*, p. 196.

10 THE FIRST NIHILIST: *FATHERS AND CHILDREN*

1 *Ottsy i deti*, written between the summer of 1860 and the end of 1861, published February 1862 in *Russki vestnik*.

2 Emel'yan Pugachëv, Cossack leader of a vast insurrection (1773–4) against Catherine II and co-star of Pushkin's historical novel *The Captain's Daughter* (1836).

3 L. 1214, to K. K. Sluchevsky, 26 Apr. 1862. Sluchevsky (1837–1904), a minor poet, was at that time spokesman for the Russian students in Heidelberg.

4 A quotation from A. S. Griboedov's 1823 comedy, *Woe from Wit* (*Gore ot uma*), Act IV, sc. iv.

5 L. 1215, to A. I. Herzen, 28 Apr. 1862. Herzen (1812–70), a memoirist and publicist of genius and an old friend of Turgenev, self-exiled to the West, edited in London the influential left-wing journal *The Bell* (*Kolokol*).

6 L. 1206, to A. A. Fet, 18 Apr. 1862. Fet (1820–92) was a major lyric poet.

7 Remember the publication of 'A Backwater' without the present fourth chapter and the tardy addition of ch. xxxv to *A Nest of Gentry* only in response to criticism.

8 About one-quarter longer than *A Nest of Gentry*, about three-fifths longer than *Rudin*.

9 D. I. Pisarev, 'Bazarov', *Sochineniya*, vol. II (Moscow, 1955), sect. 10, first published in *Russkoe slovo*, March 1862.

10 'On the Subject of *Fathers and Children*' (Po povodu *Ottsov i detei*), W. XIV, 102.

11 Both born in 1814. For 'demonism' as a characteristic of the superfluous men of the 1830s, see Seeley, 1952.

12 L. 1214, to K. K. Sluchevsky, 26 Apr. 1862.

13 Adapted from Rosemary Edmonds' translation, *Fathers and Sons* (Harmondsworth, 1965), p. 234; borrowed or adapted from the same translation are my versions, above, from ch. xv, 271 and ch. x, 239.

14 Soviet scholars have suggested that Bazarov's fight with Pavel Kirsanov in ch. XXIV may contain autobiographical material from Turgenev's quarrel and near-duel with Tolstoy in 1861 (*W.* VIII, 620, n. to p. 357); but obsessed, perhaps, by the left-wing tradition that Bazarov is a portrait (or caricature) of Dobrolyubov, they seem to have missed the affinities between Bazarov's style of quarrelling and Tolstoy's: e.g., Bazarov's 'slander' of Pushkin vies in perversity with Tolstoy's notorious pronouncement: 'Bronchitis is a metal': A. A. Fet, *Moi vospominaniya – 1848–89* (Moscow, 1890), part I, ch. III. There is, too, a delicious irony when Bazarov, the professed foe of Romanticism and traducer of Pushkin, unconsciously echoes the Romantic misanthropy of Pushkin at twenty-three, writing (September–October 1822) to his younger brother Lev: 'Vous aurez affaire aux hommes que vous ne connaissez pas encore. Commencez toujours par en penser tout le mal imaginable, vous n'en rabattrez pas de beaucoup' (You are going to have to deal with people, of whom you have had no experience till now. Always begin by thinking of them as badly as possible: you won't have to reduce [your estimate] by much).

15 Bazarov's scorn for Pavel Kirsanov's 'principles' challenges comparison with Tolstoy's 1856 attacks (Fet, *Memoirs*) on the 'convictions' of Turgenev and his fellow liberals; his later reduction of principles to 'feelings' is arguably analogous to Tolstoy's postulate of a 'moral instinct' at the root of motivation. It is unlikely that Turgenev had any conscious thought of Tolstoy in creating Bazarov; but Tolstoy – for all his utterly different political and philosophical outlook – would have fitted Arkadi's definition of a nihilist (one who looks at everything critically, defers to no authority, takes on trust no principle, however widely revered) quite as neatly as Dobrolyubov.

16 D. N. Ovsyaniko-Kulikovsky, *I. S. Turgenev, Sobranie sochineni*, vol. II, *Slavistic Printings and Reprintings* (The Hague, 1969), ch. I, especially p. 44.

17 Granjard, *Tourguénev* (Paris, 1954), p. 306.

18 Granjard, *ibid.*, p. 311, also uses the phrase 'foreign body' in reference to Bazarov's love, but does not develop the simile.

19   (Die then. Thy death was sweet, fulfilled thy mission.
    What we on earth call genius is the urge
    To love, for only love to life lends worth.
    But human love is all too soon forgot,
    So for great souls it is a happy lot
    To die, as thou didst, for a love divine.)

Alfred de Musset, 'A la Malibran', 1836, st. XXVII. María-Felicia García Malibran (1808–36) was the elder sister of Pauline Viardot and a singer of at least equal stature.

20 The ennobling function of love and the coupling of love and death are, of course, ubiquitous motifs in Romantic literature.

21 For a fair and beautifully formulated presentation of the political

aspect, context and (undiminished) relevance of the novel, see Isaiah Berlin's Romanes Lecture, *Fathers and Children* (Oxford, 1973/72).

11 THE LEGACY OF NIHILISM: 'ENOUGH'; *SMOKE*

1 Only one – 'Klara Milich' – has the scene laid in post-Emancipation Russia; 'Spring Torrents' deals with Russians in 1840 – but Russians outside Russia; 'Song of Triumphant Love' is a tale of Renaissance Italy.

2 It may be objected that 'Phantoms' was conceived in the mid-fifties and that Turgenev returned to the idea in October 1861 – after the completion but before the publication of *Fathers and Children*. However, what was set down at that date was no more than a skeleton; the writing 'took off' only in the spring of 1863: it was only then that the idea received its emotional charge.

3 'Dovol'no', begun spring 1862, written mainly in 1864, first published in the 1865 edition of Turgenev's *Works*.

4 L. 4560, to M. M. Stasyulevich, 20 May 1878.

5 Like the younger man in the 1845 poem *Conversation* (Razgovor).

6 This is not to suggest that Turgenev was thinking of Dante when he wrote it (he had plenty of such memories himself), and still less that Dostoevsky would have been thinking of Turgenev. Such associations might have resonances for a reader.

7 Dostoevsky, who had begged to publish – and had in fact published – 'Phantoms' in his journal, *The Epoch* (*Epokha*) in 1864, mercilessly parodied both 'Phantoms' and 'Enough' in pt III, ch. 1 of his 1872 novel, *The Devils* (*Besy*).

8 *Dym*, written between November 1865 and January 1867, published March 1867 in *Russki vestnik*.

9 Arguably 'A Hamlet of the Shchigry District', 'Lebedyan'', 'Spring Torrents'.

10 See E. I. Kiko's commentary to *Smoke*, W. IX, especially pp. 507–8. The series of letters in *The Bell* entitled 'Ends and Beginnings' ('Kontsy i nachala') did not name Turgenev but were widely known to be addressed to him.

11 Richard Freeborn, *Turgenev: The Novelist's Novelist* (Oxford, 1960), ch. 6, p. 144.

12 The primacy, in this sense, of the love story has been recognized by a minority of critics, from N. K. Mikhailovsky (if he was the author of the anonymous review of *Smoke* in the journal *Glasny sud*, 30 May/11 June 1867) to A. Yarmolinsky, *Turgenev* (New York, 1961), ch. 27, p. 242: '*Smoke* is primarily a love story.'

13 *Besy*, published 1871–2, intended by its author as 'a pamphlet'. It is widely recognized that some of Turgenev's themes foreshadow themes in later works by Dostoevsky.

14 A. B. Muratov, 'Geidel'bergskie arabeski v "Dyme"' in *Literaturnoe Nasledstvo*, vol. 76 (Moscow, 1967), summed up in the sentence, p. 88: 'So Turgenev did not sin against the truth.'

15 The rôle of astrology in the Reagan White House offers a piquant *pendant* to the attempts to mesmerize the crayfish – and timely support for the plaints of the deceased artist (in 'Enough') about the imperceptible rate of change in human nature.

16 For a fictional example see the attempt to inveigle prince Stepan Kasatski into marrying Nicholas I's ex-mistress in Tolstoy's 'Father Sergius' ('Otets Sergi'). The circumstances were different in that Kasatski was in love with the girl before he knew of her connection with the Emperor.

17 L. 1728, to M. V. Avdeev, 6 Feb. 1867: 'napisan v rode dlya menya novom'.

18 L. 1844, to D. I. Pisarev, 4 June 1867, in reply to Pisarev's letter to him of 30 May 1867: quoted in the notes to *Smoke*, *W.* IX, 530–1.

19 This 'original splitting' of the central hero is handled interestingly by A. B. Muratov, *I. S. Turgenev posle 'Ottsov i detei'* (Leningrad, 1972), in the chapters (not numbered) on Litvinov and Potugin. According to him, this split is motivated and justified by Turgenev's inability to discern in the Russia of the later 1860s 'any real power uniting positive principles with a capacity to carry them into effect' (p. 103).

20 'Hamlet and Don Quixote', *W.* VIII, 173–4.

21 This was the designation adopted by the Dostoevsky circle and others of like mind in the 1860s; they professed views with close affinities to Slavophilism.

22 A. S. Pushkin, *Evgeni Onegin*, ch. VII, st. xxii; V. G. Belinsky, 'Sochineniya Aleksandra Pushkina, "Stat'ya vos'maya"' in Belinsky, *Sochineniya v trëkh tomakh*) (Moscow, 1948), vol. III, pp. 518–19: discussed in A. B. Muratov, *I. S. Turgenev posle 'Ottsov i detei'*, p. 58, citing I. Eiges, 'Znachenie Pushkina dlya tvorchestva Turgeneva' in *Literaturnaya uchëba* (1940), 12.

23 In his 1852 review of Ostrovsky's play *The Poor Bride* (*Bednaya nevesta*), *W.* V, 391.

12 'THERE ARE MORE THINGS IN HEAVEN AND EARTH'

1 See the commentaries to the individual stories in *W.* IX and XI. For two such approaches see: N. Natova, 'O "misticheskikh" povestyakh Turgeneva' in *Zapiski russkoi akademicheskoi gruppy v SShA* (1983), vol. XVI, 113–49; A. B. Muratov, *Turgenev-novellist: 1870-e–1880-e gody* (Leningrad, 1985), fourth essay: 'Tainstvennye rasskazy'. Natov's paper addresses the autobiographical sub-text of 'Song of Triumphant Love' and 'Klara Milich'; Muratov's relates the tales to Turgenev's philosophy, with special reference to the same two stories and to 'The Dream'.

2 L. V. Pumpyansky, according to Muratov, *Turgenev-novellist*.

3 'Prizraki', published January–February 1864 in Dostoevsky's journal *Epokha* (*The Epoch*).

4 See E. I. Kiko's commentary to 'Phantoms', *W.* IX, 470; and A. P.

Mogilyansky, under 'Variants', *ibid.*, pp. 377–8.

5 The portrayal of the singer is so indeterminate as regards period that she could be taken to be a living woman. In that case, the scenes with figures would divide into two trios rather than three pairs: the dancers as foils to the historic figures, the singer as foil to Paris and St Petersburg: in each trio an example of what humanity can and should be opposed to examples of what humanity has been and is.

6 L. 1402, to V. P. Botkin, 8 Dec. 1863: 'Eto ryad kakikh-to dushevnykh dissolving views – vyzvannykh perekhodnym i deistvitel'no tyazhëlym i tëmnym sostoyaniem moego Ya.'

7 'Sobaka', written 1864, published 1866 in *SanktPeterburgskie Vedomosti*.

8 See *W.* IX, 497: Turgenev had related it to friends and acquaintances as early as 1859 – soon after he first heard it.

9 The Old Believers were schismatics who clung to the rites of the Orthodox Church as they had developed and been practised in Russia before the seventeenth-century reforms of Patriarch Nikon.

10 'Son', written January–May 1876, published January 1877.

11 Cf. the Gospel according to Matthew, 5.28: 'But I say unto you that whoever looketh on a woman to lust after her hath committed adultery with her already in his heart.'

12 For an enthralling panorama of Indian thinking on such matters see Wendy Doniger O'Flaherty, *Dreams, Illusions and Other Realities* (Chicago, 1984). O'Flaherty's Indians would have no difficulty with what we have considered stumbling-blocks in 'The Dog' and 'The Dream'.

13 L. 4172, to William Ralston, 22 Jan. 1877.

14 E.g., G. F. Perminov, *W.* XI, 529 and A. B. Muratov, *Turgenev-novellist*, pp. 74–81. They, no doubt, take our last interpretation of the story title as not only the obvious but the only conceivable one.

15 L. 113, to Pauline Viardot, 11–14 Aug. 1849 (under 13 Aug.).

16 'Rasskaz ottsa Alekseya', written at the beginning of 1877, published in May of that year in *Vestnik Evropy*.

17 Charles Rycroft, *The Innocence of Dreams* (London, 1979), pp. 147–8.

18 For a mid-century equation of reason, science and the pagan joy of life with Satan but an opposite reaction, see Carducci's hymn to Satan (*A Satana*). Giosuè Carducci (1835–1907) is generally regarded as the greatest Italian poet of the second half of the nineteenth century.

13 THE YEARS THAT ARE NO MORE

1 L. 2454, to M. V. Avdeev, 25 Jan. 1870: 'immediate present' is *sovremennost'*, with overtones of topicality, 'relevance'; 'of today' is *sovremennye*; 'exemplar' is *propisi*.

2 'Istoriya leitenanta Ergunova', begun spring 1866, written mainly January–February 1867, published January 1868 in *Russki vestnik*.

3 Corresponding roughly to the last twelve or thirteen chapters.

4 L. 2454, to M. V. Avdeev, 25 Jan. 1870, in which he was again defending himself against a charge of 'mysticism', based on this very scene.

5 L. 1905, to P. V. Annenkov, 5 Oct. 1867: *o eë beznravstvennosti zaranee rastrubili v publike*: this was in advance of publication, so the judgment must have been spread by people who had heard it read.

6 'Brigadir', written February–May 1867, published January 1868 in *Vestnik Evropy*.

7 L. 2208, to Maréchal, 17 Jan. 1869; Maréchal (first name unknown) was an employee of Turgenev's French publisher, P.-J. Hetzel.

8 See L. M. Lotman's commentary, *W.* XI, 438–40.

9 Letter to Turgenev, 20 June 1868, in Maurice Parturier, *Une amitié littéraire: Prosper Mérimée et Ivan Tourguéniev* (Paris, 1952), p. 192.

10 'Strannaya istoriya', written in the summer of 1869, published January 1870 in *Vestnik Evropy*.

11 See Prosper Mérimée's letter to Turgenev, 25 Mar. 1870 (also cited *W.* x, 479); the story had already appeared in German translation in 1869 and in French translation in 1870. Those ultra-patriots would have been astounded to learn that 120 years later their Vasili, dirty and ignorant as he is, could compare favourably with some of the most popular televangelists of the premier nation of the West: Vasili does live his creed.

12 When proof-reading the German translation, Turgenev insisted on keeping the original Russian word, *yurodivy*, subjoining a footnote:

> Yurodivy designates in Russia certain fanatics who, like [. . .] Indian fakirs, wander through the land thwarting the machinations of the Devil. They are regarded with pious awe and treated with deepest respect by the [common] people, who hold that their entry into a house brings good fortune and seek to interpret the most senseless utterances of these idiots as divine revelations and prophecies.

13 1854/5–1857/8; 'Yakov Pasynkov', 1855; *Rudin*, 1855; *A Nest of Gentry*, 1858; *On the Eve*, 1859.

14 The destiny of the earlier Sof'ya is determined by her self-will, which is a symptom of a pride arguably stemming from a repressed excessive humility.

15 'Stuk ... stuk ... stuk!' written in the autumn of 1870, published January 1871 in *Vestnik Evropy*.

16 L. 4164, to S. K. Bryullova, 16 Jan. 1877. 'Self-centred' renders *samolyubivy*; if 'vain' were not ambiguous, it might be nearer the mark.

17 See 'Enough', ch. XIV.

18 L. 3417, to A. P. Filosofova, 30 Aug. 1874: 'all I wanted to indicate to you was [my] right to work on purely psychological – not political and not social – problems, and the timeliness (or appropriateness) [of doing so]': 'ya khotel tol'ko ukazat' Vam na pravo i umestnost' razrabotki chisto psikhicheskikh (ne politicheskikh i ne sotsial'nykh) voprosov'.

19 A. A. Bestuzhev (1797–1837), Decembrist, poet, critic, author of short stories, used in the 1830s the pen-name Marlinsky. His highly coloured Romantic tales enjoyed a great vogue, which was punctured by Belinsky's criticism.

20 So did Pierre Bezukhov, the hero of Tolstoy's *War and Peace*, to convince himself that he was destined to assassinate Napoleon – and that was long before Marlinsky.

21 *The Devils* (also rendered: *The Possessed – Besy*), pt III, ch. VI, sect. II.

22 'Chasy', written July 1874–November 1875, published January 1876 in *Vestnik Evropy*.

23 'The Dream', which we have ranged among the 'tales of mystery', was written after 'The Watch' but published simultaneously with the first half of *Virgin Soil*, in January 1877.

24 'The Watch' is supposed to be related in 1850 by Aleksei, who was 15 in 1801, so born in 1786 and 64 in 1850; Ergunov must have been born around the beginning of the century to be a naval lieutenant in 1826/7, and has just died in 1866/7 – presumably in his mid-60s.

25 The military settings in 'The Duellist' and 'The Jew'; the military and shopkeeper settings in 'Petushkov'.

26 Cited in the commentary to 'The Watch', *W.* XI, 515. For Baburin, the 'republican' protagonist of 'Punin and Baburin', see ch. 14.

14 DOWN MEMORY LANE

1 'Two Friends', 'First Love', 'An Unhappy Girl', 'A King Lear of the Steppes', 'Spring Torrents'.

2 'Neshchastnaya', written summer 1868, published January 1869 in *Russki vestnik*.

3 Turgenev in his notes names Mikhail Bakunin's father (Aleksandr Bakunin, 1768–1854) as one model for Ivan Koltovskoi; but we find very similar characteristics (joined to a somewhat different temperament) in Herzen's masterly portrayal (*My Past and Thoughts – Byloe i dumy*, pt I, ch. v) of the men of that generation as a group and, in great detail, of his father (I. A. Yakovlev, 1767–1846), who also preferred to beget his children out of wedlock.

4 According to Turgenev's notes, Susanna was born in 1808, her mother married Ratch in 1816 and died in 1822, her father died in 1825, Ratch remarried at the end of 1827. My 'five … years' are, of necessity, approximations: 1822–7, from her mother's death to her meeting with Mikhail and 1829–34, from Mikhail's death to her acquaintance with Fustov, on the assumption that this had begun about a year before the opening of the story.

5 'Stepnoi korol' Lir', written February 1869–April 1870, published October 1870 in *Vestnik Evropy*.

6 Cf. Ovid's comparison of the disarray of his household on his last night in Rome with that of Troy in the night of its capture by the Greeks:

Si licet exemplis in paruis grandibus uti,
    Haec facies Troiae, cum caperetur, erat.

Tristia, I, III, 25–6

(If one may use in a lowly case a lofty example, / Such in the hour of its capture was the appearance of Troy.)

7 *Glava*: lit. head, chief.

8 'The reason I had this idea, madam, was because I want to decide personally, while I am alive and still here, who is to have what, so that the recipient shall enjoy what I have bestowed and feel grateful and carry out [my will] and [see] his father's and benefactor's award as a great favour . . .' The sentence is left unfinished and is strikingly clumsy, not to say confused.

9 As pointed out by Nina Brodiansky, 'Turgenev's Short Stories: a Revaluation', *Slavonic and East European Review* (December 1953), 78.

10 'Veshnie vody' (also rendered: 'Torrents of Spring', 'Spring Freshets', 'Spring Floods', etc.), written between the middle of 1870 and the end of 1871, published January 1872 in *Vestnik Evropy*.

11 Pointed out by Leonard Schapiro in the essay appended to his translation of the work, *Spring Torrents* (Harmondsworth, 1980), pp. 231–2. Schapiro instances the conclusion of ch. 24 and the last sentence of the penultimate paragraph of ch. 32.

12 In both Italian and German 'Rozelli' would be spelt with an 's'.

13 E.g., 'il paese del Dante' (for *di Dante*), 'il antico valor' (for *l'antico valor*), 'segredezza' (for *segretezza*). If Pantaleone speaks the purest Italian (*lingua toscana in bocca romana*), it is presumably due to his training as a singer and surely not because he hails from Varese (Lombardy) or Senigallia (Marche). 'Spazzette' (for *spazzole*) is dialectal; so, presumably, is 'segredezza' (contradicting the claim that Pantaleone speaks the purest Italian). The meaningless 'L'ira . . . da verso il fato' is probably for *L'ira di avverso fato* as heard by Turgenev at the opera.

14 Even if Gemma had accepted Klüber under pressure from her mother and for the sake of her family, we should note that in the discussion on the relative merits of art and trade (X, 29–30), she sides with her mother against Sanin and Pantaleone.

15 The villains in *An Imprudence* (1843) and 'Three Portraits' (1845/6) are not victims of infatuation: they indulge, or try to indulge, their passion entirely at the expense of its object.

16 Turgenev's friends were horrified by the picture (XLIII, 150) of Sanin on the cramped front seat of the carriage bound for Paris, facing Polozov sprawled in comfort on the rear seat, enjoying the pear Sanin has just peeled for him, under Polozova's gloating gaze.

17 Γ. M. Dostoevsky, *The Brothers Karamazov* (1879–80), pt I, bk III, ch. III.

18 Cf. Pushkin: 'All, all that threatens our destruction / Holds for the

hearts of mortal men / An unaccountable delight': from the Chairman's song in *Feast in Time of Plague*.

19 He is supposed to have admitted once his need to have a woman's heel on his neck pressing his face into the mud (Fet, *Moi vospominaniya*, vol. I, ch. VI, p. 159).

20 L. 2864, to P.-J. Hetzel, 2 May 1872.

21 On the 'demons' of the 1830s, see Seeley, 1952.

22 L. 2534, to Countess M. F. Sollogub, 26 July 1870.

23 'Punin i Baburin', written between December 1872 and February 1874, published April 1874 in *Vestnik Evropy*.

24 It appears to have gone unnoticed in the critical literature.

25 'Punin and Baburin', I, 168; 'Diary of a Superfluous Man', under 20 March (p. 181).

26 Letter to Turgenev, 19 Apr. 1874, cited *W*. XI, 501.

27 L. 3332, to P. V. Annenkov, 24 Apr. 1874.

28 '*Plemyannitsa*. Roman Evgenii Tur', *W*. III, 368–86 (p. 383).

15 SEEDS OF REVOLUTION: *VIRGIN SOIL*

1 S. G. Nechaev, 1847–82. For an outline of his career and significance, see Franco Venturi, *Roots of Revolution* (New York, 1973), a translation of his *Il Populismo Russo* (Turin, 1952), ch. 15.

2 Alias *The Possessed*, first published in *Russki vestnik*, 1871–2.

3 Shatov is one of several 'heroes' of the novel, important as expressing some of his author's cherished beliefs.

4 *Nov'*, written mainly January–July 1876, published January–February 1877 in *Vestnik Evropy*.

5 Venturi, *Roots of Revolution*, ch. 14, p. 350.

6 Bazarov appears at the very beginning of the brief thaw that followed Nicholas I's death, and was not given time to take advantage of it.

16 THE LAST WRITINGS

1 February 1877–September 1880. 'Father Aleksei's Story' was published in May 1877 but had been written in January of that year. The first couple of pages of 'Song of Triumphant Love' were jotted down in the autumn of 1879, but the story was then laid aside for over a year.

2 Writing, but not creation: in the last year of his life Turgenev continued to make plans, and within a fortnight of his death dictated, in French, the short story 'Une fin'.

3 Not counting a five-page children's story, 'The Mother-quail' ('Perepëlka'), intended for a children's journal but published (December 1882) in a book together with three short stories by Tolstoy.

4 'Starye portrety', written September–November 1880, published 1/13 January 1881 in the newspaper *Poryadok*.

5 'Otchayanny', written October–November 1881, published January

1882 in *Vestnik Evropy*. The rendering 'A Desperate Character' has misleading associations in English; the Russian title consists only of the adjective used as a substantive, corresponding to German 'Ein Verzweifelter', French 'Un Désespéré'.

6 Misha was born in 1828, and his father had been past his first youth when he married, so in his 30s or 40s, which would put his birth back in the 1790s or 1780s.

7 The prototype of Misha was a distant cousin of Turgenev.

8 'Pesn′ torzhestvuyushchei lyubvi', written mainly in the second half of 1881 (begun autumn 1879), published November 1881 in *Vestnik Evropy*.

9 Turgenev translated into Russian and published in 1877 two of Flaubert's *Trois contes* ('Hérodias' and 'La Légende de Saint Julien l'Hospitalier'). Matteo Bandello (1485–1561), from whom Shakespeare may have derived the story of Romeo and Juliet, was the most considerable Italian story-writer of the sixteenth century.

10 We are meant to believe that it happens to Litvinov and Tat′yana – and we do see Insarov's last twenty-four hours of life.

11 In contradistinction to 'Une fin', dictated to Pauline Viardot in French.

12 'Posle smerti'/'Klara Milich', written autumn 1882, published January 1883 in *Vestnik Evropy*.

13 L. 5605, to Zh. A. Polonskaya, 1 Jan. 1882.

14 As witness P. V. Annenkov's letter to Turgenev (dated 1 Oct. 1882) on first reading the story: cited *W.* XIII, 576.

15 'I meet – I take' vies in terseness and pithiness with Efrem's philosophy of life ('Journey into the Woodland') expressing two equally impressive, not to say awesome, personalities.

EPILOGUE

1 'Perlustration', with the general meaning of 'survey', 'inspection', was used in Russia to designate the unauthorized opening and inspection of private correspondence by officialdom.

2 L. 1215, to A. I. Herzen, 28 Apr. 1862: 'As regards God, I am of the same mind as Faust: "Wer darf ihn nennen? / Und wer bekennen: / Ich glaub'ihn? / Wer empfinden / Und sich unterwinden / Zu sagen: ich glaub'ihn nicht?"' ('Who can name Him? / Who – declare: / "I believe in Him? / Who can feel / And [yet] venture / To say: "I do not believe in Him?"'), *Faust*, pt 1, 'Martha's Garden'.

3 L. 2454, to M. V. Avdeev, 25 Jan. 1870: 'That [survival in works of art] is the only immortality I acknowledge.'

4 L. 79, to Pauline Viardot, 29 Apr.–2 May 1848, under 1 May.

5 *Ibid.*

6 'A Sea Crossing' ('Morskoe plavanie').

7 'A Dog' ('Sobaka'): not to be confused with the similarly titled short story.

8 'Werde, der du bist' (Friedrich Nietzsche, *Also sprach Zarathustra*, pt IV, 'The Honey-offering'). The existential message, implicit in the novels as wholes and more particularly in the personalities of their heroines, is contradicted in many of the stories – most explicitly in the 'tales of mystery' and 'Enough'. Another Turgenevan antinomy.

9 Genesis, 32.24–32.

10 L. 1034, to P. V. Annenkov, 27 Feb. 1861.

11 The principle of courtly love had been that love and marriage were mutually exclusive; Turgenev, as a realist and an enemy of 'systems', does leave room for exceptions or anomalies, such as Davyd's marriage to Raisa, and for apparent anomalies like the Brigadier's relation to his Agrippina – one-sided as it obviously was – though he takes care only to tell us about these (as distinct from showing them).

12 'Porog', written May 1878, illegally printed on a leaflet distributed at Turgenev's funeral by the revolutionary group Narodnaya Volya (Freedom for the People or The People's Will: *volya* means both 'freedom' and 'will').

13 See B. M. Eikhenbaum, *Lev Tolstoi, Book I: The Fifties* (Leningrad, 1928), pt I, ch. I.

Index

The index lists references in text and notes to all historical persons except our author (whose name appears on every page); to literary works by other authors in the text; to Turgenev's literary works in text or notes; and (as a boon to non-Slavists) to all his named fictional characters in text or notes as well as the first mention and explanation of a few 'untranslatable' Russian words. When the title of a work contains the name of the protagonist, references to the protagonist are listed under the title of the work.

CAMBRIDGE STUDIES IN RUSSIAN LITERATURE

General editor MALCOLM JONES

Editorial board: ANTHONY CROSS, CARYL EMERSON,
HENRY GIFFORD, G. S. SMITH, VICTOR TERRAS